Violence in Roman Egypt

EMPIRE AND AFTER

Series Editor: Clifford Ando

A complete list of books in the series
is available from the publisher.

VIOLENCE IN ROMAN EGYPT

A Study in Legal Interpretation

ARI Z. BRYEN

PENN

UNIVERSITY OF PENNSYLVANIA PRESS

PHILADELPHIA

Published by
University of Pennsylvania Press
Philadelphia, Pennsylvania 19104-4112
www.upenn.edu/pennpress

Printed in the United States of America on acid-free paper
Bryen, Ari Z.

10 9 8 7 6 5 4 3 2 1

Library of Congress Cataloging-in-Publication Data
Violence in Roman Egypt : a study in legal interpretation / Ari Z. Bryen — 1st ed.
p. cm. — (Empire and after)
ISBN 978-0-8122-4508-0
Includes bibliographical references and index.
1. Criminal procedure (Egyptian law). 2. Criminal procedure (Roman law) 3. Violent crimes—Egypt—History—To 1500. 4. Victims of crimes—Legal status, laws, etc.—Egypt—History—To 1500. 5. Violence—Egypt—History—To 1500. 6. Egypt—History—30 B.C.–640 A.D. I. Title. II. Series: Empire and after.
KL3085 .B79 2013
345.32'05 2012041493

To my parents and my sisters

CONTENTS

Three cases of assault and battery in our city justice courts so far this week are another indication of returned prosperity. Times have been so hard the past few months that when a man got mad at another he would swallow his wrath, go home, and pound his dog. Now that the good times have returned, he gets into a scrap with the cause of his anger and winds up with a round in the justice court.

—Town Newspaper, Wisconsin, October 1897,
cited by Michael Lesy, *Wisconsin Death Trip*.

INTRODUCTION

The Presentation of the Self in Everyday Life

Pain may be a human universal; writing about one's own pain is not. When historians see individuals transforming pain into narratives that complain about neighbors, local officials, or family members, we would do well to pay attention. These narratives about pain and injury invite a series of questions: What can we learn from the ways that people experience, describe, and complain about violation, pain, and injury? In what ways, and under what circumstances, can we use a narrative about violence to give an account of the ways in which non-elite individuals theorized their own behaviors? In what ways can accounts of pain—and the redemption and socialization of pain through petitions—contribute to a historical account of empires?

These questions are hardly unique to the ancient world. And they are tricky enough for social historians, especially those of an anthropological bent. They become yet more complex when we have to take into account that, in the Roman world at least, we have our accounts of pain and violation only because they have been mediated through legal structures. This is so not only in the narrow sense that these narratives were attempts to participate in the legal arena by asking authorities to judge and punish violators, but in the broader sense that the practice of defining what counts as a violation was already contingent on particular sets of legal categories. This fact of legal mediation in the writing of non-elite history is thereby complicated not only because a layer has been added to the analysis, but also because such a history runs up against a deep and persistent disciplinary division.

In the historical tradition, one might say, individuals exist in the subjunctive, always as an endless series of possibilities, capacities, and complexities; law exists in the imperative, a series of commands, reductive and violent. Individuals make their world within dense and overlapping reciprocal networks; within these networks they share stories, rituals, gods, meals, and families. Law reduces networks to flowcharts of authority, abstracting those within the networks and treating them as replaceable units of analysis. Individuals exist in time and space; law tries its best to develop an allergy to such categories. The project, then, would seem to be built on a fundamental tension between two different visions of how to map the social world, and the histories which emerge from it tend to be stories of the conflicts between these two irreconcilable ways of imagining such a world. They are normally tragic stories, for no matter how crafty a litigant might be, no matter how well he or she might negotiate the complexities of a judicial system, the law nonetheless frequently wins.

The above diagnosis could be faulted in many ways: social historians, it could be objected, have always romanticized non-elites to an intolerable degree. Humans are not endlessly capable, but radically bounded by structural and environmental factors, as well as by various mental demons of their own making. Law is not divorced from social relations, but deeply embedded. Nor is it unidirectional or transcendent. Drawing a line between law and society is anyhow a flawed project, because it merely replicates a typically "legal" claim—the claim, made most often by practitioners of law, that law is *not* the social or the everyday, that it is something that has a different essence (should we wish to be metaphysical), a logic and language fundamentally its own, and a capacity to remain innocent of or at least insulated from the work of everyday life.

Objections could be multiplied, but they begin to feel thin to historians. And this is not because these objections are wrong (they are not), or because historians are unphilosophical people (though they sometimes are). They feel thin because, if we take the primary task of social history to be that of giving an account of the reasoning that our subjects gave for their behaviors, then these objections seem to have held little weight *for them*. They took problems to court. They asked for judgment. They fell into stunned silence or joyous relief at the reading of sentences. They moved through a social world wearing (and watching, and interpreting) scars from judicial whips and rods. Alternatively, these objections begin to feel thin because so much of social history is anyhow done on the back of law's records: in societies in which literacy is not widespread we can count on finding non-elites in judicial archives, where their understandings of themselves were contested by others. Think here only of Carlo Ginsburg's monumental work on inquisitorial records. Even in societies with abundant documentation and high literacy rates judicial records have proven a boon, given the vagaries of archival preservation.

But here we have come no closer to a method, and no closer to an answer as to whether the results will be entirely predictable when we pair social history with the history of the subject before the law. What we need is an explanation of why people found these structures so congenial in the first place, why law served as an important category *to them*—a richer explanation as to why, given the tremendous stakes and the possibility of disaster, someone would have been willing to move from open-textured capacities and possibilities to the world of judgments. And here I am loath to accept explanations that cast subjects as mechanistically responding to some sort of external factor—that these practices of "going to law" somehow emerged or persisted "because of" culture or class or status or identity, ideology or false consciousness or bad faith, litigiousness or prickliness or honor, or out of a rational choice to maximize gains vis-à-vis other social actors. This is not to deny the existence of any such factor; it is to deny all of them a priori causal status. It is to do so because these explanations—in fact, even the logical form of these explanations—strike me as being, at the very least, deeply inhumane. They smell of the kind of social theory that historians have often rightly distrusted: cold, abstract, and mechanistic—in many ways, the doublet of law itself.[1] Such theories, it seems, have smuggled law's most frustrating and mystifying elements into their own projects.[2]

This is not to say that social theory is useless to historians (it is not). It is to say that, if we wish to remain true to the humane project of social history, easy explanations are not to be had, and the usefulness of any theory will be judged by its capacity to do hermeneutic service, rather than provide a ready account of causation—that is, it will be judged by its ability to open up more possibilities and richer understandings, not to wrap the world into a neat and tidy package. This was, I take it, the stance of E. P. Thompson, and one reason his work has proven enduring.

The world may not be neat and tidy, yet people often wish it to be. This brings me to the central thesis of this project: when the social world—with its possibilities, networks, and participants—becomes, for whatever reason, overwhelming, unlivable, or intolerable, law may provide a means to rectify this situation. It does this not because it is necessarily a source of fair judgments or because it is per se a source of power (though it can be), but because, through its compressions, fictions, translations, and abstractions, it provides a manageable and simplified framework—a conceptual language—for people to rethink themselves and their relationships. It can serve, in however imperfect and attenuated ways, as a source for people to theorize themselves and their behavior—to answer the question "Who am I, where do I fit within my world, and how can I render that world tolerable?" As with social theory, law's most important contribution to social life is hermeneutic.

As the title to this Introduction indicates, I have chosen to let Erving Goffman serve as my jumping-off point for this study. Goffman is perhaps the least systematic of social theorists; he was at his best as a diagnostician of human behavior. His central claim, to simplify greatly, is that human behavior and interactions are aimed at the goal of inhabiting a tolerable universe. Human beings do this by a series of small maneuvers, enacting delicate scripts that structure conduct and make it regular, predictable, knowable, or at least capable of being explained. But when these scripts fall apart, or when there is dissonance between the person and the script, repair work needs to be done, for these dissonances make the world fundamentally unlivable. But what happens when people are cast in a script which they find horrid or objectionable? How do they change it? What were the mechanics behind this process of changing a script? Here Goffman's answers tend to be unsatisfactory, or at least depressing (for often, in the case of his other famous book, *Stigma: Notes on the Management of Spoiled Identity*, the script cannot be changed). What I will argue, in the course of this book, is that, in Roman Egypt at least, law provided one mechanism for changing these scripts. It did this because of the particular ways in which it interacted with narratives.

My strategy is this: to take narratives (in this case, petitions concerning violence) seriously and to read them sympathetically; to try, insofar as possible, to work out the logic of the claims that petitioners are making, to place these claims within both local and comparative contexts, and to propose a model for making them "make sense" to a historian that comes closer to explaining the way that they might have made sense to a petitioner in the Egyptian countryside. Two caveats are important. First, "sympathetic" reading, here, does not involve having to like, appreciate, or enjoy one's informants. It does not entail a political commitment to sympathize with or romanticize nonelite people. If anything, the people who wrote petitions in Egypt are very much like any group of people who tend to complain: they lie and exaggerate, they whine; they are occasionally funny or clownish, periodically pitiable; sometimes we might suspect that they are a bit thuggish. Reading sympathetically simply entails that when they make claims we take them seriously, and try to understand the social, legal, and institutional contexts in which claim-making takes place. Second: when I speak of comparison, I mean comparative method, not comparative evidence. Bluntly put, I do not believe that the latter category has any meaningful purchase as a method, at least not in the sense that ancient historians have applied it in the last few decades—as a way of coping with the fact that our sources are incomplete and fragmentary by substituting information from "better documented" societies. Comparative method, here, is used in the ways described by Jonathan Z. Smith: as a stance that mistrusts easy analogies and coincidences, and tries instead to develop a rich language of difference.[3] Whether I have been successful in this will be judged by what follows.

What follows also tries to accomplish a larger goal, namely, that of outlining a dialectical model of imperial law and governance on the basis of this particular genre of narrative complaint. I attempt this through two main lines of inquiry. First, I try to show how violence "worked" in day-to-day life in Roman and Late Antique Egypt. This involves outlining the ways violence was discussed, how it was acted out in towns and villages, where it fit in disputes between individuals and families, how it served to govern, shape, and alter interpersonal relationships, and how it was transformed, through the language of law, into legal complaints, courtroom hearings, and institutionalized punishments. As I hope to show in what follows, violence has always had a peculiar role in the history of Roman Egypt. The discussions of Egyptian violence in literary sources from the Roman period—which portrayed Egypt as a violent place, a hardscrabble backwater filled with superstitious inhabitants particularly unsuited to civil government, and held in place only by force of arms—has had major historiographical consequences for writing the history of violence in Egypt. Specifically, it has at times forced historians to engage in apologetic treatments rather than close analysis of Egyptian violence.[4]

An analysis of the style of violence is a central part of this study, but in addition I hope to contribute to the ways we understand the Roman legal system in the provinces, and, at a broader theoretical level, to how we understand the relationship between law and society in general. This involves several related things. It involves outlining what a bottom-up view of the law might have looked like in Roman Egypt, clarifying what we think we mean when we speak of provincials entering the field of legal contest, and giving an account of both the rules and the relationships that were meaningful in a Roman province, as well as what Žižek calls the "metarules" or Searle calls the "background"—the correct system of applying rules in the first place.[5] It goes without saying that both of these categories—the rules and the ways to apply the rules properly—were constantly changing and precisely the object of contest. It also involves explaining more precisely why people chose to alter their relationships through the legal sphere in the first place. When we explain these phenomena properly, law begins to look like a rather different creature from what historians (and in particular, ancient historians) often take it to be: rather than a system of rules to be applied correctly or erroneously or a simple imposition of imperial power, law emerges, paradoxically perhaps, as both a field of contested practice and a simplifying language through which individual petitioners can redefine themselves and their universe of personal relationships.

These are perhaps less than modest goals, and if it were possible to achieve them it would probably represent the culmination of a career or a lifetime, rather than the product of a short and restricted study. But I hope that it will be possible to essay some tentative answers to some of these questions, to push the evidence farther than has been done previously, to find ways of making old documents say new things, and to present, through a detailed study of violence, some models through which these larger questions can be pursued. What follows will not be the last word on violence, law, or society in Egypt, but will serve three functions. First, I hope to complement some recent trends in ancient history and papyrology, especially the laudable efforts in the last twenty or so years that have sought broaden the scope of the issues on which papyri can be brought to bear.[6] Second and more important, I hope to contribute to some larger discussions of how to write social history from legal documents, especially where the content of the documents reflects actions that are, necessarily, viewed as aberrant, problematic, or contested either by an individual or by the community at large.[7] Finally, taken as a whole this work is an attempt to write provincial history from the bottom up, as a series of complicated transactions and conversations, as well as to bring individual choice and agency into the picture.[8]

The argument proceeds in two parts. Part I is largely an exercise in brush-clearing. I begin in Chapter 1 by giving a close reading of one petition, and present some of the questions that will guide what follows. In Chapter 2 I discuss the significance of the fact that our documentation comes from Egypt, and that Egypt was a part of the Roman Empire. Here I deal with the matter of Egyptian exceptionalism, and begin to describe some of the institutional features of government in Egypt which I consider important to understanding what follows. Because one of the stories that was told by the Romans about Egypt was that it was "violent," in Chapter 3 I turn to a discussion of violence, and the import of such a term within contemporary historical and critical projects. From there I highlight some possible ways these contemporary categories can be reappropriated for dealing with ancient material. In Chapter 3 I also deal with the question of language, since, for reasons I discuss, violence and language are intimately connected. In this particular context, however, the language I am primarily interested in is mediated language, that is, the consequences of our documentation being intertwined with scribal traditions and practices.

Part II turns back to the world of petitioners and their claims. In Chapter 4 I discuss narrative techniques, and begin to outline the ideology that underpins petitioners' claims. I argue here that the rhetorical moves in petitions point to a world in which personal dignity is insecure and subject to constant evaluation by peers and neighbors, rather than being connected to rigid positions on a clearly delineated social hierarchy. This insecurity is rooted in an equalizing ideology that can be recovered through a careful analysis of the papyri. As a consequence of this ideology, however, social relationships are complex and multifaceted, and no clear patterns of deference emerge from the world that petitioners describe. Chapter 5 continues the argument, providing an explanation of how the narratives did their work in a legal context. Here I address in greater detail a problem raised in Chapter 2, namely, the consequences of pluralism and localism for understanding petitioners' claims and strategies. Chapter 6 returns to petitioners and their opponents, and presents a model for understanding the role of violence in structuring the dynamics of interpersonal relations in Roman Egypt. A conclusion follows, as do appendices. The appendices contain translations of my primary sources, as well as a brief introduction to papyrology addressed to nonspecialists.

The central concepts that structure the argument are fiction, translation, metaphor, and narrative. These are concepts drawn from literature, not "social science" or "legal science."[9] The format I have chosen is that of a historical essay, not a comprehensive monograph or an edition of texts that treats all remaining extant evidence seriatim. My notes mark intellectual debts, document my claims about papyri, and pick the occasional fight. They are necessarily selective in their citations of secondary literature.

* * *

The question of sources structures nearly all historical projects, but is particularly acute for non-elite social history in the ancient world. For a variety of reasons that take their origins in various disciplinary configurations, the strong spine (if not the entire central nervous system) of ancient history has traditionally been the "literary" sources: works that have been passed through the medieval manuscript tradition, preserved because of their status as "classics," and copied and read in the Renaissance and thereafter as sources of humane value. "Literary," here, refers primarily to sources existing within this chain of preservation, not to sources of a particular genre (thus literary sources include poetry, but also history, epistolography, rhetoric, and technical manuals, for example). Though it is important not to paint with too broad a brush, the basic conclusion of many ancient historians is that these sources are frequently very useful for reconstructing political and military narratives and of mixed utility for reconstructing the cultural world of male elites, but they can be made to do little work for telling us about the lives of the vast majority of the inhabitants of the ancient world, Roman or otherwise. The reason given for this is that the literary sources do not tend to reflect reality, but rather to make tendentious and normative claims about it; their purpose was not to provide a record of sober analysis, but to position our largely aristocratic ancient authors within their societies. Phrased differently, literary sources are artifacts of elite "self-fashioning"—a term I am uncomfortable with. (All it seems to tell me is that language is positioned and performed—but when is language not a matter of speaking from somewhere? In what sense then would someone ever *not* be self-fashioning? And if all texts are *only* self-fashioning, then does the historical project not collapse into the study of comparative narcissisms?) Still, as a diagnosis of what the literary sources *do* say about non-elites, this assessment seems fair. Romans writers were, unsurprisingly, not great fans of their social inferiors; they tell us little about them, and what they do tend to tell us is that their inferiors were, well, inferior.

"Documentary" sources provide one way around this problem. (It is conventional, in ancient history, to distinguish literary sources from "documentary" ones—namely, inscriptions and papyri.) Inscriptions record massive amounts of information regarding administration, official careers, and burial practices, to name but a few categories. Making history from inscribed documents is still very much a work in progress, despite huge advances over the last two hundred years. This progress has improved substantially our knowledge of the ancient world, and given insights into the precise ways in which the literary tradition distorts matters. But inscriptions were an expensive technology. While they served to monumentalize things that individuals thought important, they are hard to use to write non-elite history.

It is papyri that provide the greatest promise for this sort of project. While they are found in a variety of parts of the Roman Empire, Egypt provides our greatest concentration of them. Starting in the late nineteenth century, they began to be published by generations of careful scholars, on whose work and expertise this study rests. Still, they are not an "even" data set, even within Egypt. Recovered papyri tend to come from two main areas, the Fayyum basin and the excavated cache of documents preserved in the garbage mound of the city of Oxyrhynchos. A few come from other places as well: the western Oases, for example. They come primarily from concentrated areas of population—towns, cities, and villages, not predominantly agricultural areas. Their preservation is also chronologically uneven—the second and fourth centuries are well represented, whereas information for the fifth century, for example, is spotty. Chronological preservation also varies geographically. Additionally, while many thousands of papyri have been preserved, large numbers remain unpublished. What publications there are (and there are many) are the product of shifting editorial interests, from the earliest phases in which social history was subordinated to literary and legal history, to the more recent editorial interests in archives and record-keeping. As for the content of the documents themselves, what is published is rarely a straightforward record of personal beliefs, but is almost exclusively mediated through scribes and literate professionals composing on behalf of a largely illiterate society. Additionally, though papyri initially were considered to have much promise for social historians, they are not representative of the population as a whole. Though all who work with papyri will concede this point, it is still largely unclear and hotly debated what segment of the population they do represent.

These difficulties aside, papyri in general, and petitions concerning violence more specifically remain an important data set. The people writing them were significantly different from the writers of the literary tradition. They were non-elites in any meaningful sense of the term. Here, for reasons that will become apparent, I have focused on petitions from the first six centuries of Roman rule in Egypt: a period from the Roman acquisition of Egypt in 30 B.C. until, more or less, the age of Justinian in the sixth century A.D. Justinian is formally my endpoint, but I have resisted treating the sixth century in a rigorous fashion: this is because one major cache of sixth-century papyri, the papers of Dioskoros of Aphrodito, are currently being reedited by the able hands of Jean-Luc Fournet and his team of students. But the pre-Justinianic papyri are important in a different sense: they come from a period before the introduction of the first properly comprehensive promulgation of Roman law, Justinian's *Corpus Iuris Civilis*—that is, they come from a period in which law was largely uncodified and, despite imperial queasiness with this fact, also still developing. I have little to say about the preceding Ptolemaic period. There is certainly a story to be told here, but since I lack the linguistic capacities to deal with the demotic evidence, someone else will have to tell it. And for the purposes of preserving my already limited sanity, I have restricted myself to material from Egypt, though we have petitions concerning violence from other places as well.

PART I

The Texture of the Problem

CHAPTER I

Ptolemaios Complains

Sometime between A.D. 145 and 147, Ptolemaios, son of Diodoros, sent a petition to Lucius Valerius Proculus, prefect of the province of Egypt (*praefectus Aegypti*), the highest magistrate in the land and a man appointed directly by Emperor Antoninus Pius. His complaint recounted a violent incident with a man named Ammonios, also named Kaboi. According to Ptolemaios, Ammonios was sent to attack him by another man, Isidoros, son of Mareis. This Isidoros held a privileged position in the area, being one of the *nautokolymbetai* ("sailor-divers")—apparently (since we only know the term from Ptolemaios' complaint) a group of people in charge of the administration of water in the Fayyum—no unimportant task in an area where careful management of water could mean the difference between security and starvation. In recompense for this important service, Ptolemaios goes on to explain, Isidoros and his fellow *nautokolymbetai* were excused from liturgies (compulsory public services—a redistributive scheme of mandatory "gifts" of public goods by the wealthy, and increasingly in the Roman period, by anyone foolish enough not to produce an excuse to avoid paying for them). Because of the nature of his position, Isidoros was excused as well from the burdensome poll-tax. Lest we be misled into treating Isidoros' services to the community as an index of a magnanimous character, Ptolemaios explains further: Isidoros is personally a nasty individual who makes money on the side by forging official leases for personal gain. Ammonios, Isidoros' subordinate, is no better: a man incapable of living moderately, his behavior had brought him to public attention on a previous occasion. Ptolemaios, by contrast, is a quiet person. He holds an official lease, for which he has given security, and in addition he pays his taxes—great sums of them, at that. He is a model inhabitant of Rome's empire: a landholder, a stakeholder; presumably in general he is resistant to raising a fuss, but who could abide officials acting illegally? When he was violently treated by Ammonios and Isidoros, when he was thrown out of his house by them, and when they beat him until he paid them money to stop, he had no choice but to avail himself of the intervention of their superiors. The emperor would have guaranteed it, and Ptolemaios knew that the prefect himself would have wanted as much as well.

Accordingly, Ptolemaios went to the scribe of his local village, and through a combination of stock phrases and idiosyncratic rhetoric detailed his complaints against his local enemies. We know that in other cases he drafted his own petitions, since we can match the signature at the bottom of this particular complaint with the handwriting on some of his other documents; in this case it is unclear if he drafted an initial version, but certain (because of the distinct handwriting) that a scribe wrote this version for him, not least because of the necessity of making several copies—probably three or four in total.[1] Once these copies of the original complaint were made (and likely after a process of negotiation that would produce the final version), the scribe would have given the copies back to Ptolemaios to submit on his own behalf—generally in person at the prefect's annual assizes, though in this case we know they were sent, since Ptolemaios tells us that the assizes for this year were delayed due to the upcoming Nile flood.[2] Of the copies one has survived; it was purchased by B. P. Grenfell and F. W. Kelsey in Egypt in March 1920, and brought by Kelsey back to the University of Michigan, where it is now housed in a temperature- and humidity-controlled room on the top floor of the Hatcher Graduate Library. Other documents relating to Ptolemaios have come to light as well, and reside in locations as diverse as Cairo, Florence, Geneva, Hamburg, New York, Oslo, and Madison.

This particular papyrus, published according to standard papyrological notation as P.Mich. III 174 (document number 174 contained in the third published volume of documents from the Michigan collection), is, if nothing else, a model of good preservation. From the annotations on the bottom of the papyrus, we can tell which copy this was: it was one of those that he had sent to the prefect. A copy would have remained in the prefect's archives, and another would have been returned to Ptolemaios, bearing two bits of text. One is that of whichever member of the prefect's staff was in charge of handling this particular petition. He instructed Ptolemaios to present his petition to the *strategos*, the chief magistrate of the Arsinoite nome, the administrative division which included the Fayyum and Ptolemaios' home town of Theadelphia. Finally, there is a fourth hand which might be that of the prefect himself.[3] This fourth hand provides the six crucial letters in this document: *apodos*: "return it"—that is, give the subscribed petition back to the petitioner, and let him bring it himself to the *strategos* who would ultimately be responsible for handling Ptolemaios' lawsuit. It was this phrase that represented the moment in which the state acceded to the demands for justice from its subjects, and this small Greek word was responsible for setting the institutional mechanism of justice in motion:

> Λ̣ουκίωι Οὐαλερίωι Πρόκλωι ἐπάρχωι Αἰγύπτου π̣αρὰ Πτολ̣[ε]μ̣αίου Διοδώρου τοῦ καὶ Διοσκόρου τῶν ἀπὸ τοῦ Ἀρσινοείτου νομοῦ. τῆς ἐ̣μ̣φύτου σ[ο]υ, ἡγεμὼν κύριε, εὐεργεσίας εἰς πάντας φθανούσ̣ης καὶ αὐτὸς τυχεῖν δέομαι. εἶδός τί ἐσ̣τιν ἐν τῷ νομῷ̣ ἐν ἀριθμῷ̣ ἀνδρῶν οἳ καλοῦνται ναυτοκολυμβηταί, οὗτοι δημ[ό]σιοι ὄντες καὶ τῇ τῶν ὑδάτων διοικήσει ὑπηρετοῦντες προσμένοντές τε τοῖς κατ[ὰ] καιρὸν αἰγιαλοφύλαξι καὶ κατασπορεῦσι, διὸ καὶ ἀφίονται παντὸς ἐπικεφαλαίου καὶ πάσης λ̣ειτουργίας ἔτι δὲ καὶ ἐκ τοῦ δημοσίου σιτοῦνται καθ' ὃ οὐκ ἐξὸν αὐτοῖς καθόλου ἑτ[έ]ρ̣α̣ τινὶ πραγματείᾳ̣ παρενχειρεῖν. τούτων εἷς τις Ἰσίδωρος Μαρεῖ ἀνὴρ π̣ά̣νυ το[λ]μήεις καὶ αὐθάδης τῷ̣ τρόπῳ̣ δι' ὑποβλήτων νοθεύων τὰς κυριακὰς μ̣ισθώσεις χάριν τοῦ διασεί<ει>ν καὶ ἀργυρίζεσθαι καθ' ὃ καὶ ἀποδείξω ἐπὶ τοῦ ῥητοῦ ἐπῆλθεν̣ καὶ ἐμοὶ δι' ἑνὸς τῶν ὑποβλήτων Ἀμμωνίου τινὸς ἐπικαλουμένου Καβοι ἀνδρὸς ἐπιμέμπτου καὶ διὰ τὸ ἀκόσμως βιοῖν προγραφέντος τυγχάνοντι οὐσιακῷ μισθωτῇ καὶ ἱκανοὺς φόρους διαγράφοντι εἰς τὸν κυριακὸν λόγον καὶ πρὸς τὴν μίσθωσιν ἱκανὰ ὑπαλλάξαντι οὐκ ἐῶν προσευκαιρεῖν τῇ μισθώσει ἀ̣λλὰ καὶ τοῦ οἴκ̣[ου] ἐκκλείων καὶ ὕβρεις παρέχων μέχρι καὶ διέσεισέν με ἀργύριον. ὅθεν ἐπὶ σὲ τὸν π̣άντων ἀντιλήμπτορα κατέφυγον καὶ ἀξιῶ ἐπειδὴ τοῦ παρόντος παρητήσ̣ω τὴν εἰς τὸν νομὸν ε̣ἴσοδον κελεῦσαι γραφῆναι τῷ τῆς Θεμίστου καὶ Πο̣λέμωνος στρατηγῷ̣ διακοῦσαί μου πρὸς αὐτ[ὸ]ν διὰ τὸ τὰς ἀποδείξεις δύνασθαί μ̣ε̣ ἐπὶ τῶν τόπων παραστῆσαι ὑπὲρ τ̣ο̣ῦ̣ ὑβρίσθαι καὶ διασεσεῖσθαι ἵνα δυνηθῷ̣ ἐν τοῖς εὐτυχεστάτοις τοῦ μεγίστου Αὐτοκράτορος καιροῖς καὶ ἐν τῇ ἐπαφρο[δ]ίτῳ̣ σου ἡγεμονίᾳ̣ ἀνεπηρεάστως ἐν τῇ ἰδίᾳ διαζῆν καὶ ὦ βεβο[η]θημένος. διευτύχει.
> (hand 2) Πτολεμ̣α̣[ῖο]ς Διοδώρου ἐπιδέδωκα καθὼς πρόκιται.
> (hand 3) ὁ στρατηγὸς τοῦ νομοῦ τὰ δέοντα ποιήσει.
> (hand) ἀπόδος

> To Lucius Valerius Proculus, prefect of Egypt,
> From Ptolemaios, son of Diodoros, also called Dioskoros, one of

> those from the Arsinoite nome. Your inborn benevolence, lord prefect, reaches all, and I ask to receive it as well. There are a certain number of people in my district who are called *nautokolymbetai*. These men are public officials and are in charge of the administration of water, and are attached to the shore-wardens and cultivators, and therefore they are also relieved of the entire poll-tax and exempt from every compulsory public service. They are even fed at public expense since they are completely prohibited from engaging in any other sort of work. One of these men is Isidoros son of Mareis, a truly reckless man with a surly character, who through his henchmen counterfeits official leases for the sake of extortion and profit—all of this I will prove to you at trial. Isidoros attacked me as well, by sending one of his henchmen, a man named Ammonios also known as Kaboi, a man who is worthy of blame and who has been proscribed on account of his immoderate lifestyle. He came after me despite the fact that I am the holder of an official lease and that I pay a great deal of money into the official treasury, and that I gave security for my lease. But this man does not allow me to enjoy my lease, but instead he shut me out of my house and beat me until he extorted money from me. Therefore I flee to you, the protector of all, and I ask you, since for the moment you have delayed your assizes in our nome, to order a letter to be written to the *strategos* of the division of Polemo and Themistes telling him to hear my case against him, since I am able to bring proofs before him of the violence and extortion, so that I can continue to live unmolested in my private property, enjoying the most happy times of our great emperors and of your gracious governorship, and so that I may be helped. Farewell.
> (hand 2) I, Ptolemaios son of Diodoros, have submitted the aforementioned petition.
> (hand 3) The *strategos* of the nome will do what is fitting.
> (hand 4) Return it.

Ptolemaios is an odd character, even by the standards of authors of Egyptian papyri. Because we have a number of his papers, and—equally important, for this context at least—a number of his petitions, we can recognize both an idiosyncratic style of complaint and an inability to live peacefully with his neighbors. In two other roughly contemporaneous petitions, we find Ptolemaios in trouble with a man he describes as the local loan shark; he complains

Figure 1. *P.Mich.* III 174. Digitally reproduced with the permission of the Papyrology Collection, Graduate Library, University of Michigan.

about the violence the man's assistants use against him, but also admits that he owes them the money and requests only that he not be made to pay a penny more interest than what is legal.[4] He also complains that this loan shark—who it turns out, from another of Ptolemaios' petitions, is also the son of a former *gymnasiarch*,[5] a position of honor in the community—is keeping his case from being heard by the local court (that of the *strategos*), which may indicate either paranoia on Ptolemaios' part or a probably reasonable policy of avoiding him on the part of the other villagers. In a different case, he complains that another of his enemies, a man named Sarapion, had insulted the nome *strategos* (why *Ptolemaios* chose to complain about this is, of course, obscure).[6] One is tempted to imagine that he grated more than just a little on the other members of his village.

In addition to his habit of complaining to high authorities about the unacceptable behavior of his neighbors, it appears that Ptolemaios also fancied himself a bit of a *litterateur*: this petition—like his others—is marked by odd syntax and a general bombast largely absent from petitions of the second century, though somewhat more common in late antiquity (that is, from the fourth century on).[7] He enjoys odd words: when describing Isidoros as "reckless" Ptolemaios prefers an archaism (τολμήεις, rather than the more typical τολμηρός); Ammonios is not just an attendant or a subordinate (ὑπηρέτης) but a "henchman" (ὑπόβλητος), a term which also—and probably this is intentional—means "suppositious child," and which therefore also constitutes an insult to Ammonios' family.[8] "Goon" would capture it well in English. In other petitions, he is prone to clichéd platitudes: "Of all the horrid things in life, the worst is for free men to suffer violence"—a sentiment repeated, with only minor variation, in two of his petitions.[9] Whatever he was, Ptolemaios was *not* a simple peasant suffering under the weight of official venality, begging abjectly to retain a shred of rights in his person and property.

It is harder, however, to decide where to place Ptolemaios on a social scale. The editor of one of his other petitions had originally concluded from a fragmentary line that he was a veteran, or at least a child of veterans settled in the Fayyum, but this has become doubtful, and others suspect that the papyrus in question has been misread.[10] This, unfortunately, leaves us with little. It is probably of some significance that his petition was answered in the first place. Of the many petitions presented to the prefect in the first five centuries of Roman rule, probably only a minority ever received any sort of decisive action; the rest were shuffled to the desks of other officials in an ancient ritual of buck-passing.[11] Even to get access to the prefect (or even a member of his staff) to deliver a complaint usually meant lining up with what must have been a loud, unruly throng of people once a year when the prefect made his annual assizes (an event known by its Latin name *conventus*; the Greek inhabitants of Egypt called it the "settling of accounts"—*dialogismos*—or, in Ptolemaios' case, simply his "entrance"—*eisodos*). Within several days of work at the *conventus*, many hundreds of petitions would have been reviewed and processed. One crucial papyrus gives a number: more than 1,800 petitions were submitted over three days at a stop in the *conventus* of 209.[12] The prefect would not handle most of them in person, though members of his staff would, provided that the petitioners got the documentation right and brought the relevant supporting evidence, and that they were heard before the Nile began to flood (it being considered sacrilegious for the ruler to travel along it during that time).[13] In this case, Ptolemaios' complaint had reached the prefect despite (or because of?) this lack of attendance in the nome.[14] Special cases—that is, those of great importance or, perhaps more likely, those of important people—might be heard at this time, but more likely would be passed down the chain of command, as was the petition of Ptolemaios.

The prefect was not the only individual who would receive petitions. Some could be sent to the *epistrategos*, another Roman official, whose reply was probably as likely as that of the prefect himself. Most often petitions were sent to the *strategos*, the chief magistrate of the nome. However, individuals could also petition centurions, especially if they lived in out-of-the way places; certain high-ranking soldiers if their cases concerned abuses by military officials; officials of the church (in late antiquity); and a number of other individuals (such as the *eirenarch*, *riparios*, or *nyktostrategos*) who composed what I will simply refer to as the "legal system" in Roman and late antique Egypt.[15]

With the endorsement from the prefect's office on his petition, Ptolemaios could then go to the *strategos* of the nome, who would be under pressure to hear his case. He could have gone to the *strategos* in the first place, and possibly have received the same thing, but given his evident dissatisfaction with the structures of local government it makes a certain degree of sense that he would seek to go to the top first. If the local *strategos* was in fact sympathetic to those who felt that they were being harassed by him and his constant petitions, the prefect's signature was a meaningful goad. If the *strategos* ignored Ptolemaios (again), Ptolemaios might choose to complain again to the prefect, though this time not about Isidoros, but about the state of the administration of justice in the nome. Going directly to a higher authority would, most likely, make sure that the local officials had an extra incentive to pay attention to his complaint.

If Ptolemaios succeeded in getting the attention of the *strategos*, this would have been the beginning, rather than the end of his legal headaches. Isidoros and Ammonios might have been "summoned" to appear before the relevant magistrates; they may also have been arrested and confined before trial.[16] But what this process might have actually achieved at the end of the day is remarkably unclear. One of the most frustrating aspects of the papyrological record is that, while we have numerous papyri that preserve complaints, we have little in the way of evidence for how the process was subsequently handled, and even less that might tell us how, or even if, conflicts and disputes were brought to a close.

For the present purposes, however, it is sufficient to speculate on the possibilities, even if this means pushing beyond the limits of what Ptolemaios' petition actually tells us. On the assumption that the *strategos* chose to bring the relevant parties in for a hearing, there may have been some sort of a trial. There are a fair number of these "reports of proceedings" preserved on papyrus, but none that can be shown to be the outcome of a specific petition.[17] If there were proceedings, Ptolemaios' assailants could choose not to show up, which would complicate things further, or the relevant magistrate might choose to send the petition to other officials—perhaps even back to the prefect. But if by some fortuitous accident all went as planned—the *strategos* chose to hold a hearing, and the assailants attended—what might have come of this is still somewhat obscure.

The position of *strategos* was an unenviable one. His title was a relic of the Ptolemaic period, but in the Roman period he was in charge of a number of things, not least of which was that he had to oversee the payment of taxes, as well as being the magistrate of both first and equally often final resort for civil cases (such as interpersonal violence, which was classified as a private relationship of obligation between two people, rather than a crime). He was usually an urban Greek-speaker, drawn from the ranks of a local ruling class, serving a term of roughly three years. He would have been, until probably the start of the fourth century when he ceases to be attested in the papyri, appointed by the prefect and *epistrategos* to serve in a nome other than the one from which he came.[18] This was a reasonable policy designed to prevent favoritism. But the end result was probably that the *strategos* worked in a vacuum.[19] This would have had the effect of making the administration of justice risky, not least because it would necessarily be grounded in a policy of mollifying the local bigwigs on whom he was dependent for the collection of taxes. Most likely, he would have been tempted to ignore certain people; still, if pushed to decide a case, or even to punish, the *strategos* could be brutal.[20] Ptolemaios himself knew this, and in another petition makes clear that the *strategoi* were capable of applying whippings and beatings.[21] It would be rare, however, and probably counter-productive, to use corporal punishment on a man like Isidoros—at least if we trust Ptolemaios' description of his position. Ammonios—again, if we choose to believe Ptolemaios—would likely have been beatable—*if* he was not under Isidoros' protection. The attackers might alternatively be forced to pay a monetary penalty to Ptolemaios, or they might have been let off with a warning, after being forced to make a humiliating statement that they would no longer bother him—essentially an ancient version of a restraining order, accompanied by an oath to the emperor for good measure.[22] Nevertheless, and this cannot be emphasized enough, the kind of interpersonal violence that Ptolemaios describes was a private or civil wrong (a "delict" in Roman terminology), rather than a public or criminal wrong. As such, it was not of primary interest to the state, and there is no evidence that the kinds of increasingly brutal penalties that were so typically attached to public or criminal cases—such as deportation, condemnation to the mines, or being thrown to animals—would have been at stake in his case.[23]

* * *

Knowing these things—or more accurately, reasonably suspecting them—only leaves us with a package of problems, both interpretive and epistemological. We could frame the inquiry at several levels.

• We could use this document as a source to evaluate the performance characteristics of an ancient empire. Is Ptolemaios' petition an angry and petulant letter of complaint from a cantankerous man—something not worth reflecting on except as a vignette, a source of occasional "color" in our otherwise serious accounts of economies, identities, and armies? Is it instead a righteous protest against a broken system, evidence of a growing level of corruption in the running of the Roman provinces? Or conversely, could we assume that in any system things will go wrong, and that what this document tells us is that the system was functioning *well* in the second century?—After all, the prefect did accept the complaint, and allow official measures to be taken.

• We could similarly ask questions about that nature of rhetoric in the ancient world. Does Ptolemaios' complaint preserve a local rhetoric? Is this the authentic voice of an injured man relatively low on the social scale (at least compared to our extant literary authors)? Or does the intrusion of formal legal language through the hand of a scribe leave us with something more approaching a form letter—a document, embellished to be sure, that is fundamentally no different from the many other petitions that were filed in the Roman Empire and that have been preserved on papyrus? If we could do the philology carefully and comparatively enough, could we excavate some sort of "true" or "authentic" feeling from this complaint? Does the fact that Ptolemaios wrote in an idiosyncratic style make it more or less likely that *he* sincerely believed the claims in his petition? If, on the other hand, we choose to avoid these questions of truth and authenticity, is it nonetheless significant that formal legal vocabularies have interpenetrated the languages of towns and villages on the margins of a vast administrative state? Should we treat Ptolemaios' complaint, in other words, primarily as an artifact that preserves or presents evidence of linguistic and bureaucratic hegemony and ideology—or as an artifact that does not?

• We could also ask a group of questions about law, and about the operation of law in society. Did Ptolemaios' complaint succeed in getting the prefect's attention because he followed all the rules, requirements, and formalities of the legal system in Roman Egypt? Is there any evidence that he knew the rules in the first place? Did the scribe who made copies of the petition know the rules? Did the governor know them? What were these rules anyway, and did they change over time? Does the fact that Ptolemaios wrote a petition to Roman authorities indicate that he violated the rules and requirements of village life—a sort of ancient "code of the street" that ensured everyday cooperation and dispute-containment so that the collective did not starve? Or does the existence of his petition testify to the irrelevance or nonexistence of these rules in the first place?

These are all important questions, and the list is far from exhaustive. They also tend to be the questions that are asked of these documents by papyrologists and historians. In what follows some of them will be addressed; others, I fear, we have no possibility of answering—or at least, I have not figured out answers to them yet. But they are also, in my view, second-order questions. They use individual documents like Ptolemaios' petition to speak to larger, preexisting questions; they attempt, in other words, to use the particular as a way of confirming or refuting the general: either Ptolemaios knew the rules or he did not, either the Roman government showed signs of corruption in second-century Theadelphia or it did not, either we can use his petition as the source of an authentic voice or we cannot.

This book, however, tries to come at these questions from a somewhat different angle. Instead of trying to use papyri such as Ptolemaios' complaint as a source for hypothesis-testing, I want instead to try to treat these complaints as being potentially theory-generating. We cannot forget what we already know about history, rhetoric, or sociology, of course, and this is not the point. Nonetheless I hope to show that it is worth starting from the bottom and building outward, writing a largely subjective, perception-based history from the papyri.[24] From reading these complaints closely, what can we learn about individuals living in a premodern Empire and how they perceived their world? What do these people tell us about what it means to live in (or run) an imperial system in which people are entitled to complain about their friends and neighbors, officials and rivals? What contribution do these complaints make towards the creation of a common culture, to the rule of law, and to imperial governance? And why is violence—and its accompanying narratives of wounded bodies and reputations—so central to all of this?

Building an interpretive framework for answering these questions, a methodological place to stand, is the central goal of this book. It involves work from the bottom up, reconstructing local worlds as they interact with imperial rules and realities of power. As such it is an exercise in the microhistory of ancient empires. But where microhistory has responded effectively to the challenges of "master-narrative" and "big" history, it has a tendency of slipping into antiquarianism at its worst, and occasionally, even at its best, into what can only be called "But-ing": a practice whereby microhistorians insist that every narrative is surely more complicated than what a historian presents, and as such, imperfect or limiting.[25] While I am sympathetic to a desire to complicate problematic master narratives, that is not the only goal of this book. The goal is to work from the bottom up *and* the top down, to generate a genuinely dialectical model of social interaction in a Roman province. This involves a process of reconstruction, but also an explanatory model of how individual perception and claim-making can come to interact with ruling institutions, contributing to the realities of a premodern empire and the forging of a common, tolerable—if also shifting and contested—*nomos*.[26]

* * *

This book is about violence, and, in particular, interpersonal violence, and the narrative complaints that emerge from instances of it. It is therefore also about fighting, bruising, complaining, whining, negotiating, and lying; the main characters are petitioners and their friends, enemies, families, henchmen, audiences, bureaucrats, and rulers; its main goal is to move from bruises and black eyes to larger claims about law, politics, justice, power, and empires—and especially to make claims about how these powerful ideas and structures were activated by, altered by, and imposed on individual people. I start from the assumption, which I will defend in greater detail in what follows, that violence offers a privileged territory for these explanations. For now, it will suffice to say that violence is a category that is unique in that everyone agrees that (a) it exists, in the sense that it was and it remains a meaningful way of categorizing behavior, and (b) it's always wrong when it happens to you (whether it is wrong when it happens to someone else is another matter entirely). Nobody, however, agrees what precisely it consists of, and this is what makes it interesting.

I also assume—for reasons I also hope to justify—that there is something special about the act of complaining, whether about violence or, for that matter, anything else. A complaint is, at its core, a claim on someone else's attention. It is a demand that somebody else recognize and respond to your pain, and if not respond, then at least acknowledge the feelings of another person—someone, by definition, who is at a different place on the hierarchy of power.[27] As a genre, it demands that a petitioner articulate, if only in bare outlines, a normative vision of his or her own world, and link that vision to a particular package of lived experiences. Sociologically speaking, certain institutions and relationships have to prevail in order for people to complain, and others for their complaints to be acted on; when these categories, relationships, and institutions do not exist they have to be invented. In short, complaints about violence are not just a source for realia of the ancient world that we can suppose to have existed anyway—that neighbors fight, that people do not enjoy pain, that the strong will sometimes take advantage of the weak. They give us, instead, a privileged perspective on an institutional world and the relationships it generates, tolerates, and sometimes invalidates. We can learn a great deal from these relationships, and how they adapt, change, and, in some cases, are reinvented when people avail themselves of them. And it hardly needs to be added that the act of complaining is interesting because it is political, both in the narrow sense that it involves a process of making claims on others, but also in the wider sense that complaints can change the balance of power in a given society—usually only at the margins, but sometimes in a much broader sense. As I write, young, unemployed people, having come to perceive themselves as disadvantaged and disenfranchised, have decided to complain. The people to whom and about whom they are complaining are justifiably terrified.

These two categories—violence and complaint—are a combustible mix, and as such they offer an unparalleled opportunity for historians. Conflict in general, and violent conflict in particular, forces individuals to articulate what they think they deserve, and forces them to transform notions of right and wrong into discernible rights and obligations. Complaining about violence was a meaningful act, a refusal to tolerate what someone else thought was deserved, a positive assertion of personal agency that sought to preserve dignity and redeem a victim in the eyes of those around him or her. The ability to call another individual's actions "violence" must not be dismissed as inconsequential or trivial, and if at the end of the day little was actually achieved through the act of petitioning, then it is therefore no less important to ask why individuals continually availed themselves of it. There are many hundreds of petitions preserved from the six and a half centuries of Roman rule.[28] Of these, there are roughly one hundred thirty that discuss violence.[29] Each represents, in its own way and through a stylized, bureaucratic, yet idiosyncratic vocabulary, a vision of the world as it should be.

CHAPTER 2

Violent Egypt

The Romans took over Egypt from the preceding Ptolemaic monarchy in 30 B.C., inheriting a developed and legally plural society with a strong bureaucratic infrastructure. They held Egypt as a province—or a group of provinces—until the Arab conquest in A.D. 640. The question that guides this chapter is, "What precisely does that mean, and what does the fact of empire contribute to a history of violence?" This question can be answered at several levels: culturally (by asking how Egypt fit within a Roman conceptual geography of the peoples that populated its empire), institutionally (by describing the governmental offices and bureaucratic arrangements that preceded Roman conquest and documenting how they shifted and transformed over time), and politically (by identifying the loci of power in provincial society and mapping them in an imperial hierarchy). These levels of analysis do not exhaust the possibilities: legal structures, which I take to be a privileged field, are also central, but as I will explain in greater detail further on, should not be described in the same way as cultural, institutional, or political structures, since one of their peculiarities in imperial contexts is that they can also serve to alter such structures. In addition, the challenge of locating Egypt in its imperial context is complicated by the unique climatic conditions that have allowed for the preservation of a large quantity of papyrological material; accordingly, it is possible to "check" in greater detail than in other provinces claims from Roman literature about the style of administration in Egypt. This ability to check and evaluate the literary sources has had two major historiographical consequences. First, it has often forced historians into falsifying, modifying, or (very rarely) affirming the claims of literary sources (the traditional, privileged canon of evidence from which ancient history is written) on the basis of papyrological documentation. At its best this can be an enlightening exercise, but in some cases it results in the history of the province being written either as tragedy or apology, instead of detailed and dynamic social analysis. Second, when attempts to make sense of both these conflicting bodies of evidence fail, it has resulted in scholars appealing to the notion that Egypt occupied some sort of "special place" in the Roman world.[1]

This chapter describes some of the basic institutional arrangements that prevailed in Egypt, while trying to avoid this sort of methodological impasse. Important to my central claims is a sub-thesis, namely, that while there is a convenient disciplinary division of labor between traditional historians of the Roman Empire and papyrologists, the papyrological and literary material—as well as evidence for the institutional arrangements generated by Roman provincial governors serving short (usually three-year) terms—do not constitute independent traditions that need to be checked against one another. They are, each in their own way, responses to the transformation of imperial governance and society in the first centuries A.D., and as such are differing sides of the same coin. That is, while they do periodically make claims that can be falsified or checked, they are also traditions that encapsulate ideas about what it means to govern and be governed, to rule an empire and to live in one. Both traditions therefore evolve pari passu, as part of a conversation on governance. It is, of course, a conversation between unequal partners, but as I hope to show, the gradation of inequality is less steep that some might imagine, since these inequalities were complicated, rather than reinforced, by legal arrangements.

Before moving to this analysis it is important to offer a disclaimer. The majority of this study is written from a synchronic perspective, since this seems to be the most profitable way to approach a genre of document that persists over a long period of time and is found in multiple parts of Egypt. Yet although this study will assess evidence from a broad chronological spectrum (from Augustus to the reign of Justinian, more or less), it is worth noting at the outset that Egypt was—and remains—a historical place, and as such has never been a stable entity, either "on the ground" or as part of a conceptual framework. It is true that some stereotypes die hard, and over the course of their long lives they serve to structure institutions in a particular way. The idea of a "violent Egypt" is one of these stereotypes, although I hope to show that even this one had a complex history. Accordingly, I will begin with how an imperial power came to understand its subject peoples and what role interactions with subject peoples played in the creation of these stereotypes. I will move from there to the question of institutions, and then to the role of papyri in writing the history of Egypt under the Romans. I close with reflection on the problems raised by the question, "was Egypt a particularly violent place?"

* * *

If we were to begin to understand Egypt from the perspective of an elite Roman living in the high Empire—say, from the period after the end of the Julio-Claudian dynasty and the civil wars of A.D. 69 through the middle of the third century—we would begin with literary sources, and conclude, after sorting through a variety of obiter dicta (since Egypt is not the subject of a extant "ethnographic" analysis or monograph after the early first century A.D.[2]), that it was a strange and violent place. Given that it was both strange and violent, other elements of its governmental infrastructure would seem to make more sense. It was governed in a practically unique way as compared to other provinces, namely, by a prefect of the equestrian rank who answered directly to the Emperor.[3] Senators (or even other powerful equestrians) were banned from visiting the province without special permission (the unexpected visit of Germanicus in A.D. 19 being a source of chagrin for the Emperor Tiberius).[4] The population as a whole was carefully structured into discrete "ethnic" groups (a problematic term, to which I will return): Alexandrian citizens, citizens of a few special "Greek" cities, Jews, and "Egyptians" (everyone else, irrespective of descent). This political and geographical isolation had consequences for social mobility into the highest echelons of Roman society (social mobility at other levels being a far more vexed issue): Egypt produced no senators until late antiquity, and relatively few equestrians. Even acquisition of Roman citizenship was difficult: Alexandrian citizenship, it appears, had to be obtained first. No colonies or municipia were located in Egypt. Symbolically important organs of local government and autonomy—town councils (βουλαί)—were absent throughout the Egyptian countryside (with the exception of the Hadrianic foundation of Antinoopolis in 130) until the visit of Septimius Severus in the beginning of the third century.[5] Egypt was therefore seen primarily as a fertile area, and, since it was populated by people who were fundamentally defective if not downright seditious, its basic role in the Empire was to be subjected to agricultural strip-mining.[6]

The story, so told, is a tragic, almost lachrymose history;[7] a counter-narrative could be posed, a narrative of resistance, in which the rich stories of individual people that can be extracted from the papyri are marshaled as a critique of the Roman tradition, a rebuke to the racist imagination of the imperial power.[8] In this counter-narrative, the Romans would be ignorant of the "true" facts on the ground, wrong about the intrinsic nature of the Egyptians (or the Greeks, or the Jews, or the Alexandrians), and, like all colonizing powers, guilty of having erroneously treated the oppressed as being in some way timeless and without a historical trajectory, and/or as an "other" who served as a textual mirror for imperial self-definition.

There is something slightly ironic about this position: while there is nothing per se wrong with trying to reconstruct distinctive perspectives from the "bottom up" (and indeed this is a central aim of this study), nor with emphasizing a disjuncture between elite literary sources and realities on the ground, to do so at the expense of treating either viewpoint (that of the imperial center or the subject population) as uncomplicated and homogeneous is bad historical practice. And, as with all attempts to smooth over historically dynamic processes, some key elements are lost in the process. While it is true that Roman authors of the high imperial period tended to cast Egypt (and Egyptians) as strange and violent, these claims have a history, and one that is more complex than can be accounted for by a simple accusation of imperialism, racism, Orientalism, or self-defining "othering."[9]

The Roman understanding of Egypt from the high Empire onward as strange and violent has, quite obviously, two parts. The "strange" part has a long history, dating back certainly to Herodotus, but probably originating in Hecataeus of Miletus. Herodotus famously saw Egypt as a place of inversion, an opposite of Greece, yet also a place whose very existence was a subtle critique of Greek culture, since many of the things that the Greeks claimed to be special about themselves was equally part of Egyptian self-definition, and furthermore, since a fair number of "Greek" practices had Egyptian roots.[10] While interesting commonalities between Greek and Egyptian culture could certainly be found, other aspects of Egyptian culture were harder to reconcile—in particular, the Egyptian preference for theriomorphic deities. It was also largely agreed that the Egyptians were best governed by powerful monarchs.[11] This dynamic tension, it seems, was profitably exploited by the Ptolemaic monarchs who ruled Egypt prior to its absorption into the Roman Empire.

This emphasis on difference—and the role of ethnographic writing in crafting difference—is well understood by scholars. What is more interesting for the purposes of this study is the emphasis on "violent"—and this seems to be largely an invention of the Romans, and in particular, of the Romans of the late first and early second centuries.[12] While Rome had been in contact, in some capacity or another, with the preceding Greco-Macedonian Ptolemaic monarchy since the third century B.C., it does not seem that it ever took a particular interest in generating detailed knowledge of the peoples of Egypt.[13] It is not until the age of Augustus that we have a serious description of Egypt, namely, in the seventeenth and final book of Strabo of Amaseia's *Geography*. Strikingly, Strabo is largely neutral on the character of Egyptians, and is in some ways positive (with the exception of a textually problematic passage in which he quotes Polybius).[14] If anything, the criticism he levels at Egypt is at the level of the Ptolemaic monarchy, which he presents as degenerate and incapable of governing. Their degeneracy led to Augustus' intervention to "stop the drunken violence" (ἔπαυσε παροινουμένην) and replace the monarchs with "wise" men (σωφρόνων)—the prefects of Egypt (17.1.12). The Egyptians of the *chora* or countryside, however, are in Strabo's account generally peaceful: it takes only three cohorts to maintain order, and even at that these cohorts are understaffed. The warlike nomads surrounding the Nile valley are themselves not a particular threat, either (17.1.53).

It is in the period between Strabo and Tacitus that it seems that the tradition of Egyptian violence comes to play a role in stock descriptions of the inhabitants of the province. The *locus classicus* is Tacitus' *Histories*, describing the state of the provinces during the civil wars which followed the death of Nero:

> Aegyptum copiasque, quibus coerceretur, iam inde a divo Augusto equites Romani obtinent loco regum: ita visum expedire, provinciam aditu difficilem, annonae fecundam, superstitione ac lascivia discordem et mobilem, insciam legum, ignaram magistratuum, domi retinere.

> Egypt—along with the armies that control it—has since the time of Augustus been ruled by Roman knights who have the role of kings. This seemed a good policy to keep domestic control over a province that is hard to access, full of grain, fickle and hostile because of superstition and wantonness, ignorant of laws, and unacquainted with government.[15]

The string of complaints about Egyptian character is striking in its pointed delivery. The fact that it comes from a "serious" historian like Tacitus makes it, at first glance, damning to the Egyptians. Naphtali Lewis even elevated these discrete criticisms to chapter headings in his justly famous survey, *Life in Egypt Under Roman Rule*, a formidable example of the sort of history "against the grain" that I alluded to earlier. But there is a danger in reading Tacitus in a wholly un-ironic manner here. The reference to kings is particularly telling: Tacitus knew well that the Roman equestrians walked a fine line between ruling like kings and being agents of the Emperor. Cornelius Gallus, the famous first prefect of Egypt, came too close to independence, denigrated the Emperor's reputation, and lost his life. The prince Germanicus, alluded to earlier, riled the Emperor Tiberius when he visited Egypt in A.D. 19. And, as Benjamin Kelly has argued, Tacitus' narrative of Germanicus' visit to Egypt in the *Annales* is pregnant with doubt about the nature of government at Rome, with Egypt (in this case Pharaonic Egypt) again serving as a mirror for the development and trajectory of one-man rule at Rome.[16]

Outside of the framework of Tacitus' overarching claims about the politics of kingship and governance, it remains to understand the insults to the Egyptians themselves. These are indeed part of an emerging pattern: the combination of strangeness (expressed here as religious fervor) and violence (inability to be governed) evident from the *Histories* of Tacitus can similarly be found in the work of his slightly younger contemporary, Juvenal, who combines both in his fifteenth *Satire*, and who focuses specifically on the inhabitants of the *chora* (the countryside, or rather, the entirety of Egypt excluding Alexandria). Here, the Egyptians not only worship strange monsters (*portenta*)—cats, dogs, fish, apes, birds, and crocodiles—they spend their time fighting over whose gods are best. This leads to implacable hatreds between villagers, in the case of this satire, between Ombo and Tentyra:

> inter finitimos uetus atque antiqua simultas,
> inmortale odium et numquam sanabile uulnus,
> ardet adhuc Ombos et Tentura. summus utrimque
> inde furor uolgo, quod numina uicinorum
> odit uterque locus, cum solos credat habendos
> esse deos quos ipse colit.

> Between these neighbors, Ombo and Tentyra, there is an old and venerable grudge, an immortal hatred, a wound that cannot be healed, one that still burns. There is the greatest hatred of each people for the other, since each place hates the gods of the other one, since they think that the gods that they worship are the only ones that deserve to be worshiped.[17]

Accordingly, the members of each village spend their time assaulting their neighbors on feast days: while their neighbors drunkenly revel (since the Egyptians, according to Juvenal, are particularly adept at this), the opposing village sneaks in and attacks. Noses get broken, cheeks scratched to the bone, eyes lacerated. But the fun of inter-village brawling could potentially be dismissed, were it enough to satisfy the malefactors. It was not:

> terga fugae celeri praestant instantibus Ombis
> qui uicina colunt umbrosae Tentura palmae.
> labitur hic quidam nimia formidine cursum
> praecipitans capiturque. ast illum in plurima sectum
> frusta et particulas, ut multis mortuus unus
> sufficeret, totum corrosis ossibus edit
> uictrix turba, nec ardenti decoxit aeno
> aut ueribus, longum usque adeo tardumque putauit
> expectare focos, contenta cadauere crudo.

> Those who inhabit neighboring Tentyra with its shady palm trees turn back, fleeing quickly from the charging Ombites; but one of them, running too fast and afraid, slips, falls, and is captured. He is sliced into a multitude of bits and pieces, so that one corpse will serve many. The victorious crowd devoured the whole thing, gnawing down even his bones—they didn't cook him down in a stew pot, or even make kebabs of him, thinking it too long even to wait for a fire. Instead, they were happy with just his raw corpse.[18]

Conflict over strange gods that are not even gods leads to the joy of pointless violence, which even then does not satisfy until it ends in an orgy of cannibalism. Devouring enemies raw, of course, involves violating two basic elements of humanity: violation of the taboo on cannibalism, but also the rejection of minimally dignified modes of preparation (cooking).[19] In this, the Egyptians are worse than the other uncivilized members of the Empire as a whole, who are at least capable of being taught civilized habits.[20]

Satire is meant to be funny, and this one undoubtedly is. Going farther than that, however, is perilous. It is unclear, to begin with, whether Juvenal's poem is a hateful slander or a learned joke (or both): Ombo and Tentyra are not neighbors, which may be a sign that the poet speaks tongue-in-cheek. Divining any sort of truth about Juvenal and his beliefs (or the beliefs of those he satirizes) from his poetic persona is a fraught exercise.[21] But bracketing the question of belief, there is nevertheless a commonality between Tacitus' characterization of the Egyptians and Juvenal's abuse: the Egyptians are violent and irascible, hard to control. They are crazed about religion. They are hard to assimilate. Moreover, they have no interest in these processes, feeling no sort of self-critical shame about their penchant for violence. Accordingly, in the Roman tradition the Egyptians are also famous bandits (or famous for their bandits), who play a feature role in Lucian's *Toxaris* and a bit part in Philostratus' *Life of Apollonius* (3rd cen. A.D.).[22] The author of the *Historia Augusta* (like Juvenal, a complex and satirical text) sums up the tradition well: "the Egyptians, as is well known, are fickle, raving mad, boastful, violent; they are also liars, children, always striving after revolution even in their public gossip, makers of verse, writers of epigrams, astrologers, soothsayers, and folk-healers."[23] As proof, the author introduces a (phony) letter of Hadrian, supposedly written to a certain Servianus, in which Hadrian accuses the Egyptians of multiple perversions, ranging from religious confusion (the Christians are actually worshippers of Serapis, and the priests of Serapis are actually Christians; but it does not matter, since what they in fact all worship is money) to unusual and shameful ways of impregnating their chickens.

What seems most striking is the relative consistency of this tradition of violent seditiousness over time: once it appears, it canonizes quickly and with a minimal degree of meta-commentary. While other members of Rome's empire eventually come to be integrated, and their elite classes taught to blend, if sometimes imperfectly, into the broader culture of civilized men, Egyptians still belong to a rough and nasty part of the world. This tradition persists at least into the late fourth century. Roughly contemporary with the *Historia Augusta*, Ammianus Marcellinus describes the Egyptians as "mostly darkened, with a look that is more gloomy than mournful; skinny and dry, they get heated up at any disturbance; they are quarrelsome and they are the bitterest debt-collectors. It is shameful among them if they cannot show whip marks on their bodies acquired from not paying their taxes. No torture has yet been invented harsh enough to get a hardened bandit from that region to give up his true name unwillingly" (22.16.23). More of the same, perhaps, but nevertheless intriguing in light of a vignette from earlier in the same book of Ammianus' narrative:

> Per hoc idem tempus rumoribus exciti variis Aegyptii venere complures, genus hominum controversum et adsuetudine perplexius litigandi semper laetissimum, maximeque avidum multiplicatum

reposcere, si conpulsori quicquam dederit, ut levari debito possit, vel certe commodius per dilationem inferre, quae flagitantur, aut criminis vitandi formidine, divites pecuniarum repetundarum interrogare. hi omnes densati in unum, principem ipsum et praefectos praetorio graculorum more strepentes interpellabant incondite, modo non ante septuagensimum annum extorquentes quae dedisse se iure vel secus plurimis adfirmabant. cumque nihil aliud agi permitterent, edicto proposito universos iussit transire Chalcedona, pollicitus quod ipse quoque protinus veniret, cuncta eorum negotia finiturus. quibus transgressis mandatum est navigiorum magistris ultro citroque discurrentium, nequis transfretare auderet Aegyptium, hocque observato cura perpensiore evanuit pertinax calumniandi propositum, et omnes spe praesumpta frustrati redierunt ad lares. unde velut aequitate ipsa dictante lex est promulgata, qua cavetur nullum interpellari suffragatorem super his quae eum recte constiterit accepisse.

At the same time a large number of Egyptians arrived (at Constantinople), roused up by a number of rumors. Egyptians are a difficult race of people, who customarily take the greatest pleasure in complicated litigation. If they have ever handed something over to a debt collector, they are particularly eager to ask back many times what they paid, so as to lighten the debt if they can, or to do better through stalling. And they summon rich men to court for extortion, since due to fear they are eager to avoid the charges. All these people came into the city as a crowd, interrupting the emperor and the praetorian prefects as they whined like jackdaws, trying to get back money that they swore that they had paid, rightly or wrongly, to all sorts of people some seventy years ago. Since nothing else could be accomplished at the court, the emperor posted an edict demanding that they all cross over to Chalcedon, and promised that he would come over as soon as possible and take care of their claims. Once they had crossed an order was given to the ferry captains who crossed back and forth over the strait not to carry any Egyptian passengers. This law was carefully observed, which put an end to their attempts at blackmail, and they all went back home with their hopes dashed. As a result, a law was passed almost as if justice herself had declared it, that no patron could be harassed on account of sums that he had lawfully accepted.[24]

In this case, the problem, it appears, is not that the Egyptians are allergic to government, but rather that they complain too much. This is a telling detail: though Ammianus thinks that they have made up all of the charges, there is something ironic in that at the heart of his complaint is the claim that the Egyptians are now doing precisely what they are supposed to be doing: filing petitions and relying on the imperial legal system. On one reading, then, it would appear that the Romans are hateful bigots, and the Egyptians cannot catch a break.

At the same time, however, Ammianus' emphasis on litigiousness might provide some insight into the genesis of the stereotypes of Egyptians in the Empire. As I have noted above, the stereotype of the ungovernability of Egypt seems to arise in the late first century A.D. One place to locate the source of the stereotype could be found in the riots between Alexandrians and Jews in A.D. 38—riots that were continuous, in some sense at least, with a Jewish revolt that lasted well into the second century. These riots were certainly brutal, leading to embassies to Emperor Claudius and famously documented not only by Philo of Alexandria's *In Flaccum* and Claudius' response to the Alexandrian and Jewish embassies, but they also led to the creation of a difficult and problematic literature, the *Acta Alexandrinorum*, a body of literary texts masquerading as legal documents and claiming to demonstrate the bravery of the Alexandrian ambassadors who end up confronting the emperor and being put to death.[25] At the same time, there is reason to place this discrete episode of violence in a broader historical context. Historical events, no matter how violent, do not automatically lead to particular stereotypes; there has to be reason to read them in particular ways. I would suggest that the historical context for this reading of Egyptian violence is to be found in political and conceptual sea-changes in the nature of imperial government and society.[26]

The dynastic watersheds of the late first century marked a series of changes in the ways in which the Romans began to think of the imperial project, and the role of discrete peoples within the project. While the Flavian dynasty had begun a process of installing a new aristocracy and marking off conquered peoples from Rome as a whole, these processes of reinterpreting the provinces come to a different sort of fruition under the Antonines.[27] These cosmopolitan emperors took an increasing interest in the provinces in a different sense: first, in the promotion of a common urban culture within the provinces;[28] second, by analogy, by marking off distinct and homogenous "urban" cultures from their native surroundings (such being the case, for instance, with Hadrian's foundation of Antinoopolis).[29] It should be added that this urban culture—or at least an idealized version of it—frowned on lower-order people taking their cases to court, preferring that these people stay in what the imperial powers imagined to be their proper places in the social hierarchy.[30] At the same time, it is reasonable to suspect that this transformation of provincial culture took place against a complex backdrop of social mobility in the Empire, of the sort that was emphasized in a seminal article by Greg Woolf on the "epigraphic habit" in the western provinces. For my argument, the most important of Woolf's points come in his emphasis on provincial agency: provincial participation in the epigraphic "culture" of the Roman world, he emphasized, was not simply a matter of provincials copying metropolitan practices. It was instead a means of asserting a stable identity in a rapidly shifting world.[31]

Woolf's argument can be expanded, mutatis mutandis, and used to explain the complex dialectic that I suggest led to the crystallization of these Roman literary stereotypes in the high empire. Ammianus provides the clue by making the link between violence and litigiousness, which is then racialized through the description of the Egyptians' bodies as skinny, dark, dry, and prone to overheating. Even if we reject Ammianus' judgment that litigiousness is a sign of a violent character, his emphasis is interesting, and seems to correspond to certain realities in the province itself. If we track the number of petitions submitted in Egypt over the first three centuries A.D. (for Ammianus an index of litigiousness, and therefore ungovernability) we see a significant uptick in the late first century. (We similarly see strategies for keeping people *out* of the courts run by imperial powers: the introduction of new systems of local jurisdiction in the form of "The Law of the Egyptians," for example.[32]) The charts below give a sense of the concentration of legal activity across time: the first is the total count of petitions from the first three and a half centuries of Roman rule in Egypt from the appendix of the recent monograph of Benjamin Kelly. The second counts the petitions in the first twenty volumes of the *Sammelbuch griechischer Urkunden aus Aegypten*. The *Sammelbuch* (SB) collects documents published internationally in unindexed journals; it is presented here in order to correct for editorial biases that might have gone into forming a particular collection represented in the aggregate count, or for "clumps" of relevant data that emerge from counting a particular archive (such as the large archive of petitions from first-century Euhemeria). The data have been "smoothed" in one important way: for petitions that are datable only on the basis of paleography, the "middle" date has been entered into the database (so for a papyrus of the third century, a date of 250 has been entered; for a papyrus of the second or third century, 200). The third chart is an aggregate count of published documents of all sorts that have been entered into the *Heidelberger Gesamtverzeichnis der Griechischen Papyruskunden Ägyptens*, a comprehensive database of papyrological sources.

Table 1. Petitions by Year—Sammelbuch

Year	*Number of petitions*
30 B.C.–1 B.C.	5
1 A.D.–50 A.D.	12
51 A.D.–100 A.D.	12
101 A.D.–150 A.D.	16
151 A.D.–200 A.D.	27
201 A.D.–250 A.D.	26
251 A.D.–300 A.D.	3

Table 2. Petitions by Year—Kelly 2011

Year	*Number of petitions*
30 B.C.– 1 B.C.	20
A.D. 1– 50 A.D.	103
51 A.D.– 100 A.D.	45
101 A.D.– 150 A.D.	129
151 A.D.– 200 A.D.	143
201 A.D.– 250 A.D.	96
251 A.D.– 300 A.D.	31

Table 3. Documents by Year—HGV

Year	*Sum of quantity of documents*
50 B.C.–1 B.C.	579
1 A.D.–50 A.D.	1,334
51 A.D.–100 A.D.	1,982
101 A.D.–150 A.D.	5,099
151 A.D.–200 A.D.	4,355
201 A.D.–250 A.D.	2,326
251 A.D.–300 A.D.	1,655

Charts like these, of course, are clumsy instruments. In many ways they compare apples to oranges: the HGV count includes not only papyri, but also ostraca. They cannot represent geographical distribution. The relative quantities of material in the three charts are radically different. They cannot account for generic variation in the aggregate data (the HGV count). They cannot account for subjective changes in the quality of the documentation—differences in the tone of a petition, for example. But in spite of these flaws they give some sense of how the quantity of petitions varies according to the quantity of our published material as a whole. The uptick in petitions in the second century would seem to have some significance in light of the shifts in the discourse about Egypt among elite Roman authors.

The stereotype of lawless, violent Egyptians, it appears, was being generated at roughly the same time (late first and early second centuries A.D.) as the inhabitants of Egypt began using the courts regularly, that is, when they began to integrate themselves into the Empire by refusing to settle their own problems privately. The claims of a violent Egypt are therefore more plausibly a reaction to the solidification and regularization of Roman rule over others and the responsibilities that this entails for a ruling power rather than a set of stable generative stereotypes. And as the Egyptians became more entangled in imperial systems of government, the stereotype was able to retain its currency. As I will argue in greater detail in the chapters that follow, the use of courts is somewhat analogous to the situation that Woolf describes for inscriptions: courts (and the judgments that they produce) were ways of bringing temporary stability to dynamic and complex interpersonal relationships. While the chronologies of these two different moves toward stability are slightly different (the process Woolf describes takes place over the course of the first century, whereas the evidence from the papyri begins to pick up in the late first and continues to rise in the second), they are nevertheless part of a single, dialectical process that emerges with the transition from the charismatic Julio-Claudian dynasty to the newer, stable, and increasingly bureaucratic world of the Flavians and Antonines. The stereotypes that emerge from writers like Tacitus grappling intellectually with the development of empire are as telling as the actions of Egyptian litigants.

* * *

While potentially useful for explaining the nature of imperial stereotypes, this sort of analysis has its limits. First and foremost, it leaves vague the precise definition of "Egyptian" and gives no clues as to what that designation might have meant to someone living in the Egyptian countryside (the *chora*, the main source of papyri). Second, while stereotypes are easy enough to identify, there is not necessarily a correlation between a particular stereotype and the institutional framework that an imperial power sets up "on the ground," much less a direct correlation between an idealized institutional flow chart and the way that these institutional relations actually worked.

We can begin with the question of the relationship between "Egypt" and "Egyptians." As mentioned above, four distinct "classes" of people inhabited Egypt: Alexandrian citizens, citizens of a few select Greek cities (Naukratis, Ptolemais, and eventually Antinoopolis), Jews, and everyone else (Egyptians), which would have included descendants of "Greek" colonists who did not have a privileged citizenship.

There is reason to think that this system of classes/citizenships was meaningful for the ways that people interacted with the imperial government, at least in some respects. Philo of Alexandria records, for example, that Egyptians were subject to harsher forms of corporal punishment than non-Egyptians, in this case, both Alexandrians and Jewish elders.[33] One advocate in a case in the first century thinks that the Egyptians are in general supposed to be treated harshly by the law.[34] Egyptians were famously singled out for harsh treatment by Caracalla, who expelled a number of them from Alexandria (the expulsion edict is ironically found on the very papyrus that documents the grant of citizenship in 212).[35] These brief mentions aside, the main source of evidence concerning relations between groups is a papyrus relating to the office of the *Idios Logos*, the representative of the emperor's accounts in Egypt. Since the province was treated, from conquest onward, more or less as the personal possession of the emperor, this official would have been his chief financial representative on the ground. The papyrus in question, the *Gnomon* or "guide," lists the rules accumulated from the age of Augustus onward. A number of these rules penalize crossing status-boundaries: various forms of intermarriage are forbidden; Egyptians who "pick children up from the dung heaps" (illegally adopt or enslave their potential social betters?) are fined a quarter of their property at death; Roman soldiers acting as citizens when not properly discharged are fined a quarter of their property; Egyptians who try to register as citizens of the Greek cities are fined; and so on.[36]

At first glance the mere existence of such a list of rules seems to indicate a harsh and oppressive regime bent on keeping people of differing social status carefully separated according to rank. These classes, however, are fundamentally juridical ones, and as such, they are suspiciously neat. The realities were more complex. Putting aside, for the moment, the complex problem of how status was inherited and transmitted (in practice rather than in theory), it is to begin with unclear how these distinctions were maintained: the Roman army (lightly staffed, according to Strabo) was never intended to be a proactive internal police force, and the Roman government (also lightly staffed) would have been ill suited to policing the choice of domestic sexual partner or the transmission of an inconsequentially small inheritance unless someone actively complained about it.[37] The attempts of the Roman governors to get parties to register their inheritance documents were notoriously unsuccessful.[38] Yet even accepting that the rules contained in the *Gnomon* were well enforced (and I think this is doubtful, for reasons I will explain in a moment), and therefore that these juridical distinctions were meaningful parts of lived reality for the ways in which people interacted with their neighbors or with their government, there is nevertheless very little evidence that these juridical categories can be mapped to a sense of identity, and if they can, it remains unclear under what circumstances a concept like "identity" might be a meaningful analytical category for the study of violence or of social relations in general. I will return to these questions in Chapter 4, but for the present it will suffice to note a few things. First, while there is sometimes a temptation to think of these juridical classes as living in completely separate spheres, this is highly doubtful: in light of the papyrological evidence, we should instead imagine a high degree of intermixing of populations, even when such a mixture was incapable of being represented through juridical language.[39] Thus papyri amply document newly discharged veterans (Roman citizens), as well Antinoopolite citizens, interacting in the countryside with Egyptians,[40] or Egyptians living in Alexandria.[41] This does not, of course, mean that these people liked each other, or were interested in overlooking a degrading legal status to focus on the content of their neighbors' characters.[42] It means that they did not conscientiously move in separate geographical, political, or social spheres, and, in light of what we know about mobility in other imperial/colonial contexts, there was likely to be the kind of cross-pollination of ideas, language, and culture that makes for situations that are also juridically complex. The evidence of onomastics points similarly to overlap: a Greek ephebic inscription, for instance, lists new citizens with names like Sarapammon, Sarapion, and Aphrodisios son of Annoubias.[43] Second, while there are a few statements from the papyri that we might classify as "politically incorrect" slurs directed at Egyptians,[44] there is very little to give us insight into each community's (if this is indeed the right word) self-perception.

This gulf between imperial administrative rules and local realities is indicative of some larger issues about what it meant for Egypt to be a province, and therefore relevant to how we should imagine the relations between empire and subject in the Roman period. The Roman government's desire to keep the population distinctly ranked by ethno-juridical status was in tension with its ruling ideology, namely, that it was a responsive and rational empire that was accountable to its citizens.[45] And in Egypt, this claim was particularly meaningful, since Egypt had a long tradition, particularly under the preceding Ptolemaic monarchy, of allowing its subjects the right to complain and giving them officially sanctioned avenues to obtain redress. It is at the intersection of this ruling ideology and this preexisting tradition of complaint and response that we can best understand why the segregated, carefully demarcated world of the *Gnomon* of the *Idios Logos* looks so different from the lived experience of a petitioner in Egypt.

* * *

It is from here that we can move to the actual administrative practices that characterized Egypt under the Roman Empire, and come to understand in a more robust way why complaint is such an important category of social behavior for revealing the dynamics of an ancient empire. There are two threads to this story, and both of them involve giving an account of the position of the Roman governor.

Like the *strategos* mentioned earlier, the governor of Egypt had a difficult job. He was ultimately responsible for extracting grain from Egypt to feed Rome (and later, Constantinople). This involved a delicate process of calibrating the extraction at the proper level to enable feeding the population in one area and to avoid starving the population in another. The management of grain also involved the proper management of water, as the Nile flooded only once a year and had to be properly distributed through an intricate series of canals lest everybody starve. The system of corvée labor that dug and maintained these critical veins and arteries needed to be overseen and managed, and the whole process had to be documented and accounted for. In other words, the simple task of extraction could easily be a full-time job in itself, and depended on managing the participation of individuals at many levels of the imperial hierarchy (and some who were not on this hierarchy at all), with substantial local knowledge of how to run large-scale agricultural production in geographically diverse regions (such as the Fayyum basin), without permanently and irreparably irritating any particular constituency.[46] Given that the governor's means of enforcement resembled more a sledgehammer than a scalpel, and given the scope of the challenges of extraction,[47] "best practices" probably involved trying to make as many people happy as much of the time as possible while simultaneously, if infrequently, applying spectacular levels of brutality to particular malefactors. Governors often failed (like Aulus Avilius Flaccus, at least in Philo's description), leaving their successors to clean up their messes. Such seems to have been the case when Tiberius Iulius Alexander, himself a rare example of an Egyptian governor with extensive local knowledge (and a nephew of Philo of Alexandria) acceded to the governorship of Egypt in A.D. 66:

> Tiberius Iulius Alexander declares: since I care very much about preserving the city in its fitting condition in which it enjoys the benefits which it has received from the Emperors, and in keeping Egypt in good health so that she may happily serve both the *annona* and the greatest flourishing of our present times, without being burdened by new and unjust exactions:
>
> Scarcely had I left the city (Alexandria) when I was shouted down by petitioners in both large and small groups, and from both the wealthy classes and the country farmers, who complained about the recent offenses; accordingly, I have wasted none of my efforts in setting the situation straight. So that you might have a more confident hope in all these matters concerning your salvation and profit because of the shining example to us of our safety, the benefactor of the entire race of men, Imperator Caesar Galba, and so that you know that I have concerned myself with the matters that pertain to your benefit, I have therefore made public notice concerning each of the things that I have inquired into, and I have done those things which it is allowed to me to do or to decide; and those things which are more important and which need the power and greatness of the Emperor, I will present to him with all frankness.[48]

A list of concessions to good governance follows: the elimination of compulsory service as a tax collector, the regulation of immunity, limitations on litigation concerning financial matters, among other things. The extensive text was circulated through the land on papyri and was inscribed on stone (copies of both exist), proclaiming that the governor would, henceforth, attempt to achieve a level of fairness in his extractions.

Tiberius Iulius Alexander's proclamation is fascinating, not only because it shows a detailed awareness of a series of local issues, but also because it points to the complex situation of the governor of Egypt in managing a series of constituencies who were particularly vocal in their demands. Not quite in the "place of kings" (in Tacitus' vision), Alexander had to make certain to refer issues of particular import to the Emperor himself; nevertheless, he retained a significant amount of agency. Similarly important is his relationship to the local peoples: in his inscription he presents himself as caring not at all whether the people who "shout him down" with their petitions are Greeks or Egyptians, but only that they represent both the local men of importance and the farmers who tilled the land. Both groups, he declares, have legitimate complaints, and, more important, both, he assumes, have rights that deserve to be respected.

This, then, is the second thread of the story: the idea that a ruler, to be legitimate, had to be responsive (rather than merely imposing his will by force) opens up a series of crucial possibilities for his subjects. To be legitimate meant to be a fair judge, and while it is likely that the Roman governors of Egypt (or any other province) felt this adjudication of cases to be an irksome chore, they nevertheless created an institutional framework that encouraged people to avail themselves of Roman justice.[49] This meant treating people as if they had rights by extending to them remedies that we may think of as procedural, but which were in fact substantive (since this distinction, as Alan Bowman has pointed out, would have made no sense in the Roman world).[50] It meant, above all, responding to their petitions, and finding workable solutions to numerous problems, social and economic.

What this also means is that every time the prefect, the *epistrategos*, the *strategos*, or any other official in Egypt received a petition, they were deciding what the law of the land was, and whether it should be applied, extended, or altered to fit the facts of a particular case. When these officials subscribed a petition and set the wheels of justice in motion, they were then—in a peripheral but critical sense—making law, and they were making it on the basis of people's narratives and normative claims. In the face of such diversity and colonial cultural, linguistic, and economic overlap and indeterminacy, they also ended up making law in ways that undermined the ideal of stable, discrete populations living separately from one another.

In a system that is primarily founded on local initiative (that is, when problems are brought into the legal sphere only through the choice of nonstate actors),[51] this process of law-making necessarily moves in two directions. On the one hand, there is a requirement that certain aspects of the formal law be followed: complaints must fit into a certain legal form, and certain kinds of language must be exploited to make one's case. This can be crudely categorized both as a "top down" process, in that the language and style of complaint are determined by the state, and as a "bottom up" process, in that it depends exclusively on individual initiative to bring the matter to the attention of authorities. On the other hand, formal aspects of complaining (of translating a complaint into law) were counterbalanced by the Roman state's financial need to maintain order and peace, as well its ideology of responsiveness. This counterbalance necessarily involves making pragmatic compromises which, while they were capable of being imagined as exceptions that fell outside the letter of the law, were in fact contributing to the shape of the body of rules as a whole. That is, these compromises often set precedents for future decisions. While there was no formally articulated doctrine of *stare decisis* in Roman law, people noticed precedents, and soon began to invoke them in new contexts.[52] Making a legal decision, even if it was a pragmatic compromise, nonetheless involved declaring what was justice; invoking a precedent was a way of demanding that the government, which prided itself on making just decisions, live up to the reputation it claimed for itself—namely that the individual magistrate was a moral agent.[53] That this process moves in several directions at once is a prime source of scholarly confusion.[54] While an account of the role of the legal system is of major importance for contextualizing the documents through which we understand violence, any attempt to view this dynamic system as a static, coherent, or rationalized whole (on the analogy of a "constitution" or a "basic law"—or from the perspective of the *Gnomon* of the *Idios Logos*) is bound to be frustrated.[55]

* * *

One important question, however, concerns the peculiar situation of Roman law. Roman law was famously a law for Roman citizens, to the exclusion of others. The majority of people living in Egypt (or in most other places outside the Italian peninsula, for that matter) were not Roman citizens before 212. Accordingly, there is a temptation to think the Romans would have spent most of their administrative energy dealing with the problems of Roman citizens, enforcing Roman law in their cases, and doing their best to delegate local matters to local people whenever possible.

At the level of legal technicality this is largely true, but the situation is more complicated for two reasons. One is that, despite the vast amount of legal documentation concerning both violence and other, more mundane matters, the interface between written, positive law and practical law is unclear. I believe, and outline in greater detail in Chapter 5, that there is good reason to believe that whatever the actual, written law of the province, there was in practice a substantial amount of pragmatic muddling through in day-to-day affairs, and provided that certain formal aspects of the law were followed, the Roman governors in Egypt were willing to tolerate petitions from a broad range of individuals. While not all these would necessarily receive justice, the governors attempted to serve the populace in the best way possible—provided certain rules of approach were followed.[56] The second problem, however, is more difficult, and comes to a larger question of the evidence itself. The problem, posed in its most basic form, is this: *if* there was a legal remedy for violence extended to all individuals, and *if* the government was willing to enforce it, who would *actually* have taken advantage of it? In other words, to whom was the system accessible? Could it be accessible to the defective Egyptians of Tacitus, Juvenal, and the *Historia Augusta*?

The papyrological evidence provides limited answers to these questions. First, while writing may not have been a prohibitively expensive technology, the papyri do not give us access to the entire socioeconomic spectrum of Roman Egypt.[57] As usual, the lowest of the low are excluded. This is predictable, of course, but a complicating factor is that we have very little firm evidence which indicates what percentage of the population this might be. We might surmise that it was a segment that was largely agricultural, since most of the extant papyri come from the larger towns and villages and seem to represent a class of people who look at first glance to be far from miserable and destitute. Second, it is exceedingly hard from the rhetorical narratives of petitioners to discern what their precise status was: sometimes they make reference to their citizenship or to offices that they have held, but they were not required to do so. In some ways, as I will argue, this is to be expected: going to court was about seeking to define one's status in the first place. Finally, when Tacitus and Juvenal refer to Egyptians as being violent, there is nothing that would indicate that they knew (or cared) about the complex system of ranked citizenships, but instead simply spoke in generalities about the land and its peoples. While I will deal with these issues in greater detail in what follows, it is worthwhile for the moment to consider briefly the issue of citizenship, and in particular its connection to legal access.

The legal situation in Egypt after the Roman conquest is difficult to characterize briefly, but in what follows I hope to essay a few conclusions. In

Ptolemaic procedure there were two different courts (an "Egyptian" and a "Greek") in which to judge disputes. The choice of court was based, or came to be based, on the original language in which the supporting documentation was written.[58] In the Roman period there was no such choice; judicial hearings concerning violence were held in front of magistrates, according to the *cognitio* procedure—that is, the magistrate (whether a Roman prefect or *epistrategos* or a Greek-speaker serving as *strategos*) was both presiding official and judge in legal proceedings. This break from the jury system meant that litigants of all classes would be treated by administrators who were more or less legal amateurs. And while it was a common element of imperial Roman practice to allow individual populations to be judged "by their own laws," there is little evidence that these administrators would have known what they were in the first place. Accordingly, it would be a mistake to assume that there was a major difference in the type of substantive rules to which each population would be held.[59] This is particularly true in the case of violence.

This will be a controversial statement for some. Deciphering which of the private law practices that show up in the papyri are "Roman," "Alexandrine," "Greek," or "Egyptian" has been a favorite exercise for legal historians since at least the publication of Mitteis's *Reichsrecht und Volksrecht* at the end of the nineteenth century.[60] There were certainly "Egyptian" legal materials, as the Greek translation of the Hermopolis "Legal Code" makes clear.[61] There were likewise traditional legal practices, especially in certain aspects of private law like contracts and marital property. But it is important to remember that any "local" practice was implicated in the larger administrative superstructure of the Empire itself. Several things follow from this premise: first, and most important, it is dangerous to assume that Roman law simply layered itself on top of local law, providing some kind of legal "veneer" or "superficial varnish."[62] Leaving aside the objectionable metaphor of culture-as-bookshelf, it makes sense to note, as scholars are increasingly realizing,[63] that once the Romans showed up it was *all* Roman law, because the Romans were the ones enforcing it. I write this only partially tongue-in-cheek, to emphasize that local law, when it existed (and it had a checkered history), existed only because the Romans either required it to exist or defined it into existence.[64] Second, it would be problematic to conclude, on the basis of the use of local law, that the Roman governors in charge of provinces knew anything about what its contents were, or were prepared to enforce it.[65] Additionally, while there might have been divergent legal traditions at the moment of conquest or shortly thereafter, there was a subsequent flood of legal development throughout the

Empire as a whole, through the imposition of wide-ranging legal reforms in specific regions (such as can be seen in the Flavian municipal laws from Spain) and through the constant issuing of imperial or gubernatorial edicts and constitutions, processes which likely impinge on one another, if only indirectly.[66] These developments were based on principles palatable to Romans, sent off by Roman magistrates, and enforced at the local levels. Further, individuals living in the provinces seem to have been conscious of the privileges that this flurry of documentation conveyed. Furthermore, as Gonzalez has noted in the case of the *Lex Irnitana*, sometimes the Romans themselves imagined people as *already* living by the same principles as those on which they based the laws in the first place.[67] Finally, and as a consequence of all these factors, at least so far as the question of violence is concerned, it is a fundamental mistake to draw a clear line between the world of legal practice in Egypt before the *Constitutio Antoniniana* in 212, with its divergent citizenships and status markers, and after, in a period where everyone is a citizen. This is so not only because there is so little empirical evidence for a change in the formal rules for dealing with violence in the period following the Antonine Constitution, but also because even *before* 212 there was a marked tendency toward the homogenization of legal culture.

For the question of violence, however, it is in my opinion more profitable to distinguish between private law as it was practiced by individuals and law as it was practiced by magistrates adjudicating between two parties. The Romans no doubt tolerated local legal forms, and permitted individuals to conduct private transactions according to them. They had no interest in preventing people who were not Roman citizens from writing contracts, marrying, buying, and selling. If there were a dispute over one of these things, though, and it came before a magistrate, the legal situation would have been more complicated. Roman magistrates understood local laws to be a disadvantage, and a brutal and inhumane one at that. In Chapter 5 I detail a case of this. Overall, a better way to understand the legal situation in Egypt before the grant of universal citizenship in 212 (and after it as well), especially as it relates to the question of how magistrates sought to judge, is to think of the administrative structure as being populated by a fragile network of administrators with ill-defined and overlapping competencies,[68] and laws not as coherent systems of rules that need to be followed in their entirety, but as a system of differential privileges and disabilities. These privileges and disabilities were not absolute: in the name of humanity or good governance they could be followed to the letter or ignored.[69] Roman citizenship offered the greatest number of privileges, Alexandrine fewer, metropolitan yet fewer, and so on.[70] Petitioners might be treated better or worse according to their legal status, but all had the right to attempt to approach the government for redress, even when their opponents were of a higher status. This did not mean that all people would receive equal justice, but simply that all people had a right to try.[71]

* * *

Thus far I have tried to present an outline of how Egypt fitted into the broader world of the Roman Empire at the level of imagination and administrative practice, and argued that the picture is more complex and dynamic than either ancient literary authorities or modern scholars have allowed. In particular, the realities of administering an imperial province allowed for a system that was characterized neither by wholesale, top-down repression and extraction, nor by completely reactive governance. Instead, the administration of Egypt as a Roman province was based on two approaches that were in tension with one another: a desire to mark off discrete groups from one another was undermined, in idiosyncratic ways, by a commitment to Roman self-understandings of being a just and rational empire as well as by the need to use discretion, precision, and well-calibrated strategies of extraction to manage the needs of two populaces in distinct areas. This tension is particularly evident from the workings of the legal system, which allowed for individual subjects to interact with their superiors in ways that could meaningfully shape future practice. More than a story of oppression and resistance, the realities of imperialism in Egypt made for an administrative regime that was dynamic and productive.

But at this point it is fair to ask, "But was it particularly violent?" That is, no matter how much explanation one gives of imperial stereotypes, the realities of provincial governance, and the dynamism of legal systems, was there some sort of underlying reality that made daily life in Egypt more brutal than life in, say, contemporary Rome or Asia Minor, or modern-day Topeka or Detroit? Depending on what one thinks is at stake in the question, the answers would be "yes," "it's unclear," and "what do you mean by 'violent'?"

As far as the "yes" answer is concerned, one could note that the Roman Empire, as a whole, was administered by relatively few people, the means of coercion were dispersed, and professional policing was limited—there were town guards, for example, but these were not what a modern person would think of as a professional police force, being recruited, instead, from the population of local inhabitants, and thereby ensconced in village hierarchies.[72] There is little evidence of them stopping a crime.[73] There were relatively few ways, in other words, actually to *prevent* a violent act—at least at the institutional level. Attempts to wipe out brigandage—obviously a problematic category—had only limited success; attempts to wipe out interpersonal violence in towns and villages were nonexistent.

But the lack of policing institutions does not automatically mean that a particular society is likely to be violent. Levels of violence, presumably, have fluctuated chronologically and geographically before the advent of policing in the early modern period. Even without policing, there were channels through which people could complain about the violence of others. But here things become less clear. Would the possibility that my neighbor would complain to the prefect pose a serious deterrent to my punching him in the face? Would the fact that people could try to avail themselves of justice have actually functioned to make Egypt any less violent? Would the fact that a complaint might not be given a hearing have made it a more violent place?

It is hard to measure deterrence even in modern societies with robust data collection, since one is both measuring acts that did not happen and presuming baseline levels of "violence"—a questionable technique, since violence is a phenomenon for which it is hard to give a robust causal account in the first place, even if we presume that we know what it consists of (and we do not, because, for reasons I will outline momentarily, it is not so much a thing as it is a contestable ethical claim). It also bears reminding that there is no way to approximate something like a "crime rate" from the ancient world: in part, the data are insufficient, but more important, the acts of interpersonal violence about which I am concerned were not, in the first place, crimes—they were delicts, private relationships of obligation between individuals and families, and as such, not of primary interest to the state.[74] Even if we were to engage in the methodologically questionable exercise of grouping together things that are unacceptable in modern Western society and labeling them as "crimes,"[75] we would not alleviate many difficulties, since we would often be comparing apples with oranges: robbing a traveler on a public road is different from punching a neighbor in the course of an argument, is different again from breaking into a person's home to take back something you think is yours, and is emphatically different from when the governor beats you with rods because you've failed to pay your taxes or you've finally exhausted his limited patience. Accordingly, any procedure of marking off behaviors that a modern historian or sociologist might take to be antisocial and then trying to measure them as an index of civility produces odd results. I am reminded of the line of former Washington, D.C., mayor Marion Barry, spoken during the rash of drug-related murders in the late 1980s, that "outside of the killings, DC has one of the lowest crime rates in the country." Absurd, perhaps, but also indicative of the problem: the categories by which we measure what counts as a violent place are everything, but they are also extremely hard to define in a way that is sociologically—or historically—meaningful.[76] This has consequences for comparison, whether with other regions of the Roman Empire or between ancient and modern systems. I suppose that if I were forced to choose between being dropped off in downtown Topeka or downtown Detroit, I would choose Topeka, at least if I were being dropped off at night; but given the choice between Topeka and second-century Oxyrhynchos I confess that I am at a loss to know where I would fare better, in what ways, or at what time of day.

All of which leads to the last possible answer to the initial question, itself taking the form of a question. What is one trying to communicate when one labels something as "violent," and what precisely is at stake in such a designation? It is here that we have to look to a complex modern historiography on violence, contextualize these academic perspectives in terms of their larger theoretical and political projects, and move from there back to the ancient evidence, attempting to bring these two traditions into conversation with one another.

CHAPTER 3

Violence, Modern and Ancient

At the end of the previous chapter I raised the question of the links between violence and conceptual apparatuses that purport to measure violence—crime rates, for example. The question of what can be learned through the study of something like a "crime rate" leads in turn to another problem: for better or for worse (probably for worse), we inhabit a world that exhibits a strong tendency to criminalize things that are unpleasant, to make political issues into criminal issues, and to organize state resources around the policing and protection of citizens from these criminal acts. In other words, as sociologist Jonathan Simon has argued, we "govern through crime."[1] Crime is a powerful concept in modern society. In contemporary discourse, criminality is juxtaposed to civility; crime is something that is necessarily horrid and bad; it is not supposed to happen, or at least, it is not supposed to happen "over here"—crime is only tolerable when it is on the other side of the line that separates civilization from barbarism. Within the ever-increasing universe of things that are "crimes," violent crime, however, remains the easy case. Even for those who have substantial doubt as to the effectiveness or morality of modern penal policies, there is instinctive and near-universal agreement that the "real criminals"—the violent criminals—deserve to be removed from society and sequestered elsewhere.

This is not, of course, the place to discuss the ethics of modern penal policy; I dwell on it only because our modern understandings of violence as a category which is primarily criminal have a major effect on the ways in which we understand what is at stake in labeling something an act of violence. Our insistence on treating violence as crime leads us easily to treat violence as something fundamentally other, horrid, or incomprehensible—to treat it as something that challenges the capacity of our analytical categories to describe and understand. Here the fact that our understandings of violence are mediated through our contemporary legal categories has been joined to certain moves in twentieth-century critical thought which I will outline below; this fusion of perspectives (crime and critique) has, I will suggest, led to a complicated and dangerous dead end in contemporary scholarship on violence, namely, a tendency to think that our scholarly categories and forms of disciplinary reasoning cannot possible capture what is "violent" about "violence"—or even what is meaningful or interesting about it. The end result of this is a body of contemporary scholarly literature on violence that is by turns both shrill and melancholic—a body of literature which frequently ends up apologizing for violence or being awe-struck by it, rather than engaging in a sober and reflective analysis of it.

It is this chapter's goal to describe in greater detail what was meant by a claim of "violence" in Roman Egypt, to describe what we might mean by such a claim today, and then to attempt to see how these two categories can inform one another, while also trying to avoid this particular impasse. I will defend in some detail the claim I made earlier, namely, that violence is not a thing or an act (though acts can indeed be termed violent), but instead an ethical label, one that is located within matrices of power and of what one considers acceptable and unacceptable. As with all categories of ethical and moral evaluation it is subject to contest. It is therefore also political, insofar as concerns of power will adhere in the contest over whether the label of "violence" applies. But this is not merely a question (as it is in modern society) where what is at stake is the exclusion of the perpetrator of violence from society as a whole. Instead, in a world that was largely reluctant to criminalize interpersonal acts of harm, what was at stake in calling someone's behavior "violence" was the nature of the obligation that he or she had incurred by the act of violence, and by extension, also the nature of personhood inherent in such concepts of obligation. I will unpack this idea in greater detail below.

To claim that violence should be treated soberly and analytically by scholars is not to say that it can be trivialized, or to claim that there is not something unique about it: violence does retain something distinct from other relational categories and ethical labels, since by moving into the world of inchoate emotions such as pain it also intersects with two other important categories, namely, language and subjectivity. It is related to subjectivity at least in the sense that the experience of personal violation (about which more specificity in what follows) challenges the boundaries of the self and causes those boundaries, often taken for granted, to become an object of reflection;[2] it is related to language in the sense that language provides a highly imperfect vehicle for the expression of pain, a condition that in turn affects the making of claims about pain and the forging of intersubjective bonds between the one who suffers and the one who sympathizes, or who comes to be convinced that he must sympathize.[3] Violence runs up against subjectivity and language in important and fascinating ways, and any appreciation of how violent acts come to "mean" things—in the ancient world or the modern—must take account of this dynamic, for only with this relationship in mind can we return to the world of the papyri, and the importance of the power of narration for petitioners, governors, and the law.

What follows proceeds in three parts. First, I proceed philologically and terminologically, and try to map the semantic range of the vocabulary of violence in Roman Egypt. This leads to a particular problem, namely, the question of the "authenticity" of this language, and the problems posed by the fact that such language was mediated through a scribal tradition. Petitions concerning violence were obviously mediated, but historians, I argue, have erred in taking this mediation to be a methodological problem, rather than an opportunity. This mediation gives us opportunities for understanding what is "at work" in the language that petitioners use. Still, knowing the words for violence is only a part of the equation; it does not help us to piece together the kinds of claims that are being made when someone declares someone else's actions to be "violence." This leads to a question of whether *we* know what we mean when we identify something as violence. In the next part of the chapter I move to the problems that contemporary historians encounter in writing about violence, and the challenges that modern understandings of violence pose for understanding ancient violence. Key in the modern historiographical tradition, I argue, is a divide between two traditions that follow the path of Max Weber: one group which prefers to write about violence as something ethically neutral (force), and another which writes about it as ethically problematic (violence). The distinction is valuable, I argue, because by reappropriating the violence/force distinction as a tool for understanding the claims made in the papyri we gain additional insight into the negotiations about the nature of violence, its connection with concepts of personhood, and the ways in which that personhood is redeemed through petitions once it is violated. I close by returning to my initial point, namely, about how the language of petitions—stilted, formulaic, and mediated—can come to be meaningful, and then go on to introduce a concept that will structure Part II of this book: translation.

* * *

It is best to begin with terminology. There is a relatively compressed vocabulary that can be mustered by a petitioner (or the scribe helping him or her compose) to describe a violent act. There is a good deal that is historically interesting about this vocabulary. Most important, "violence" is always understood to be prima facie wrong. That is to say, insofar as I can tell, there is no concept, in the papyrological material or in the literary or the legal evidence, of a "sufficient amount of" violence, "justifiable" violence, or "deserved" violence. There are, of course, gradations of wrong, but they never at any point blend into gradations of right. This is not to say that there was no understanding of justifiable force. There were plenty of situations in which force was deployed, in which it was understood to be explicitly or implicitly acceptable, and in which it could be either defensible by legal standards or tolerated (or approved of, or even celebrated) by society at large. It just could not, and would not, be called violence. It is a peculiarity of the words—*hybris* in Greek, *iniuria* or *contumelia* in Latin—that they simply cannot receive a positive valence.[4] *Iniuria* can be qualified as *atrox* ("heinous" or "aggravated"); *hybris* as ἀνήκεστος ("heinous," translating Latin *atrox*), or οὐ τυχοῦσα ("uncommon," "inappropriate," "unconscionable"). That is to say, when people sought to use adjectives to qualify these terms, the adjectives they used only made them worse, not better. For the Latin term, this is simply a feature of etymology: *in-iuria*, "not lawful," or broadly "not acceptable." If something is *ius*, it is broadly right. It would therefore make no sense to have something like *bona iniuria*—it is intrinsically illogical. The Greek word *hybris*, as every student of tragedy knows, is likewise never a positive thing. It is only a modern notion that recognizes that the idea of *hybris*, in its broader, fifth-century B.C. formation as something like "failing to be mindful of one's station in the world" might, in fact, be connected to a certain quality that can make a person successful. For lack of a native term we call this quality *chutzpah*. It is also a notion that is fundamentally foreign to the ancient world.

In addition to "violence" having a thoroughly negative valence, it also has a relatively restricted scale. Specifically, in Roman Egypt, all violence is personal. There is nothing, at least in the papyrological evidence, that resembles Paul Farmer's "structural violence"—an agent-less but nevertheless statistically visible suffering produced by inequality and unevenly distributed across a population.[5] This has certain consequences: Government cannot be violent; an individual magistrate can. The fact of inequality is not in itself violent; but a very wealthy individual may, as a result of this wealth, be prone to act violently (a common theme in complaints). They key term, as I indicated earlier, is *hybris*, though some petitions speak more specifically of "blows" (*plegai*), or refer simply to "nastiness" (*aedia*, a term which I will translate simply as "violence" as well, avoiding the euphemism).[6] In Roman Egypt, *hybris* has a narrower sense than it did in fifth-century Athens.[7] *Hybris* can refer to violent or offensive conduct against a person's body (a beating or cudgeling, for instance), or against a person's reputation (insults, threats, or public abuse, Loidoria). Some have mistakenly understood these terms as two different types of violence, which they are not. Rather, they are based on a different concept of personhood—a concept that encompasses a wider territory than the modern definition, being both corporeal and incorporeal, or more accurately, both physical and social.[8]

Violence appears in the papyri in several contexts. It can be used in the context of a petition asking for redress for crimes against persons in a petitioner's family (such as spouses and children), or immediate kin (such as parents or grandparents), or people in any given individual's employ (such as a tenant farmer or shepherd). It probably *cannot* be used to refer to contemptuous or injurious treatment of slaves.[9] Slaves were counted as property, and what we might call "violence" against property and financial interests was in Roman Egypt called *bia* (which can translate to "damage" or "harm," but which always indicates harm not to full people but to inanimate objects, financial interests, and slaves).[10] *Bia* could also be used to refer to coercive actions that sought to harm an individual's financial interests (in this sense it maps, albeit imperfectly, to the Roman legal category of *metus*). What is important to note here, however, is that because of the nature of legal procedures, some (if not many) petitions necessarily concern more than one issue at once. Thus, in the petition of Ptolemaios discussed in Chapter 1, Ptolemaios was complaining *both* about harm to his financial interests (the extorted money) *and* about violence (the beatings through which his opponents managed to get him to give up the money). However, though both terms can exist in a single document, they refer to separately actionable issues—for instance, to a crime against property and an incidence of violence. It is also important not to confuse violence (*hybris*) or harm to property (*bia*) with the adjectival or adverbial form of *bia* (βίαιος, βιαίως). This descriptor appears a number of times in petitions to refer to people's behavior and character (e.g., so-and-so is a violent/harmful/unpleasant person), but so far as I can tell never is used formally to define the action itself.[11] There are likewise procedural peculiarities that exist for violence but not for damage/harm, as I will outline in greater detail in Chapter 5.

In addition to the fact that the language used to describe violence is bound up with the language of wrong, the language that surrounds the core legal terms is the language of disdain, hostility, and eventually, of prayer and redemption. When petitioners are "approached" they are also "attacked" (ἐπέρχεσθαι in both cases, which also, and perhaps tellingly, means "to take to court"); they are knocked down (κατακόπτειν); "tortured" or "abused" (αἰκίζειν); and "despised" (καταφρονεῖν), to give just a few commonly recurring examples. People's opponents are joyfully overbearing: they "take confidence" (θάρρειν) in their power to get away with doing violence; they act "in the manner of thieves" (λῃστρικῷ τρόπῳ), or in the manner of tyrants (τυρρανικῷ τρόπῳ). Petitioners, in turn, wish for "punishment" (ἐπέξοδος) or "revenge" or "judgment" (ἐκδικία). In other words, despite their repetitious nature, petitions still record a rich language of scorn and insult.[12]

Nevertheless, this repetitiousness of a limited number of tropes over a long period of time should cause some concern. There is no question that these documents were mediated through a scribal tradition. This raises an important question of method: what if we are not, in fact, looking at first-person narratives that reflect an individual's subjective self-perception and evaluation of self-worth? What if what we have, instead, are various examples of how scribes would have interpreted pain? This leads to a pair of objections that might be labeled, for the sake of convenience, the skeptical position. By this I mean a belief that either (a) *all* we have in the resulting petition is the voice of the scribe or (b) even if there *is* more than the voice of the scribe, we can take no methodologically defensible epistemological position through which we could separate the scribe's voice from that of the petitioner.[13] Even when petitions vary, scribes are manipulating formulae to make a "best fit" between formal language and the experience of violence. It is further likely that even outside the bounds of scribal mediation, petitioners are lying, or at least manipulating the truth. They are creating, in other words, what Natalie Zemon Davis has called "fictions"—massaged, rhetorical, well-designed statements that were intended to resonate with broader social ideas about truth and justice.[14] They are not delivering the truth about violence; they are winking at the truth, and winking not even at their own truth, but at other people's truths, at what those other people—those who populate the legal system—consider violence. In other words, these documents tell us very little indeed about violence or how people experience it; they may tell us something about how scribes record it, or at best, how they translate it.[15]

Phrased in its most strident form, this position leaves the historian in something of a quandary. This is especially so if one thinks that the point of reading petitions is to figure out precisely what happened in X village on Y day—that is, to evaluate the ways in which petitions reflect the truth about a moment in the past. This is, of course, part of the point of reading them. And in this case the answer to the question of "how accurately do these narratives reflect the incident about which the petitioner is complaining?" would then have to be, "probably not so accurately." But in this form, the problem is overstated. Petitions were not only narratives about the past. They were future-oriented as well. They sought to produce judgments and rearrange social relationships as a result of a past violent act. As such, they were political moves in local dramas, both in the sense that they sought to produce a set of actions, and that they sought to change the contours of a certain balance of power. By making this small change in our historical perspective (that is, by moving from a concern about truth in the past to attention to the ways in which petitions produced truths that would shape the future), scribal mediation of the language of violence comes to look less like a problem, and more like an opportunity to understand in greater detail the intricacies of the political and institutional landscape in which petitions were produced.

Anyone who watches television cop shows knows that the police work with a specific institutional vocabulary. In cop talk, as in Egyptian petitions, there is a relatively limited range of vocabulary used to describe violent occurrences.[16] The language used to describe modern situations is the product of an institutional culture that requires reasonable consistency in describing criminal actions: a police report must use this limited vocabulary to convey details that may eventually have legal repercussions. Thus, while the vocabulary itself is sparse, it is used to convey maximum amounts of information. At the same time, police reports are individualized descriptions of events, designed not only for legal purposes, but also for accurate reporting back to a community in the form of crime statistics and police blotters in local newspapers. Because of this, the language must both be a roughly accurate legalistic translation of the "facts" of the event and also be specific enough that quantifiable patterns can be extracted. While it would be silly to claim that in Egypt there was a desire on the part of the government to extract specific data on this aspect of local life, the comparison is still instructive: petitions were the product of a legal tradition, and as such are relatively consistent in their language. Complainants sought to get their point across to authorities forcefully; they used specific language that was laden with meaning to do this. But this does not mean that petitions were merely forms to be filled out. Descriptions of violence had to resonate with a body of institutional presumptions to the degree that they had to be recognized as complaining about violence in order to start institutional processes in motion in the first place. But they also had to tell a particular form of story, and that story had to be individualized.

It is worth arguing from example. The following two petitions come from the Kronion archive from Tebtynis. Both are from the year A.D. 48, both are addressed to the *strategos* Apollonios, and both are written in what appears to be the same hand. The first dates to the fifth of January, the second to the fifth of February. Furthermore, in both petitions, the name of the assailant, Patynion, is the same (though his patronymic is subtly different). These two documents are the most similar examples that I have found in the petitions about violence. Unlike other documents I discuss in the text, I have printed the papyri below to reflect the original layout of the documents, and preserved the original spellings of the words:[17]

Ἀπολλωνίῳ στρατηγῷ Ἀρσινοείτου
παρὰ Πετσίριος τοῦ Φουλήμι-
ος τῶν ἀπὸ Ταλεὶ τῇ ε τοῦ
Τῦβι τοῦ ἐνοστῶτος η̣ [ἔτους]
Τιβερίου Κλαυδίου Καίσαρος
Σεβαστοῦ Γερμανικοῦ
Αὐτοκράτορος. ἐμοῦ ὄντος
ἐργασζομένου ἐν ᾧ μεμίσ-
θωμε παρὰ Ἰσχυρίωνος
τοῦ Πτολεμαίου περὶ Ταλὶ
ἀμπελῶνος, εὗρον ἐπ᾽ αὐ-
τοφῴρωι Πατυνίωνα
Ἡρακλίδου καὶ τὸν τούτου
ὑ̣ε̣[ιὸ]ν .[......] . . ἐ̣λάνον-
τας ἡ̣μ̣ιένους δη̣[.....] . .
ἐν τοῖς παρεσπαρμένοις
λαχάνοις καὶ ἐμοῦ λογο-
πυουμένου πρὸς αὐτοὺς
καὶ ὕββριν μοι ἐπεταίλε-
σαν οὐ τὴν τοιχοῦσαν ἔτι
δὲ καὶ ἐκ τοῦ τοιούτου ἔδο-
κάν μοι ἀφιδέστερα πληγὰς
πλήρους εἰς τὰ παρατυχό-
ντα μέρη τοῦ σώματος

κ̣α̣ὶ̣ π̣ρ̣ο̣[σέ]π̣α̣ι̣σ̣ο̣μ μοι εἰς τὴν
πλευρὰν τ̣ο̣ῖ̣[ς] γρόνθοις
ὥσται νῦν κατακλεινην εἶ-
ν̣αι κ̣α̣ὶ̣ κ̣ι̣νδυ̣νε̣ύ̣ε̣ι̣ν̣ τῷ̣
ζῆν. διὼ ἀξι̣ῶ̣ι̣ γρ̣ά̣ψ̣α̣ι̣
τῷ̣ τῆς Ταλεὶ ἀρχεφώδῳ̣
ἐκπέμψε τοὺς ἐνκαλου-
μέν[ο]υς ἐπὶ σαὶ πρὸς τὴν ἐ-
σομένην ἐπέξοδον.
εὐτύχι.
(The date, name, and description of the petitioner follow)

To Apollonios, *strategos* of the Arsinoite nome,
From Petsiris son of Phoulemis, one of those from Talei. On the 5th of Tubi of the present 8th year of Tiberius Claudius Caesar Augustus Germanicus Imperator, while I was working in the vineyard that I rent from Ischyrion, son of Ptolemaios, in Talei, I myself saw Patynion son of Herakleides and his son . . . leading mules . . . in the vegetable patches. I had a discussion with them and they did inappropriate violence to me, and what's more, they beat me unsparingly with many blows all over my body. They laid into my side with their fists, so now I am laid up and in danger of losing my life. Therefore I ask you to write to the *archephodos* of Talei to send the accused to you for forthcoming punishment. Farewell.

Ἀπολλωνίῳ̣ στρατηγῷ̣ Ἀρσινοείτ(ου)
παρὰ Παποντῶτος τοῦ Παποντῶτο(ς)
τῶν ἀπὸ Ταλὶ τῆς Πολέμωνος με-
ρίδος λεγο(μένου) Ψεναμτῖτο(ς) γεοργοῦ
τῶν ἀπὸ Ταλεὶ τῆς αὐτῆς μερίδος.
ἐπιβάλλον(τός) τινος λη̣στρικῷ̣ τρόπο
εἰς ἣν ἐχο ἐν προγεγραμμένη̣ κό-
μη̣ Ταλὶ οἰκίαν καὶ ἤρωσάν μου
δοκοὺς δέκα καὶ ὅλμον, καὶ ἐ-
μοῦ τὴν ἀναζήτησιν πυουμέ-

νου σὺν τῷ τῆς κώμης Ταλεὶ ἐ-
πιστάτῃ εὗρον ἀπ' αὐτοφώρωι
ἐν τῇ Πατυνίωνος τοῦ Ἡρακλήου
οἰκίαν ἀπὸ μέρους τῶν ἠρμέ-
νων δοκῶν δοκοὺς πέντε , καὶ
ἐμοῦ λογοπυουμένου πρὸς αὐ-
τὸν περὶ τούτων ὕββριν μοι
ἐπετέλεσον οὐ τὴν τοιχοῦσαν
καὶ ἐν τῇ συμπλωκῇ ἐξέπε-
σον παρ' ἐμοῦ εἰς τὸ ἔδαφος
ὃ εἶχον ἐπὶ τῶι ὤμῳ μου
παιδίον ὥσται ἐκ τοῦ τοιούτο(υ)
κινδυνεύειν τοῦ ζῆ̣ν̣. διὼ
ἀξιῶ γράψε τοῖς τῆς
Ταλεὶ ἐπιστάταις ἐκπέμ-
ψε τὸν ἐνκαλούμενο(ν) Πατυ-
νίωνα ἐπὶ σαὶ πρὸς τὴν ἐ-
σομένην ἐπέξοδον.
εὐτύχ[ει].
(The date, name, and description of the petitioner follow)

To Apollonios, *strategos* of the Arsinoite nome,
From Papontos, son of Papontos, one of those from Talei in the division of Polemon and a farmer of the land called Psenamtis, in the same division of Polemon. Someone entered the house which I have in the aforementioned Talei in the manner of thieves, and took ten beams and a millstone. When the commander of Talei and I made an investigation, I myself saw five of the aforementioned beams in the house of Patynion son of Herakleos. When I had a discussion with him about this he used inappropriate violence, and in the melee a small child who was seated on my shoulder fell down to the ground, and because of this is in danger of losing his life. Therefore I ask you to write to the commanders of Talei and to have them send the accused man, Patynion, to you for forthcoming punishment. Farewell.[18]

Both documents tell stories with similar language, and both are fine examples of well-preserved first-century petitions—long and thin papyri, narrations

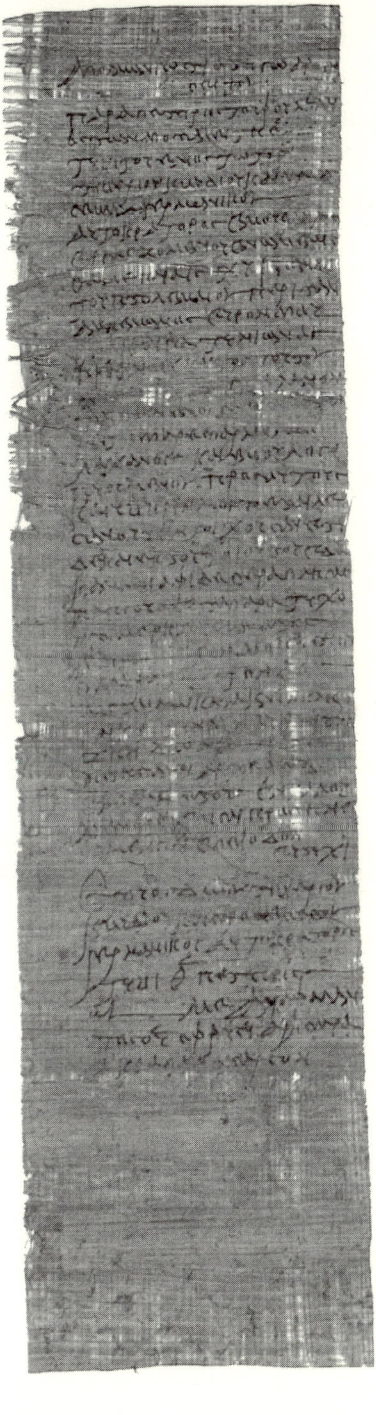

Figure 2. *P.Mich.* V 229. Digitally reproduced with the permission of the Papyrus Collection, Graduate Library, University of Michigan.

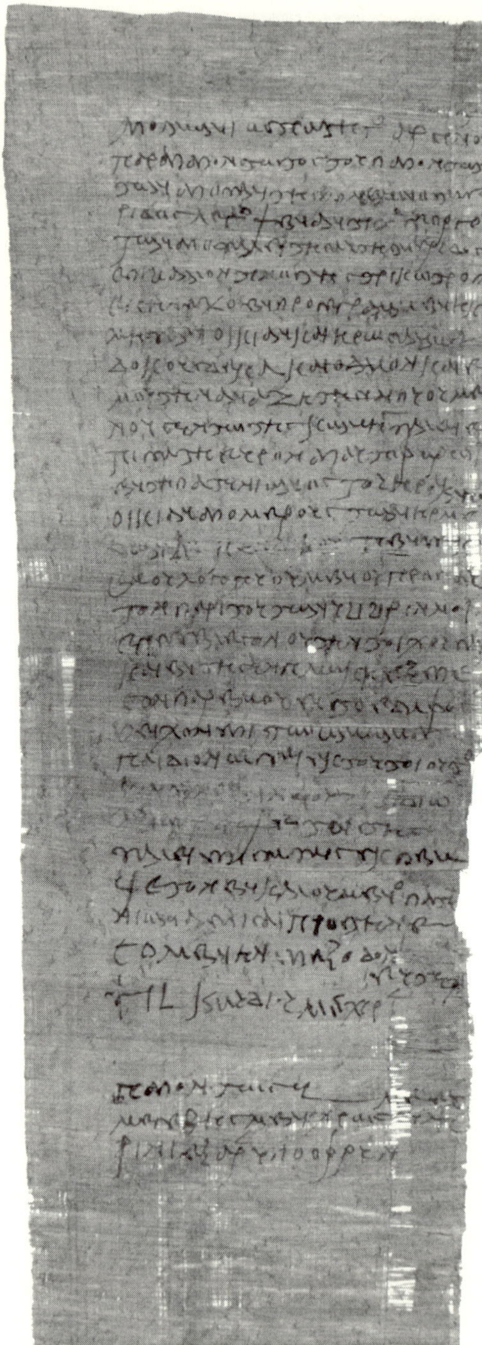

Figure 3. *P.Mich.* V 230. Digitally reproduced with the permission of the Papyrus Collection, Graduate Library, University of Michigan.

that are short and to the point without excessive amounts of language. The formula for the address at the top of the papyrus and the formula for the request are personalized, but essentially the same, even down to the ways in which they present the text visually. Space is left at the bottom of both documents, perhaps to fill in any subsequent bureaucratic endorsements. More important, there are stock phrases and legal boilerplate used to frame the complaint itself: not only is *hybris* present as a legal term (and identically misspelled), but the same verb is used in both papyri to describe the way that it is employed. In addition, it is qualified as *ou tychousa* (inappropriate, aggravated) in both papyri. Both petitioners mention that they "had a discussion" (i.e., a verbal confrontation) with the assailant, and use the same term (*logopoieisthai*). The comparisons could be extended.

These two documents have striking similarities, but it should be immediately obvious that they are telling different stories. In one (229), the story focuses on a seemingly unplanned act of violence, coming on the heels of a violation of property; in the other (230), there is also a violation of property, but the violence here is certainly not planned. In the second document (230) the petitioner is trying to convey that Paytnion is the thief himself. Likewise, in the first case, the violence is described at greater length, focusing on the blows to "all the parts of the body," whereas in the latter document, any personal injuries received by the petitioner have been subordinated to the injuries to and grave condition of the child he claims to have been carrying on his shoulder.

That both of these documents are mediated through a scribe, and probably through the same scribe, makes them a good test case for asking some questions about the nature of narratives in the papyri, and what the proper methodological guidelines should be for using these documents as sources for individual experience. No tidy solution to this problem is possible, given that there is little evidence for the ways in which these documents were composed. Nonetheless, it is worth making three main methodological suggestions.

First, the temptation to isolate scribal intrusions into the narrative, strip them from the text, and then look at the remainder is methodologically problematic. Certain kinds of legal boilerplate show up in all petitions, but to attribute this to the hand of the scribe alone is to enter dangerous territory. There are good reasons for thinking that there is an interactive process going on when petitions are composed, and that the interface between the scribe and the speaker is a dynamic one.[19] In Chapter 5 I detail a case of how the draft of a petition is turned into a final (or at least a subsequent) version, and how the appropriate legal language is inserted into the document to bolster the position of the petitioner and clarify her legal complaint. Additionally, we know precious little about scribes, and to vest them with such agency in a process of complaint is risky. For the moment, however, it will suffice to note that the insertion of certain kinds of legal boilerplate into these documents is not a mere formality.

Second, legal language is loaded. The words themselves carry meanings, and these meanings would be critical for the ways that the complaint was subsequently processed by magistrates. The form of the document was likewise important. As scholars have recently cautioned, papyri must be imagined not only as texts, but as artifacts.[20] As such, we must imagine how the document would have been read. It was necessary to make it look like a petition, so that the *strategos* or the relevant members of his staff would know exactly what they were looking at the instant that they unfolded it—as Traianos Gagos once pointed out, it is probably no accident that the physical shape of petitions in the Roman period remains so consistent.[21] No mistakes could be made about this, and thus we also see that certain documents have labels telling the reader what they were. P.Mich. V 229 does this: on the verso, it declares that it is the petition (*hypomnema*) of Petsiris of Talei. Form had to be gotten right.[22]

Third, the idea that scribes hold a monopoly on legal words is dangerous. Legal anthropologists have, in the last twenty or so years, reminded us that while legal language *may* come from the "top down,"—though it need not—it can be appropriated and made meaningful to large segments of the population that are not responsible for its initial genesis.[23] In contemporary life legal words are used with great frequency and precision precisely because they are packed with communicative force, even we often use them in ways in which they were not originally intended. For instance, if a police officer touches me menacingly, I know to shout "police brutality" (at least if there are witnesses present). If he subsequently arrests me, I know to remind him that "I'm not resisting." Certain legal words worked themselves into the popular vocabulary in Egypt as well: in a letter from a man named Demarchos, he tells his sister Taor, "I want to acknowledge that you wrote me about what Agathinos did to me. If I live a while and return to my homeland I will get satisfaction for myself (ἐκδικήσω ἐμαυτόν)."[24] Demarchos' use of the verb *ekdikein* is unusual in a letter that is otherwise overwhelmingly concerned with mundane matters, but the term is common in legal documents. Likewise, in a letter with otherwise mangled language, a son writes to his father inquiring, "who . . . is the one who has done violence to you?" (ὕβριν σοι πεποίηκεν).[25] In the next chapter I look in greater detail at a personal letter that is almost exclusively concerned with violence. But for the present purposes it should suffice to note that the kinds of language that were critical for activating legal action were also, to a certain extent, part of the larger vocabulary. What is important, then, is to see the final product (the petition) as a carefully shaped narrative, one that goes out of its way to exploit certain kinds of language to fashion the narrative itself into a formal complaint. This was an interactive process that took place between the scribe and the victim, and the resulting narrative must be treated as a whole, boilerplate and all.

* * *

Properly deciphering the technical terminology of violence and outlining the cultural and institutional matrices from which that terminology comes is the beginning, rather than the end, of the problem violence poses for historians. Getting the words right, while important, will not tell us what violence "meant" for someone living in Roman Egypt. Simply knowing the semantic range of *hybris* cannot explain what was at stake in making a claim of violence, how violence came to challenge a petitioner's sense of self, or how that sense of self was redeemed through the writing of a petition and the subsequent legal processes. And just as philology cannot inform us about what violence "meant" for our subjects, so too it fails to explain what violence "means" for us. At stake here are not just theoretical questions, but questions of method as well. With what sort of epistemological distance should we write about violence? Is it a concept that can be understood through the conventional forms of reasoning available to historians? Or is there something inherent in violence that challenges the capacities of historians? Can we genuinely know someone else's pain or trauma? Do we actually know what *we* mean when we say "violence"? And if we do not, then why is that the case?

These are, of course, complex questions. They are made even more so because they are informed by a long discussion taking place in contemporary social theory concerning the interface between modernity and violence. It is a debate which evolves alongside, and is likely intertwined with, the penal and criminological revolutions of the nineteenth and twentieth centuries that brought us "governing through crime." The result of this discussion is that scholarly accounts of violence proliferate, and violence has come to be a label applied promiscuously to a wide—and ever increasing—variety of social phenomena (pari passu with the increasing criminalization of a diversity of social phenomena). Nevertheless, it remains odd that, in spite of the "genealogical" turn in the modern social sciences which seeks to subject every central analytical category to the scrutiny of the historicizing eye, "violence" has thus far largely escaped such a treatment. Yet it is crucial that it should be so analyzed, both for its own sake and to outline its cross-cultural applicability.

In the section that follows I attempt to outline, provisionally and in broad strokes, something of the modern discussion of violence; to mark out the path we've taken that makes the concept of violence so challenging to historical writing. The goal is not to cover everything that has been labeled "violent" or "violence," but rather to understand why this label has come to be so important and so amenable to marking a diversity of acts and relationships; what it is, in other words, that people think is at stake when they declare that something unexpected is in fact "violence." Here a caveat is important: what follows is not a proper intellectual history that traces in detail threads of thought through various philosophical "schools"—it is an attempt to gesture at what I think are key moments in this history when certain conceptual doors were opened up. Once these doors were opened, other thinkers—sometimes with irreconcilable ideas and commitments—often walked through them. The second part of this chapter attempts to cleave from this mass of literature a few central, threading concepts that might support some sort of rigorous cross-cultural application, differentiating what might be of broad methodological applicability from what should remain historically contingent. In this part I turn back to the world of the papyri and to their particular language of complaint, as well as to the distinction between force and violence, in an effort to better understand the force of the label of violence (pun intended) within these categories.

* * *

A genealogy of the concept of violence, or at least of violence as a sociologically significant concept, should begin with Max Weber. There are two reasons for beginning with Weber, one historical and the other linguistic. The historical point is the easier one: Weber's thesis, variously expressed, that the modern state successfully claims a monopoly on "the legitimate use of physical force within a given territory" has proven fruitful in the social sciences generally, so much so that even though it is often subject to critique from a variety of perspectives it remains a pithy and original formulation. The difficulties inherent in Weber's thesis—that even modern states often fail to control territories effectively, that they often delegate their monopoly unwillingly, that premodern and modern state-building projects differ in aims and scope, that legitimacy is often up for grabs, that force is not always or necessarily physical—need not detain us here. The more important matter for the comparative study of violence is linguistic: Weber uses a single, ethically neutral term (*Gewalt*) for violence. Contemporary discussions, especially in sociology and political science, of "state violence," "legitimate violence," or the "monopoly on violence" that translate the German terms (*staatliche Gewalt, Gewaltmonopol*) are still deeply influenced, methodologically speaking, by the ethical ambivalence of the original term.[26] Yet this ethical neutrality is hard to translate into English, in which we tend to make a distinction between violence and force—the former being unjustified, the latter ethically neutral or at least unsuspicious. That Weber's *Gewalt* can be and has been translated both ways should make us alert to the agenda of the broader historiography of violence.[27] While it may be useful for large-scale sociological comparison to rid ourselves of this distinction between force and violence (or even between legitimate and illegitimate force),[28] failing to be alert to the ethical position of those who choose to write about violence (instead of force, or vice versa) ends up obscuring some critical moves and currents in twentieth-century historiography.

To contextualize this problem, we can point again to Weber, and the tradition of historical sociology that is anchored in his work but finds its real starting point in Norbert Elias's *Civilizing Process* (originally published in 1939). To paint in broad strokes, this tradition posits a dichotomy between violence and social order, and seeks to explain the ways in which order contains violence, usually by incorporating it within legitimate institutional frameworks. This tradition, in its least intellectually sophisticated manifestations, can be a teleological narrative of the ways in which contemporary liberal order is fashioned (or fails to be fashioned) from chaos and uncertainty; more recent work, such as that of Charles Tilly or Douglass North, has substantially improved on this teleological tendency while keeping the basic insight that institutions—both formal and informal—can lower incentives for actors to "defect" (to cheat or to use violence) in transactions, and thus promote stability, safety, and growth.[29] To say that institutions *can* control violence is not, of course, to argue that they necessarily succeed in so doing, or that institutional configurations cannot sometimes promote violence.[30] It bears adding as well that this perspective does not always entail optimism: one only need think of the pessimism that marks the climax of Weber's *Protestant Ethic*, a bleak vision of man trapped in the iron cage of bureaucratic rationality. Mutatis mutandis, a similar pessimism about human paralysis in the face of the rationalization of institutions extends to Foucault's diagnosis in *Discipline and Punish* of the carceral revolution in contemporary society.

While Weberian pessimism about the disenchantments of modern rational governance is a key part of the tradition of historical sociology, a different reaction to the same processes that Weber described emerged in the wake of World War II. In particular, it is a thread in the critical tradition that emerges from a deep anxiety about the nature of industrial progress and Enlightenment rationality, based more on Marx and Nietzsche (and, to an overlooked degree, on Kierkegaard, about which more below) than in traditional German sociology—though it was certainly indebted to Weber. It is these postwar German thinkers who contributed the most to the problems that a study of violence today entails, and it is worth mapping a few key moves in this line of critical thought to approach an answer to why contemporary scholars are so comfortable with applying the label of "violence" to such a broad range of phenomena.

While the sociological tradition prized a value-neutral approach and therefore relied upon the ethically ambiguous sense of *Gewalt*, the same cannot be said of the critical projects of the late twentieth century. To give a potted narrative of their development, one could say that, from the middle of the nineteenth century to the middle of the twentieth, the world witnessed the advent of new technologies for both mass production and mass destruction (or, depending on one's perspective, for both simultaneously). These technological developments, claiming to emerge under the banner of progress, culminated in two events: industrialized genocide in bureaucratically rationalized and technically sophisticated death camps, and the nuclear attacks on Japan. The rapidly changing technological horizon was joined to an increase in political consciousness (not least in scholarly circles) of the fragile and sometimes dubious bases of political power and sovereignty. This political consciousness was linked to the technological changes in large measure through the writings of the Frankfurt school, whose emphasis on total critique was rooted in Marx and Nietzsche, but when translated into an American landscape (not least through the work of Marcuse) came to serve as a catalyst for the intellectual and political revolutions of the late 1960s, and from there has informed contemporary critical projects.[31]

The experience of comprehensive destruction in general, and of a technologically sophisticated genocide in particular, guided inquiry. While this appeared in a variety of manifestations, one place to start would be with Hannah Arendt's *Origins of Totalitarianism*, in which, through attempting to explain Nazism as a species of "radical evil," she argued that the nature of the concentration camps—spaces in which "everything is permitted"—led to a form of human experience that defied the categories of language, law, and even ethical thought. Tellingly, "crime" is her point of reference:

> We attempt to understand elements in the present or recollected experience that simply surpass our powers of understanding. We attempt to classify as criminal a thing which, as we feel, no such category was ever intended to cover. What meaning has the concept of murder when we are confronted with the mass production of corpses? We attempt to understand the behavior of concentration-camp inmates and SS-men psychologically, when the very thing that must be realized is that the psyche *can* be destroyed even without the destruction of the physical man; that indeed, psyche, character, and individuality seem under certain circumstances to express themselves only through the rapidity or slowness through which they disintegrate. The end result in any case is inanimate men, i.e., men who can no longer be psychologically understood, whose return to the psychologically or otherwise intelligibly human world closely resembles the resurrection of Lazarus. All statements of common sense, whether of a psychological or sociological nature, serve only to encourage those who think it "superficial" to "dwell on horrors."[32]

The link here between the tremendous violence of the concentration camps and the problem of moral (or legal) judgment, if not explanation, is brought to the fore through recourse to the language of religion (Lazarus). These links are critical: totalitarianism, through its vision of technologically perfected and socially dis-embedded modernity (camps), opens up a space in which men can finally realize their Enlightened potential (anything and everything)—only to find that this transgression of previous limits is in fact a species of nihilism which erodes even the categories of understanding. Hence, the recourse to the language of the miraculous, and in particular, to the image of Lazarus, a man who moves across the space of life and death. The image of Lazarus is key to Arendt's argument in more ways than one: not only is he something miraculous in the sense that he cannot be understood according to traditional categories (if at all), but insofar as he can be understood, it is in the sense that his resurrection marks the boundaries between life and death that Arendt's Nazis disregarded: namely, in ways which require a transcendental policing ironically missing in the modern and disenchanted world.

Arendt is not unique here in linking violence and late modernity with the language of religion and miracle, or in linking this package of features to a claim that totalitarian violence challenges our power to understand and describe. Arendt is less clear, however, on whether it is actually in the nature of violence that it confounds such categories, or whether this is an optical illusion of sorts—that is, that extreme violence only *appears* to be incapable of description or cognition.

Arendt's claim that totalitarian violence challenges our categories of understanding did not emerge from a vacuum. It is part of a larger conversation on the nature of reason and enlightenment that played out over the course of the mid-twentieth century among thinkers as diverse as Heidegger (Arendt's teacher) and those of the Institute for Social Research (the Frankfurt School of critical theory). In many respects our current discourse on (and discomfort with) violence is linked to this discussion as much as it is to our legal categories, albeit in the former case perhaps more tangentially. The basic claim—shared by Heidegger and the Frankfurt school—was that the instrumental, scientific reason prized by the Enlightenment had become fundamentally dehumanizing. It is this dehumanization that is productive of violence,[33] and not just particular acts of violence against particular individuals, but, because the violence perpetrated on the vulnerable is actually a species of self-hatred,[34] this instrumentally rationalized system promotes a violence which pollutes all participants in it. As Adorno and Horkheimer put in it in the section of *Dialectic of Enlightenment* dealing with anti-Semitism:

> The enlightened self-control with which adapted Jews effaced within themselves the painful scars of domination by others, a second kind of circumcision, made them forsake their own dilapidated community and wholeheartedly embrace the life of the modern bourgeoisie, which was already advancing ineluctably towards a reversion to pure oppression and reorganization into an exclusively racial entity. Race is not, as the racial nationalists claim, an immediate, natural peculiarity. Rather, it is a regression to nature as mere violence, to the hidebound particularism which, in the existing order, constitutes precisely the universal. Race today is the self-assertion of the bourgeois individual, integrated into the barbaric collective. The harmonious society to which the liberal Jews declared their allegiance has finally been granted to them in the form of national community. They believed only that anti-Semitism disfigured this order, which in reality cannot

> exist without disfiguring human beings. The persecution of the Jews, like any persecution, cannot be separated from that order. Its essence, however it may hide itself at times, is the violence which today is openly revealed.[35]

Reason—true reason, not coldly instrumental reason—can critique this system, but fundamentally, in its modern, technological instantiation, "Enlightenment is totalitarian."[36]

There are two important moves here: first, the extension of the violence of totalitarianism from death camps to the entirety of late modernity meant the opening up of a vast territory in which one could locate, expose, and critique the violence that was now revealed to structure everyday life and practice. And the experience of the twentieth century meant that this could be extended beyond the boundaries of Europe proper to include the European colonial experience writ large (and the thorough nastiness of the violence of nineteenth-century colonization and twentieth-century decolonization made this task both easier and more timely).[37] Additionally, the sense that the demise of Nazism in World War II did not in fact end the progress of modern totalitarianism, but simply allowed it to appear in newer and seemingly more benign clothes, necessitated turning critical attention to modern society and exposing its violence through an analogous process of critique.[38] A sense that violence lurked in every corner and was a central social ordering principle (and a morally questionable one, in contrast to Weber, who was only pessimistic) resulted in the profusion of the use of the term today, in which we find, to draw from the table of contents of one recent collected volume, that there is, at the very least, state violence, structural violence, everyday violence, symbolic violence, interpersonal violence, and gendered violence.[39] In its specific manifestations, violence can be anything from punching another individual in the nose to anything generally coercive or even unpleasant (and here we can include all forms of social ordering), on the assumption that order is possible either because (a) it ultimately rests upon the eventual likelihood of violence, regardless of whether such violence is ever actually employed; or (b) because ordering proceeds from power, and power in itself is reducible to acts of violence.[40] In this process of marking things as violent and exposing them to the critical gaze there was never any need to produce a method by which types of violence could be disassociated from one another: since all forms of violence could be equally traumatizing (and therefore equally valid opportunities to expose the dynamics of power), a system of distinguishing which forms of violence might be more important than others would have been fundamentally an imposition of power, and hence of violence, and hence culpable. The downside to this critical move, however, is obvious: history quickly comes to look very much like Foucault's reading of Nietzsche, in which:

> Humanity does not gradually progress from combat to combat until it arrives at universal reciprocity, where the rule of law finally replaces warfare; humanity installs each of its violences in a system of rules and thus proceeds from domination to domination. The nature of these rules allows violence to be inflicted on violence and the resurgence of new forces that are sufficiently strong to dominate those in power. Rules are empty in themselves, violent and unfinalized; they are impersonal and can be bent to any purpose. The successes of history belong to those who are capable of seizing these rules, to replace those who had used them, to disguise themselves so as to pervert them, invert their meaning, and redirect them against those who had initially imposed them; controlling this complex mechanism, they will make it function so as to overcome the rulers through their own rules.[41]

To continue in this vein rapidly exposes one of two problems, depending on how one approaches the analysis: at one level, if all is violence and violence is everywhere, then violence is also nowhere and nothing particularly remarkable—it's just turtles all the way down. In this sense, the concept becomes sociologically useless; it has the additional disadvantage of making the writing of the history of violence along these lines excruciatingly boring.

The other way that these moves have changed historical discourse on violence is perhaps more important, as well as being both philosophically and methodologically dangerous. To return to Arendt's move in bringing the language of religion to bear on questions of totalitarian violence, we could say that, if violence is both everywhere and nowhere, then it is not sociologically empty, but instead paradoxical in the Kierkegaardian sense: that is, it implies or induces a critical stance in which violence can only be beheld with a *horror religiosus*, observed with awe but not understood, because, like the sacrifice of Isaac, it suspends the ethical and as such touches on the sublime or the indescribable.[42] This is the second legacy of critical theory, namely, the involvement of the language of religion and mystified awe in the study of violence. While initially proposing to expose the violence of the Enlightenment by marking it as mythical, it is no small irony that subsequent critical projects often have come to echo their own objects, returning to the language of religion in a sort of inversion in which acts, images, or descriptions of violence come to exercise a power of fascination;[43] from this fascination it is only a short step further to where violence can be treated as something transcendent, sublime, or even joyous: think here, for example, of Jean-Paul Sartre's glorification of revolutionary violence in the end of his preface to Fanon's *Wretched of the Earth*, where violence has became therapeutic, purgative, and humanizing;[44] or of the ludicrous mutterings of Jean Baudrillard, expressed with what can only be described as tittering glee, in the aftermath of September 11, 2001, in which actor is indistinguishable from victim, in which what is real is inextricable from what is fiction, in which the ethical has been overtly suspended, and all that matters is the putative purity of a collective sacrifice.[45]

* * *

To return, briefly, to Arendt, and from there to the problem of how historians should treat violence: it is to Arendt's credit that she came to understand the nature of the methodological impasse that her early use of the term "radical evil" provoked: she rejected the term in *Eichmann in Jerusalem*, explaining in a letter to Gershom Scholem that "I changed my mind and. . . . It is now my opinion that no evil is 'radical,' that it is only extreme, and that it possesses neither depth nor any demonic dimension. It can overgrow and lay waste the whole world precisely because it spreads like a fungus on the surface. It is 'thought-defying,' as I said, because thought tries to reach some depth, to go to the roots, and the moment it concerns itself with evil, it is frustrated because it finds nothing. That is its banality. Only the good has depth and can be radical."[46] It is not the task of historians, fortunately, to identify, in the same ways as may be critical for normative political theory, what has genuine or radical depth. It is, however, the job of historians to avoid or untangle concepts that are "thought-defying," to subject them to scrutiny, and to avoid methodological paths that lead only to hopeless irrationalism. This is the task for understanding violence, one with which ancient historians have likewise grappled (in many respects unsuccessfully).[47] The fact that such a broad range of concepts might fall under the rubric of "violence" has led to hand-wringing and despair, and to the dismissal of the problem, in the words of Bruce Frier, as "all but intractable, especially because it is virtually impossible to define and depends so much on the perspective of the observer."[48]

It is unfortunate that Frier dismissed the problem, however, primarily because his central insight is correct. Violence is not so much a thing to be defined as it is a label used in a process of defining the actions of another, and locating those actions (and sometimes also the motives and character) of others within a discourse of claim-making. In other words, using the label "violent" to describe an action or a person is a way of declaring unacceptable something that another thought appropriate, natural, or necessary.[49] By applying the label of violence, individuals engage in a process of actively challenging the legitimacy of what might otherwise be understood to be innocuous, necessary, or well deserved, unmasking these things for what they "really" are. It is not that it "depends so much on the perspective of the observer," but rather that it depends on the perspective of both the victim and the observer—the receiver of the complaint—and ultimately, on whether the observer can be convinced and—just as important—can convince others that the label of violence is correct.

Two examples might be brought to bear here. The first comes from a cache of documents, largely petitions, surviving from Euhemeria, a small town at the edge of Lake Moeris in the Fayyum in the first century A.D. The petitions are largely addressed to the *epistates phylakiton*, the local commander of the guards (police chief would be a misnomer, as his function was not policing in the contemporary sense). The commander of the guards was sent petitions from villagers complaining of a predictable set of annoyances in village life: theft, trespass, interpersonal violence, and the like. He had to make decisions about which complaints were reasonable and required official attention, and when he decided that a complaint did, he would forward the petition to the *archephodos*, who, it appears, was in charge of "arresting" or "sending" the people about whom the petitioner complained.[50] Among the petitions one stands out:

> Ἀθηνοδώρωι ἐπιστάτῃ φυλακιτῶν παρὰ Ἰσίωνος δούλου Χ[α]—
> ιρήμονος ἐξηγητοῦ. τῇ Σεβαστῇ β τοῦ ἐνεστῶτο(ς) μηνὸς Παῦνι
> τοῦ β (ἔτους) Γαίου Καίσαρος Σεβαστοῦ Γερμανι[κ]ο(ῦ)
> παραγενομένου μου εἰς Εὐημέρειαν τῆς Θεμίστου μερίδ(ος) περὶ
> μετεώρων ἐλ[ογ]οποιησάμην πρὸς Ὀννῶφριν Σίλβωνος τῶν ἀπὸ
> τῆς κώμης ὑπὲρ οὗ ἔχω πρὸς αὐτὸν ἐνεχύρου, ὃς δὲ ἐκ τοῦ ἐναντίου
> ἄλογον ἀηδίαν μοι ἐπιχειρήσας παρεχρήσατό μοι πολλὰ καὶ
> ἄσχημα καὶ ἐνειλούμενός μοι ἀπώλεσα πινακίδα καὶ ἀργυ(ρίου)
> (δραχμὰς) ξ, ἔτι δὲ καὶ ἐτόλμησεν φθόνους[51] μοι ἐπαγαγεῖν αἰτίας

τοῦ μὴ ὄντος. διὸ ἀξιῶ γράψαι ἀχθῆναι αὐτὸν ἐπὶ σὲ πρὸς τὴν δέουσαν ἐπέξοδον. εὐτύχ(ει).

To Athenodoros, commander of the guards,
From Ision, slave of Chairemon the *exegetes*. On the 2nd of the present month of Pauni, *dies augusta*, in the second year of Gaius Caesar Augustus Germanicus, I was present in Euhemeria of the division of Themistos due to some unfinished business, and I had an argument with Onnophris son of Silbon, one of those from the town, about a pledge that I have from him. But he, for his part, treated me with irrational violence, abused me in many unpleasant ways, and beat me. I lost my account book and 60 silver drachmas. Still he dared to cast envy at me, though for no good reason (?). Therefore I ask that you write for him to be brought before you for the necessary punishment. Farewell.[52]

A lot can be learned about the power of the label of violence and related claim-making discourses from this story of a confrontation between two men (or a man and a slave) in an Egyptian village. On the one hand there is the account-balancing slave, Ision, charged by his master to collect a series of debts; on the other hand, the assailant, Onnophris, resists him. Behind Ision's narrative there may lurk many potential stories about motives, both his own and Onnophris', and there are some tempting details in Ision's description. It is interesting, for example, that Ision loses his πίναξ—his account book—in the melee, and given that the argument itself is about the settling of accounts, it seems possible that Onnophris could have been venting his anger over a financial situation both upon Ision's body and upon the documentation of the ins-and-outs of their previous interactions. The accusations of envy, though grammatically bungled, may also speak volumes about how Ision perceived the nature of their relationship. Envy proceeds from a perceived imbalance in the "right" power distribution in a relationship or set of relationships, and points to the suspicions that ensue when these feel out of order.[53] In this case, despite his formal status as a slave, Ision was hardly powerless: this is in part because of the large range of abilities that slaves in the Roman Empire were allotted on behalf of their masters, but also, significantly, because he was the agent not just of any master, but of a fairly important one: the *exegetes* was connected to the office of the *strategos*, and in charge of citizenship lists and the appointment of guardians.[54] Likewise, there are the details of the violent acts themselves: Onnophris' "irrational violence" (ἄλογον ἀηδίαν), his abuse, and his threats are recorded in the typical, indignant language of complaint—a language that presumes that Ision had dignity capable of injury in the first place. Onnophris, it appears from the petition, did not agree.[55]

When Ision wrote this petition, he made a public claim about the ways in which he deserved to be treated, sought to get the upper hand in defining the terms of his relationship with another individual, and attempted to involve external authorities in the relationship between himself and another (free) man. As with all claims, his was subject to contest, not just subsequently by his opponent in the courtroom, but also by local authorities (the observers, in Frier's formulation), who could use their power to decide whether such a claim could be convincing or not.[56] In this case it is fortunate that this petition comes from an archive, for here we can better understand the workings of this process: while most of the Euhemeria petitions were subscribed by the *epistates phylakiton* and sent on to the *archephodos* with instructions that the *archephodos* "arrest" the malefactors and thus begin legal proceedings, Ision's petition has no subscription.[57] In other words, it appears that Ision's claim of violence was rejected. One way to frame this would be to say that local authorities decided that what Onnophris had used was merely justifiable force, not unacceptable violence, and he used it against a slave who deserved it, not a man who had rights worth taking the state's time in defending. Presumably Chairemon, Ision's owner, could try again by suing Onnophris for damages, but in such a case Ision would be presumed to be a piece of property, not a man.

The second example is not papyrological, but comes instead from the jurisprudential literature. (Here it bears adding that Roman jurisprudence was not a hermetically sealed and independent tradition of thought, but was instead forged in tandem with empire.) The passage in question comes from the *Digest*, and is woven together from excerpts of Ulpian's and Paulus' commentaries *On the Edict* (both from the third century, but here discussing the opinion of Salvius Julianus, who worked in the second century). In book 9 of the *Digest* the opinions of the jurists are set out on the question of Aquilian liability, namely, the relationship of obligation that results from unlawfully causing harm to slaves and chattels. But the text then turns to the case of teachers, and a teacher who kills or wounds a slave during a lesson. Here the jurists are certain that the teacher is liable under the Aquilian law if he kills or wounds the slave, but the jurists then turn to the question of how to deal with a teacher in the case where he uses violence against his free-born charges:

> sutor, inquit, puero discenti ingenuo filio familias, parum bene facienti quod demonstraverit, forma calcei cervicem percussit, ut oculus puero perfunderetur. Dicit igitur Iulianus iniuriarum quidem actionem non competere, quia non faciendae iniuriae causa percusserit, sed monendi et docendi causa: an ex locato, dubitat, quia levis dumtaxat castigatio concessa est docenti: sed lege Aquilia posse agi non dubito: (*Paulus libro 22 ad edictum*) praeceptoris enim nimia saevitia culpae adsignatur.
>
> He (Julianus) says: a shoemaker, in the course of teaching a freeborn boy who was a son-in-power, struck his (the boy's) neck with a shoe last, since the boy did not sufficiently perform the task he was taught. But as a result, the boy's eye was knocked out. Julianus said that the action for *iniuria* does not apply, since he did not hit the boy with the object of causing injury, but with the object of teaching and admonishing. He doubts whether the action on hire applies, since the right of lightly chastising is granted to teachers. But I do not doubt that the Lex Aquilia applies: (Paulus, *On the Edict* book 22) since an excess of brutality on the part of the teacher is a reason for assigning fault.[58]

The *Digest* passage is interesting, not least because it mirrors certain moves that were made in defining the relationship between Ision and Onnophris. In the case discussed by the jurists, the question is put as to the nature of the relationship that occurs when there is violence between two free men who have unequal degrees of power over one another. The question, put in one form, is whether the striking of the child should count as violence or as force; certainly teachers have the right to strike the children they teach: so long as this is done for the purpose of "teaching and admonishing," this is justifiable force, and no further relationship results between the two parties. But Ulpian and Paul *do* think that a claim can be made for Aquilian damages, if only as an *actio utilis*,[59] if the instructor's violence crosses from acceptable to brutal. But in this case a series of wires have to be crossed for the legal operation to proceed properly: the praetor would write up a *formula* for Aquilian damages, and the judge would have to decide whether such a line had been crossed. But this would presumably require treating the free pupil through a fiction as though he were a slave, and allowing the suit to his father in his capacity—again fictional—as the boy's "owner."[60] The jurists' moves in this argument reflect the same kind of intellectual slippage—though this time in the opposite direction—as that which prevails in the quarrel between Ision and Onnophris, and raises, however obliquely, a set of questions as to what kinds of relationships (of personal status and of obligation) can or must be assumed when the term "violence" (here, *iniuria*, a term I will return to below) is applied to certain kinds of acts. Here the injury to the boy cannot be characterized as violence between free and independent men (*iniuria*), for they are incapable of having a relationship of equals, at least in the sense that violence is prohibited between equal men, for here the right to harm lightly and for the purpose of correction is granted to one of them; nor, for the same reasons, as a relationship of contract (since the teacher was allowed, under such a contract, to use limited amounts of force); instead, the last available option is to treat the boy as a damaged slave, and allow his father—like Chairemon in the imagined alternative to the case of Ision—to sue under the Lex Aquilia. Were the boy in question not an imaginary construct of the jurists, one would imagine that he, like Ision, would have felt this to have been an affront to his dignity.

From here we can return to the question of how violence is best understood as an ethical label, and propose that the force/violence distinction I discussed above can be reappropriated as a methodological guideline for the study of violence: more than just an artifact of divergent scholarly traditions, the English distinction between (potentially justifiable or morally neutral) force and (unjustifiable) violence is precisely what is at stake in defining the relations between Ision and Onnophris and the shoemaker and his pupil, and is central for understanding the scope of the term "violence" in the papyrological evidence in general. And there is a good deal at stake in this distinction, in two senses. First, violence—or the ability, legally speaking, to feel pain as a result of violence—is intimately connected with ideas of personhood. I will deal with this more momentarily, but for the moment it will suffice to say that personhood is also connected to the ability to enter into certain kinds of interpersonal relationships, in particular, the relationship that results (or does not result) from an act of violence or force. To wit: someone can be "forced" to do something legitimate or justified—to pay taxes, to abide by the terms of a contract, or to make a shoe properly.[61] Once the force has been applied, provided it is justified, the relationship between the two individuals is over. The taxes have been paid or the shoe stretched correctly, and the government or the teacher does not subsequently owe that individual recompense for having had to resort to force. But when someone commits an act of violence—or when someone labels someone else's actions as an act of violence—there is a claim of a subsequent relationship between the individuals in question. Violence opens avenues of redress, but additionally creates and transforms individual relationships, construing victim and violator as legal equals bound together through obligations. The offender subsequently *owes* something to the victim, and the two are henceforth bound in a relationship of debt and repayment until the issue is settled—if indeed it ever is. The act of giving the label of violence, as in modern discourse, implies that one finds another's actions to be inappropriate or unpalatable. But unlike modern discourse, the label of violence does not implicitly try to relegate the violator beyond the line that distinguishes civilization from barbarism; instead, the idea is that violence has created a subsequent, albeit inverted, relationship—a new relationship of obligation wherein the violated dominates, albeit only in the sense that his obligation will be redeemed before a judge. This is because one man's violence is often another man's force, and the correctness of the label "violence" has to be worked out politically, that is, through public claim-making and contestation.

* * *

The quarrels between slaves and debtors and shoemakers and students lead to another point about violence, one hinted at in the previous section: there is a connection between violence and personhood, and particularly how one perceives oneself as a person (that is, one's subjectivity), in two senses of the term. One sense is legal, and is reflected in the ways law connects the power to claim things as violence with questions of status, expressed most starkly above in the movement between free and slave, but to one extent or another implicitly in every violent conflict. The ways in which law constructs and impinges upon subjectivities through the language of personal status and obligation is an important part of my narrative, and an element to which I will return below. But for the moment, it is profitable to begin with a wider sense of the term subjectivity, that is, with how people come to understand themselves and their place in the world, and how violence connects with these elements of self-perception.

At one level one could say that, while all people are vulnerable in some way or another, in any given society (and for current purposes we can take this term as being unproblematic) there are differential degrees of vulnerability. How and where one can be injured, by whom, and with what sorts of result to a person's sense of self and self-worth is a product of culture, though it is in the nature of these cultural categories that they are often precisely what are being contested in the case of a claim of violence. Two examples will again suffice. The first comes from Pierre Bourdieu's classic discussion of the contested dynamics of vulnerability in Kabyle society in Algeria, in which he describes honor as a game to be played between equals, a dialogue of challenge and riposte in which the worth of both the offender and the challenger was open to public scrutiny. When challenged, a man could reply, presuming himself to be the social equal of his challenger; by the same token, he could choose to ignore the insult, marking the offender as someone not worth responding to while similarly declaring his own person as invulnerable to the hostilities of those who were lower ranked. The ideals, however, were complicated by the realities:

> To choose not to reply may have different meanings, even contradictory ones. The offender can, by his physical force, his prestige, or the importance and authority of the group to which he belongs, be superior, equal, or inferior to the person offended. If the logic of honour presupposes the recognition of an ideal equality of honour between the two parties, popular consciousness is nevertheless not unaware of inequalities in fact. He who cries, "I've got a moustache too!" is answered by the proverb: "The moustache of the hare is not that of the lion." In this way a whole casuistry, spontaneous and extremely subtle, may develop.[62]

The dynamic process of challenge and riposte (or refusal to counter the challenges of another) that Bourdieu describes can be compared with a letter of the younger Pliny, describing the murder of Larcius Macedo, a senator and ex-praetor, but also himself a descendant of slaves (and for this reason, according to Pliny, a harsh and unpleasant master), by his own slaves in the baths. The first part of the letter describes the murder itself (I will return to this part below). After reflecting on Macedo's death, Pliny pauses to recall another incident in which Macedo had been subjected to violence in the baths, considering it a sort of an omen:

> addam quod opportune de eodem Macedone succurrit. cum in publico Romae lavaretur, notabilis atque etiam, ut exitus docuit, ominosa res accidit. eques Romanus a servo eius, ut transitum daret, manu leviter admonitus convertit se nec servum, a quo erat tactus, sed ipsum Macedonem tam graviter palma percussit ut paene concideret. ita balineum illi quasi per gradus quosdam primum contumeliae locus, deinde exitii fuit.

> I will offer another detail which just came to mind concerning this same Macedo. When at Rome, he was in the public baths when a noteworthy, and, as his death has proven, ominous incident occurred. A Roman knight was tapped lightly by Macedo's slave so that he could pass by; the knight wheeled around and slapped not the slave, but Macedo himself, so hard that he nearly fell over. In this way, the baths were for Macedo like a path, leading first to violence (*contumelia*), and finally to death.[63]

The contrast between these two texts, both dealing with the ethics of violence and the nature of vulnerability, is striking, to pun just slightly (and, it bears mentioning, yet another good empirical reason for jettisoning the nonsense about "Mediterranean" societies that continues to return, in zombie-like fashion, to scholarly inquiry). The delicate casuistry of Bourdieu's Kabyle society that provides a commentary on how the game of honor should be played (often with telling mistakes and misunderstandings) is answered quickly by Pliny's Roman knight, who strikes instinctively and derogatorily at his social inferiors (an open-handed slap possessing the same degrading and emasculating force it has today, it appears). The only accident here is that in this case the open hand lands on the knight's vast superior in social rank; the assumption remains that the knee-jerk delivery of punishing violence to a slave who had the audacity to invade a superior's personal space (by his touch, and by his request that the knight yield a way through the crowd) is perfectly reasonable and acceptable. The lesson, for Pliny, seems to be that the baths are dangerous, for when the markers of invulnerability are checked at the door you may well end up violently humiliated by your social inferiors. But in a wider sense, these texts demonstrate how violence is enmeshed in a society's broader discourse about who can be rightly injured and how, and similarly within notions of who can feel pain and who can complain about feeling it. In this sense, it contributes to a person's subjectivity, since when people come to notice that they have been victims of violation they reflect, through their written complaints at least, but probably more broadly in ways that we cannot see, on precisely who they are (and how this contrasts with who they *think* they are, and/or who *others* think they are) and where they fit into society.

This is so not only in general terms, but in particular ways as well. One of the most important contributions of anthropology in recent decades has been to draw attention back to the physical body, and in particular, to how subjectivity is affected by the physical body, how it is or how it comes to be perceived.[64] Violence plays an important role in this process as well. To return to Pliny's letter on Macedo, this time to the narration of Macedo's death:

> lavabatur in villa Formiana. repente eum servi circumsistunt. alius fauces invadit, alius os verberat, alius pectus et ventrem, atque etiam—foedum dictu—verenda contundit.
>
> He was bathing in his villa at Formiae. Suddenly slaves surrounded him. One of them grabbed his throat while another one beat his face, another beat his chest and belly, and also—horrible to say—pounded his private parts.[65]

Pliny's description of the assault on Macedo is presented through the lens of privacy and vulnerability (both literally and figuratively); it is made more horrifying by playing on fears that are endemic in slave systems. The slaves' violation of Macedo deprives him of certain protections to his body that are guaranteed by his rank, and does this by harming him in places that are off limits to others. The language of the body is central to this, and provides a way into the question of how subjectivity is based upon—and similarly can come to structure—ideas about the body. Throughout petitions—and likewise in the subsequent claim-making process—bodies are on display, being written about as wounded and marked, swollen and bruised, violated and exposed. This is so not only in the first-person narratives of petitions, but, since the power of observation was spread throughout society, in other contexts as well. In contrast to Pliny's Macedo, a report from a public doctor gives a hint of the power of the official gaze in the Egyptian context, and the amount of parts that would have been on display:

> (hand 14) ρϛ
>
> (hand 1) [Οὐαλερίῳ] Ἀμμωνιανῷ τῷ καὶ Γεροντίῳ λ[ογισ]ṭ[ῇ] Ὀξυρυγχίτου [παρὰ Αὐρηλίου] Σαραπίωνος Ἡροδότου ἀπὸ τῆς λαμ(πρᾶς) καὶ λαμ(προτάτης) Ὀξ[υρυγχιτ]ῷṿ πόλεως δημοσίου ἰατροῦ. [ἐπεστάλην τῇ] χθὲς ἡμέρᾳ, ἥτις ἦν Μεχεὶρ κϛ, ἐκ βιβλιδίων [ἐπιδοθέ]ṿτων σοι ὑπὸ Οὐαλερίου Νουνδιναρίου [- ca.9 -]traces ὥστε γενέσθαι ἐν ἐποικίῳ αὐṭοῦ Π̣ . . .[. . . .]ειω καὶ ἐπιδεῖν τὴν περὶ τοῦ πλη[γέντος (?) . . . . . .] . . .ṭου καὶ̣ [. . .] φ̣ύλακος Μουεῖτος διάθεσιν καὶ ἐγγράφως σοι π̣[ρο]σφωνῆσαι.

ὅθεν ἐν τῷ ἐποικίῳ γε̣[νόμενος] ἐπεῖδον τ̣ὸ̣ν̣ αὐτὸν Μ[ο]υ̣εῖν κλινήρη ὄντα ἔχοντα κατὰ μὲν τοῦ βρ̣έ̣γματο̣ς διαίρεσιν μετὰ ψιλώσεως [τοῦ] ὀ̣σ̣τ̣έ̣ο̣υ καὶ κατὰ τῆς κορυφῆς τραύματα δύο μετ̣ὰ ψιλώ̣σ̣ε̣ω̣ς τοῦ ὀσ[τέ]ου καὶ κ̣ά̣[τ]ω̣θεν τούτων τραύματα [. . . ἐ]πὶ τοῦ δεξιοῦ μέρους τῆς κεφαλ̣ῆ̣ς καὶ κατὰ τοῦ ἀριστεροῦ κροτά[φου -5-6-] . . . . οἰδήματος καὶ κατὰ τῶν̣ . . . .[-ca. 2-] [τοῦ] ἀ̣ριστεροῦ ὠτί[ου οἴ]δημα μετὰ πε̣λ̣ι̣ώ̣μ̣ατος καὶ κατὰ τῆς δεξιᾶς ὠμο[πλάτης κα]ὶ̣ τοῦ ὤμου οἴδημα μετὰ πελιώματος [καὶ κ]ατὰ τῆς δεξιᾶς χει[ρὸ]ς κατὰ τοῦ μεγί̣σ̣τ̣ο̣υ̣ δακτύλων πλῆγμα μετ' ο̣ἰ̣δ̣[ήματο]ς καὶ κατὰ τοῦ βραχίονος τῆς δεξιᾶς χειρὸς οἴδημα μετ[ὰ] π̣ελιώματος καὶ κατὰ τοῦ ἀριστεροῦ μηροῦ τρῶ[σιν . . . .] .[.] .ως καὶ τοῦ γονατίου ἄνωθεν τρῶσιν καὶ ἐ̣[πὶ] τ̣ο̣ῦ δεξιοῦ μη̣ρ̣οῦ τρώσεις δύο πέρας εἰς πέρας [κ]α̣ὶ̣ κ̣ατὰ [πάσης τῆς] ἀριστερᾱ̣ς π̣λ̣ε̣υ̣ρᾶς τρῶσιν· ὅθεν προσφωνῶ.

(ἔτους) ι [καὶ] η τ[ῶ]ν̣ κυρίων .[.] . . ἡμῶν Κωνσταντίνου καὶ Λ[ικινίο]υ̣ Σε̣βαστῶν, ἐπὶ ὑπατ[ε]ί̣ας Καικ̣ι̣ν̣ί̣ο̣υ̣ Σαβε̣ί̣[νου] καὶ Οὐεττίου Ῥουφίνου τῶν λαμ̣π̣ρ̣ο̣τ̣ά̣τ̣ω̣ν̣ Μ̣ε̣χ̣[εὶρ κζ].

(hand 2) Α̣ὐ̣ρ̣ή̣λ̣ι̣ο̣ς̣ [Σαρα]π̣ίων ἐπιδέδωκα π̣ρ̣ο̣σ̣φωνῶ̣ν̣ ὡς πρόκειται.

Page 106

(hand 1) To Valerius Ammonianus, also called Gerontius, *logistes* of Oxyrhynchos,

From Aurelius Sarapion son of Herodotos, public doctor from the glorious and most glorious city of the Oxyrhynchites. Yesterday, which was the 26th of Mecheir, on account of a petition submitted to you by Valerius Noundinarios I was sent . . . to go to the village of P—, and to observe and report on the condition (?) of the wounded man . . . the condition of the guard Moueis, and therefore I submit to you this report. When I arrived at the village I observed Moueis lying in bed, with a gash on his head stripped to bone, two wounds on the top of his head with stripping to bone, beneath these wounds . . . on the right side of his head; and on his right temple . . . swelling and on his . . . on his left ear a bruise with lividity, and on his right shoulder-blade a bruise with lividity, on his right hand on the largest finger a bruise with swelling, on his right wrist a bruise with lividity, on his left thigh a wound . . . above his

> groin a wound, on his left thigh two wounds from end to end, and all along his left side more wounds. I attest to this. Year 18 of our lords Constantinus and Licinius, Augusti, in the consulship of the mot glorious Caecinius Sabeinos and Vettius Rufinus, Mecheir 27. (hand 2) I Aurelius Sarapion have submitted this report as requested.[66]

When petitioners chose to complain about violence, they were asked to reflect not only on who they are as social beings, but similarly on who they are as physical beings. The experience of pain, mediated through language, draws attention to the body and its wounds. I will discuss this process at greater length in what follows, but for the present a few comments must suffice for outlining the ways in which the experience of violation contributes to subjectivity and self-perception. The overt reflection—and narration—of the experience of being a victim of violence provides a window into the world of differential vulnerabilities that I mentioned above, and as such is a valuable source for how individuals living in an ancient empire chose to describe and classify themselves. This does not, however, make these sources unproblematic. What we see in the narratives that petitioners create is both a set of normative claims about how they *wish* to be treated, and also a narration framed at the moment when they are forced to acknowledge publicly a disjunction between their wounded bodies and their normative claims—or, in another sense, between their ideally deserving social body and their actually mistreated physical body. At the moment of violation, in other words, we are seeing not unmediated subjectivities, but deeply and problematically affected ones, which reveal themselves through highly selective descriptions. These descriptions, however, cluster in interesting and important ways, and deserve to be treated systematically.

A final issue, however, relates to the mechanics of how personhood is structured by and reflected in this narrative process, but comes from there to a broader problem, one which is both linguistic and epistemological. Namely: as I suggested above, language (in this case, the language of petition, with its accompanying narrations and claims and its stilted and repetitive terminology) is a highly imperfect technology for communicating pain. It is therefore also an imperfect tool for communicating one's self-understanding in the wake of violence.[67] This is so for three reasons. Language is imprecise and capable of misunderstanding. Pain is largely a private emotion or sensation. Language that expresses pain—if people choose to express it at all—often feels limp and inadequate to its task.[68] Finally, in the world of Roman Egypt, the language of pain that is found in petitions is delivered through a stilted, legalistic vocabulary, the product of a scribal culture that mediates or *translates* between the language of pain and the language of law. Though working through all the details of these problems would be beyond the scope of this chapter (and working through them in the detail necessary would require a deep and wide-ranging philosophical anthropology), let me make a suggestion: translation and fiction, like obligation, are powerful metaphors, and they work in multiple directions. What matters in the case of a petition is not some underlying truth or reality of what actually happened, nor simply the ability of the words in the petition to move a higher power to sympathy. What ultimately matters is what comes to be accepted as truth in a particular moment in a particular society. And this is precisely what is interesting about law. When people framed their narratives about wounded bodies and personal pain, they were setting administrative wheels in motion, and they and the people they accused would subsequently be responsible for details placed in their narrations. The reason why this worked was that by translating some version of their painful experiences into the proper legal categories, by writing them up in petitions that would be passed around to high officials, petitioners thereby made those feelings and experiences "true"—because, at least in some sense, the truth of law is capable of flattening out the truth of facts and experience.[69] *Traduttore, traditore,* of course, and this is precisely the power of these narratives, and why people sought refuge in them in the wake of violence.

PART II

From the Language of Pain to the Language of Law

CHAPTER 4

Narrating Injury

In the course of a fight, aim counts. This is a purely practical matter, especially in cases where your opponent has a chance at hurting you, too. Luckily, there are certain parts of the human body that are tenderer than others. In the heat of combat it sometimes pays to aim directly at those parts. Eyes are good, as are noses, throats, and genitals. Fists are good implements because it is relatively straightforward to aim a hand; hands have the added advantage that they can subsequently be unclenched for pulling, scratching, and ripping; they can be withdrawn quickly to guard an eye, nose, or throat. Kicks can pack more power, but the foot is a clumsy tool, and largely single-purpose: it has greater effective range, but its defensive purposes are limited. Having a stick or a club tends to put you at an advantage, especially vis-à-vis an unarmed opponent. Not only does it increase effective range, but, thanks to torque, it can serve as a particularly brutal weapon, capable of shattering the bone of a defensively placed forearm, or cracking a skull in a case where your opponent fails to keep up his guard. Found objects—rocks and the like—can do damage from a distance, but are hard to aim. As a rule of thumb it generally helps to have friends on your side.

Violence is physical, and when people fight they generally do their best not to lose. The best way to do this is to prevail quickly, to make certain your opponent is hurt to a degree sufficient to have him—or her—withdraw. Or give up and beg for mercy. Or be knocked unconscious. People who are good at fighting, especially if they fight when cornered (for instance, when someone else goes to "have a discussion" with them), do not tend to think these tactics through. They try to harm, and to harm severely and quickly. They land kicks and punches where they can. They use what weapons they can find. They aim for the tender parts. In cases where people plan an attack this is somewhat different, of course, but even the best laid plans can and generally do go awry, and effective violence will have to be improvised. The possibility of being harmed sets off defensive instincts that raise the blood pressure, quicken the breathing, and cause the body to release endorphins. The pleasure of harming an opponent you fear—or loathe—may well do the same.

These "facts" of violence—with their improvisations, their instinctive moves, and their contests of pain delivery—are markedly different both from the narratives which emerge from violent encounters, and from the symbolic repertoire of scornful gestures that may precede or follow a violent attack. These facts—where one strikes, how, and how many times—are often spur-of-the-moment decisions. One may go to a neighbor's house with a club, to be sure, but in general one has to be a violent specialist to know with a reasonable degree of certainty in advance precisely *how* one is going to end up hurting that neighbor—where, in other words, that club is going to end up, and how hard one is going to swing it. Professional boxers, one type of violent specialist, train for years to know how best to calibrate a punch, how to save their energy for later rounds, and how to tire out an opponent; they know the rules and regulations well, but are reliant on chances and split-second opportunities for delivering harm and pain. British bare-knuckle boxers (part of an unlicensed but highly lucrative subculture) are perhaps a better comparandum: they too have mastered a set of techniques, but when describing their practice they emphasize their creative and instinctual exploitation of opportunities offered them unwisely by their opponents.[1] There were not many violent specialists in Roman Egypt.

To move from this world of improvisation to the world of narration implies a series of important changes, transformations, and translations. Fighting is visceral, instinctive, neurological, exocrine; in this sense, pain is very much its counterpart. In narrative, nothing is left to chance. Where your opponent hit you is not based on where you happened not to protect yourself; it demands to be explained, to have meaning, to be rationalized and accounted for. It is no longer a punch, a kick, or a scratch; it is a deliberate, calculated move in a village drama, framed in a chronological sequence, accountable to a temporal logic of increasing (or, by contrast, shocking) venality, abusiveness, or cruelty. It is the magic of the petition—the narrative of violence—that it serves as the point of entry for a legal contest in which not only is a petitioner given the opportunity to choose how to rationalize the conduct of his or her assailant and his or her visceral instincts and place them within an intelligible causal frame, but also, if the petition is accepted, the assailant will have no choice but to reply in the identical register of discourse.

The narratives of petitioners, in other words, produce a series of transformations in the script of the interaction between the two parties, to put the issue in Goffman-esque terms.

This chapter, and this second section of the book as a whole, concentrate on these narrative transformations. In what follows I lay out, in broad strokes, the ways in which petitioners tell stories about their attackers, their characters, and their tactics. From close readings of petitions, despite their mediated, rhetorical, and transformative nature, a complex world is revealed: a world in which petitioners claim for themselves the status of social equals with respect to their neighbors, opponents, and communities. The world that petitioners describe is one in which personal dignity is insecure and subject to constant evaluation by peers and neighbors, rather than (as current scholarly consensus holds) being connected to rigid positions on a clearly delineated social hierarchy.[2] This world is in tension with, but also sustained by, an equalizing ideology of personal and social inviolability that can be recovered from the papyri. In such a world, while social relationships are complex and multifaceted, no clear patterns of deference emerge from the world that petitioners describe. The consequence of this social flatness is that victims of violence use law to claim their place in a normative world in which all reputations are contestable, all (free) individuals relatively equal (at least in the sense that they think of themselves as essentially inviolable), and all attackers responsible for the suffering that they impose on such similar people—irrespective of actual differences in rank or power. This ideology of social flatness influences not only the ways in which petitioners account for the actions of their opponents, but also how they choose to explain their own wounded bodies, how they choose to describe their pain, and how they frame narratives of how they came to end up as victims of violence. What follows is largely descriptive, but the focus should remain on the processes of narrative and rationalization: the narratives of petitions were initial attempts at making and imposing meaning, but they would come to mean other things as well, both legally and in the world of towns and villages.

* * *

Offenders in the *chora* are largely well known.[3] To be sure, an offender may bring friends and relatives whom the victim either cannot identify or chooses not to identify. But genuinely random assaults are rare.[4] In those cases, individuals would sometimes still write petitions, asking that they be "kept on file" (ἐν τῷ καταχωρισμῷ) so that "the account would be preserved" (πρὸς τὸ μένειν μοι τὸν λόγον), on the assumption that petitioners would eventually find out who was responsible and proceed from there. But more often, petitioners know precisely who is responsible, and describe in varying amounts of detail the intricacies of their interactions beforehand. There are two main ways to handle the fact that one knows one's attackers: either a sense of indignant surprise that a petitioner was attacked in the first place, or a claim that such an attack was in fact a predictable outcome of the defective character of the neighbors. These two strategies, while formally contradictory, can nevertheless be combined. Such is the case with a woman named Aurelia Ataris, who wrote two petitions on successive days to Flavius Abinnaeus, a garrison commander in Fayyum in the fourth century:

Φλαυίῳ Ἀβιννέῳ ἐπάρχῳ εἴλης στρατιωτῶν διακειμένων ἐν κάστροις Διονυσιάδος παρὰ Αὐρηλίας Ἀτᾶρις θυγ<ατ>ρὸς Μέλανος οὐετρανο(ῦ) γεουχούσης ἐν κώμῃ Ἑρμοῦ πόλει. κατὰ τὴν τρίτην τῶν ἐπαγομένων, οὐκ οἶδα τίνι λόγῳ ḳαὶ λῃστ[ρ]ικῷ τρόπῳ χρησάμενοι, πρὸς ὥραν δεκάτην, ἐμοῦ ἀπ̣αιτοῦντός μου τὸ χρέος τῶν χρεωστεῖ μοι, ἀπέḳλ̣εισέν με ἐν τῇ οἰκίᾳ αὐτοῦ Πολείον ἅμ̣α τῷ υἱῷ Ὡρίωνος τọῦ εἰρηνάρχου Ἀπίωνι καὶ τῇ ἀδελφῇ τοῦ Πολ(είονος) Κυριακῇ καὶ ἀπέκτεινάν με ταῖς πληγαῖς· φυγῇ ἐχρησάμην ἀπὸ τῆς οἰκίας αὐτοῦ καὶ ἀπέβαλα ἐμαυτὴν ἀπάνωθεν ἀπὸ τῆς ὕβρεως αὐτῶν καὶ τῆς βίας ἣν ἔπαθα ἀπὸ αὐτῶν καὶ πρὸς θάνατον ἀνάκειμαι. δι' αὐτὸ τοῦτο ἀξιῶ καὶ δέομαί σου τῆς φιλανθρωπίας, κύριε, τούτους συνλαβέσθαι καὶ παραπέμψ[αι] αὐτοὺς τῷ κυρίῳ μου δουκί· αὐτοῦ γάρ ἐστιν τοὺς τὰ τοιαῦτα τολμῶντας ἐκδικεῖν· καὶ τούτου τυχὼν χάριτά σοι ὁμολογήσομαι, κύριε. διευτύχει.

Αὐρηλία Ἀτᾶρις ἐπιδέδωκα. ὑπατείας τῶν δεσπ̣[ο]τῶν ἡμῶν Κωνσταντίου τὸ δ καὶ Κώνσταντο[ς τὸ γ] Αὐγούστων, ἐ̣π̣[αγομέ]ṿῳ̣ṿ γ.

To Flavius Abinnaeus, *praefectus alae* of the soldiers stationed in the camps of Dionysias,

From Aurelia Ataris, daughter of Melas the veteran, a landholder in the town of Hermopolis. On the third intercalary day at the tenth hour, I do not know why, and acting in the manner of thieves, when I was collecting a debt which he owes me, Poleion shut me up in his house, and along with Apion, the son of Horion the *eirenarch*, and Poleion's sister, Kyriake, and they practically beat me to death. I

> fled from their house and threw myself from it, escaping the violence and the damage that I suffered at their hands. Now I am at death's door. Therefore I ask you this, and beg your benevolence, lord: arrest these men and send them to my lord, the *dux*, for it is his job to punish people who dare to do such things. Once I achieve this I will owe you thanks, lord. Farewell.
> I, Aurelia Ataris, have submitted this. In the consulship of our masters Constantius for the 4th time and Constans for the 3rd time, Augusti. Third intercalary day.[5]

Ataris' petition is interesting for several reasons. First, as is clear from what she says, she knew her attackers well enough not only to name them, but also to have extended credit to one of them in the past. This need not indicate that relations were previously cordial; it may merely indicate that she knew where to find him if he failed to pay his debts—that is, that he was a part of the normal social architecture of the village. And as a known person herself, Ataris would have known that she had rights that could be enforced in the future: as the child of a veteran, she had access to certain types of power—not least, the ability to write to a man like Abinnaeus, who served as a conduit between her and the *dux*, the military governor (from the late third century the administrative responsibilities of the prefect were divided between the *praeses*, or civil governor, and the *dux*). She could, if necessary, thereby bypass other local administrative and judicial organs. In her situation, this was a valuable possession, not least because in asking her debt back from Polelon she was also assaulted by Apion, the son of the local guard (the *eirenarch*), a man recruited from the ranks of the local villagers to provide for day-to-day security.[6] (Apion appears to have taken advantage of this connection, and appears in other places in the Abinnaeus archive as a local malefactor, acting in concert with others.[7]) Additionally, from the fact that Ataris wrote her petition to Abinnaeus on the day of the attack itself—and wrote another one, with only slight differences, the next day—it would appear that she was aware of her options for finding her way to justice.[8] Whether this would have emboldened her in her dealings with the other villagers, we cannot know.

Ataris' language in describing the attack is interesting largely because it is undermined by the other facts that she reveals. She claims that she "do[es] not know why" she was attacked, a claim that recurs in other petitions, and which we can readily doubt. Thus, in another fourth-century petition from the Hermopolite nome a woman named Aurelia Eus claims that, in spite of her possible incursions onto her neighbor's land, she was assaulted for reasons she cannot understand by a man named Isakis, accompanied by a group of women. She claims this in spite of the detail that she adds toward the end of the petition, namely, that Isakis had done the same thing to her husband—who, it seems, had the good sense to flee.[9] A similar claim is advanced by two men from Oxyrhynchos who had the audacity to tell some of their neighbors to take care of their share of the canal work, and were accordingly assaulted.[10] The pattern is not only late antique: in a similar complaint from the first century Satabous, a priest from Soknopaiou Nesos reverts to the language of surprise and incomprehension when, in the course of an extended dispute with another priest, Nestnephis, he was assaulted after Nestnephis stole his millstone for no particular reason.[11]

Aurelia Ataris makes another claim which raises eyebrows, if only because, again, it seems to be contradicted by the rest of her narrative: she claims that her attackers acted "in the manner of thieves" (ληστρικῷ τρόπῳ). This is odd: petitioners not infrequently complain that their opponents acted in the manner of "thieves" or "bandits," but this usually indicates that they snuck onto an opponent's property, not that they were confronted in their own homes or in public by the petitioner him- or herself. The term is most often used for home-breaking and theft, which can sometimes be accompanied by violence.[12] This does not exhaust the possibilities, however: the claim that offenders acted "in the manner of thieves" can simply be another way of expressing surprise. Thus, in a petition concerning a land dispute, a man complains that his neighbor and his children came onto his land "in the manner of thieves . . . wishing to farm it" (βουλόμενοι αὐτὰ γεωργῆσαι), and when he remonstrated (as usual, "had a discussion") they beat him with "clubs and swords" (μετὰ ῥοπάλων καὶ ξιφῶν).[13]

There probably were, to be sure, some cases in which people were genuinely surprised by their neighbors' behavior. Thus, for example, a goldsmith complains that a customer came into his store, feigned interest in some of his merchandise, and then beat him up and stole a gold bracelet.[14] But it is nevertheless interesting that the language of surprise is evident in petitions in which petitioners, by their own admission, have preexisting and potentially hostile relationships with people they know. At one level, it may be that a claim of surprise construes the petitioner as innocent and undeserving, and their opponents as combustible and irrational. It is unsurprising, of course, that petitioners would try to do this. Alternatively, petitioners may not be trying to communicate shock, but rather making a claim that their opponents' behavior is *incapable* of rational justification. Either way, these claims of "not knowing" are a strategy like any other: by placing the onus of producing an explanation on the offenders, petitioners can choose to explain some elements of the offense and withhold information about others.

While the language of shock and surprise plays a role in some petitions, in others petitioners are quite clear about why their opponents did what they did: they were rotten people. Here petitioners avail themselves of a rich language of motives, language not confined to petitions concerning violence. Ptolemaios, whose petitions were featured in Chapter 1, describes his opponents as morally bankrupt in various ways: he characterizes a man to whom he owes money as being the leader of a group of "cheap slaves and parasites" (δούλων εὐώνων ἢ καὶ . . . ὀψωνιαζομένων), and claims that his opponent (also named Ptolemaios) is also "by nature nasty and violent, who lives the life of a moneylender and does every sort of forbidden, foul thing" (ạὐ̣θάδης τῷ τρόπῳ κ[αὶ βί]ạị ọς, δανειστικὸν βίοṿ ζῶν καὶ πράσσων ἀνόσια πάṿ[τα] ἀ̣πειρημένα).[15] In another petition, Ptolemaios describes the same man as "nasty and violent by nature because he thinks himself a ruler and that completed matters are his business" (αὐθάδης τῷ ἔ̣θ̣[ει(?) καὶ] βίαιος διὰ τὸ δοκεῖν αὐιọ̀ṿ ἀρχοντικὸν εἶναι καὶ πράγ[ματα ἐπι]τηδε<ύ>ων ἀπ[η]ρ[τισ]μ[έ]να).[16] Other petitioners describe their opponents as "reckless" and "worthless."[17] And while some opponents are immoral, others are unhinged madmen (or madwomen). Such is the case in an Oxyrhynchite petition from the third century describing an encounter with the wife of a local cook. The petition is interesting for its unusual vocabulary:

> Αὐρηλίῳ Ἀλεξ[άνδρῳ τῶν] ἐπὶ τῆς εἰρήνη̣[ς] παρὰ Αὐρηλίου Ἀ̣ [. . . . . . .
> τοῦ] καὶ Ἀφύγχιος ἀγωṿ[οθετήσαν]τος τῆς Ὀξυρυγχε̣ι̣τ̣ῶν
> πόλ̣[εως]. ἑσπέρας τῇ διελθούσῃ ἡμέρᾳ Διδύμη τις, γυνὴ Ἀγαθοῦ
> Δα̣[ί]μονος μαγείρου, παριοῦσα τὴν οἰκίαν μου καὶ εὑροῦσα με
> ἑστῶτα μετὰ τῶν ἡμετέρων, ἐξύβρισεν ἡμᾶς ῥητοῖς τε καὶ ἀρρήτοις,
> γυνὴ ἀναιδείᾳ μεγίστῃ καὶ θράσει κεχορηγημένη· ἔπειτα ἐπισ̣χ̣όντι
> μοι αὐτὴν παραινοῦντος ἀποσχέσθαι ἡμῶν διὰ τὸ τῆς ὥρας ἄδηλον
> εἰς τοσοῦτον ἀπονοίας ἐλθοῦσα ἐπιπηδήσασά μοι, ἀνασεσοβημένη
> τοὺς τρόπους, ἐξέτεινεν καὶ τὰς χεῖρας καὶ ἔτ̣[υ]ψέν με καὶ
> διελοιδορήσατ[ό τισι τῶν] περιεστώτων θυ[γατριδῶν] οὓς
> ἐμαρτυράμην, ο̣[ὐ μόνους δέ,] ἀλλὰ καὶ ἕνα τῶν τ̣[ῆς ἡμετέρας]
> πόλεως δημοσίων [παρόντα]. τοσαῦτα οὖν πεπον̣[θὼς ἐγὼ] ὁ τυχὼν
> πεπλ̣[ηγμένος δίδω]μί̣ σ̣ο̣ι̣ τὰ βιβλί[δια ἀξιῶν σε] κελεῦσαι ἀχθῆ[ναι

αὐτὴν ἐπὶ] σέ, ἵνα τῆς πρὸ[ς ἅπαντάς σου] [εὐε]ρ̣[γε]σί[ας] τ̣ύ̣χ̣[ω.
διευτύχει].

To Aurelius Alexander, one of those in charge of the peace,
From Aurelius A—, also known as Aphynchis, former *agonothete* in the city of the Oxyrhynchites. Yesterday evening a certain Didyme, wife of Agathos Daimon, the cook, appeared at my house and, finding me standing there with my family, did violence to us, in ways both sayable and unsayable. She is a completely shameless woman, well furnished with bravado. When I tried to restrain her and advised her to keep away from us, because of the darkness of night she reached such a peak of insanity that she attacked me, since she is naturally hot-tempered (?), reached out and struck me, and cursed out some of my granddaughters who were standing nearby. I have presented them as witnesses, and not only them, but also one of the officials of our city who was present as well. Having suffered such things and finding myself wounded, I submit to you this petition, asking you to order her to be brought before you, so that I may receive the benefaction you extend to all. Farewell.[18]

Being confronted at night by a woman like Didyme was likely to be an unpleasant experience, but recourse to the language of bad temper is much less common than recourse to the language of power. Didyme's family perhaps could have countered such a claim with a defense that she was a lunatic, and therefore incapable of bad intent (*dolus*, to use the Roman legal category). But when petitioners complained that opponents were motivated by the power of their position within a village or city, they made a claim that would have resonated well within their social world, as well as with the Roman government's ruling ideology—perhaps too rarely followed in practice[19]—that allowing the strong to take advantage of the weak constituted a failure of proper government, and hence could call into question the legitimacy of the rulers themselves.[20] Petitioners fill their complaints with descriptions of the locally powerful taking advantage of their positions, language that escalates starting in the late second and third centuries, and which features prominently in petitions from late antiquity. Attackers are described as wealthy and powerful: they "take confidence" in their wealth and power,[21] they use their "power in the area" to commit violence,[22] they make certain that righteous petitioners cannot access courts.[23] They "look down on" or "despise" (καταφρονεῖν) their victims for all sorts of reasons: for one petitioner's "lack of meddlesomeness, appearance, and . . . [ ]"; on another for his "weak vision"; the condition of yet another's feet—whatever that means.[24] They are "unsatisfied" (μὴ ἀρκεσθείς) when they only abuse a petitioner lightly—implying that they take a sense of joy in the abuses.[25] A petition from Kellis in the Great Oasis combines a series of these tropes into a single complaint:

> [Φ]λαουίῳ Φαυστίνῳ τῷ διασημοτάτῳ ἡγεμ̣ό̣νι vac. παρὰ Αὐρηλίου Γε̣νᾶ Οὐώνσιος κωμάρχου κώμης Κέλλεως [τ]ο̣ῦ Μωθ̣ίτου νομοῦ. κώμαρχος κ̣[λ]η̣[ρ]ωθείς, κύριε, τῆς ἡμετέρας κώμης μετὰ τῶν ἄλλων λ̣ειτουργῶν̣ ὑπὸ παρουσίᾳ τοῦ διαδόχου τ̣ο̣ῦ̣ ἐ̣ξάκτορος καὶ τῶν ἐν τέλει ἁπάντων κατὰ τὸ σύνηθες ἐποίησα τοὺς [λ]ε̣ι̣τ̣ο̣υργοὺς πάντας τὴν τ̣ύ̣χ̣η̣ν ἑαυτῶν τῇ στρατηγικῇ τάξει διδόναι κατὰ τὸ ἔθος καὶ ἕκαστ̣[ος ἡμῶν κα]θεξῆς ἐκληρώθη <εἰς> λειτουργείας, μόνον δὲ Ταα τινα τὸ ὄνομα κληρωθέντα μεθ' ἡμῶν̣ \[-ca.?-]την/ ὀ̣ψ̣ω̣ν̣ι̣α̣στὴν ὄντα Ἁρπο[κ]ρ̣α̣τ̣ίωνος ἄρξαντος μετῆλθον ὥστε καὶ αὐτὸν προσοκνεῖν τῇ δημοσίᾳ χρείᾳ μετὰ τῶν [σ]υ̣λ̣λ̣ε̣ιτουργῶν. ὁ δὲ θαρρῶν τῇ δυναστείᾳ τοῦ αὐτοῦ Ἁ̣ρ̣π̣ο̣κρατίωνος πολλῇ οὔσῃ ἐπὶ τῶν τό[πων] ἧττον̣ ἐφρόντισεν τῆς ἐμῆς μετριότητος. κατασχεθέντος δὲ ὑπ' ἐμοῦ καὶ τοῦ κοινωνοῦ [μ]ου Γενᾶ τοῦ ἄλλου κωμάρχου ὁ προειρημένος Ἁρποκρατίων πολλῇ τυρρανίᾳ χρώμενος ἐπὶ τ̣ῶν τόπων συμμάχους τοῦς ἑαυτοῦ παρέβαλέν μοι μετὰ ῥοπάλων, οἵτινες ἐπῆλθόν μοι ὡ̣ς ἐν πολέμῳ μέσῳ πληγαῖς θανασίμοις συνκόψαντές με καὶ τὸν δημόσιον λειτουργὸν π̣αρ' ἡμῶν ἀπέσπασαν τόν τε ἀριστερὸν ὀφθαλμὸν ἔπληξαν καὶ τὰς πλευρὰς συνέκοψαν· ἔτι πρὸς θαν̣ά̣τ̣ο̣υ̣ ὢν ἐπὶ τήνδε τὴν τῶν λιβέλλων ἐπίδοσιν ἦλθον μὴ [[τι]] ἀνθρώπινόν τι παθῶ πρὸ τῆς ἐκδικίας καὶ ἀνεκδίκητός μου εἶ̣ν̣\αι/ ὁ φόνος . . .
>
> To the most eminent Flavius Faustinus, *praeses* (of the Thebaid), From Aurelius Gena, son of Ouonsis, *komarch* of the town of Kellis in the Mothite nome. I was appointed as *komarch* of our town, lord, and along with the other liturgists in the presence of the vice-exactor and the other officials, as is customary, I made the liturgists declare their status to the office of the *strategos* in the customary fashion, and each of us in turn was selected by lot for his liturgy. But a certain man named Taa was selected with us, the client of

> Harpokration, the former *archon*. I had to go after him alone to get him to participate as well in public works along with the other liturgists. But this man is confident in the power of this Harpokration—which is quite great around here—and scorned my modestness. When he (Taa) was being held back by me and by my colleague Gena, the other *komarch*, this aforementioned Harpokration, acting like a great tyrant, sent against me the *symmachoi* of the area, who are under his control, bearing clubs. These people attacked me as if in the midst of war, and thrashed me with deadly blows, dragged the public liturgist away from us, and hit me in the left eye and thrashed my sides. Since therefore I am at death's door I present to you this petition, lest I die before judgment and my murder go unpunished.[26]

The petitioner continues in the same vein, noting that Harpokration's παῖς (son or slave, in this context probably his slave, though it is unclear), a man named Timotheos, has been involved in several attacks against the petitioner and his family: though the text is fragmentary, the petitioner recounts at least one incident involving Timotheos doing something to (presumably stealing or driving off) his brother's pigs; publicly humiliating the said brother by stripping off his clothes in public and forcing him to flee the town; and stealing wine from the petitioner's house. The language fixates on the disproportionate amount of power of those attached to Harpokration, ranging from the abuses of his "caterer" Taa, to his use of the *symmachoi*—probably armed assistants of the *riparii*, charged with enforcement of the public peace.[27]

In Aurelius Gena's petition his enemies scorn him because they are well connected, but it is evident that he, too, holds a position of some influence in his village. Later in his petition he reveals that, in spite of the potentially mortal damage done to him, he and his fellow liturgists seem to have disarmed the *symmachoi*—he offers as a witness to their misdeeds a man named Pebos, who "has their clubs at his house, since he took them from the *symmachoi*" whose names Gena then gives. Thus, though his petition documents his helplessness with respect to his well-connected enemies, we again may suspect that there is more to this story. Was Gena himself perhaps a source of social tension in Kellis? As a man nominating his fellow townspeople for liturgies, he certainly could have made their lives complicated: there is every reason to suspect that in the process of assigning burdensome public duties there was at least a micro-, if not macrophysics of insult and score-settling. Liturgies are often said to be assigned to someone for the sake of "protecting" or "shielding" one's friends (σκέπη) or for "insulting" or "threatening" one's enemies (ἐπηρεία).[28] Regardless of the truth of the matter, Gena now claims that his enemies are powerful enough not to do what he has told them to do, that they scorn his decision-making, and that they responded to his commands with violence for which they were now going to be held legally responsibly through Gena's petition.

Whether we should trust Gena's descriptions of Harpokration and his allies is a harder question: Roger Bagnall has argued persuasively that the violent rich who are portrayed in petitions are probably not so much richer—if at all—than the people who complain about their actions.[29] This is important, but it may well be beside the point, for two reasons. To begin with, we might confess that we have very little means of knowing how powerful a petitioner was vis-à-vis his or her opponent: at some level this is part of petitioners' strategies, but it is also because we as scholars have a particularly underdeveloped vocabulary for understanding the workings of power in the Egyptian countryside—or anywhere else in the Roman world, for that matter. Wealth is not the same as power, or at least it is a poor proxy. As to how something actually got done in a village or town, we are poorly informed; we are even more poorly informed about who could block something getting done. Neither should we presume that the person who could get something done—or keep something from being done—would have been the same in a town or a city, or even from town to town. Here an administrative flowchart probably is worth less than an admission of helplessness in the face of what was probably a complex and constantly shifting distribution of power. I am reminded of one of James Redfield's rules of academic administration (academic departments being in some sense analogous to the worlds of towns and villages in having complex distributions of actual power and tangled webs of historical interpersonal dynamics that are impenetrable to outsiders): in the course of making any academic decision, there is usually only one person whose opinion matters for that particular decision, and that person is usually smart enough not to get stuck being department chair. So petitioners may be lying or exaggerating the local power of their opponents, but at the end of the day there is very little we can do to prove them wrong. Secondly, this is probably part of the point. More important, perhaps, while it would not be surprising to hear that the strong take advantage of the weak in any given society, what is surprising is that being strong is a matter of suspicion in the first place: that the language of wealth, shot through with claims of personal rottenness, is also the language of imbalance in the proper distribution of social power (and thus social power would appear, a fortiori, to be properly distributed only when perfectly evenly distributed). It therefore has value for historians even (or perhaps especially) when petitioners are potentially lying. In spite of the strong tradition in the ancient literary sources which links wealth to beauty and beauty to moral virtue, there is little evidence that this package of ideals has any resonance in the *chora*. In the world of petitioners, wealth and power are only additional evidence of an opponent's defective character.

* * *

Petitioners not only try to make sense of the motives and characters of their assailants, but they also try to make sense of the manner of the attack. They catalogue a wide range of violent acts, ranging from attacks with weapons of various sorts (like the clubs of the *symmachoi* described by Aurelius Gena), to fists and kicks, to violent language. While it is tempting to arrange them in a hierarchy of unfortunate things that may be inflicted on someone, this is not the point of a petition. Harm to the social person in a petition is counted as being as bad as harm to the physical person—though it bears mentioning that cataloging and producing evidence of the harms that violent language causes is much harder. And harm to the physical person, as I will demonstrate below, is generally framed as harm to the social person.

Violence in Egypt consists of what we would today call assault (whether or not there is an accompanying battery), or what Roman jurists would have called *iniuria*. The jurists accepted a wide variety of actions that could be counted as violent:

> iniuria autem committitur non solum cum quis pugno puta aut fuste percussus vel etiam verberatus erit, sed etiam si cui convicium factum fuerit, sive quis bona alicuius quasi debitoris, sciens eum nihil sibi debere, proscripserit, sive quis ad infamiam alicuius libellum aut carmen scripserit, sive quis matrem familias aut praetextatum adsectatus fuerit, et denique aliis pluribus modis.
>
> Iniuria is committed not only, for example, when someone is hit or beaten with a fist or a stick, but also if someone raises a clamor about someone; or if someone advertises a sale of someone else's estate as if that man were a debtor, while knowing that he owes nothing; or if someone writes a song or a pamphlet for the purpose of

> slandering someone; or if someone follows around a matron or a youth; and in many others ways as well.[30]

There is no evidence that petitioners read Gaius, but the fact that their claims of injury fit in general quite comfortably within Roman juristic definitions does seem to be evidence that there was something of a mutually comprehensible legal *koine* in the Hellenistic and Roman period Mediterranean basin, at least so far as injury goes (there are important consequences to this, which I will return to below and in the next chapter). But within these apparently coherent definitions, the texture of the narratives does change over time. Petitions become more florid starting in the second century, pari passu with the increase in the number of preserved petitions. That is, as the relationship thickens between Egypt as a province and its Roman rulers, petitioners speak more freely, place more of their public affairs on display, and tend to weave narratives about themselves and their opponents that try to define an increasing number of the aspects of their relationships. In contrast, early petitions tend to state facts perfunctorily. A petition from first-century Oxyrhynchos from the archive of Tryphon the weaver, although fragmentary, can serve as an example:

> Σώται στρατη[γῷ] παρὰ Τρύφων[ος Διον(υσίου)] τ[ῶν] ἀπ'
> Ὀξυρύγ[χων πόλεως.] ὀψίτερον τῆς ὥρας τ[ῇ] Σεβαστῇ τοῦ
> ἐνεστῶτος μηνὸς Ἐπεὶφ τοῦ α (ἔτους) [Γαίου] Καίσαρος Σεβα[στ]οῦ
> [αἱ] γ[υν]αῖκ[ες] [Θε]ναμοῦνις ọạη̣. ης κ(αὶ) [ἡ α]ὐτῆς θυγάτη[ρ]
> Δημητρ[οῦς πρᾶ]γμα ἁπλῶς μὴ ἔχουσαι [πρὸ]ς ἐμὲ μηδὲ πρὸς τὴν
> [σύ]μβιόν μου Σαραεῦτα̣ [ἀ]λόγον ταυτῇ ἠ̣νέγκ̣αντο [καὶ συν-]
> εστήσαντο ἔνκυον [οὖ]σαν καὶ π̣ .[. . . .] . . . . [. . .]πει δ̣εκο[. .]ν
> πληγῶν [. . .] . .[. .] .[.] .[. .] . [. . ἔκ]τρωμα
> (hand 2) [.] τα[. . . . .]. ς [δι]ὸ ἐρχ[όμενο]ς ἀξιῶι [ἀ]χθῆνα[ι τὰς ἐ]νκα̣λ̣ο̣υ̣-
> μένας ἐπί σε [ὅπ]ως [τύ]χω[σ]ι [. .]ιη̣ . . .[. . .] τ. . .καί
>
> To Sotas, *strategos*,
> From Tryphon, son of Dionysios, one of those from the city of Oxyrhynchos. Late at night on the *dies Augusta* of the present month of Epeiph, in the 1st year of Gaius Caesar Augustus, the woman Thenamounis from the Oasis (?) and her daughter, Demetrous, having no issue with me nor with my wife, Saraeus, attacked her for no reason and harmed her, despite her being pregnant and . . . blows . . .

> untimely birth (hand 2) therefore I approach you and ask that the accused be brought before you so that they get . . . and . . . [31]

As with most first-century petitions, Tryphon's petition gives a minimal amount of detail. In his case this may have been strategic: from his archive we can tell that the two women who assaulted his wife were not random assailants. Demetrous was Tryphon's first wife, whom he had divorced some time prior and accused of theft.[32] Tryphon compresses these details, giving nothing about his prior relations with his attackers, their motives, or their characters. The details of the violent act, however fragmentary, are much more in focus: his wife's pregnancy, the blows, that she seems to be in danger of her life.

The matter-of-fact-ness of Tryphon's petition can be contrasted to another petition concerning violent women, this one from late third-century Karanis:

> Αὐρηλίῳ Γορδιανῷ β(ενε)φ(ικιαρίῳ) στατίζοντι παρὰ Αὐρηλίας Ταήσεως Κοπρῆ ἀπὸ κώμης Καρανίδος. βίαν καὶ παρά[νομο]ν ἐπέλευσιν παθο[ῦ]σα, τῶν ἡμετέρων [-2–3-] . . [-1–2-]μένη ὑπὸ τοῦ κατὰ πατέρα μου ἀδελφοῦ Χαιρήμωνος ἀπὸ τῆς αὐτῆς κώμης Κ[α-] ρανίδος, ἐφ' οἷς μὴ φέρο̣υ̣σα ἦλθον ἐπὶ τὴν τῶν νόμων ἐγδικίαν. νήπιος ὑπὸ τῶν γονέων καταλειφθεῖσα ἔμεινα παρὰ τῷ κατὰ μητέρα μου ἀδελφῷ Ἀμμωνίῳ διατρεφομένη, τῶν πατρῴ<ω>ν μου ἀποσυληθέντων καὶ διακατεχομένων ὑπὸ τοῦ προειρημένου Χαιρήμωνος, ἐφ' οἷς ἔτι τὴν καταδεῆ ἡλικίαν ἄγουσα τὰς ἡσυχίας ἦγον, ἐκ δὲ θεοῦ προνοίας ἐν ἡλικίᾳ γεν[ο]μένη ἀνά<γ>κην ἔσχον εἰσελθεῖν τὸν αὐτὸ̣ν {τὸν} καὶ προκίμενον Χαιρήμονα περὶ ὧν διακατέχει μου πατρῴ<ω>ν. καὶ ἅπαξ καὶ δεύτερον ἐντυχούσης μου τῷ ἐνπεπιστευμένῳ τὴν δεκαδαρχίαν β(ενε)φ(ικιαρίῳ), καὶ ἐκέλευσεν αὐτὸν ἀ[πο]δοῦναι ἅπερ ἐν κόλποις ἔχει, ἀλλ' οὐκ̣ [ἀπέδοτο]. ἐχθές, ἥτις ἦν κδ, τὰς ἑαυτοῦ θυγατέρας Κυριλλοῦν καὶ Τασουχάριον καὶ Ταῆσιν κ̣α̣ὶ̣ Τ̣ .[. .] καὶ Θατρῆν μητέρα αὐτῶν εναφι . ισμο . . .σας με πλ[ηγα]ῖς αἰκίσαντες τῶν τριχῶν περι . . . .τες καὶ τὴν [ἐσ]θῆτα διαρρήξαντες χαμαιριφῆ με ἀφῆκαν, ἐπὶ παρόντων "Ολ' καὶ Κασίου δημοσίων τῆς αὐτῆς κώμ[ης] οἵτινες ὑφ[εί]λοντό με τ̣ῶ̣ν̣ [γυ] ν̣α̣ι̣κ̣[ῶν] [-ca.?-]μι . . . .[. .] . . . . . .[-ca.?-]

> To Aurelius Gordianus, *beneficiarius* on duty,
> From Aurelia Taesis, daughter of Kopres, from the town of Karanis.
> I have suffered damage and illegal prosecution . . . by my paternal

> uncle, Chairemon, who is from the same town of Karanis. Not being able to bear these things, I have sought legal redress. When I was a young child I lost my parents, and I lived with my maternal uncle Ammonios, and was raised by him. But my paternal property was stolen and is being held by the aforementioned Chairemon. I remained passive about these matters while I was still a minor, but when thanks to the providence of god I came of age, I thought it necessary to sue the aforementioned Chairemon concerning the property which he was keeping from me. Not once but twice I petitioned the *beneficiarius* entrusted with the decadarchy, and he ordered Chairemon to return the things he was holding on to. But he did not return them. Yesterday, which was the 24th, his daughters Kyrillous, Tasoucharion, Taesis, T—, and Thatres, their mother . . . abused me with blows, pulled out (?) my hair, tore my clothes, and threw me on the floor. They did this in the presence of Hol and Kasios, officials from the same village, who pulled me away from the women . . . [33]

Though incomplete, the petition of Aurelia Taesis is otherwise an excellent example of a third- century petition concerning violence. It includes a narrative of the source of the hostilities, the names of the offenders (and their links to her uncle), the names of witnesses, and details of the violent act itself—not only the beating, but also the tearing of clothes and hair (whether in the course of the fight, as a means of winning, or as a means of additional degradation and shaming), and the fact that Taesis finds herself in the dirt at the end of the fight. As in the case of Tryphon, we also have supporting documentation that helps us to fill out the narrative, since the document comes from a family archive. The details of this documentation will be discussed in a subsequent chapter, but for the moment, it is worth simply contrasting these two petitions and their narrative choices.

Both Taesis and Tryphon use their narratives about violence to assert visions that have the potential to become legal truths. In Tryphon's case this is done by compressing a longer history into a single violent act, directed against his helpless pregnant wife. Taesis chooses to narrate a history, to describe the outlines of the long-term conflict in ways that are advantageous to her, or, if not advantageous, at least in ways that render her world comprehensible to her and hopefully also to her audience as well. In both cases, however, the narrative focus is on the physical acts themselves—violent, degrading, unnecessary, and overpowering. Tryphon's first wife and her mother will have to explain why, out of nowhere, they attacked a pregnant woman; Taesis' family will have to explain why they ganged up on a young woman who has recently come of age, and with whom they had a set of legal relations that could otherwise have been hammered out in court. In both cases the moment of physical contact, though, will be placed under a microscope, and have to be explained. What has changed, across time, is that petitioners come to place more and more of their personal history on display, asking to freeze in time more and more of what is a constantly evolving texture of interpersonal relations, and asking that officials not just validate a petitioner's account of violence, but address a whole package of complex and overlapping personal and familial bonds.

Punches and kicks were not the only ways to do violence to someone. Weapons feature in the record as well. Attacks with weapons have already come up in the context of earlier discussions, such as the clubs of the *symmachoi* that were used against, and subsequently confiscated by, Aurelius Gena and his associates. Armed attacks are a relatively small proportion of the extant papyrological documentation on violence, but still constitute an important category of violent behavior in the documentary record. Weapons can mark important connections: swords could be associated with people who seem to be part of the imperial government, especially in late antiquity.[34] Whips hint that the violence claims official status even when illegitimate: thus, a priest from Soknopaiou Nesos claims that he was illegitimately arrested and whipped when he threatened to expose a fellow priest's fraud at the local customs house.[35] More frequently, however, the weapons that show up in the papyrological record are agricultural weapons, such as clubs and axes, and, we may assume, served as weapons of convenience. Thus, for instance, in one fourth-century document from Hermopolis that will be discussed in more detail below,[36] Flavius Isidorus, a *beneficiarius*, petitions about the actions of a number of local shepherds. Though he claims to have complained about their behavior on a number of other occasions, on this occasion they assaulted his shepherd. He claims that they stripped him (γυμνώ[σαντες]), beat him with clubs (ῥοπαλῶν), and tore his clothes ([ἐ]σθῆτα διαρ[ρή-]ξαντες). Clubbings feature in other petitions as well, such as the complaint of Isidorus son of Ptolemaios, who states that he was assaulted by cowherds when he was in his fields, claiming that he had captured one of their cows that had strayed onto his land and damaged his planting.[37] He charges that the cowherds then threw him on the ground, beat him with a large club, and took the cow back. He asks the official (in this case, the *praepositus pagi*) to bring them to court so that he can prosecute his case, for both the violence and the damage done to his crops. A similar complaint involving pastoralists attacking a landowner with clubs is preserved in the Abinnaeus archive.[38]

Violence involving some kind of weapon, as we can see from the cases above, is not always a planned event. Often we see pastoral objects used as improvised weapons, such as in the complaint of a landowner who was attacked with either an axe or a set of pruning shears when he caught men trespassing on his olive orchard and cutting the branches of his date palms.[39] In a similar case, a man complains of being assaulted by a group of shepherds who used their *kolloroboi*, or shepherd's crooks, to beat him.[40]

There are other instances in the papyri of attacks with un-improvised weapons: in one, a woman complains that some unknown men had broken into her home and attacked her husband and son with swords. She requests that a public doctor come and check on their condition.[41] In another example, a man and his sons, along with another man of the village and his brother, attacked a petitioner with clubs and swords in an effort, the petitioner claims, to remove him from his land.[42] In one particularly complex petition from the archive of Sakaon, the petitioner, named Zoilos (himself related to Sakaon by marriage, and part of a family that had been intermarrying with members of Sakaon's family for two generations) charges that Sakaon had rounded up a group of men who attacked his (Zoilos') father (Melas) with clubs and swords after Sakaon removed Nonna, the wife of Zoilos' son, Gerontios, from his (Zoilos') home.[43] Zoilos' other son Pasis went to defend his father,[44] since he saw his father "being violated by utterly worthless men" (ὑ̣βριζόμενον ὑπὸ τῶν π̣α̣νκακίστων ἀνδρῶν), but, Zoilos claims, the men in turn used their weapons to assault Pasis as well. After this, he claims, they stole a large amount of livestock: a number of "sheep, sixteen oxen, and five asses"—some owned by the petitioners, some on lease.

Violence need not have always involved physical contact. Petitioners frequently make mention of violent language, often drawing attention to such violence in the context of a physical assault. Violent language has not been the subject of inquiry since Taubenschlag's studies in the first half of the twentieth century.[45] It is problematic in the sense that, although violent language features in a number of complaints, petitioners give us little by way of specifics about the words themselves.[46] This is frustrating, especially in light of how much other detail they include in their complaints. Yet there are still some telling details: most important, the language that petitioners seem to fixate on is itself described as part of an assault, rather than, say, a claim about defamation.

The most common way of describing verbal abuse is by the term *loidoria*, along with its cognates. It is a term that is attested relatively early—Ptolemaic examples abound.[47] There are several complaints from the Roman and late antique periods as well that use this term, often in connection with other methods of violent attack. Thus, for instance, in one papyrus recording a quarrel between hunters and a tax collector, the petitioner (the tax collector) claims that the hunter repulsed him "with violence and *loidoria*" when he attempted to claim a judgment against him.[48] It also appears in a personal letter from the third or fourth century, where the writer complains to an associate about the behavior of a particular slave, saying that the slave treated him "with violence as well" (μετὰ καὶ ὕβρεως), and that when he tried to get the slave to give a payment the slave was "abusive and bossy."[49] It is hard to deduce from this papyrus whether the *loidoria* was actually violent or threatening, or simply rude. Finally, in one papyrus we see a petitioner complaining about some damage to his property, as well as a physical assault that involved violence and being knocked to the ground. The top of the papyrus is damaged, but the editors record λοι̣[at the very top of the papyrus, and we may assume, based on the pattern of the evidence in general, that this should refer to *loidoria*.[50]

In one example from Oxyrhynchos, an individual named Aphynchis complains that Achilleus, a pastry cook, had attacked his slave and wounded her on the lip. Aphynchis says that he went to confront Achilleus, and Achilleus attacked him. In the course of the petition he describes the event, pairing verbal abuse with a description of other offensive behaviors:

> ἐξαυτῆς γενομένῳ μοι πρὸς αὐτὸν καὶ λογοποιο[υ]μένῳ περὶ τῆς τοσαύτης αὐτοῦ αὐθα̣δίας ἐπῆ̣λθεν καὶ ἐμ[οὶ κ]α̣ὶ̣ [ἐ]ξ̣ύ̣βισεν καὶ διελοιδορήσατό μοι οὐ μόν̣ον̣ ἀλλὰ καὶ λίθῳ με ἐνετίναξεν κατὰ τῆς κεφαλῆς.
>
> Right away I confronted him and had a discussion with him about his remarkable nastiness, but he then attacked me too, and he did violence to me and cursed me out. Not only did he do this, but he also struck me in the head with a rock.[51]

This was certainly not the only way to describe verbal abuse.[52] Didyme, the wife of the cook, who was mentioned earlier, was described as having come to the petitioner's house where she "cursed out some of my granddaughters who were standing nearby" (διελοιδορήσατ[ό τισι τῶν] περιεστώτων θυ[γατριδῶν]).[53]

In another document which survives in two copies, one in London and one in Florence, the petitioner claims that a slave woman had come to his house and assaulted his wife and young daughter. He claims that she did "inappropriate violence to my wife and my young daughter, assaulting them with foul and shameful language" (ὕβρεις οὐ τὰς τυχούσας τῇ ἡμετέρᾳ συμβίῳ καὶ τῇ παρθένῳ μου θυγατρὶ ἀνοικείοις καὶ αἰσχροῖς ῥήμασι συνήψεν).[54] In another complaint, a woman named Aurelia Eirene complains of having become involved in a quarrel with a man, perhaps one of her fellow villagers. The top of the document is missing, so we have no background to the events. The preserved part of the document begins:

> [λέγων εἰς π]ρ̣όσωπ̣[όν] μου διὰ τῆς ἑαυτο̣[ῦ] ῥινὸς βουλ̣[όμεν]ο̣ς με τοῦ ζῆν̣ ἀπ̣αλλάξαι, καὶ εἰ μὴ βοηθείας τε̣[τυχ]ήκειν ὑπὸ Παμοῦν ὁμοκωμήτου μου πάλαι ἂν ε̣ἰς ψυ̣χ̣ήν μου ἔφθακεν . . .

> . . . speaking at my face through his nose, he wished to end my life. And I would have long since been dead, if I had not obtained help from Pamoun my fellow villager.[55]

The details of the conflict are unclear because the text is lacunose. The editor suspects that the argument is over rights to a vacant lot (ψιλὸς τόπος), but the details of the actual violent encounter are unclear. One might suspect that this was an argument that became heated, rather than a planned assault. It is almost certain that there was physical violence in this situation, especially since Eirene goes to great lengths to emphasize that she was in danger of losing her life, and she claims that one of her fellow villagers intervened to end the conflict. In this case, though, it is noteworthy that Eirene should have focused on the verbal abuse as well as any possible physical abuse. As the editor notes, the act of speaking "through one's nose" (διὰ τῆς ῥινός) should certainly be taken as a contemptuous act: in an official letter from the fifth century, the writer claims that a man "snorted abusively" at him when he tried to collect taxes from him; and in an elaborate Oxyrhynchite divorce document from the fourth century an abused wife claims that her husband "said many foul things to my face, even speaking through his nose."[56] In both this Oxyrhynchite example and the petition of Aurelia Eirene the face (πρόσωπον)—is emphasized as a target of abuse in much the same way as petitioners emphasize damage done to their bodies resulting from an attack.[57] The emphasis on the face makes the act confrontational and menacing, but here the body part is also richly evocative, for it is in the face that the physical person and the social person become indistinguishable from one another.[58]

In the cases mentioned above, violent language is coupled with a physical attack. A more problematic case is that of Aurelius Sarapion from the Arsinoite nome in the fourth century.

> παρὰ Αὐρηλίου Σαρα[πίονος c.11 ἀπὸ] κώμης Φιλαδελφίας [γ]ρ[α]μματ[
> c.13] μηνὸς Μεσορὴ ἐπαγομένων [c.8] μου εἰς τοὺς γάμους ἐν τῇ οἰκίᾳ
> τῆς ἡμετέρα[ς] ἀδ̣[ε]λ̣φῆς οὐκ οἶδ' ὅπως Ἄριος υἱὸς Ἀγάμμωνος ἀπὸ
> τῆς αὐτῆς κώμ[ης] Φιλαδελφίας καιροτηρησάμενός με ἐξερχόμενον
> ἐ̣π̣ὶ̣ [Κερ]κ̣ε̣σ̣ώ̣ρ̣ο̣υ̣ς ἐκ τῆς οἰκίας ἐβουλήθη ἐπέλευσίν μοι
> ποιήσασθαι μετὰ ξίφους ἔχων μεθ' ἑαυτοῦ καὶ ἄλλους τινὰς, οὓς
> δυνήσεται ὑποβαλεῖν καὶ δύνανται οἱ ἀρχέφοδοι τῆς κώμης
> μαρτυρῆσαι καὶ οἱ οἰκοῦντες ἐν τῇ οἰκίᾳ, καὶ ἐπελθὼν πολλὰς αἰ[σ-]
> χρολογίας εἰς πρόσωπόν μου ἐξειπών. καὶ γὰρ καὶ [κα]τὰ τὸν πέρυσι
> ἐνιαυτὸν ὁ αὐτὸς πάλιν Ἄριος καὶ ὁ τούτου πατὴρ Ἀγάμμων τῶν ἀπὸ
> τῆς κώμης φυγῇ δρασαμένων ἐπελθόντες ῥιψοκινδύνῳ γνώμῃ τῇ
> ἡμετέρᾳ οἰκίᾳ καὶ φῶτα ἐπενεγ̣κ̣[όν]τ̣ε̣ς ἐνέπρησαν αὐτὴν ἐκ
> θεμελίου. ἐπεὶ τοίνυν οὐχ ὀλίγ[α] ἐστὶν τὰ τολμηθέντα ὑπ' αὐτῶν
> κατ' ἐμοῦ, ἀλλὰ ἡ[μῖν] παρ' ἕκαστα ὁ τούτου πατὴρ καὶ προειρημέν[ο]
> ς Ἀγάμμων ἐπέρχεται καὶ κωλύει τοὺς γινομένο[υ]ς μερισμοὺς ἐν τῇ
> κώμῃ τῶν δημο[σ]ίων πραγμάτων διὰ {τὸ} το̣ῦ̣τ̣ο̣ τάδ' ἐμὰ τὰ βιβλία
> ἐπιδίδωμί σοι ἀξιῶν ἀχθῆναι ἐπί σου τ[οὺ]ς προειρημένους Ἄριον
> καὶ τὸν τούτου πατέρα Ἀγάμμωνα καὶ ἐν ἀσφ̣α̣λ̣ε̣ῖ π̣α̣ρὰ σ̣ε̣[αυ]τ̣[ῷ̣]
> α̣ὐ̣τ̣ο̣ὺ̣ς τ̣ο̣ύ̣τ̣ο̣υ̣ς ἔχειν καὶ ἱκα[ν]ὰ ἀξιόχρεα α[ὐτ]ο̣ὺ̣ς ἐπ̣α̣ν̣α̣γκασθῆναι
> παρασχ[εῖν] ὑπὲρ τῆς σωτη[ρίας] μ̣ο̣υ̣ . . . . . μ̣ι̣ ἑτέρων . . . . ων οὐ γὰρ
> ἀ̣ν̣[. .] ω̣ν̣ . . . . ἐ̣ν̣τ̣ε̣ύ̣ξομ̣α̣ι̣ τῇ μείζονι ἐξου[σίᾳ̣.]
> διευτύχει.

From Aurelius Sarapion . . . from the town of Philadelphia, (a scribe) . . . in the month of Mesore on the ? intercalary day . . . (I was going) to a wedding at my sister's house. I do not know how, but Arios son of Agammon from the same town of Philadelphia waited for me to come out of the house to go to Kerkeosiris, and tried to attack me while bearing a sword. He had some others with him, whom he can identify. The *archephodoi* of the town and those living in the house can attest to this too. He attacked me, shouting many abusive words at my face. And last year this same Arion once

> again, along with his father, Agammon, who are among those in the village who have taken flight, attacked our house with reckless intentions, and bearing torches they burned it down to its foundations. Whereas, therefore, the offences that these men have dared to do to me are not few, and whereas the father of this man, the aforementioned Agammon, attacks and in every case is preventing the public service assignments which are taking place in the town, I submit my petition to you, and ask that the aforementioned Arion and his father be brought before you, that they be held securely in your presence, and that they provide a sufficient surety account of my salvation . . . others . . . I will petition the higher power. Farewell.[59]

The narrative here is complex, and a number of things are the subject of complaint: first, the initial attack, done by Arion, in the company of others, and carrying swords; second, the burning of Sarapion's house the previous year by Arios and his father Agammon; finally, the actions of Agammon in preventing tax assessments in the village. All three are the subject of the same complaint, as is evidenced by the request of Sarapion that both Arios and his father are the people he wants confined by the official, even though it does not seem that Agammon participated in the initial attack. Sarapion likewise does not request that the men who helped Arios in the initial attack be brought up, but we may surmise that he intends to pursue them in some way, since he asserts that he will provide their names.

In the examples cited above verbal abuse is either paired with physical abuse, or it seems to presage physical abuse (in the form of a threat). These are both forms of violent action. But here the petitions have collapsed important social distinctions in interesting ways. Petitioners make no attempt to rank these forms of violence: in writing a petition, being hit with a whip or a club is just as much an act of violence as being cursed out by a neighbor or having him (or her) speak violently through his nose. But other sources of evidence make clear that verbal violence, while still counting as violence, was distinguishable from other sorts of physical violence. Thus, a fragmentary guild charter from the first century B.C. specifies that fines will be levied for a variety of offenses by one member to another: verbal abuse or a slap in the face (λοιδορήματος ἢ ῥαπίσματο[ς]) will both be punished by a given fine; a beating with a club (ῥάβδου πληγῆς) probably by a higher fine.[60] The text is damaged, and the fines not preserved, but the fact that verbal abuse and face- slapping are fined equally is telling, indicating that both constitute offenses against the person. Guild charters are an interesting way of understanding prevailing morality: their purpose was not to initiate legal claims in the same sense as a petition, but they were contracts, and deposited accordingly in town archives (I will return to the power of contract later, in Chapter 6). A relatively broad range of individuals were guild members. Additionally, as both voluntary agreements documenting consensus on what constitutes a transgression and what a reasonable punishment, they are good evidence for the ways in which people sought to regulate their communities morally, as well as a prime source of evidence for trying to understand the relative value placed on certain types of actions. Thus, we should understand the fining of certain types of behaviors as reflecting relative types of abuse within a community, and the potential that each form of behavior had for damaging community relations.[61]

In a similar way, a problematic and tantalizing personal letter from the fourth century A.D. reveals the relative degree of damage that could be done by verbal abuse, but also the relative ranking of different forms of violence. The text is frustrating because of its murky grammar and diction, but hints at the important consequences that could come from verbal altercations:

> Κυρίῳ μου ἀδελφῷ Γονατᾷ γεούχῳ Ἀντωνῖ[ν]ος πλεῖστα χαίρειν. πρὸ μὲν [π]άντων εὔχομαι τὴν ὁλοκληρίαν σοῦ {παρὰ} παρὰ τῷ κυ(ρίῳ) θ(ε)ῷ ὅπως ὁλοκληροῦ(ντά) σε ἀπολάβω. ἀσπάζωμαι τὰ ἀβάσκαντά σου τέκνα. γινόσσκειν σε θέλω, κύριέ μου πάτρων, ὅ̣τι μέμφις μοι περὶ τῆς καμηλάτης σου ὅτι ὕβρικεν ἡμᾶς. ἐγὼ δὲ ὕβρικα Τιθοῆν ἐκ λόγο`ύ´ς, οὐ μετὰ ῥα`ύ´βδὶν, ἀλλ̣ὰ̣ ἐκ λόγους· τί οὖν ἔχει π̣ρ̣ᾶ̣γμα ὁ Πάντηρ ἐμένα ὕβρισε{ν}; ἐγὼ γὰρ ἐτήρησα τὴν φιλείαν σου τὴν ἀρχέα[ν] καὶ μέχρει σήμερον ἔχω πάλειν τὴ(ν) σ̣[ὴ]ν φιλίαν. εἰ μὲν σὺ θέλεις ἀποσπάσ̣η̣ς τὴν φιλ[ί]αν, ἔστω· γ̣ν̣ῶτι οὖν `ὅτι´ οὐδὲν αὐτῷ τῷ Πάντηρι̣ ἐποίησα διὰ σέ· οὐκ ἔξις γὰρ δραπέτων καὶ ἀγενὶ`ς ἀνθρώπων´ ὑβρίδι τὸ<ν> κω<μ>ψώτερον αὐτοῦ. διὰ σὲ ταῦ<τα> ἡμῖν ποιο`ῦ´σιν. ἐὰν ὑβρίσω Τιθοῆν ἔξις [[αυτω]] μοι αὐτῷ{ν} ὑβρίζω καὶ αὐτὸς ἐμένα, ἐπιδὴ συ`γ´κληρονόμος μού {ε} ἐστιν· ὁ ἀγενὶς γὰρ οὐκ ἔξις μοι ὕβριδι, ἐὰν μὴ {ε} ἐπιστρέψ̣η̣ς αὐτῷ. γνῶτι οὖ`ν´, ὅτι δύναμε αὐτὸν πεδεύσω· ἐγὼ διὰ σὲ οὐδὲν αὐτῷ ἐποίησα μέχρι σήμερον, καὶ ἐὰν ἔλθ̣η̣ς δύν̣η̣{ς} μαθεῖν ἀπὸ τοῦ ἀδελφοῦ αὐτοῦ.
>
> To my lord brother Gonatas, landowner, Antoninos, very many greetings. Before all things I pray for your health before the lord

> God, that I find you in good health. I greet your children—may no evil eye ever reach them! I wish you to know, my lord patron, that I have a complaint against your camel-driver because he attacked me. I did indeed attack Tithoes with words, not with a stick but with words. What business, then, has Panther to attack me? For I kept my old friendship with you and up to the present day I have your friendship still. However if you wish to withdraw your friendship, so be it! Notice, then, that for your sake I have done nothing to Panther himself. For in the future the runaway slave will not attack a man who is his better. It is on your account that they do these things to us. If I attack Tithoes in the future, I attack him against my own interests and myself attack myself, since he is coheir with me. The knave, however, will not attack me in the future, (even?) if you don't take measures against him. So notice that I am capable of teaching him a lesson. On your account I have done nothing to him and if you come you can learn (the facts) from his brother. (translated by Rea)[62]

Antoninos is being held responsible for having assaulted a man named Tithoes, and it seems that as a result of this behavior a camel-driver named Panther assaulted him. We do not know the relationship between Tithoes and Panther, but Panther the camel-driver seems to also be associated with Gonatas, and Antoninus wants to mitigate the charge. His sense of desperation is evident. He emphasizes that he used words and not weapons; the underlying assumption is that, while both are bad, words are less so. Panther too, he claims, has done violence. The effects of the fight, in this case, may eventually have been sorted out informally, by an appeal to a patron, rather than a legal authority, but since the letter is only a fragment of a larger dispute it is difficult to make hypotheses about the conclusion of this episode. It could well have been the case that the letter was sent at the same time as, or after, a petition.

That there are levels of violence should come as no surprise: in contemporary American society one would expect different outcomes—at least in terms of legally enforced punishments—from shouting obscenities at an associate or clubbing a random stranger. Yet what is interesting here is that the contrast between levels of violence brought forth by this document is deliberately expunged from petitions. In other words, though individuals might have made distinctions in private between various levels of insulting conduct, petitioners do not mark these differences in their narratives. It should not be surprising that people use different sets of criteria when speaking to one another (as in the letter from Antoninus to Gonatas) or contracting with one another (as in the guild charter), from those they use when they try to frame their relationships in legally actionable fashions. But these differences are meaningful, and evidence of the transformative process. Petitioners "discuss" or "argue";[63] offenders threaten, menace, or insult. These decisions in the narrations rationalize, in different ways, the conduct of offenders, and hold them responsible for it.

* * *

Before turning to how petitioners discuss their own bodies in their narratives, it is worth mentioning what seems to be omitted from narratives. Omissions are telling, especially when the things omitted are precisely the sorts of things that tend to feature prominently in contemporary analytical categories. As I have suggested, petitions are important ways of locating oneself socially and explaining one's position within a world. Nevertheless, those who tend to rely upon the contemporary academic's holy trinity of social relations (race, class, and gender) to figure out how people in Roman Egypt locate themselves will soon find that these categories can be made to do relatively little work, especially if we take seriously the idea that the value of a first-person narrative is that it tells us who petitioners think themselves and their opponents to be. For instance: as is clear from the preceding discussion, women feature prominently in petitions as both attackers and victims. There is a tendency—though not an overwhelming one—for women to attack other women, or at least to be present among male counterparts when attacking women, especially in cases where a group goes after an individual at home. This is the case, for example, in the petition of Aurelia Taesis, quoted above, where the daughters and wife of her uncle Chairemon attack her in what appears to be a planned assault. But as to the "meaning" of this gendered division of the labor of violence (if, in fact, there is one to begin with), petitioners say nothing at all.[64] Certainly female petitioners describe themselves as "weak" and "widowed," and ask the recipients of their petitions to pity them (especially in late antiquity),[65] but this is, to a large extent, the same thing as male petitioners were doing, too, when they attempted to generate a sense of pathos—the difference being that women in the ancient world could exploit a slightly more extensive vocabulary of weakness. Accordingly, it gives us little insight into how, or if, there was a gendered dynamic to violence, aside from being able to suspect, albeit only cautiously, that the category of victimhood might be in the first place a gendered category in antiquity.[66]

To the extent that gender is important to complaints, it is that there is a major lacuna in the papyrological evidence regarding one type of gendered violence: rape.[67] This may reflect that fact that, cross-culturally, rape is frequently under-reported;[68] or reflect that rape, like murder, would have involved criminal, rather than civil/delictual proceedings. It may also suggest that some rapes ("abductions") may have resulted in marriages.[69] This is not to say that there is no record of potentially *sexualized* violence. Such seems to be the case in a petition from early second-century Oxyrhynchos:

> Ἀρχίᾳ στρα(τηγῷ) παρὰ Ἡρακλᾶτος Παυσειρίωνος ἀπ' Ὀξυρύγχων πόλεως. τῇ διελθούσῃ ε ὀψίτερον τῆς ὥρας Ἀπολλῶς Ἡρακλείδου (hand 2) ἀπὸ τῆς αὐτῆς πόλ(εως) (hand 1) γεινόμενος ἐπὶ τῷ αὐτῷ ἀμφόδῳ ἐπῆλθεν τῇ γυναικί μου Ταaμόιτι οὔσῃ πρὸ τῆς θύρας μεθύων καὶ ἐξελοιδόρησεν καὶ ἀνέσυρεν αὐτή<ν>, παρόντων πλείστων ἀξιοχρέων ἀ<ν>δρῶ[ν] ὧν τὰ ὀνόματα ἐπὶ τοῦ ῥητοῦ δηλώσω. διὸ ἐπιδιδοὺ[ς] τὸ ἀναφόριον, ἀξιῶ ἐκδ[ι]κηθῆναι ὅπως ε[ἰ]ς τὸ μέλλον ἀνεπηρέα[στος σὺν] τοῖς ἐμοῖς φυλαχθ[ῶ. (ἔτους) ιδ (?)] Αὐτοκράτορος Καίσα[ρος] Νέρουα Τραιανοῦ Σ[εβαστοῦ] Γερμανικοῦ Δακ[ικο]ῦ [. . . . .]
>
> To Archias, *strategos*,
> From Heraklas son of Pauseirion, from the city of Oxyrhynchos.
> Yesterday, on the 5th, late at night, Apollos, son of Herakleides, (2nd hand) from the same city (1st hand) and who lives on the same block attacked my wife Taamois while she was standing in front of our house. He was drunk, and he verbally abused her and stripped her in the presence of many worthy men, whose names I will present at trial. Therefore I submit this petition, and I ask that I be avenged, so that for the future I can be unthreatened and be safe along with my family. (14th?) year of Imperator Caesar Nerva Trajan Augustus Germanicus Dacicus . . . [70]

While the violence to Heraklas' wife certainly appears sexualized, and potentially aggravated by the presence of the local worthies, stripping appears in other papyri as well, and is not exclusively a form of violence directed against women, nor against women by men: Aurelius Gena, whose petition was quoted above, records similar behavior being directed against his brother, to cite just one of several examples.

To the same extent that gender is unhelpful as a category for understanding how petitioners understood themselves and their attackers, race is similarly uninformative. "Race," of course, is a highly problematic term; "ethnicity" is a better fit for the ancient world. Semantics aside, it is to begin with a hotly contested matter as to what sociological value any such category has for Roman Egypt; or to what extent, if any, there is a sense of "ethnic identity" recoverable from the papyri. Additionally, the contours of the coherence between the juridical categories of "ethnic" identity and other forms of potential ethnic self-identification (e.g., linguistic identity) have, in my view, never been adequately described. But to the extent that ethnic identity—in either its juridical sense or in the sense of an affective bond between people who think of themselves as possessing some common source of descent or other marker of historical corporate identity—features in petitions, there is precisely one example. Gaius Iulius Niger, a Roman veteran living in Karanis, complains that he has suffered violence at the hands of an Egyptian (ὕ[βριν] πέπονθα ὑπὸ ἀνθρώπου Αἰγυπτίου, 5).[71] At the end of the document he restates the distinction, "I ask, as a Roman who has suffered such things at the hands of an Egyptian . . . " The most natural reading of this document would see the "ethnic" claim here being primarily juridical, not affective: a (recently enfranchised?) Roman citizen is upset since the provincial dared to infringe on the rights of an individual with a protected status. The Egyptian in question seems to have been a person of some importance in the village, being the scribe of the *epiteretes* (the supervisor of tax collection) of the village of Karanis.[72] The dispute in question seems to have escalated from an economic transaction that went awry. Since we cannot reconstruct a major portion of the narration in this document, we cannot know what particular thing was the source of the complaint. What seems most likely is that we are looking at a particularly crass and privileged individual whose comments obscure what is otherwise a general trend in Egypt.[73]

It is interesting, to be sure, that there is little in petitions about violence that reflects ethnic identity; but the petition of Niger, if he uses his "ethnic" terms in a juridical sense, points to yet another interesting category for locating oneself in a social world: rank and class. Unlike gender and ethnicity, which have played a relatively minor role in explaining the dynamics of violence in the papyri, class ("status") has played a feature role. In reviewing the results of petitions to the *epistrategos*, Naphtali Lewis concluded that "The existence of a single judiciary provided a single process for all, but that did not *ipso facto* dispense equal justice for all. Roman Egypt was a class-driven and class-riven society."[74] Leaving aside, for the moment, the question of what sorts of sociological, historical, or anthropological criteria should be brought to bear in deciding whether a given society was particularly "class-riven," the relative roles of class and rank have played a feature role in writing the history of the Roman world, though Roman historians generally prefer to use the term "status," rather than class (I will use them interchangeably in what follows). And there is no doubt that within Roman society writ large there were multiple badges of rank, as well as an aristocracy that in general failed to repopulate itself, and hence concerned itself with the relative value of those who were admitted into its ranks. The jurists were not innocent of these distinctions, either, and went to great lengths to specify that certain groups of high-ranking individuals (senators, equestrians, and town councilors) were protected from increasingly harsh criminal punishments. But to generalize from these facts a social system that accounts for everyone in society and imagines each of its members as being carefully sifted according to a well-defined social place and enmeshed in clearly delineated bonds of reciprocity is a risky endeavor. This is the problem raised by an analysis in which status serves as the primary analytical axis.[75]

The classic statement of the view that status is the main factor that we should use to make sense of petitions comes from Roger Bagnall's 1989 article, "Official and Private Violence in Roman Egypt." Here Bagnall advanced the argument that weak people might be willing to suffer violence without making complaints since, as in Lewis's view, Roman justice was largely inaccessible to weaker parties, and the Roman legal texts presumed the ability of individuals of higher status to take advantage of people of lower status:

> Some of the cases in that book [Bruce Frier's *Casebook on the Roman Law of Delict*] concerning *iniuria* contain striking pointers to the variability of Roman law in tolerating either verbal or physical assault on individuals, depending, as Gaius puts it, on the act, the place, or the person (*Inst.* 3.225): "for example, if a magistrate suffers *iniuria*, or *iniuria* is inflicted on a senator by one of low degree." The converse was true: just as *iniuria* was more serious if directed by one of low status against one of high status, it was less serious if directed by one of high status against one of low status. Gaius puts it succinctly, again: "But if someone raises a clamor against a slave or strikes him with a fist, no formula is published, nor is one given lightly to a plaintiff" (*Inst.* 3.222). Even the wearing of slave's clothing by the (free) victim could be cause for denial of

> action for accosting a maiden (Ulpian, *ad Edictum* 57, *D.* 47.10.15.15). The distinction was not only one of slave and free, for a freedman's access to action about *iniuria* was limited, too, "for why should the patron be denied mild punishment for the raising of a clamor that is not indecent?" (Ulpian, *ad Edictum* 57, *D.* 47.10.11.7). The extensive discussion of *iniuria* in Book 47 of the *Digest* refers often to the status of the parties involved, and naturally enough, since the key element in *iniuria* is the intentional damage to the reputation of the victim. One without a reputation cannot suffer *iniuria*; it is injury to the sense of honor that counts.[76]

Bagnall sought to find places where *iniuria* was "tolerat[ed]"; but in fact, the passage from Gaius says no such thing, but rather it specifies how *iniuria* could be aggravated (since aggravated violence, *iniuria atrox*, changes procedures for the valuation of injuries). He also argued, on the basis of the passage cited, that if it was the case that it was worse when done to someone of high status, it was therefore "less serious" if inflicted against one of lower status. True enough, perhaps, though "less serious" must not be equated with generally acceptable, and the fact that the passage in Gaius specifically refers to a senator being struck by a *humilis persona*—that is, a person without protected rank, should give pause. The illustration of this, however, comes from a passage from Gaius concerned not with people of *lower* status—that is, not a senator—but with slaves, people with virtually *no* legal status as people, and freedmen, who suffered serious legal disabilities, but also a number of protections.[77] Specifically, the passage illustrates that *mild* chastisement (*levis coercitio*) of freedmen is acceptable, *if* it is delivered by a patron—not by any individual.[78] Slaves and freedmen then are collapsed, in this argument, into a general class of people without "reputation," which in turn is collapsed into the broader category of people without "honor."[79] This tendency to see the world as roughly bifurcated into elites and masses is not specific to Egypt, of course, but would only seem to further undermine Bagnall's point that the relative status of the parties is what matters in a violent encounter.[80]

These problems aside, the question remains: to what extent should we follow a line of thinking that takes status as a general guide to understanding the nature of violent interactions in the papyrological record? That is, to what extent was a petition for redress the outcome of an interaction in which two people of roughly equal status fought it out for precedence in an Egyptian village or city? Would people of lower status be expected to suffer violence quietly? As I noted earlier, status is a hard thing to trace in general, and more so in the papyrological record when petitioners are being deliberately obfuscatory. Bagnall himself notes that even the distinction between free and slave could be blurry in Egypt.[81] In some cases, we can trace important features of the status of individual petitioners, especially if they identify themselves by their occupation at the start of a petition, or as individuals of a certain rank after the grant of universal citizenship in A.D. 212, but in such cases it is often hard to see the status of the assailants. One way out of this problem would be to imagine that petitioners were all of the same basic social rank in the first place, and therefore the language of status was irrelevant and thus absent from complaints. This is Bagnall's solution, one which *ex hypothesi* cannot be proven, but which is suggestive. At a juridical level it may well be true: many petitioners seem to share the same juridical position as their opponents, as most were probably "Egyptians" before the grant of citizenship in A.D. 212, and all were Roman citizens thereafter. This would not explain the theme of "powerful and abusive" opponents outlined above, but such language could be dismissed as an exaggeration (at the expense of the insight into the ethical claims petitioners made about the proper distribution of power in a social landscape).

But the fact that only with rare exceptions do petitioners emphasize the discrepancy in formal status relations between themselves and their assailants is telling. As scholars we can trace status relationships in the documents using certain criteria (drawn from legal and literary sources). Status is important to us as a tool for historical analysis. However, the question that is more important in this context is what the petitioners themselves thought important. To look at the status relationships through the eyes of the petitioners, we need to have some clue to show that these questions of status were an issue of substance to them—some sort of normative statement, even if rhetorical, that a dissonance in status was a material factor in how one chose to write a petition, or even if one chose to write a petition. And we largely do not have this, save in the cases in which people complain about the exaggerated power of their opponents—precisely the opposite, that is, of what Bagnall argues. (Gaius Iulius Niger's petition, as I noted earlier, is the exception to the rule concerning juridical rank.)

The language of rank does not appear in complaints about violence except in one particular and very telling sense: petitioners distinguish sharply between free and slave, and carefully patrol the line that separates the two. This sort of status claim is part and parcel of seeing the world as socially flat, since it fundamentally levels all sorts of social distinctions other than freedom, in which all men and women are fundamentally rights-bearing individuals who are inviolable. But when the line between free and slave was in danger of being crossed we can see how vigorously it was protested. A petition from the Great Oasis can serve as an example.

> Σατρίῳ Ἀρριανῷ τῷ δι[ασημο]τάτῳ ἡγεμόνι παρὰ Σύρου Πετεχῶντος νεω[τέρου] ἐξωπυλίτου ἀπὸ τοπαρχίας Κύσεως τῆς Ἱβιτῶν π[όλεως]. ἠγαγόμην ἐμαυτῷ γυναῖκα [ὁ]μόφυλον Τσεκ[. . ἐλ]ευθέραν ἐξ ἐλευθέρων γονέων, ἐξ ἧς καὶ πεπαι[δοποίη]μαι. ἐπεὶ οὖν Τάβης θυγάτηρ Ἀμμωνίας ἐξωπυλ[ίτου καὶ .] .ις Λελῶι(?) ὁ ταύτης ἀνὴρ ἅμα Ψενήσει καὶ Στρά[τωνι υἱοῖ]ς αὐτῶν ἔργον ἀνάξιον τῆ[ς] ἅπασι πρυτανε[υομένης] παιδείας, ἴδιον δὲ τῆς ἀπὸνοία[ς α]ὐτῶν ἐνεαν[ίευσαν, καὶ τ]οὺς προκειμένους σύμβιόν [τ]ε καὶ παῖδας ἐ[μοὺς εἰς τ]ὴν ἑαυτῶν ἑσ[τ]ίαν καθεῖρξαν, δούλιο[ν ζυγὸν ἐλευ]θέροις προσάπτοντες, ὧν ἅπαν μὲν [πέφυκεν ἐλ-]εύθερον, ἐλεύθεροι δὲ νῦν περίεισι συγγε[νεῖς ἀ]δελφοί, ἐμὲ δὲ ὅτι ἀντεῖπον συλλαβόντες ἀ[ναξίαι]ς πληγαῖς ᾐκίσαντο, ἀναγκαίως περὶ πο[λλοῦ] τὴν ὁρμὴν ποιούμενος πρὸς τὸ σὸν μεγαλεῖ[ον, ἡγε-]μὼν δέσποτα, τάδε μαρτύρομαι, διαπεμφθήσ[εσθαι] τῷ σῷ μεγαλείῳ διὰ τοῦ . . .[.] .νιος τοῦ καὶ ἐπι[τυχόντ]ος τοῦ βοηθοῦ αὐτοῦ ἐμ[οὶ ὑ]π' αὐτῶν αἰκιζο[μένῳ] καὶ τυπτομένῳ, καὶ ἀξιῶ [τοὺς μὲ(?)]ν προειρημέν[ους μ]ου παῖδας τῆς παρανό[μου φυλα]κῆς ἀνεθῆνα[ι, τοὺς] δὲ ἀντιδίκους ἐφ' ἱκανοῖς [κενηθῆναι ἐπὶ σε - ca.11 -] ατίζοντας δ . . . .αι προσ[- ca.24 -] αὐτοὺς θλιβομένους [. . . . . .]ν χρησαν[. . . . . τ]ῆς ἐπὶ τοῦ ἀχράντου σου [δικαστη]ρίου κρίσ[εως . . . . . .]η τὴν καταφυγὴν ποι[ούμενος ἀ]ποδείξω [τοὺς ἐξ ἐν]αντίας τήν τε κατ' ἐμοῦ [ἐπήριαν] καὶ τοῦ γέν[ους τὸ]ν παράνομον ἀνδρα[ποδισμ]όν. εὐτύχει. [(ἔτους) ιε] καὶ (ἔτους) γ καὶ [(ἔτους) α τ]ῶν κυρίων ἡμῶν [Μαξιμι]ανοῦ καὶ Σεου[ήρου Σ]εβαστῶν καὶ [Μαξιμί]νου καὶ Κ[ωνσταντί]νου τῶν [ἐπιφαν]εστάτων Και[σάρων] Φαμενώθ.
>
> [Σύρος] Πετεχῶν[τος ν]εωτέρου ἐξωπυ[λίτης ὁ] προκείμ[ενος ἐ-]πιδέδωκα. ἔγραψα [ὑπὲρ] αὐτοῦ γράμ[ματα] μὴ εἰδότος Αὐρήλιος [. . . . .] ειος ὁ κα[ὶ . . . .]ε.

To the most eminent Satrius Arrianus, governor (of the Thebaid), From Syros son of Petechon the younger, *exopylites* from the toparchy of Kysis in the city of the Hibites. I married a woman of my own sort, Tsek—, a free woman from free parents, and I have had

> children with her. But then Tabes, daughter of Ammonia, the *exopylites*, and Leloi, her husband, along with their children Psenesis and Straton, did a deed unworthy of the *paideia* that is enjoined upon everyone, but characteristic of their folly. Acting brashly, they confined my aforementioned wife and children in their home, attaching a slavish yoke to free individuals, though every one of them was born free, and have siblings who are still living who are also free. When I confronted them they seized me and abused me with undeserved blows. I considered it necessary to approach your highness, my governor and master, and to testify about these things, and to have my testimony sent to your excellence through —nis, who furnished me help as I was being abused and beaten by them, and I ask that my aforementioned children be freed from their unlawful detention and that my opponents be secured at your court . . . pressured . . . the judgment of your immaculate courtroom . . . with recourse to you I will convict my opponents of the insult to me and the illegal enslavement of my family.
> Year 15 and Year 3 and Year 1 of our lords Maximianus and Severus, Augusti, and Maximinus and Constantinus, most noble Caesars, Phamenoth ?. I Syros, son of Petechon, the younger, the aforementioned *exopylites*, have submitted this. I, Aurelius NN, also known as NN, wrote on his behalf since he is illiterate.[82]

Syros identifies himself as an *exopylites*, "one living outside the gates." Youtie has convincingly argued that the *exopylitai* were low-status individuals, concerned with taking care of the dead and associated with the professional buriers, the *nekrotaphoi*.[83] He does not identify himself as an Aurelius, as would be expected in the fourth century. He is insistent, however, on his family's free status, and by implication, his own. This would be expected in a petition that might be complaining of enslavement, even though the reasons for the "enslavement" of his family are unclear.[84] His language, moreover, exploits a term related to class and status: he charges that the deeds of his opponents are "unworthy" of the *paideia* (education, civilized conduct) that is "enjoined upon everyone"—which perhaps is a reference simply to common codes of behavior and morality. Still, the inclusion of *paideia* in this complaint—especially within the larger discourse about freedom and slavery—has unmistakable overtones of status-consciousness—except, perhaps perversely, only to claim that what marks out society's elites (*paideia*) is actually enjoined upon *all*—even *exopylitai*.[85] And when we probe deeper into Syros' complaint, we see that the question of status is still more complex: rather than complaining about people of higher status, we see that one of his opponents, at least, is the child of an *exopylites*. As for the status identity of the remainder of the opponents, specifically the identity of the husband, he says nothing. We may guess that like is married to like, and that the entire group shared a relatively low status relative to their social milieu as a whole.

But Syros' petition allows us to see in a clearer fashion what was also at stake in the petition of Ision the slave and in the Roman legal rules concerning the application of the Lex Aquilia to free individuals (above, Chapter 3): one's "status" as a person (not one's relative social or juridical status) is what is being challenged by a violent act. And this is the case, as I suggested earlier, not only in the sense of "am I a free person or a slave?" but also in the broader sense of "who am I with respect to my understanding of myself, my neighbors, and my opponent?" These are clearly very different things, and largely irreconcilable; they speak to the limitations of the conceptual distinction free/slave to account for the multiplicity of forms of social ordering that make life livable. This, however, is a failure of local thinking, not scholarly thinking—and there is no requirement that a particular ideology be consistent in order to be usable (in fact, it is inherent in the definition of ideology). As in the case with Ision and the wounded free boy in the passage from the *Digest* discussed in Chapter 3, in making both these sorts of claims at once certain wires have to get crossed.

* * *

Here Syros' petition is instructive, because it is an exaggerated form of what all petitioners do: all petitioners are worried about being treated as if they were objects, not people. And to a degree, they're right: the experience of violence, and the capacity that violent assaults and ensuing pain have to dissociate one from one's body mean that, in a particular way, petitioners' wounded bodies—both social and physical—become objects in their petitions, things to be reflected upon, bearing wounds to be catalogued. The emphasis in these narratives, instead of being on modes of social location such as race, class, and gender, is largely a discourse of wounded bodies, and in particular, bodies with wounds that were publicly visible. Here wounded bodies are on public display, marked out and stigmatized, open to the gaze of neighbors, and capable of being "read" as an index of the dissonance between the person one thinks one is and the person that another has shown that they are not.

As in the case of violent language, petitioners are careful to describe the parts of their bodies that are the target of their opponents' aggressions. Several documents, for example, focus on violence to the head and face. Thus in a petition from the Hermopolite nome in the fourth century, a woman named Aurelia Thaesis expresses shock at the actions of her brother and her sister-in-law:

> [Αὐρ]ηλίῳ Δι[οκλεῖ . . . .] πρα̣[ιπ(οσίτῳ) ιβ πάγου] νομοῦ [Ἑρμοπολεί]του [πα]ρὰ Αὐρηλία[ς Θαήσ]ιος Παθερμουθί[ο]υ̣ ἀπ̣[ὸ] [κώμ]ης Πεννη[. τοῦ] \ὑ/πὸ σὲ πάγου. ὁ ὁμο[γνήσ]ιός μου ἀδελφ[ὸς . . .]σσος συνοικ[εῖ μοι] καὶ μηδεμιᾶ[ς ἀμ]φισβητήσεως [οὔσης] πρὸς ἀλλήλ[ους ἐ]κ [τ]υχόντων ἐπῆλ[θέν] μοι μετὰ τῆς [συ]μβίου αὐτοῦ Ῥίας, καὶ [κατε]νεγκόντες εἰς τὸ ἔδαφος πληγαῖς ἱκαναῖς με κατέκτ̣ει[να]ν γρόνθοις τε καὶ λακτί[σ]μασιν καθ' ὅλων τῶν σωμάτων ὡς καὶ ἐπὶ τῶν ὄψεών μου τὰ οἰδήματα φαίνεται, ἡμιθανῆ καταστήσαντες, οὐδὲν ἧττον [κα]ὶ̣ τὴν περὶ ἐμὲ ἐσθῆτα περιέσχισαν. [ὅ]θ[ε]ν οὐ δυναμένη ἀφησυχάσαι γυνὴ [ἀσθε]νὴς καὶ χήρα ἐπιδίδωμι τῇ ἐπιεικείᾳ [σο]υ τάδε τὰ βιβλία [μο]υ̣ τοσ̣οῦτο μαρτυραμένη [κ]αὶ ἀξιοῦσα τῆς παρὰ σοῦ ἐκδικίας τυχεῖν. διευτύχει.
> [ὑ]πατείας Σεργίου καὶ Νιγρινιανοῦ τῶν λαμπροτάτων Φ[αρ]μοῦθι ιβ. Αὐρηλία Θαῆσις Παθερμουθίου ἐπιδέδωκα. Φλ(αούιος) Ἀμμώνιος οὐετρανὸς ἀξιωθ(εὶς) ἔγραψα ὑπ(ὲρ) αὐτῆς γράμμα[τ]α μὴ εἰδυίης.

> To Aurelius Diokles . . . *praepositus* of the 12th pagus of the Hermopolite nome,
> From Aurelia Thaesis, daughter of Pathermouthis, from the town of Penne—in your pagus. My full brother, —ssos, lives with me, and there has never been any dispute between us. Unexpectedly, he attacked me, along with his wife Rhia. They pushed me to the ground with a considerable number of blows and with punches and kicks all over my body, so that now there are bruises on my face. They beat me half to death, and what's more, they even tore my clothing. Therefore, since I, a weak and widowed woman, am not able to be passive about this, I submit to your clemency this petition attesting to this and asking I be avenged by you. Farewell. In the consulship of the most glorious Sergius and Nigrinianus, Pharmouthi 12. I, Au-

> relia Thaesis, daughter of Pathermouthios, have submitted this. I, Flavius Ammonius, the veteran, wrote on her behalf as requested, since she is illiterate.[86]

Thaesis' petition incorporates a number of features found in petitions already cited: she emphasizes her sense of surprise; she knows her attackers; she emphasizes her weakness and her widowhood. She is specific about the violence itself: though her brother and his wife use punches and kicks "all over [her] body," she specifies the locus of the wounds as the face, which is presented not simply as a target of the violence but as proof of it as well. Perhaps not accidentally the term used for "bruises" (*oidemata*) is a term otherwise found exclusively in doctors' reports, not in petitions.[87]

Damage to the face is specified in another fourth-century petition as well, in which a woman named Aurelia Demetria describes an ongoing conflict with a man whose name is not preserved, but who was probably her previous husband. She claims he broke into her home and "beat me mercilessly and broke my hands and as a result I also have black eyes from all of the (blows)" (τύψας με [ἀν]ελεῶς κλά[σα]ς καὶ χεῖρά μου ὡς καὶ τὰ ὑπώπια ἔχω ἀ̣φ' ὅλων τ̣ῶν ω.[. . .].).[88] The references to the cheeks and face in these two petitions may perhaps be understood as a reference to "black eyes"—a highly visible mark of injury which is notoriously slow to heal. Thus we see in a trial transcript from the fourth or fifth century (the only trial transcript recording proceedings in a case of violence) that men are questioned by the *praeses* of the Thebaid concerning an assault which has left a mark on the victim's eyebrow (*ophrys*). The transcript begins by noting that the wounds are still visible even at the time of the trial.[89] As in verbal violence, the face here is not just a tender part; it is also a locus of personhood, and therefore these facial injuries not only are painful, but are socially disfiguring as well. Injuries to the eyes, in particular, are socially damaging, and not only because they are prominent: the eyes are the portal to the soul in the ancient physiognomic tradition; they reflect, in their physical shape, the deeper nature of the person bearing them; they can harm by casting jealous glances.[90] They are, in other words, an extremely social part of the anatomy.

In addition to parts of the face, injuries to the head are also specified in complaints. Thus, using a locution comparable to the petition of Thaesis, a shepherd claims that another group of shepherds (it seems) attacked him while he was pasturing a group of animals. He specifies that "they beat me many times with their shepherds' crooks, beating me on my head and on the other parts of the body" (πληγὰς πλείστ[α]ς ἐπέθηκάν μοι κολλωρόβοις πλήξαντας τὴν κεφαλὴν κ̣α̣[ὶ] τ̣ὰ̣ ἄλλα [μ]έρ[η τ]οῦ σώματος).[91] Aiming at the head, while not quite a tender part, is often important for ending a fight quickly. But again, like the face, the language of heads is social as well: it too is a locus of personhood, in its capacity to allow one to "count" in society (and be counted), as well as in the sense that the head is a locus of punishment. Unsurprisingly, given that this was a society in which the census played a large role and in which the power of the governor to deprive of life was well understood, this was known in Egypt. Thus, describing his opponent's character, the petitioner in a fragmentary fourth- or fifth-century document claims that he can reveal things about his opponent "for which one head would not suffice for punishment" (ἐφ' οἷς οὐκ̣ ἂν α̣ὐ̣τ̣ῷ̣ π̣ρὸς τ̣ι̣μωρία̣ν ἀρκέσει κεφαλὴ μία).[92]

The danger of having one's wounded body exposed to public scrutiny is well expressed in a petition from the papers of the *beneficiarius* Flavius Isidorus. This document, written in Isidorus' own hand, describes an attack against a shepherd. It is clear from the way Isidorus contextualizes the attack that this was part of a larger set of conflicts—earlier in the document he claims he had petitioned against the offenders on several occasions—but this seems to be the only time that the conflict turned violent:

> οἱ δὲ γυμνώ[σαντες] ε[ὐθ]ὺς μετὰ ῥοπαλῶν πρ[. . . .]ν̣ . . . τὴν ἐπικιμένην α[ὐτοῦ ἐ]σθῆτα διαρ[ή]ξαντες ἀφ[εί]λαντ[ο], ἔπειτα κατέκοψα[ν] π̣[ληγ]αῖς αὐτὸν κατά τ[ε] τῶν σκελῶν καὶ κατὰ τῶν ἄλλων μελῶ̣[ν] τοῦ σώματος, ἡμιθανὴν αὐτὸν καταστήσαντες ὡς κα[ὶ] φαν̣ε̣[ρ]ά ἐστιν τὰ προσφωνηθέντα ὑ̣π̣ὸ̣ τῶν ἐπιθεωρησάντων τὰ πλήγματα, ἀδήλου ο[ὔ]σης τῆς ἑαυτοῦ σωτηρίας. διὰ το[ῦτ]ο καὶ νῦν ἐπιδίδωμι τῇ σῇ λογιότητι τούσδε μου τοὺς λιβέλλου[ς] μαρτυρόμενος καὶ ἀξιῶν τούτο[υς] ἐν ἀσφαλεῖ εἶναι μέχρις τῆς εὐτυχοῦς ἐπιδημίας τοῦ κυρίου μου τοῦ ἄρχοντος· ἑτοιμότατα γὰρ ἔχω ἀπελέ̣γ̣ξαι ἐν τῷ ἀχράν<τῳ> αὐτοῦ δικαστηρίῳ τούτους λῃστὰς ὁμολό[γ]ους καὶ ζῶα ἀπελ<ηλ>ακότας πολλάκις καὶ Ἰωνᾶν τὸν προκίμενον φονέα ἀποδεῖξαι.

> . . . but once they stripped him, straightaway with clubs they . . . they tore apart the clothes he was wearing and stole them, then they pounded him on the legs and on the other parts of his body, leaving him half-dead, such that the marks from the blows attested

> by those who came to see them remain apparent. Whether he will survive is unclear. Therefore I submit this petition to your eloquence, attesting to this and asking that they be held securely until the blessed visit of my lord, the governor. For I am absolutely ready to interrogate these confessed thieves and constant cattle rustlers in his immaculate courtroom, and to show that the aforementioned Ionas is a murderer.[93]

The violence that took place here was part of a deliberate attempt to humiliate the shepherd. The emphasis on the stripping of clothes, as in other petitions, highlights the exposure of the shepherd's body; it is a long walk (or crawl) home indeed with one's personal areas exposed to the public gaze, and yet another visible sign of injury.[94] It is similarly a form of humiliation that is sexualized. But in addition to the ripped clothes of his shepherd, Isidorus highlights, among the other parts of the body that were injured, the shepherd's legs. The blows to the legs are visible evidence of the fight, as Isidorus makes clear: anyone who comes can see them. The emphasis is on the blows to a visible, public part of the body. Isidorus, moreover, reminds the *riparios* to whom he addresses the petition (as petitioners do frequently in late antiquity) that he is ready and willing to force the assailants to explain their actions in the courtroom. He will interrogate them—he will force them to make sense of their violence. He will force them, in other words, to respond in the language of law—where every punch counts, and nothing is left to chance.

* * *

When petitioners recount violence, they make claims about their opponents, but they let their bodies speak for themselves.[95] These bodies—out of sorts, in pain, wounded, and on parade—are the objects of narration. In a sense, these descriptions echo Simone Weil's famous essay on the *Iliad*, where violence turns attackers into wild animals and irrepressible forces of nature, and turns victims to stone—or worse, to slaves.[96] Weil's language here is fitting: in a society in which all free men are equal, and all unequal men are slaves, the experience of narrating one's suffering, along with the objectification that this entails, crosses precisely the wires between free and slave, man and object, that I alluded to earlier. Weil perhaps reified violence overmuch, but she did succeed in capturing one of its fascinating effects—the power of violence to make humanity feel contingent, discontinuous, or inert, in the sense of frozen or out of sorts. Still, the analogy must not be pushed too far: petitioners in Egypt were not inert—they were neither rocks nor slaves. Narrative is objectifying, but it is redemptive as well. It is perhaps ironic that its redemptive features can be activated only by placing oneself on display, objectifying and humbling oneself. But this does not turn a person into an object. A narrative—however mediated and however imperfect—has two purposes: one is to communicate pain and pathos, and only real men and women, not objects or slaves, are entitled to feel pain. The other is to place this pain on display, and in so doing to rouse the sympathies of other, more powerful individuals, and through them to enter a realm of contest where, as in a petitioner's narrative, every action must have meaning. This is the realm of law.

CHAPTER 5

The Work of Law

Writing a petition meant asking for something; as such, it was undoubtedly an experience fraught with tension. It is perhaps easy for us to forget this, living as we do in modern societies where the divisions between ruler and ruled are not so pronounced, and where a sense of rights has been so richly cultivated and carefully articulated that these rights can be taken for granted—so much so that they can be spoken of as "self-evident." But it is worth remembering that every time an Egyptian petitioner sent off a request, an official was told that he needed, in essence, to get busy doing his job, or to start doing it better. The existence of a petition meant that something had gone wrong, and it was his job to fix it. Roman officials tried to take that job seriously, in no small part because the smooth running of the machinery of the Empire was fundamentally dependent on a promise to its inhabitants. The promise was relatively simple: the government would continue to be just and responsive so long as taxes were paid, grain was shipped, and certain basic rules were followed. But this promise was also an abstraction, and it required that certain problems be worked out in somewhat messier detail. When a farmer in the Fayyum decided to make the government keep its promise, he would have to interact with some extremely powerful people. He would do this by using the legal system.

"Using the legal system" is an important phrase, and one worth unpacking. At one level it is a compact way of saying that the individual petitioner would have to engage in a series of encounters, discussions, arguments, and transactions with people who were powerful—more powerful, by definition, than he was, and probably more powerful than he could ever hope to be. He would engage in these transactions, moreover, so that he could force these powerful officials to do things—to punish his opponents, to keep him safe, to help him get his way, and so on. He would similarly ask that the legal system, and the powerful people who controlled it, validate his vision of himself and his claims about his normative universe. This would involve writing, waiting in line, arguing, and being pushed from venue to venue to await a decision; the enforcement of that decision would probably involve repeating the same process over again. To an individual petitioner, trying to force officials to do things must have felt like pushing a large rock uphill, with the coordinate threat that the rock might at any moment roll backward and squish him.

But "using the legal system" is more than the sum total of the interactions between a petitioner and an official. Law is a complex business: as I suggested earlier, legal systems, even outside of imperial encounters, have the power to create, maintain, and enforce certain types of truths; to validate some claims and quash others; to generate, through the creation and maintenance of records of practice, knowledge of individual subjects; and to frame subjects as juridical beings, in whom rights and obligations are vested. These legal practices are slippery and contested, even in societies in which a population is relatively homogeneous and where there is a relative consensus as to the legitimacy and discrete competencies of political and judicial institutions; they are far more complex in imperial encounters in which participants enter the sphere of legal contest speaking diverse languages, approach those in power with varying levels of mistrust, and potentially disagree not only about the legitimate "rules" that govern a particular encounter, but also about the correct means for enforcing (or not enforcing) these rules.

This chapter is primarily concerned with the shape of these encounters—with questions of what petitioners were trying to achieve when they wrote their narratives, with what those in charge of them were willing to do on their behalf, and with the results (such as we can reconstruct them) of these encounters. Whereas in the last chapter I focused on the creation of narratives and questions of self-perception, this chapter is largely about powerful third parties. (In the final chapter I will return to petitioners and their relations with their adversaries.) These powerful third parties—governors, *epistrategoi*, *strategoi*, and others—are essential to the operation of law and legal interactions. As I hope to show, this is not only because they hold the formally authorized means of violence (since it is unlikely that at the end of the day they would ever bring great violence to bear on petitioners' opponents). In the adjudication of disputes, and particularly of disputes that take place in an imperial encounter, they are important simply by virtue of the fact of their being different and variously distant, that is, by virtue of their formal or institutional location outside the immediate dynamics of community relations.

This distance—and the power connected to it—is a consequence of the legal pluralism that characterizes empires. Distance and pluralism are themselves just sides of the same coin, namely, that empires tend to emphasize, thrive upon, and govern by the maintenance and enforcement of difference.[1] The fact of difference—in its various manifestations as pluralism or as distance—is both advantageous and complicating: that officials might work with presumptions about right and wrong different from those of petitioners complicates these encounters, but does not render them impossible to manage; nor does it reduce the creation and enforcement of "law" to simply an act of colonial violence, albeit in a cleaner toga. There were processes of translation and persuasion involved in making claims of law, as would be expected in cases where the fact of difference was a key structuring principle. It is not sufficient, then, to imagine that the legal system only provides a venue for disputes.[2] To a certain extent it does provide this, but it also transforms those disputes, not least by integrating powerful individuals into the dispute itself, but also by transforming the nature of the complaint itself.[3] We tend to doubt that that *any* act of translation can be as good as the original; I will argue, instead, that at some levels it was better, and that correctly achieving these acts of translation and transformation was precisely the goal of petitioners in the first place.

* * *

It is best to begin by giving some account of what petitioners want, or, at least, what they claim to want, and move from there to see how these requests "fit" with what the legal system, at least in its formal structure, claimed it was prepared to do for petitioners. This is an important exercise, for two reasons: at a basic level, because in presenting a history from the "bottom up" it matters a great deal to begin with what people said they were doing; second, and more important, because there is an assumption in the scholarly literature that petitioners simply want a return to the status quo, to find some way of mediating their differences with their opponents, and to go back to the business of daily life.[4] At the core of this idea are two assumptions about law, both of which can be traced back, mutatis mutandis, to the Romantic conceptions of *Volk* generated by Herder and brought to the study of law by Savigny, conceptions that reemerge periodically in legal history and anthropology, especially in the service of projects mistrustful of Enlightenment natural law traditions.[5] The first assumption is that there is a fundamental and insurmountable division between those who make (positive) law and those who have to follow it; as a consequence of this division the relationship between the two groups (law makers and law followers) is one of imposition; and therefore the provincial legal system—in all of its manifestations—was something fundamentally foreign and distasteful to those on the receiving end of law's commands. This assumption has as its corollary a second assumption, namely, that a legal system—or, at least, a system of dispute processing and resolution—is something that is most effective when it is bound to culture, by which is meant a package of distinctive, exclusive, authentic—and therefore preferential—modes of dealing with problems. Accordingly, the ideal means of dealing with disputes, violent or otherwise, is to keep them within a local context, and settle them by a process of mediation.[6]

In the writing of Roman history these claims have often been taken as axiomatic;[7] still, in addition to being capable of theoretical critique (which I will attempt below), they are also empirically falsifiable. We can begin with the claim, advanced most forcefully by Deborah Hobson, that petitioners were not seeking to have their opponents punished, but rather that they simply desired a return to the status quo ante. In other words, that the goal of using the legal system was not retribution but rather recompense.[8] Yet, as Benjamin Kelly has rightly pointed out, this is at best only partially accurate.[9] In petitions concerning violence, at least in petitions of first instance, petitioners *always* ask for punishment, for hearings, and for legal action; they *never* ask for mediation, reconciliation, or a return to the status quo ante. When violence is accompanied by the taking of, or harm to, property, petitioners *also* ask for recompense.[10] When there is no violence, it makes sense that petitioners would function according to a system of strict compensation for loss. Two examples are instructive as to the differences between harm to the person and harm to property:

> Φ[λ]αουίῳ Ἀπολλωνίῳ στρ(ατηγῷ) Ἀρσι(νοΐτου) Ἡρακλ(είδου) μερίδος
> παρὰ Σοήρεως Πακύσεως ἀπὸ κώ(μης) Σοκνοπαίου Νήσου. ὁ
> ἀδελφός μου Ὀννῶφρις ἐτελ(εύτησεν) [ἄ]τεκνος ἐπὶ κληρο(νό)μ(ῳ̣)
> ἐμοί, καταλείψας μοι [..] καμήλους τρεῖς οἵτινε̣ς λ̣[...]ρ.[.]...[.].[.]ρ̣
> ἐμοὶ ἦσαν. Σαταβοὺς δ̣.[..]επ̣[...].αρ̣π̣εινο̣ς. ἀλόγως ἐπῆλθέ μ̣[οι κα]ὶ̣
> βιαίως ἀπέσπασεν [τ]ο̣ὺ̣ς καμή[λο]υς, περὶ ο̣[ὗ(?) κ]α̣ὶ̣ τότε σοι
> ἐνέτυχο(ν) διὰ Μέλ[α]νος δούλο[υ μ]ου, αὐτὴ ἐν ἀσθενίᾳ̣ τυγ[χ-]
> άνουσα, καὶ [ἐ]πέταξας ἕνα τῶν περ[ί] σε ὑπηρετῶν ἐπαναγκάσαι
> αὐτὸν ἀπ[ο]καταστῆσα[ί] μοι τοὺς καμήλους, ὃς μαθὼ̣ν [α]ὐτὸ τότε
> ἀφανὴς ἐγένετο. ἐπεὶ οὖν μέχρι τούτου οὐκ ἀποκατέσ̣τ̣ησέν μοι

> αὐτούς, τυγχάν[ω] δὲ τῇ ἔναγχος τῶν θρεμμάτων ἀπογ[ρ(αφῇ)] ἀπογρ(αψαμένη), ἀξιῶ νῦν χλω[ροφ]αγούντων [αὐ]τῶν ὑπὸ τὸν Σαταβοὺν [- ca.16 -].μ( ) [.]ị δẹς οὐκ ἔ̣χ̣ο̣υ̣σ̣α
>
> To Flavius Apollonius, *strategos* of the Arsinoite nome in the division of Herakleides,
> From Soeris from the town of Soknopaiou Nesos. My brother Onnophris died without children and his inheritance went to me, leaving me . . . three camels which . . . they were mine. Satabous . . . without reason approached me and forcefully seized the camels, concerning which I petitioned you at that time through my slave Melas, since I was sick. You ordered one of your agents to compel him to return my camels, but he (Satabous) found this out and disappeared. Since up until now he has not returned them to me, and since I just registered them in the latest registration of livestock, I now request that since they are eating green food under (the control of?) Satabous . . . [11]

Though the scope of the request in this papyrus is not preserved, it still serves as evidence of what was desired in the previous petition. While the details of the relationship between the petitioner and Satabous are unclear, the way that she discussed the previous petition (the one delivered through the slave) seems to indicate a relatively straightforward case of theft followed by a request for restitution (without, it appears, a punitive element). By the time of this second petition the matter has become more complicated, since not only is there still the need for restitution but the petitioner is also liable for the taxes on the livestock.

Another example is also instructive, if not entirely straightforward. This petition involves a case of breaking and entering and theft. The petitioner claims that two men, Pakysis and Panouphis, had broken into his storehouse and absconded with a quantity of goods while he was out of town. He found that the culprits were his downstairs neighbors who had reached his things by a hole they made in the ceiling, and he demanded recompense. Four copies of this petition are extant:

> διελεγχόμενοι δὲ οἱ ἔνδον οἰκοῦντες ὡς ἐξ αὐτῶν ἐπηρείας τοῦτο γεγένηται ὑπέσχοντο διά τε τοῦ τῆς κώμης ἀρχεφόδου καὶ διὰ ἄλλων δώσειν εἰς τὸν λόγον τῆς κλοπῆς πυροῦ ἀρτάβας ἑπτά. ἀλλ'

ἐπεὶ τῇ μὲν ὑποσχέσει συνέθεντο, τῇ δὲ ἀποδόσει μέχρι νῦν οὐχ' ὑπήντησαν, ἀναγκαίως τὴν ἐπίδοσιν τῶν βιβλιδίων ποιοῦμαι, ἅπερ ἀξιῶ ἐν καταχωρισμῷ γενέσθαι εἰς τὸ μένειν μοι λόγον πρὸς τοὺς ἐνκαλουμένους Πανοῦφιν Στοτοήτεως καὶ Πακῦσιν Καννεῖτος. διευτύχει.

Once those living in that house were interrogated, (they admitted) that they did this because of their malice, and promised in front of the *archephodos* of the town and others that they would give seven *artabas* of grain as payment for the theft. But although they made this promise, they have not up till now given them to me. Therefore of necessity I submit this petition, and ask that it remain on file so that my account will be preserved against the accused, Panouphis, son of Stotoetis, and Pakysis, son of Kanneis. Farewell.[12]

The difference in language and procedure between this case of theft and cases of violence is instructive. Complaints recording violence to the person and harm to property share a number of features: they generally come fast on the heels of the harm in question, use the same techniques of naming and shaming their opponents, and ask for recompense. In this petition, there was an intervening period of time between the matter of complaint and the petition itself. The petitioner also states that he tried to manage the problem locally and by consent (through a sworn agreement, a *hyposchesis*) before he involved the authorities at a higher level. From another copy of the same complaint (this one addressed to the centurion), we can tell that the seven *artabas* was, oddly enough, *less* than they had stolen.[13] Likewise, the petitioner does not ask for additional restitution, but rather that his petition remain on file—a course of action that leaves the matter open to prosecution. In this case, it seems, the petitioner is using the legal system as a way of applying pressure to gain recompense from the thieves and enforce an existing agreement (the one he claims was made in the presence of the *archephodos*), not for the immediate purpose of pursuing the case in court.

In cases where violence is involved along with damage to property, petitioners often are clear that they wish for both compensation and punishment. Thus in a relatively early petition, a man complains that a group of individuals with whom he had made a series of financial arrangements chose to beat him up rather than returning what they owed him. The man filed a petition about assault, but then the attackers chose to beat him up again, this time stealing back a cloak which they had given him as security for a loan. He petitions again, asking that the offenders be brought "before you so that I can get back the fodder and the wheat and our cloak and that they can get what they deserve." This "get what they deserve" (ạụ̓τοὶ δ̣ὲ τύχωσι ὧν προσήκει), is a punitive request, clearly marked out from the compensatory request with the particle δέ.[14] These two-part requests are relatively common, even considering that many petitions are missing their bottom parts as a result of the vagaries of preservation. Thus, in a case of physical and verbal assault coupled with damage to a farm (this part of the narrative is not preserved, but the request is), a man asks that the offender be brought before an official for punishment (*ekdikia*), and that the petition be kept on file for the upcoming *conventus*, where he will pursue both the issue of "the damage to my farm and the things which he dared to do to me" (περί τε τοῦ βλάβους τοῦ κλήρου καὶ ὧν ἐτόλμησεν).[15] Similarly, in a case from the fourth century a petitioner complains of being assaulted by his neighbors after their cow had damaged his crops. He asks that the men be hauled before the *praepositus pagi* "on account of both the sowing and the violence" and that his account be preserved to be heard at the court of the *praeses* (καὶ περὶ τῆς σπορᾶς καὶ περὶ τ̣ῆ̣ς ὕβρεως τηρεῖσθαι ἐμοὶ καὶ τὸν λόγο̣ν̣ ἐπὶ το ἡγεμονικοῦ δικαστ̣η̣ρίο̣υ̣).[16] Examples could be multiplied.[17]

The two-part request, however, is only one of the options petitioners could employ. In some cases where there was both violence and damage petitioners could simply ask for "punishment" (ἐπέξοδος)—this punishment could be "fitting" or "necessary" (δέουσα) or "forthcoming" (ἐσομένη). These sorts of requests are fairly common early in the Roman period (such as in the Euhemeria petitions), and are not exclusive to mixed attacks against person and property, nor are they exclusive to violence alone.[18] Petitioners similarly request *ekdikia* (punishment, revenge, or judgment).[19] They similarly ask to be "free and free from violence" (ἐλεύθερον καὶ ἀνύβριστον) or "free from abuse and threats" (ἀνύβριστον καὶ ἀνεπηρέαστον).[20] While this may appear to be a request, in most complaints in which individuals ask to be kept safe after a violent incident they are also requesting that legal measures be taken against their opponents as well.[21] The late antique evidence likewise accords with this model: in cases where petitioners ask for individuals to be restrained against them following a violent attack, they also ask for a chance to bring the case to court and see the offender punished.[22]

These requests should not be understood as being somehow "vague"—in spite of the fact that we know very little of what particular sort of thing "punishment" would consist of (a point I will return to momentarily).[23] They are in fact specific; they just speak to a basic and difficult problem involved in the pricing of injury. In instances in which there is damage to property and person, the damage to the property is the easier to quantify. Sheep can be returned or paid for, broken walls repaired, and ruined objects reckoned in cash or barter. But how can one quantify a punch in the face? An insult? It is hard to put a price on personal dignity, especially if the price has to be structured to take care of not only the physical damage, but also the perceived threat to personhood and standing. Some legal systems have tried to price these injuries. In the law of the Salian Franks or in the Burgundian Code certain attacks are to be paid for by certain fines, and these fines are adjusted by rank.[24] But offering set prices for violence is just one choice among many (and not a terribly useful one, legally speaking, given the vagaries of inflation).[25] In the case of the barbarian codes, these prices also come from a world in which law made a more strident attempt to mark status and social position.[26] It is true that particular institutions tended to set prices for violent and insulting behavior—such as in guild charters in which certain behaviors and misadventures were billed to the member at a certain fixed rate[27]—but this style of thinking is fundamentally foreign to the Roman legal system, which in this period did not set fixed fines for damages. Rather, damages to tangible goods were set according to market values. In terms of personal delicts like *iniuria/hybris*, the Roman system was yet more fluid and allowed the prosecuting party to state what he or she thought was a fair compensation for a wounded body (except in the case of *atrox iniuria*, in which the praetor would set the price); the judge (and later the magistrate, once *iniuria* began to be tried *extra ordinem*, as it always was in Egypt) was to evaluate compensation *ex bono et aequo*—according to what is right and fair. This refusal to work from a schedule of prices for bruises and wounds also opened up yet another way in which petitioners could decide who they were, and advocate for what they thought they were worth.

But the fact that the provincial legal system tended to resolve wounds into cash should not lead us to conclude that a pocketful of coin was the only or even the primary goal of a petitioner. Simply being able to show one's opponents that one was not willing to suffer passively can sometimes be satisfying in itself.[28] Having one's opponents "brought" or "hauled" (ἀχθῆναι) before an official proves that they, too, can be made to do things they are unwilling to do. A possible clue to this dynamic comes from a petition from third-century Oxyrhynchos: a woman complains that a man named Eudaimon has assaulted her son-in-law, and that she submitted a petition concerning this. Eudaimon, however, was strong enough to have the petition quashed (ἐξίσχυσεν τὰ βιβλίδια ἀθετηθῆναι) "so that he wouldn't appear liable to prosecution" (ἵνα μὴ φανῇ ἐπελευστικός).[29] The word in question (*epeleustikos*) is rare, and caution is necessary in interpreting its sense:[30] to be "sue-able" or "liable to prosecution," it seems, carries the sense of being compellable, vulnerable, subject to scrutiny, and forced to respond in register of law. Even for the powerful this could have the potential to be a frightening experience—a governor or even a *strategos* could happen to be in a bad mood that day, and issue (or carry out) threats. Thus in a papyrus from the fourth century, a man (in this case, a council member) who owed a debt to a local large landholder claims to have received a summons and "withdrew to the Great Oasis because of the fear of the courtroom in my heart," where he spent "four straight days and nights, parched."[31] The possibility of using institutional mechanisms to bind one's opponents, and prove that they were not, in fact, inviolable, must not be overlooked as something meaningless. In fact, in the fourth century and later the references to courtrooms are increased, and petitioners are often specific about wanting to pursue matters in the legal system.[32] One petitioner looks forward to his opportunity to show in court that his assailants are "sworn thieves" and that one is a murderer;[33] yet another declares at the end of his petition that he is not afraid to take the matter to court.[34]

The emphasis on punishment, hearings, and arrests is not exclusive to accounts of violence, but should make us wary of any claim that victims of violence merely desired cash compensation. Nor are there any petitions that lead us to think that the petitioner wished to return to the status quo ante after a violent assault on the petitioner or on his or her family. Coupled with this impressive avoidance of compensatory requests, we might add that there is virtually no evidence that, once a particular behavior was deemed "violent," it could then be taken out of the realm of adjudication and made subject to a procedure for mediation, either formal or informal. Thus, of the 41 *dialyseis* or mediation agreements from late antiquity collected by Gagos and Van Minnen, almost all concern issues of property, payment, and inheritance—that is, things that are contractual disagreements, rather than matters of personal harm.[35] If we read some narratives in petitions closely and carefully, there might be hints that individuals attempted to handle disputes locally—sometimes petitioners confess that they tried to discuss some matter with an offender, and that this failed or resulted in more violence, and therefore they brought the disputes to the attention of legal authorities. Even if we look to nonlegal documents like personal letters to try to shed some light on this problem, the results are slim: there is little evidence that violence was settled extra-legally. One writer expresses what may perhaps be a sentiment of what might be construed as revenge.[36] Another urges his associate to compel others to do his bidding μετὰ στρεβλώσεως, which was translated by the original editors as "with torture" but in its context more likely should be construed as "use pressure."[37] Yet another cryptically writes to his sister saying, "if anyone has injured you, let me know his name by letter."[38] At the same time, these three threats—if that is indeed what they are—are counterbalanced by yet other letters in which individuals urge one another to pursue redress against violence through the legal system,[39] or suggest that obnoxious individuals be avoided.[40]

Given, then, that petitioners request punishment and retributive action (whether in cash or by the humiliation of their opponents), it is fair to ask what the likelihood was of their achieving this, and what it would have looked like if they did manage to achieve it. It is a frustrating aspect of our extant documentation that there is no clear-cut answer to this question. Certainly Roman governors could be brutal if they so chose; local officials could as well (though whether they were entitled to be so is a trickier question). They were not afraid to issue threats: thus, in a record of proceedings originating perhaps in Alexandria, the prefect presides over the case of a freedman accused of ingratitude by his former master, and (so it appears, since the text is fragmentary) promises to beat the ungrateful freedman with rods if his patron accuses him in court again.[41] In addition to damages, magistrates could also choose to inflict corporal punishment on the defendant. Thus it is clear from an edict that the governor, while limited in the type of individual he could beat and how, had the ability to inflict corporal punishment on his subjects:

> Αὐρήλιος Ἡρώδης ὁ διασημότατος ἡγούμενος Θηβαΐδος λέγει· τὸ τὴν διὰ τῶν ἱμάντων ληṭαρι[.]ων ἐπιχωρίως οὕτω καλουμένων αἰκίαν ὑπομένειν ἐστὶν μὲν καὶ ἐπὶ τῶν δουλικὴν τύχην εἰληχότων ἀνιαρόν, οὐ μὴν κατὰ τὸ παντελὲς ἀπ'ηγορευμένον, ἐλευθέρους δὲ ἄνδρας τοιαύτην ὕβριν ὑπομένειν οὔτε τοῖς [νόμοις] ἀκόλ[ου]θọṿ ἀδικίαν τε [ἔ]χον ἐστὶν ἐṿ [- ca.33 -].ạτε
>
> Aurelius Herodes the most distinguished governor of the Thebaid declares: the subjection to disgrace by lashing which is called *letar* . . . in the native language is grievous for those of slave status, but not entirely prohibited. But for free men to undergo such *hybris* is not in accordance with the laws and is unjust . . . [42]

Two important things emerge from this document. First, the *praeses* thinks that this punishment, while not *totally* forbidden, is in fact grave, even when applied to slaves. Echoing the world of petitioners, this edict reproduces the ever-important distinction between free and slave, and adds that the free do indeed suffer *hybris* when treated slavishly. Second, he acknowledges that those imposing these punishments—that is, agents of the state—can commit *hybris* like anyone else. Still, this edict should not be mistaken as somehow benign: while lashing was for slaves, free men could still be beaten with rods.[43] Likewise interesting is the characterization of the role of the *strategos* by the ever-verbose Ptolemaios son of Diodorus, who characterizes the behavior of an individual who he charges is exceeding his authority. The crucial but mutilated passage is: "to be *strategoi*, that is, to rule and to prevent and to crush and to beat and strike free men and to whip them like slaves." (στρατ̣ηγεῖν τοῦτ' ἐστὶν ἄρχειν καὶ κωλ̣ύ̣ειν [κ]α̣ὶ ἀ̣λ̣ή̣θ̣ε̣ι̣ν̣ κ̣α̣[ὶ] τοὺς ἐ̣λευθέρο̣υ̣ς τ̣ύπτειν καὶ παίειν καὶ μαστιγο̣ῦν ὡ̣ς δ̣ο̣[ύλο]υ̣ς).[44] Finally, in a bilingual copy of court proceedings from the fourth century we see the interaction of the *praeses* and a slave who was involved in an attack on a city councilman:

> Filammon d(ixit): ὁ υἱός μ[ου] ἐκινδύνευσεν ἀποθανεῖν διὰ τὰς πληγάς. Fl(avius) Leontius Beronician(us) v(ir) c(larissimus) pr(aeses) Tebaei(dis) d(ixit): τίνος ἕνεκεν ἐπῆλθες τῷ βουλευτῇ; et ad officium d(ixit): τυπτέσθω. et cumque buneuris caesus fuisset, Fl(avius) Leontius Beronicianus v(ir) c(larissimus) pr(aeses) Tebaei(dis) d(ixit): ἐλευθέρους μὴ τύπτητε. et ad officium d(ixit) parce. cumque pepertum ei fuisset, Fl(avius) Leontius Beronician(us) v(ir) c(larissimus) pr(aeses) Tebaei(dis) d(ixit): εἰπὲ ποῦ ἐστιν τὸ χρυσίον ὅπερ ἥρπασας . . .
>
> Philammon said, "My son is in danger of dying from the blows!" The most glorious Flavius Leontius Beronicianus, governor of the Thebaid, said: "Why did you attack the city councilman?" And he said to the *officium*: "Let him be beaten." And after he had been beaten with oxhide whips, the most glorious Flavius Leontius Beronicianus, governor of the Thebaid, said: "Don't beat free men." And he said to the *officium*: "Spare him." The most glorious Flavius Leontius Beronicianus, governor of the Thebaid said, "tell me where is the money you stole?" . . . [45]

Precisely what is going on in this interaction is hard to reconstruct: it may be that the slave here is being tortured, which would have been necessary to extract his testimony. If it is torture, then the insistence that he be "spared" before answering questions is strange—unless it means "spare him for now—if he stops answering, we'll beat him more later." It may also be that the governor was choosing to inflict a bit of punishment on the slave, after his patience had been worn down by a long and contentious hearing. Philammon, whose son, the city councilman, has been injured, may have succeeded in provoking the rage of the prefect. In this case, after having the slave beaten sufficiently, the *praeses* sends him off with a piece of advice for the future: not to beat free men (stated in the imperative). We may imagine that there was no reason for punishing the slave financially when, as in this case, his master (who would normally be liable for his behavior) is not present in the courtroom. The *praeses* then moves on to the charges of theft against the slave, where we might imagine that compensation would have been a more pressing issue. The papyrus breaks off shortly thereafter, but the importance of corporal punishment in the courtroom, especially in recompense for a different violent act, is nonetheless important. At the same time, though we may see instances in which behavior was punished by lashes, we have no evidence of some of the other punishments known from criminal courts being used in civil cases: thus we have no evidence of exile, condemnation to the mines, or forfeiture of property being requested in cases of violence.[46] This may again be part of the gap in the available evidence, but even this is significant: there is no indication in the Egyptian evidence that courtroom procedures for violence ever had a "criminal" aspect.

At the same time, it is immediately obvious that all of these "punishments"—or, in the case of the Alexandrian freedman, the threat of punishment—were directed against slaves. Whether free men would have succeeded in getting their opponents so punished is harder to discern. There is one tantalizing hint, from relatively late in the period under consideration. It is an oath that seems to emerge from a case of violence, and comes from Herakleopolis:

> Σεπτιμ<ί>ῳ Φλαουιανῷ πρωτεύοντι Ἡρακλ(εο)πολίτου παρὰ Αὐρηλίας Μαύρας θυγατρὸς Θεοδώρου ἀπὸ κώμης Πεενσαμοὶ ιγ πάγου τοῦ αὐτοῦ νομοῦ. ἐπειδὴ Ἰουλιανὸ̣ς Ν̣εμεσίωνος ὁμοκω̣μήτης μου καὶ σύνοικος προσῆλ̣θ̣ε̣ν τ̣ῇ̣ σ̣ῇ̣ ἐ̣ν̣τ̣ρεχείᾳ αἰτ̣ι̣ώ̣μεν̣ό̣ς με περὶ ὕβρεως, ἡ δὲ σὴ [τύχη] ἀκόλουθ̣α̣ [το]ῖ̣ς νόμοις πράττουσα μεταπεμ̣ψαμένη μ̣[ε] παρενε̣[..]σεν μηκέτι πρὸς αὐτὸν ἀμφισβητ̣ε̣ῖν, κατὰ τ̣[ο]ῦ̣το ὁμολογῶ ἐπομν̣υμένη τὸν θεῖον καὶ

σεβάσμιον ὅρκ̣ο̣ν̣ τ̣ῶ̣ν δεσποτ̣ῶ̣ν ἡμῶν Ὀνωρίου <καὶ> Θεοδοσίου τῶν αἰωνίων Α̣ὐ̣γούστων ἐντεῦθεν μὴ διαφέρεσθαι πρὸς τὸν προλεχθέντα μ̣ο̣υ σύ̣ν̣ο̣ικον Ἰουλιανὸν μηδὲ ἀμφισβητεῖν περὶ τῆς τ̣υ̣χ̣ο̣ύ̣σ̣η̣ς προφά̣σ̣εως, ἀλλ' εἴπερ ἐκείνου προκαταρξαμένου ὕβριν ὑπομείνω, ἐμὲ ἐπάναγκες ἀνελθεῖν καὶ δηλῶσ̣α̣[ι τοῖς] νόμοις καὶ τῇ [σ]ῇ̣ ἐ̣[π]ι̣ε̣ι̣κ̣ε̣ί̣ᾳ̣ ἀ̣ν̣υ̣π̣ε̣[ρ]θ̣έτως, εἰ δὲ φανείη[ν ψευ]σαμένη, ἔνοχος [ἔσο]μ̣αι τῇ ἐκτί̣σ̣ε̣ι̣......ων δύο καὶ τῷ ἐπηρτημένῳ περὶ τούτου κ̣ι̣[ν]δ̣ύνῳ καὶ ἐ̣π̣ερωτηθ̣[εῖσ]α̣ ὡμολόγησα.

To Septimius Flavianus, *proteuon* of Herakleopolis, from Aurelia Maura, daughter of Theodoros, from the town of Peensamoi in the 13th pagus of the same nome. Since Ioulianos, son of Nemesion, my fellow townsman who lives in my home, has approached your skillfulness accusing me of violence, your good fortune has done according to the laws and sent for me . . . not to dispute with him. Accordingly, having sworn the divine and august oath by our lords Honorius and Theodosius, eternal Augusti, I agree that from here onwards I will not quarrel with my aforementioned housemate Ioulianos, nor will I dispute with him on any pretense. But if that man starts a quarrel, I will refrain from violence; instead I will approach you, and right away demonstrate this to the laws and to your skillfulness. If it should appear that I am lying, let me be liable for payment of . . . two, as well as the penalty threatened on account of this. Having been asked, I agree.[47]

Were we to have additional information on the dispute between Ioulianos and Maura, we could probably make a better assessment of this document. The fact that there is, to my knowledge, only one such papyrus dealing with violence in this manner necessitates caution. Still, a number of features raise interesting possibilities. First, this appears *not* to be a *dialysis*, or mediation agreement, but rather a unilateral oath. It emerges from Ioulianos' original petition to Septimius Flavianus, who, it appears, enjoins the oath on Maura, whereas in mediation agreements parties either agree among themselves about the best solution or bring in another party (rather than the original recipient of the petition) to settle the issue.[48] The precise relationship between Ioulianos and Maura is similarly problematic: were they landlord and tenant? If they are related or married (which I doubt), family language has been elided. It appears that whatever transpired between them, they continued to live in the same house. As for the penalty section, it is unfortunate that the amount in question is lacunose, and little can be learned from the vague reference to the additional penalty. Who would have possessed the papyrus? Would a copy have been given to Ioulianos, as protection in case of Maura's persistence in the quarrel? Or would it have remained on file, with the potential to be activated later? Should we even assume that Maura was guilty of a serious offense in the first place? What if the offense was trivial, Ioulianos' petition full of exaggerations, the evidence of violence slim, or any number of other possible circumstances prevailed? If that were the case, this papyrus might not reflect a solution to violence at all, but rather an attempt by Septimius Flavianus to do the best job possible to stop Ioulianos from complaining, while simultaneously making sure that the quarrel would not escalate.

But let us assume, for the moment, that Maura actually did violence to Ioulianos, and that this papyrus represents one possible way of solving the problem. What, then, would this oath have achieved? To those who tend to think that human beings can be reduced to rational calculators of potential gains and losses, the answer would have to be "very little." Maura gets off lightly. Simply having to swear that she will no longer do violence to him costs relatively little. She hands over no money. She is not beaten with rods or threatened. She may have to do this in the future, should she persist in her bad behavior, but reinitiating proceedings might be laborious for Ioulianos. And here we would have to assume one thing and conclude another: first, that "law" is just a bigger stick with which to hit your opponents, and second, that petitioners aren't very good at using it. To invoke, again, the language of rational choice, we could say that petitioners appear to be playing a game with very low stakes, and playing it quite poorly. We may even conclude that they're playing the wrong game to begin with: with so little that could possibly result from legal action, a better choice would be to ignore violence in the first place—and since it appears that they do not, we would have to conclude that petitioners were somehow largely irrational.

There is, however, another way out of this problem, one that does not postulate that a cultural practice that persists over multiple centuries is somehow irrational. What has Ioulianos achieved? He has won. His narrative has been validated. Maura is not untouchable after all. She is humiliated in public. More important, she is not to quarrel or to dispute with him "for any reason." Ioulianos has, as I suggested earlier, successfully prevailed upon a third party (Septimius Flavianus) to perform an act of translation, reducing his relations with Maura, whatever they were (and they are *intentionally* obscured in her oath), into a prohibition on dispute, whatever its causes. The solution is to flatten these relationships, and in so doing it accords well with petitioners' normative claims about how the social world should work. And here it matters little whether or not his initial accusation was true or proven, for now Ioulianos has achieved, through his act of translation, a state in which things are legally true. Compensation in cash or in Maura's pain is lagniappe (which is not to say it is undesirable). Ioulianos has a restraining order, the upper hand in their relationship, and more important perhaps, legally validated knowledge of who he is vis-à-vis her. He is a person not to be touched.

* * *

Legal systems, of course, are more than a black box that pops out institutionalized judgments and punishments once petitioners insert their claims. There are rules, too, not just for slotting particular complaints into particular categories, but also for how complaints, once classified, are to be evaluated, and by whom. There are practices of knowledge and recording that structure these systems. And of course there are people: some people might have the authority to make judgments or delegate cases, others may be tasked with recording discrete legal moments, still others may be asked to use force—either in apprehending the accused or in carrying out authorized punishments. As is well known, law masks its violence by claiming to adhere to some sort of system, by depersonalizing judgments by claiming simply to apply rules, and by appealing to ideologies of fairness and righteousness. At this point it is fair to ask: What were these rules? Did petitioners know them? Did governors? How were they applied in practice, and what were the consequences of their application? How did they come to "mean" things?

These are hard questions, even for modern societies in which legal anthropologists have the ability to interrogate their subjects, conduct diachronic surveys of legal knowledge, and access well-kept courtroom records. Even if ancient historians could avail themselves of such data sets the problem would not be thereby alleviated, since at the core of all of these questions lurks the broader issue: what does one mean by "law"? What form did it take? Where was it located? How ought we to distinguish between legal order and social order? Even granting that we could make this distinction, where would we locate the line—or horizon—distinguishing between the two? Of course, to attempt a philosophy of law would be beyond the bounds of this study. However, it is reasonable to put forward a few methodological guidelines that could serve in giving some structure to how we should evaluate petitioners and their strategies with those who were in charge of them. Here I advance two main claims: in the world of Roman Egypt two main things that marked out something as being distinctly "law," rather than something else. One of these, as I suggested earlier, was the fact of difference or distance, by which I mean that legitimate judges were ideally external to, rather than embedded within, local systems of social ordering. The second is the fact of writing, and in particular, authorized writing. These two things marking out "law" from other sorts of order interact in fascinating ways in the legally plural system of Roman Egypt, and have consequences not only for the study of violence but for the dynamics of provincial law in general.

* * *

As I stated above, the Roman legal system—in the provinces and elsewhere—was characterized by legal pluralism. I began to sketch these dynamics in Chapter 2, where the discussion turned more on the realities of practice than on the conceptual possibilities that plural systems open up. Legal pluralism, like law itself, is a term that carries much baggage.[49] At its core, a legally "plural" regime is one in which there are multiple systems of law that coexist at a given time. Thus, in Roman Egypt (at least prior to the Constitutio Antoniniana in A.D. 212 which theoretically bound most inhabitants by Roman civil law), one could recognize pluralism in that Roman law existed alongside the *ius gentium*, the "law of peoples," by which Roman governors would, in theory, judge those not bound by various practices of the Roman civil law (*ius civile*). In this case, simply by way of example, a governor could decide that the child of two Romans (or a Roman and a woman with whom he was granted *conubium*, the right to create a lawful Roman marriage) would be under the power (*potestas*) of his father, giving his father a series of rights over his son and his son's property; the same would not necessarily, in theory, be true in the same way of the son of two Egyptians, who were not bound by the rules of the *ius civile* concerning the power over children.[50] (That at the level of theory the Romans themselves often decided the contents of the *ius gentium*, and that the *ius gentium* did not necessarily bear any relationship to how a particular community organized itself, are problems that need not detain us here.[51]) By a similar token, pluralism in Egypt could be recognized by the multiplicity of citizenship statuses, and the increasing willingness (to the extent that this is the correct term) of the Roman government to allow (or force) Egyptians to formalize various practices and to live by them—in one case by the introduction, in late first or early second century, of a "law of the Egyptians."[52] For the sake of clarity, I will follow John Griffiths in calling these forms of legal pluralism "weak legal pluralism."[53] Weak pluralism designates a plural regime in which the state nevertheless monopolizes law-creating or delegates these powers to various authorized groups while preserving distinctions among its subjects. It can take various forms: the state can recognize and legitimate different practices, allowing them to stand as semi-autonomous systems of jurisdiction. The Romans did this in Judaea, for example, by allowing the Sanhedrin to regulate itself in certain matters relating to religion;[54] they did this also in late antiquity, by allowing the church to take cognizance of certain matters (the *episcopalis audientia*).[55] Similarly, Roman authorities did such a thing in Egypt by permitting guilds to regulate the behavior of their members. Alternatively, in a system of weak pluralism a central power can treat local patterns of practice not as "law" but as "custom," and allow such customs to persist, provided they do not impinge on central state prerogatives.[56] These examples of weak pluralism, it should go without saying, are merely reference points on a spectrum; they do not exhaust the possibilities.

Weak legal pluralism is "weak" in the sense that the state is and remains the source of law-deciding authority; alternative legal orders exist and are recognized only at the discretion of the state, and can be disposed of by similar discretion.[57] Strong legal pluralism, on the other hand, entails a claim that "law" can exist independent of state authority.[58] In such a system, different groups create and reinforce normative orders, define what is right and wrong, use tactics of social control to enforce these normative visions, and thus make law as well. These tactics of social control can be more or less formal or effective—they range from shaming and moral censure, at one end, to brute violence against transgressors of the normative order at the other.[59] Strong legal pluralism may exist to attempt to block the intervention of a state power (resistance), may simply choose to ignore such a power (as in cases where strong legal pluralism exists because the state cannot or chooses not to reach a particular group of individuals, such as in mountainous regions),[60] or may insist that the state itself validate its claims (as in the making of certain kinds of rights-claims).[61] In strong plural orders, law is genuinely "bottom up," grounded in a group's collective consciousness of right and wrong; to use Robert Cover's terminology, through their "jurisgenetic" impulses communities create law as a "bridge" which links normative commitments, historical experiences, and collective narratives to what could, should, or might be. States (or empires), in turn, are not jurisgenetic; they are "jurispathic"—they block or kill these multiple normative orders, imposing authority through judicial violence. As Cover explains:

> Modern apologists for the jurispathic function of courts usually state the problem not as one of *too much* law, but as one of *unclear* law. The supreme tribunal removes uncertainty, lack of clarity, and difference of opinion about what the law is. This statist formation is either begging the question or misleading. To state, as I have done, that the problem is of too much law is to acknowledge the nomic integrity of each of the communities that have generated principles and precepts. It is to posit that *each* "community of interpretation" that has achieved "law" has its own *nomos*—narratives, experiences, and visions to which the norm articulated is the right response. And it is to recognize that different interpretive communities will almost certainly exist and will generate distinctive responses to any normative problem of substantial complexity.[62]

The problems that "strong" legal pluralism entails are legion, both in the work it can be made to do as a theoretical category and in structuring judicial practice.[63] But Cover's central insight is largely useful: the idea that there are "too many" sources of law in a given society is a good diagnosis of the situation in Roman Egypt. This abundance of law—and the idea that a magistrate's job was to be "jurispathic"—is relevant in two senses in Roman Egypt. First, because although there was a formally nested and ranked system of citizenships, in terms of legal practice people within each category frequently disagreed with one another about these rules and asked outside authorities to intervene, not only to "clarify" each community's rules, but also to overturn them. This is the problem that I defined earlier as "distance" and "difference." Second, the formal structure of Roman governance set up a system which was tolerant of a broad degree of narrative freedom, provided only that certain signaling words were used within the narrative to identify the nub of the complaint. In this limited but critical sense, the Roman government allowed for "strong" pluralism. This is the problem I defined earlier as that of writing, and of authorized writing in particular. Both of these features of Roman justice in fact undermined the formal commitment of the legal system to weak pluralism, producing an advantageous system for petitioners.

To throw this matter into greater relief, it is worth looking at two judicial decisions and their contexts before addressing specifically how the Roman legal system handled violence. The decisions both are cited in the lengthy petition of the late second century A.D., the "Petition of Dionysia." In the following chapter Dionysia will take center stage along with a few other interesting petitioners, but for now it will suffice to note that her petition (one of the longest extant) originates as the result of a petition by her father, in which he accuses her of using violence against him. As a result, he hopes to be able to cause her to divorce her husband, and reintegrate her into his house. He claims, furthermore, that he is allowed to do this on the basis of the "Law of the Egyptians." As a response, Dionysia produced an account of their quarrels, and cited a number of precedents that, she claimed, denied that the law gave her father the power to do this. Two of these citations are relevant to the question of pluralism. They are separated by roughly forty-five years:

> ἐξ ὑπομ[νηματισ]μῶν Πακωνίου Φήλικος ἐπιστρατήγου. (ἔτους) ιη θεοῦ Ἀδριανοῦ, Φαῶφι ιζ, ẹṿ τῇ παρὰ ἄνω Σεβεννύτου, ἐπὶ τῶν κατὰ Φλạụή̣σ̣ι̣ος Ἀμμούνιος ἐπὶ παρούσῃ Ταẹịχήκει θυγατρὶ αὐτοῦ πρὸς Ἥρωνα Πεταήσιος. Ἰσίδωρος ῥήτωρ ὑπὲρ Φλαυήσιος εἶπεν, τ̣ὸ̣ν οὖν ạἰτ̣ι̣ώ̣μενον ἀποσπάσαι βουλόμενον τ[ὴ]ν θυγατέρα αὐτοῦ συνοικοῦσαν τῷ ἀντιδίκῳ δεδικάσθαι ὑπογύως πρὸς αὐτὸν ἐπὶ τοῦ ẹ̣[πι]σ̣τ̣ρ̣ạτ̣ήγου καὶ ὑπερτεθεῖσθαι τὴν δίκην ὑμῖν ἵνα ἀναγνωσθῇ ὁ τῶν Αἰγυπτίω[ν νό]μος. Σεουήρου καὶ Ἡλιοδώρου ῥητόρων ἀποκριναμένων Τειτιανὸν τὸν ἡγεμονεύσαντα ὁμοίας ὑποθέσεως ἀκούσαντα [ἐξ] Αἰγυπτιακῶν προσώπων μὴ ἠκολουθηκέναι τῇ τοῦ νόμου ἀπανθρωπίạ ἀλλὰ τ[ῇ] ἐπι[νοί]ạ τῆς παιδός, εἰ βούλεται παρὰ τ[ῷ ἀνδρὶ] μένειν, Πακώνιος Φῆλιξ· ἀναγνωσθήτω ὁ ν[ό]μ[ος. ἀ]ναγνωσθέντος Πακώνιος [Φῆ]λιξ· ἀνάγνωτε καὶ τὸν Τειτιανοῦ ὑπομ[ν]ηματισμόν. Σεουήρου ῥήτορος ἀναγν[όντος], ἐπὶ τοῦ ̣ιβ (ἔτους) Ἀ[δρια]νοῦ Καίσαρος τοῦ κυρίου, Παῦν[ι] ̣η, Πακώνιος Φῆλιξ· καθὼς ὁ κράτιστος Τ[ειτ]ιανὸ[ς] ἔκρινεν, πεύσονται τῆς γυναικός· κ̣ạ̣ὶ̣ ἐκέλευ[σε]ν δ̣ι̣' [ἑρ]μ̣η̣νέως αὐτὴν ἐλεγχθῆν[α]ι, τ̣ί̣ βούλεται· εἰπούσης, παρὰ τῷ ἀνδρὶ μένειν, Π[α]κώνιος Φῆλιξ ἐκέλευσεν ὑπομνηματι[σ]θῆναι.
>
> ἐξ ὑπομνηματισμῶν Οὐμβρί[ου] δικαιοδότου. (ἔτους) ϛ Δομιτιανοῦ Φαμεν[ὼθ.] Διδύμη ἧς ἔκδικος ὁ ἀνὴρ Ἀπολλώνιος πρὸς Σαβεῖνον τὸν καὶ Κάσιον, ἐκ τῶν ῥηθέντων· Σαραπίων· μετ' ἄλλα τὰ πρόσωπα Αἰγ[ύ]πτια ὄ̣ν̣τ̣ạ παρ' οἷς ἄκρατός ἐστιν ἡ τῶν ν[ό]μων ἀποτομ̣[ί]α· διοριζόμενος γάρ σοι λέγω [ὅ]τι Ạἰ̣γ[ύ]π̣τ̣ι̣οι οὐ μόνον τοῦ

ἀφελέσθαι τὰς [θυγατ]έρ[ας ὧ]ν ἔδωκαν ἐξουσίαν, ἔχουσιν δὲ καὶ ὧν ἐὰν κ̣α̣ὶ̣ ἴδια κτήσωνται μεθ' ἕτερα· Ο[ὔ]μβρι[ο]ς Σ̣α̣βείνῳ̣· εἰ ἔφθακας ἅπαξ προῖκα δ[οὺς τῇ θυγ]ατρί σου, ἀποκατάστησον. Σαβεῖνο[ς· τ]οῦτον μα̣..... α̣ἴ̣τοῦμαι. Οὔμβριος· τῇ θυγατρ[ὶ] δ̣ή̣. Σαβεῖνος· τούτῳ τῷ ἀνδρὶ οὐθὲν [προσ]ή̣κ̣[ει] συνεῖναι. Οὔμβριος· χεῖρόν ἐστι ἀνδρὸς ἀφαι[ρεῖσθαι]

From the *commentarii* of Paconius Felix, *epistrategos*. (Year) 18 of the divine Hadrian, Phaophi 17. In the upper division of the Sebennyte nome, in the case of Phlauesis son of Ammounis in the presence of his daughter, Taeichekis, against Heron son of Petaesis. Isidorus the advocate spoke on behalf of Phlauesis, saying that the man in question wishes to take away his daughter who lives with the defendant. Recently his case was judged at the court of the *epistrategos*, and the case was deferred so that the law of the Egyptians might be read. Severus and Heliodoros, the (opposing) advocates, replied that Titianus the former prefect heard a similar case concerning Egyptians, and he decided not in accordance with the inhumanity of the law, but according to the decision of the daughter, whether she wished to remain with her husband. Paconius Felix said, "Let the law (of the Egyptians) be read out." When it was read, Paconius Felix said, "Read out also the *commentarii* of Titianus." Severus the advocate read out, "(Year) 12 of Hadrian, Caesar, our lord, Pauni 8, etc." Paconius Felix said, "As his highness Titianus has decided, they will ask the woman." And he ordered her to be asked through a translator what she wanted. She replied, to remain with her husband. Paconius Felix ordered the decision to be recorded. (A.D. 133)

From the *commentarii* of Umbrius, *iuridicus*. Year 6 of Domitian, ? Phamenoth. Didyme, whose advocate was her husband, Apollonius, against Sabeinos also called Kasios. From the transcript. Sarapion (among other things) said: "The parties are Egyptians, and the severity of the law is untempered for them. I declare to you that Egyptians not only have the power to take back from their daughters what they gave (in marriage), but also (they have power over) whatever the daughters acquired for themselves. After other things, Umbrius said to Sabeinos: "If you have already given your daughter

> a dowry at one time, restore it." Sabeinos said, "this" . . . Umbrius: "Indeed: to your daughter!" Sabeinos: "She should not be with this man." Umbrius: "It is worse for her to be taken from her husband." (A.D. 87)[64]

Multiple layers of legal behavior are reflected in Dionysia's complaint, and I will come to these later. For current purposes, the legal decisions within Dionysia's petition (itself composed in A.D. 187) provide firsthand evidence that magistrates adjudicating disputes had access to a number of sources of law. These sources included Egyptian law, decisions of previous magistrates, and whatever knowledge of imperial law they kept in their heads. In addition, these sources of law were available not only to adjudicating magistrates, but to individual litigants.[65] Presumably they were not *widely* available, and scholars tend to assume that Dionysia had some level of legal assistance in gathering these decisions together and presenting them.[66] But that they were available at all indicates that there was in fact a relationship between positive, statutory law and legal practice. It is the details of this relationship, however, that are particularly interesting, especially in terms of the ways that this mass of law was understood by judges. In this particular case, a series of judges seems to have looked at and understood the Egyptian law, and come to the conclusion that they had a substantial disdain for it. When pressed to pit moral principles against the technical law of the land, they preferred, in this case, to judge according to principles, and then also in accordance with precedent.[67]

Provincial officials would have sought to act within the rules; in fact, at the highest levels some had handpicked staff members with legal expertise.[68] At the same time, the running of a province—and especially the administration of justice—was a complex and delicate affair. Rules were important, but so were pragmatic solutions to problems. There may be a helpful analogue found in the legal-anthropological writings on American small-claims courts. In a situation in which the proper legal solution could have been particularly harsh (as it is confessed to be in the two decisions quoted above), officials might try to avoid enforcing the law in order to prevent what they perceive to be a more substantial social rupture. In the American system this can be done by issuing a number of continuances in the hope that the problem will eventually resolve itself without legal intervention; judges can likewise try to force parties to mediation to produce a compromise solution which, as a result, will keep the legal system out of people's personal relationships.[69] In the case of the citations in Dionysia's complaint, neither of these two options was possible—both parties insisted on a legal solution to the problem at hand—but the judges in previous cases took umbrage at the "severity" of the laws, and tried to work out a solution that was ethically palatable.

As I stated in Chapter 2, pluralism, at least within an empire, was in some way predicated on the thinking that particular systems of local ordering or local law were inferior or distasteful. And petitioners—in this case young women—agreed, and asked that the Roman governors who had previously granted the right of a community to organize itself (through "Egyptian law") revisit the consequences of this decision, and evaluate their cases on the basis of precedents, as well as moral judgment. The precedents did not accord with "the law," and thus it is fair to say that, in this case, there was too much law (contradictory law), and that the judges were being asked to be jurispathic.[70] What was a catastrophe for Cover turns out, on this reading, to be an advantage for at least some petitioners.

One reason for this is that, modern ideological sensibilities aside, pluralism can be an ugly and brutal thing. This is especially so in the case of conflict, and in the case of violence. Petitioners who know their assailants, who have multiple, complex, and overlapping ties with them, often are clear that having their case end up *back* in their own community is the last thing they want—at least without the stamp of a powerful third party to guide the proceedings. Some complain that they have been stymied from the beginning, kept from courts by their opponents—in one case cited above, for instance, the petitioner claimed that a complaint about violence was "quashed" (ἀθετηθῆναι).[71] Neighbors and fellow villagers can be counted on to lie; a tantalizing glimpse of this process is evidence from an ostrakon from the eastern desert:

> Λονγῖνος Νομερίωι τῶι τιμιωτάτωι φιλτάτωι καὶ ἀδελφῶι πλῖστα χαίρειν καὶ διὰ παντὸς ὑγιαίνειν. λαβὼν τὸ ὄστρακον παρὰ τοῦ σμαραγδαρίου τοῦτο ἐν ῷ̣ μοι γράφις κεχρῆσθα̣ι̣ Κοδράτῳ̣ (δραχμὰς) ξ εἰς οἶκον ὁμοῦ πίν̣ο̣ν̣τ̣ε̣ς, ε̣ὐθέως ἔγραψα καὶ ἔπεμψά σοι ἀντιφώνησιν διὰ τῶν καμηλιτῶν τῶν μετὰ τῶν κιβαρίων ἀναβεβηκότων. ἐποιήσαμεν τοὺς ἄρτους σου καὶ ἀνεκάλυψας κεράμιον καὶ ἐπίνομεν ἐπ' ἄριστον ἐγὼ <καὶ> σὺ αὐτός. εἰ ἐν ἐκείνῃ τῇ ἡμέρᾳ ἦν, γράψον μοι. εἰ δὲ εἰς λόγον δελφακίων πάλι<ν> γράψον καὶ ἀνάμνησόν μοι. ἐγὼ ἕτοιμός εἰμι τοῦ μαρτυρῆσαι, μόνον ποίωι χρόνῳ καὶ εἰς τίνα{ν} τρόπον ἔλαθε. γράψον ἵνα οἱ λόγοι συνφωνήσωσιν, μὴ σὺ εἴπῃς ὅτι ἐν ἐκίνῳ τῶι χρόνῳ ἔλαβες, καὶ ἐγὼ ἄλλῳ. πότερον εἰ ἔλαβε πρὶν ἀνενέγκῃς Ἡραεὶν ὧδε ἢ{ι}

> οὔσης αὐτῆς ἢ μετὰ τὸ καταβῆναι αὐτήν ο.. εἰς ταχὺ καὶ μὴ πολλοὺς λόγους ἀλλὰ πρὸς ἃ λελάληκες αὐτ[ῷ.] ἀσπάζου Ἡραεὶν καὶ Ἀβάσκαντον. δὸς αὐτῶι δέσμην κράμβης.
>
> Longinus to Numerius, his most honored brother, many greetings, and wishes that you are well in everything. Having received this letter of yours from the emerald-worker in which you write that you lent to Quadratus 60 drachmas when we were drinking in your house, I immediately wrote you back and sent you a reply through the camel-drivers who have come up bringing food. We made bread and you and I both finished off a *keramion* (of wine)—if it was that day, write to me. Also write and remind me if it was the day of the accounting for the pigs. I am ready to testify for you, except that I have forgotten at what time and in what way. Write to me so that our accounts agree, lest you say that you got it at that time and I say at another time. Also, whether he (Quadratus) got it before you brought Herais, that is, whether she was here or after she went away . . . quickly and without a lot of words, but just what you've said to him. Greet Herais and Abaskantos. Give him a head of cabbage.[72]

Aside from lying and subverting the legal process, neighbors use violence. They are likely to use more violence, and more effective violence, than magistrates. This is the problem in the first place, and a good reason to doubt the claim that petitioners wanted to split the difference and be reintegrated within the very structures that caused them harm to begin with.

There is another thing to be learned from the citations in Dionysia's petition: it is important to be wary of any explanatory model that sees magistrates as rigid, algorithmic processors of facts and data into straightforward legal categories, for these categories (and their relationship to the meta-categories) are often the object of contest in the first place. Magistrates could use a combination of precedent, local law, Roman law, and personal ethics to decide a case. Magistrates were ultimately responsible to imperial authorities for their decisions. At the same time, it is important not to imagine that any given official acted as a little Pliny, scrupulously sending letters of inquiry to the emperor on minor points of detail. Sometimes they would consult imperial authorities, as petitioners themselves sometimes did when dissatisfied with a judgment.[73] At other times, unlike Pliny's rhetorical presentation, the authorities in Egypt functioned according to a messier, more diffuse system.

The legal decisions quoted in Dionysia's petition highlight an important cluster of problems entailed in studying legal behavior in Egypt. With something as complex as her petition, we can see with much greater resolution than in a papyrus of fifteen lines the many different interests that need to be taken into account when presenting a model of legal behavior or knowledge. We should be wary about judging the motives or knowledge of a petitioner on the basis of little or nothing. Petitioners do not always present a case as careful and as well-researched as Dionysia's, but there is ample evidence that petitioners did know something about the law when they presented their requests to authorities, as Katzoff has made clear.[74]

Still, the legal issues at the heart of Dionysia's complaint concern marriage, not violence (though violence was also involved). Because marriage relationships were central to the distribution of property (in addition to being central to community harmony, and thus to the extraction of resources from those communities) they were the target of much imperial intervention and juristic thinking. Violence, however, is juristically far less interesting, and intentional harms have never been a major engine for transformative projects in legal theory.[75] Presumably, like pornography in American obscenity law, a judge was just supposed to know it when he saw it. But this failure of the legal system to theorize violence had advantages, too. As a corollary to the idea that there was "too much law" in some areas, in others there was very little at all—it was not abundantly self-contradictory, but rather open-textured and amorphous. So far as the making of legal decisions is concerned, this amounts to basically the same thing.

The basic definitions of violence in juristic law were relatively easy to understand. Anyone capable of "bad intent" (*dolus*) was capable of inflicting violence; anyone capable of inflicting it was also capable of suffering it (*qui iniuriam pati possunt, et facere posse*: 47.10.3, Ulpian, *ad Edictum* 56). The right to bring suit, however, was more limited. That right was given primarily to heads of households, who were given the right to sue for *iniuria* done either to themselves or to members of their family under their control.[76] As stated above, injuries were priced by the parties, unless the violence was considered aggravated (*atrox*). In this case, the person who estimated the damages changed.[77] As to the scope of violence, Roman tradition appears to have been comfortable with a broader definition of the action. Under Roman law, the scope of what was considered violence was largely the same as what was considered violence in the papyri—namely, violence against the person and his (or her) reputation. There are of course some differences: there was no praetor in Egypt, so what was at stake in defining violence as "aggravated" (*atrox*, *anekestos*) is less clear; children, unless they were Roman citizens, were not under the power of their fathers, and accordingly the scope of who could petition on whose behalf was wider. Family members petition on each other's behalf, as do employers in some cases. One personal letter shows two members of the same injured group petitioning at the same time, though such a strategy might be officially frowned upon.[78] These rules, furthermore, are not strikingly dissimilar to the rules concerning violence in the case of Alexandrian laws recorded on the famous third-century B.C. *Dikaiomata* papyrus.[79]

Briefly, then, the rules on violence would have allowed, in a way not dissimilar to the decisions cited in Dionysia's petition, a broad array of factors both legal and (formally) nonlegal to be brought to bear by petitioners and magistrates alike—provided, of course, that the petitioner was to be counted by the magistrate as a full and capable person (the problem discussed in the previous two chapters). Nor is it misleading to use the Roman juristic tradition here. Under the system in Egypt from Augustus through late antiquity, the law simply declared that people would be given actions in certain cases, not what was to count as being contained within each category. An edict of the prefect lists cases that the prefect will hear:

> ὁ ἡγεμ̣ὼν διαγνώσετα̣ι περὶ φόνου, περὶ λ̣ῃστειῶν, περὶ φαρμακείας, περὶ πλαγιαρίας, περὶ ἀπελατῶν, περὶ βίας σὺν ὅπλοις γεγενημένης, π(ερὶ) πλαστογραφίας, καὶ ῥ̣ᾳδιουργίας, [π(ερὶ) ἀ]ν̣-ῃ̣ρημένων [δι]αθ̣ηκῶν
>
> π(ερὶ) ὕβρεως ἀνηκέστου π(ερὶ) ὧ̣ν ἐ̣ὰν μέμφωνται ο[ἱ] ἐλ̣ε̣υ̣θερώσαντες ἀπελευθέρους ἢ γονεῖς πα̣ῖ̣δ(ας). οἱ λοιποὶ οὐκ ἄλλως ὑπ' ἐμοῦ ἀκουσθήσονται εἰ μὴ ἐπικαλεσάμενοι κα̣ὶ̣ παραβό̣λ̣ιον θέντες τὸ τ̣έ̣[ταρτον] μέρος ἐκ τιμήμ̣α[τος περὶ(?)] ο̣ὗ ἐδ̣ικάσθῃ
>
> The prefect will hear (cases) concerning murder; concerning theft; concerning poisoning; concerning kidnapping; concerning driving off of animals; concerning *bia* done with weapons; concerning forgery and fraud; concerning cancellation of wills;
>
> concerning *atrox iniuria*; concerning things for which manumittors might blame freedmen or parents children; the remainder will not otherwise be heard by me unless those making the appeal also put

> down a payment of one quarter part of the matter which is being judged.[80]

There is no set of "tests" here for determining which facts needed to prevail to place a case in one of these categories; the definitions were worked out on a case-by-case basis by a combination of the assertions of the petitioners and the judgment of the magistrates in charge of proceedings. Far from being rigid and doctrinaire, then, the Roman legal system in Egypt and the principles that guided legal thinking were by modern standards fluid and flexible. This fluidity, however, should not be understood as an innate flaw of the provincial legal system. In contrast, it is of great advantage to the user: the flexible nature of a legal system is directly correlated with the likelihood that an individual will use it. In other words, the more flexible and vague, the higher the chance that people see the institutions as capable of having the capacity to accommodate their claims and narratives.[81] This is not to argue that all aspects of the legal system can be understood through a rational-choice model in which individuals make arithmetical calculations of risk and gain (it cannot, for reasons I outlined above). However, it is important to note that a flexible system permits a great deal of individual agency in the way in which problems are defined and magistrates approached, and provides an opportunity for individuals to try to bend the system to fit their particular problems.

* * *

This openness of the legal categories was confined in a key way: petitioners had to use particular "signaling" words to buttress their claims. This was not particularly constraining, and there are some limited occasions where one can see these strategies being played out. Specifically, there are a few cases where different versions of petitions concerning the same event have been preserved. There is one case of violence in which I have been able to find evidence of the drafting process, but there are likely to be others. Without checking the differences between the published version and the often unpublished duplicate, one cannot be sure.[82] In the second case there are successive but different petitions sent to different magistrates, and differences in the way that the claim (and its relation to law) is signaled. While having identical copies of the same document is not uncommon (due to the necessity of different parties having documentation),[83] the fact that there are versions that differ is of great import. When these are compared side by side, we can use them as evidence of the types of rhetorical and personal strategies employed by petitioners to accomplish their ends. In what follows two different complaints are investigated. In the first, a local priest of the god Soknopaios complains about the violence of another priest. He petitions first the local centurion, and then the prefect. In the second case, a woman petitions the *riparii* concerning violence done to her by her neighbors. Both a draft and a final copy of her complaint are preserved.

The first set of documents comes from Soknopaiou Nesos in A.D. 14, from a priest named Satabous. He complains that a fellow priest named Nestnephis has both assaulted him and stolen a mortar from him. One petition is to the prefect:

> [Μαγί]ωι [Μ]αξίμω[ι] [παρὰ] Σαταβο[ῦτ]ος τοῦ [Ἑρ]ιέως τῶν ἀπὸ τῆς Σεκνεπαί[ου Νήσο]υ τῆς Ἡρακλεί[δου] μερίδος [ἱερ]έων. τῆι λ [τοῦ Π]ạχὼṿ τοῦ μγ [(ἔτους)] Καίσαρος Νεστνῆφις Τεσήους [ἄλογ]ον ἀηδ[ί]αν μο[ι] στησάμενος μετὰ τῶν [παρ' αὐτοῦ] ὕβρισέṿ με καὶ [π]λείους μοι πληγὰς ἐνέτεινε[ν] ἐ[ξέλα]σίν μοι νοησάμε[νο]ς, ἔτι δὲ καὶ βιασάμε[νο]ς [ἐλθὼν με]τὰ τῶν αὐτῶν καὶ ἑτέρων νυκτὸς λ̣ῃστρικῷ τρόπωι [... ἐκ τ]οῦ ὑπάρχοντός μοι ἐν τῆι κώμηι μυλαίου ἐξε[τό(?)]πισεν ὅλμον, ὑπὲρ ὧν καὶ ἔγκλημα κατε[χώρ]ισα Διο[νυ-] σοδώρωι. σοῦ οὖν καὶ δι' ἐκθεμάτων [ἀπα]γο[ρ]εύ[σαντος] μί[σ] γεσθα[ι τὰς] τοιαύτας ὕ[βρεις] καὶ [πληγάς], ἀ[ξιῶ δικ]αιοδο[τη-] θῆναι, ὅπως ἐγὼ [τυγχά]νω ἀν[τει]λημμένος, ὁ δ' ἐγκαλούμενος [πρ]ὸς ἑτέρων ἐπίστασιν τύχηι ὧν προσήκει. εὐτύχει.

> To Magius Maximus,
> From Satabous son of Herieus, one of the priests from Soknopaiou Nesos in the division of Herakleides. On the 30th of Pachon of the 43rd year of Caesar Nestnephis son of Teses did irrational violence to me along with those associated with him. He did violence to me, laying many blows upon me with the intention of driving me off. Even though he was overpowered, he came with his family and some others at night in the manner of thieves . . . they removed the mortar from the mill that I have in the town. Concerning these things I have also filed a complaint with Dionysodoros. Since you have prohibited through edicts the mixing of such violence and beatings, I ask that you administer justice so that I may be assisted and the accused and may get what he deserves as a deterrent to others. Farewell.[84]

The other petition is to the centurion:

> [Λ]οκρητίω[ι ἑκατοντάρχηι παρὰ Σαταβ]οῦτος τοῦ [Ἑριέως νεωτέρου τῶν ἀπὸ κώμης Σοκο]νοπαίου Ν[ήσου τῆς Ἡρακλείδου μερίδος. ὑπά]ρχει μοι ἐ[ν τ]ῆι Σοκον[οπαίου Νήσωι οἰκί]α, ἥτις ἦν μύλαιον, ἐν̣ ἧι̣ ὅ̣λ̣[μον αὐτὸς ἐπι]κρατῶ, ἔτι [.]λαι τ[οῖ]ς π[ε]ρὶ ἐμὲ [... .... ἀ]κολούθως τινί ποτ[ε] λόγῳ Ν[εσθνῆφι]ς Τεσήους ἱερεὺς τῶν ἀπὸ τῆς [αὐτῆς Νήσο]υ ἐπιβαλὼν λῃστρ[ικῷ τρόπῳ νυκτὶ τῆι φ]ε-ρούσηι εἰς τὴν α το[ῦ Π]αῦνι τοῦ [μγ (ἔτους) Καίσα]ρος ἐπὶ τὸν σημαινόμενον ὅλμον [ἐλθὼν με]τὰ πολυχειρίας ἀπη[ν]έγκατο. ὧι [καὶ ἐνεκάλ]εσα ἐπὶ Διοφάντου τοῦ διαδεχομένου [Διονυσόδω]ρον τὸν στρατηγὸν Ἀ[ρσι(νοίτου) δι'] ὑπο[μνήματος,] ἐφ' οὗ καὶ δικαιολογηθ[έν]των ἡ[μῶν κατ]ε[κ]ρίθη ὁ ἐγκαλο[ύμε]νο[ς ἀπ]ο-κατα[στῆσαι] τὸν ὅλμον. τούτου δὲ μὴ βουλομέ[νου ἀποκα]ταστῆσαί μοι [τοῦτον,] ἀλλὰ καὶ [π]ρὸ[ς πάντα ὕβρε]ις εἴς με καὶ τοὺς παρ' [ἐμ]οῦ ὄ[ντα]ς [οὐ δεούσα]ς συντελουμένου οὐ μόνον, ἀλλὰ καὶ [ἐν τῇ κώμ]ῃ πληγὰς ἐπιφέρει μ̣ο̣ι, οὐ δυνάμ̣ε[νος ὑποφέ]ρειν τὰς αἰκίας ἀδικίας κινδ[υ]νεύ[ων τὴν ἐμὴν οἰκί]αν προλιπεῖν τυγχαν[..] ...[- ca.13 - ἀ]ξίαν [- ca.10 - ἀναφ]όρι[ον]
>
> To Lucretius the centurion,
> From Satabous, son of Hericus, the younger, one of those from the town of Soknopaiou Nesos in the division of Herakleides. In Soknopaiou Nesos I have a house which was a mill, in which I have a mortar, still . . . to those around me . . . (I don't know) for what particular reason Nestnephis, son of Teses, a priest, one of those from this same Soknopaiou Nesos, came upon it in the manner of thieves on the night before the 1st of Pauni of the 43rd year of Caesar. He went to the mortar in question and with the help of many others took it away. For this reason I accused him in a petition before Diophantes who was acting on behalf of Dionysodoros as the *strategos* of the Arsinoite nome, and concerning this we prevailed in court and the accused was ordered to return the mortar. But he is unwilling to return it to me, and instead always directs inappropriate violence against me and my associates; not only this, but also he beats me up in the town. Since I cannot tolerate his abusive injustices and since I am in danger of having to leave my home . . . fitting . . . copy.[85]

While the date of the attack is clear, there is not an exact date for either petition. SB I 5235 comes somewhat before SB I 5238, since in 5235 Satabous mentions having petitioned the *strategos*, while in 5238 he refers to the *strategos*' decision. It is an unfortunate limitation of the evidence that neither of the two is a petition of first instance.

In the first of the two documents the focus is unmistakably on Nestnephis' violent actions. Satabous does not present the prefect with the background to the story, but moves quickly to describing the violence itself, and emphasizing that it was senseless and inappropriate (ἄλογον ἀηδίαν). Whether this particular construction has a legal valence is unclear: these words appear in other petitions as well,[86] but are not exclusively legal terms—ἀηδία occurs in a number of personal letters,[87] and may refer just to generalized nastiness or unpleasantness, but could also euphemistically refer to violence as well. Irrespective of whether this phrase has a legal meaning, Satabous's complaint immediately moves to terms that do—*hybris*, *plegai*, and the *exelasis* that Nestnephis was planning. All of these terms correspond to specific legal categories. Satabous moves on to call the *exelasis bia*, and inserts into his complaint that the actions were done at night (possibly an aggravating factor),[88] and in a "thievish fashion"—a common piece of legal boilerplate. The complaint then turns to the most specific act of financial damage, the theft of the mortar. Satabous indicates that he has filed a claim already with Dionysodorus, whose station he does not mention. From this we may perhaps infer that the content of the complaint was less important in Satabous' appeal to the prefect than simply the fact of showing that he has taken pains to work out the problem in a legal fashion. As further emphasis of his attention to legal detail, Satabous reminds the prefect that such behavior is prohibited by edicts (*ekthemata*). The mention of an edict that prohibits "mixing together such *hybreis* and *plegai*" (whatever that means) is placed within a genitive absolute construction, while the main clause of the sentence is the request for justice proper. Satabous, in other words, uses an appeal to a specific statute as a justification for his request. He requests that justice be done, but also appeals to a broader legal principle—that Nestnephis ought to be punished not only for what he has done in this particular case, but also in other instances. This construction (ἐπίστασιν ἑτέρων or ἐπίστασιν ἄλλων) is relatively common in Ptolemaic petitions,[89] but also fits well within the broader context of the complaint.

In his petition to the centurion, the conflict is described differently. Since there is no independent date for this document, it is impossible to say how much time has elapsed between this petition and the previous one, but the conflict has developed.[90] Between the complaint to the prefect and that to the centurion, another petition has been filed, this one with the assistant to the *strategos*, Diophantes. The result of that petition was a decision compelling Nestnephis to restore the mortar to Satabous, a decision which Nestnephis ignored. The centurion, Lucretius, was an individual of much more local significance than the prefect.[91] That he was also known personally to Satabous can be deduced from other documents in his dossier: Lucretius, along with the *strategos* and the *basilikos grammateus*, had been appointed by the prefect to judge a case involving Satabous three years earlier (A.D. 11).[92] In this presentation, Satabous changes the priorities of his complaint somewhat. Rather than focusing on the violence that took place on the night in question, Satabous describes the theft (the outstanding issue), and relegates the violence to the end of the petition. In contrast to the earlier document, in this case the violence is presented as ongoing and directed against both himself and members of his family. The violence in this document is presented as a result of ignoring the decision of the *strategos*. In this respect, the violence here should be understood as a *local* complaint—an action that undermines the respect for law and order that ensures the successful running of the village on a day-to-day basis. Unlike the complaint to the prefect, in this complaint Satabous does not need to appeal to a statute; simply disobeying those in charge is more than sufficient to justify legal action. Furthermore, this second petition makes use of the language of exasperation: Nestnephis "not only" uses outrageous *hybreis* against Satabous and his family, "but also beats me up in the village." The construction that signals this exasperation, οὐ μόνον . . . ἀλλὰ καὶ is a relatively colloquial, indignant phrasing with no substantive legal import, but wholly consistent with the tone of this appeal.

On the whole, these two petitions use different strategies. The complaint to the local official includes background information, emphasizes public humiliations (Nestnephis assaulting him in the village), offenses to Satabous' family, and an out-of-control assailant who threatens to disrupt the harmony of the village. The complaint to the prefect frontloads the legal language, provides no background, and is an assertion of rights under the law. This earlier complaint also makes use of much more legal language, and justifies itself by reference to the prefect's decrees rather than a larger set of (self-evident) injustices. These narrative choices cannot be accidental, but instead are related to broader strategies for approaching government officials. That these choices can be made in the first place, however, is a prime indicator of how savvy petitioners could be with their complaints. Petitions must not be read as form letters drafted mechanically and sent off to whichever offical was available. They are conscious and calculated attempts to frame individual complaints in legal language, and petitioners chose the language they used with care.

The process through which these decisions were made can be seen by comparing two drafts of a single petition concerning a violent incident in fourth-century Hermopolis. The documents (*P.Cair.* inv.10269 and 10270) were originally published by Goodspeed as a single text (*P.Cair.Goodsp.* 15 [A.D. 362]), but there are a few key differences in the texts. According to Goodspeed, both documents were written by the same scribe. The substance of the complaint is clear from both copies: Aurelia Eus charges that a man named Isakis—along with a number of his female relatives—had attacked her in her home. Bearing the brunt of the violence, however, were two other women, one named Sophia and one named Taesis. Taesis was pregnant, and miscarried as a result of the attack;[93] Sophia had something stolen from her. Eus also claims that the attackers destroyed a newly constructed wall that she had put up in her house, all in an effort to drive her out of the village—not an uncommon complaint, but different from other complaints in that she additionally claims that the attackers had successfully driven her husband and children from the village as well.

It is not entirely clear which of these documents is the draft: inv. 10269 has a fuller and more internally coherent account of the violent encounter, but some of the minor differences between 10269 and 10270 would seem to indicate that 10270 is the more polished version: thus grammatical errors in lines 7 and 10 of 10269 are corrected in 10270, but 10270 also has a grammatical error in line 5, and the narrative of the violence is rife with grammatical inconsistencies. Also, 10270 has an address on the verso, though it is not very well preserved. The case against 10270 being the final version is that the violence described is not entirely clear. While we cannot reconstruct the archaeological context for these documents, it is most likely that they were found in the same place, and that they are both private copies. It is likewise possible that they are both drafts and that another version was the one sent out. The best we can do is look at the internal logic of the narrative to determine which is the more polished copy, and in this respect 10269 is more so.

Both the published and the reconstructed texts are produced below. The differences between the two have been underlined:

P.Cair.Goodsp. 15, inv. 10269

Ὑπατείας Μαμερτίου καὶ Εὐουιτ'ταυ τῶν λαμπροτάτων.

Αὐρηλίοις Νίλῳ Γενναδίῳ καὶ Θεοδώρῳ Κωμασίῳ ῥιπαρίοις νομοῦ Ἑρμοπολίτου,
παρὰ Αὐρηλίας Εὐτὸς Φ[ί]βιο[ς ἀ]πὸ ἐποίκου Παπλώου τοῦ αὐτοῦ Ἑρμοπολείτου νομοῦ· τὰ τετολμημένα
εἰς ἐμὲ ἐν τοιαύτῃ πρ[υ]τα[ν]ευομένῃ εἰρήνῃ τοῦ δεσπότου [ἡ]μῶν βασιλέως Φλαουίου Ἰουλιανοῦ αἰωνίου
Ἀ[γο]ύστου οὐ χρὴ ἀνεκ[δί]κητα περιοφθῆναι. ἐπὶ τοίνυν κέκτημαι ἔπαυλιν κατ᾽ ἔγραφον ἀσφάλειαν
ἐπὶ τῆς αὐτῆς κώμης [πρ]ὸ ι̅ϛ̅ ἐνιαυτῶν καὶ ἐκ βορρᾶ τῆς αὐτῆς ἐπαύλεως αἰώνημαι ψιλὸν τόπον
σὺν ἐνόντι φρέατος παρὰ Τασοῦτος μητὴρ Ταυρίνου [ἐ]πὶ τοῦ αὐτοῦ χρόνου, καὶ τῆς ἐπαύλεως καὶ τοῦ
ψιλοῦ τόπου ἔσχον νομὴν [ἐ]πὶ τοῦ αὐτοῦ χρόνου ἅμα τε͂ς πράσεσι, τὴν οἰκοδομὴν πεποίημαι τοῦ ψιλοῦ
τόπου καὶ τοῦ λάκκου κεχωσμένου τὴν ἀναβολὴν πεποίημαι καὶ τὸν ποτισμὸν ἐποίουν ἀπὸ τοῦ
φρέατοις τοῖς βοεικοῖ[ς μου κ]τήσει μέχρις τοῦ παρελθόντος ἐνιαυτοῦ· καὶ πάντες γινώσκουσι
οἱ ἀπὸ τῆς κώμης τὸ τῆς [δ]εσπ[οτ]είας καὶ τὸ τῆς νομῆς. νῦν δὲ ἠρξάμην τὴν οἰκοδομὴν ποιήσασθαι
τοῦ πεπτωκότος τοίχου. οὐκ οἶδ᾽ ὅπως Ἴσακις Ἀμμωνίωνος καὶ ἡ αὐτοῦ ἀδελφὴ Ταπίωμις
καὶ Ἑ[λ]ένη Πανίτιος καὶ Ἑ[λ]ένη γυνὴ Πετερσῶτος καὶ
Τα[.] . . . εγ . . . ς ἐπῆλθάν μοι βυλόμενοι
τέλεόν με ἀναιλεῖν ὥσπερ ἐπαγγέλλονταί μοι καθ᾽ ἕκαστα, εἰ μὴ ἔτυχον βοήθειαν, Ταῆσιν καὶ
τὴν ταύτης ἀδελφὴν [Σ]οφείαν· τὴν μὲν Τάησιν βαρέαν οὖσαν ἐκ τῶν πληγῶν αὐτῶν ἐξέτρω-
σεν τὸ βρέφος τὴν δὲ Σοφίαν τὸ ὄνυδιν αὐτῆς ἀφήρπασαν, καὶ ν[ῦ]ν π[αρ᾽] αὐτοῖς ἐστιν· καὶ τὸν
τοῖχον κατάβαλαν τοῦ ψιλοῦ τόπου τυρρανικῷ τρόπῳ, βουλόμ[εν-]οι ἀφαρπάσαι παρ᾽ ἐμοῦ
τὰ οἰκόπεδα καὶ τὴν ἐν συνπτώσει οἰκείαν τῆς μητρός μου ἔν[γισ-]τα τῆς ἐπαύλεως ἔχουσα
μετὰ χεῖρας τὰς πράσις. καὶ ἐφανέρωσα τῇ μονῇ καὶ τῷ βοηθῷ [το]ῦ πραιποσίτου. θαρρῶν
ὁ αὐτὸς Ἴσακις τοῖς χρήμασι αὐτοῦ καὶ τοῦ πλούτου βούλεταί μ[α]ι ἐξελάσαι ἀπὸ τῆς κώμης

ὥσπερ τὸν πατέραν τῶν πεδίων μου ἐφυγάδευσεν καὶ νῦν ἐν ἀλλοδαπε͂ς τὴν διατριβὴν
ποιούμενος, σήμερον δὲ ὑπὲρ ἀρουρῶν πεντήκοντα ἀβροχίσ̣[τ]ου τελῶ. ἐξοφθαλμιάσας
ὁ ἐνγεγραμμένος τοῖς ἐμοῖς καμάτοις ὥσπερ πολλοὺς .[. . .].[. . .] ἀπὸ τῆς κ̣ώμης διὰ τὴν τῶν
χρημάτων στῆνος· ὅθεν μὴ δυναμένη ἀφησυχά̣ζ̣ε̣ιν τρό[πῳ μηδενὶ] ἠπίχθ[ην] ἐπιδοῦναι
τῇ ὑμῶν εὐσεβ̣είᾳ̣ [τάδε τὰ βίβ]λια ἀξιοῦσα τ . . . [c.13] φροντίδι
τὴν [.] .. λύειν τῶν [.] ε [c.12] πευτω̣ν ο [c.22] ..εν τοις
[c.28] α [c.30] .. εὐτυχεῖται

Inv. 10270 (the draft?)

Ὑπατείας Μαμερτίου καὶ Εὐουιτ'ταυ τῶν λαμπροτάτων.
Αὐρηλίοις Νίλῳ Γενναδίῳ καὶ Θεοδώρῳ Κωμασίῳ ῥιπαρίοις νομοῦ Ἑρμοπολίτου,
παρὰ Αὐρηλίας Εὐτὸς Φ[ί]βιο[ς ἀ]π̣ὸ̣ ἐποίκου Παπλώου τοῦ αὐτοῦ Ἑρμοπολείτου·
τὰ τετολμημένα εἰς ἐμὲ [ἐ]ν̣ [το]ιαύ̣τ̣η̣ πρυτανευομένῃ εἰρήνῃ τοῦ δ̣[ε]σπότου
ἡμῶν βασιλέως αἰωνίου Ἀ[γο]ύστου οὐ χρὴ ἀν̣εκ[δί]κητα περιοφθῆναι. ἐπὶ τοίνυν
κέκτημαι ἔπαυλιν κατε[γ]ρ̣[ά]φην ἀσφάλειαν ἐπὶ τῆς αὐτῆς κ[ώ]μης πρὸ ις̣ ἐνι-
αυτῶν καὶ ἐκ βορρᾶ τῆς αὐτ̣ῆς ἐπαύλεως αἰώνημαι ψιλὸν τ[ό]π̣ον σὺν τῷ̣ ἐνόντι
λάκκῳ παρὰ Τασοῦτος μητὴρ Ταυρίνου ἐπὶ τοῦ αὐτοῦ χρόνου, καὶ τῆς ἐπαύλεως καὶ
τοῦ ψιλοῦ τόπου ἔσχον νομὴν ἐπὶ τοῦ αὐτοῦ χρόνου ἅ̣μα τε͂ς πράσεσι, τὴν οἰκο-
δομὴν πεποίημαι τοῦ ψ̣ι̣λ̣ο̣ῦ̣ τ̣ό̣που καὶ τοῦ λάκκου κεχωσμένου τὴν ἀναβολὴν
πεποίημαι καὶ τὸν ποτισ̣[μὸν ἐπο]ί[ο]υν ἀπὸ τοῦ λάκκου τοῖς βοεικοῖς μου κτήσι

μέχρι τοῦ παρελθόντος ἐ[νια]υτο[ῦ]· καὶ πάντ̣ες γινώσκουσι [ο]ἱ ἀπὸ
τῆς κώμης
τὸ τῆς δ̣ε̣σποτείας καὶ νομῆς. τὴν(?) δὲ ἠ̣ρξάμην̣ τὴν οἰκοδομὴν π[οι-]
ιῆσ̣α̣σ̣θαι τοῦ
πεπτωκότος τοίχου. οὐκ οἰ̣δ̣' ὅπως Ἴσακις Ἀμμωνίωνος καὶ
Ταπίωμις γυνὴ
Σερήνου καὶ οἱ συγγενεῖς αὐτοῦ πάντες ἐπῆθον ἐμοὶ καὶ Τάησιν
Ὀννωφρ[ι]ο̣υ̣,
βαρέα οὖσαν καὶ ἐκτέτρωκεν τὸ βρέφος καὶ ταύτης (?) ἀδελφὴν
Σοφείαν ἀπέσπασ̣α̣ν
τ̣ὸ ὄνυδιν τῆς αὐτῆς Σοφίας, καὶ νῦν παρ' αὐτοῖς ἐστιν. καὶ τὸν
οἰκοδομηθὲν τοῖχον
κατάβαλαν τοῦ ψιλοῦ τόπου τυρρανικῷ τρόπῳ, βουλόμενοι
ἀφαρπάσ̣α̣ι̣ παρ' ἐμοῦ
[τ]ὰ οἰκόπεδα καὶ τὴν ἐν συνπτώσει οἰκείαν τῆς μητρός μου
ἔνγιστα τῆς ἐπαύλεως
ἁρπάσαι ἔχων μετὰ χεῖρας τὰς πράσις. καὶ ἐφανέρωσα τῇ μονῇ καὶ
τῷ βοηθῷ
τοῦ πρεποσίτου. θαρρῶν ὁ αὐτὸς Ἴσακις τοῖς χρήμασι αὐτοῦ καὶ τοῦ
π̣λ̣[ο]ύ̣τ̣ο̣υ̣
βούλεταί μ̣ε̣ ἐξελάσαι ἀπὸ τῆς κώμης ὥσπερ τὸν πατέραν τῶν
πεδίων μου ἐφυ-
γάδευσεν καὶ νῦν ἐν ἀλλοδαπες τὴν διατριβὴν ποιούμενος,
σήμερον δὲ ὑπὲρ ἀρουρῶ-
ν πεντήκοντα ἀβροχίσ̣[του] τ̣ελῶ. ἐξοφθαλμιάσας ὁ ἐνγεγραμμένος
τοῖς ἐ̣μ̣ο̣ῖ̣ς
καμάτοις ὥσπερ πολλ[οὺς c.8] ἀπὸ τῆς κ̣ώμης διὰ τὴν τῷ[ν χρημάτων]
σ̣τ̣ῆ̣ν̣ο̣ς·
ὅθεν μὴ [δυνα]μ̣ένη [ἀφησυχαζειν τρ]ό̣πῳ ο̣ὐ̣δ̣έ̣ν̣α̣ (?) ἠπίχθη̣ν̣
ἐπιδοῦναι
traces

Verso: λιβέλλους . . . . .ε̣ .φιας [ ] ἀπὸ Παπλώου

In the consulship of the most glorious Mamertius and Evittau.
To Aurelius Nilos son of Gennadios, and Aurelius Theodoros son of Komasios, *riparii* of the Hermopolite nome,

From Aurelia Eus daughter of Phibis from the village of Paploos in the same Hermopolite nome. The offenses committed against me in the time of such great peace commanded by our master, Emperor Flavius Julianus, eternal Augustus, must not be overlooked unavenged. I have had for 16 years according to a written guarantee a yard in the same town, and I have bought at the same time a vacant lot and the cistern in it on the north side of it from Tasous, mother of Taurinos. Along with the vacant lot and the yard I had a right of pasturage that I got at the same time as the purchase. I have put up a building on the vacant lot, have restored the collapsed embankments of the cistern, and I watered my cattle from the cistern up until this past year. And everyone from the town knows that I am the owner and have the right of pasturage. Now I have begun to build up the fallen wall.

Inv. 10269: I know not how, but Isakis, son of Ammonion, and his sister Tapiomis along with Helene, daughter of Panitis, and Helene, wife of Petersos, and Ta— attacked me, wishing to finish me off—as they would announce to me constantly. And they would have, had I not found help in Taesis and her sister, Sophia. But Taesis was pregnant, and they made her expel the fetus because of their blows; and they stole Sophia's donkey, and they have it still.

Inv. 10270: I know not how, but Isakis son of Ammonion and Tapiomis wife of Serenos and all of his relatives attacked me and Taesis, daughter of Onnophris, who was pregnant and expelled the fetus, her sister Sophia—they took the donkey of this same Sophia, and they have it still.

In a tyrannical fashion they knocked down the wall of the vacant lot, wishing to steal from me my building site and my mother's fallen house next to the yard, although I have the deeds of sale for it in my possession—I even showed them to the assistant of the *praepositus* at my official appearance. This same Isakis takes confidence in his money and his wealth, and he wishes to drive me from the town just as he drove off the father of my children, who is even now passing his time in other parts, and so now I have to pay taxes on 50 *auroras* of uninundated land. The accused scorns my distress just as

Figure 4. Cairo inv. 10270. Photo by Adam Bülow-Jakobsen. Used with permission.

> many . . . from the village through the power of money. Therefore, since I am unable to be passive about this in any way, I am driven to give to your piety this petition asking . . . your concern . . . release from . . . in the . . . Farewell.

Between these two texts we can see examples of how the language of violence is brought out in the drafting process. Some of the changes are without doubt merely cosmetic, such as correcting the itacism in the spelling of *praepositus* or calling the well a φρέαρ in one version and a λάκκος in the other. It cannot be accidental, however, that the description of the violence receives the most substantive set of changes and expansions. First, the family relationships of the

Figure 5. *P.Cair.Goodsp.* 15. Digitally reproduced with the permission of the Centre for the Study of Ancient Documents and the Photographic Archive of Papyri in the Cairo Museum, with thanks to the Andrew W. Mellon Foundation, the Cairo Museum, the Association Internationale de Papyrologues, and Dr. Adam Bülow-Jacobsen.

attackers are made clear: rather than just Isakis, Tapiomis, and "all his relatives" the final version presents four distinct individuals. The relationship between them is unclear, as all the women are identified only by their husbands' names. This does not preclude a fraternal or other sort of extended family relationship between Isakis and the husbands, and the reference to relatives (συγγενεῖς) in the draft would seem to confirm a family relationship. Naming is shaming; Eus's precision in identifying her attackers would surely have made subsequent legal follow-up less problematic.

In addition to expanding the list of offenders, inv. 10269 gives a fuller description of the circumstances of violence. Eus makes the claim that the violent incident was not an encounter where the violence was the product of a single individual's rounding up friends and family, but that the attackers have threatened her continuously (καθ' ἕκαστα). Furthermore, it is implicit in the description of the threat that it is a public declaration—ἐπαγγέλλω is connected to the language of public decree. That this is potentially inconsistent with Eus' claim that she doesn't know "for what reason" she was their chosen victim seems to have been of no concern in the drafting of 10269. Additionally, Eus is specific about the intentions of these attackers. The point, she claims, is to "make an end" of her. The attack, in inv. 10269, is described not as a simple assault, but rather one that involves aggravating circumstances. Such an "end" was averted only by the passing help of two other women, who were both victimized in turn. Most important, in the rewritten complaint Eus includes the words *plegai* and *apharpasai*—both legal terms. The insertion of these loaded words can only be seen as a move in the direction of formal legal language.

* * *

It is here that we can turn to the consequences of the provincial system's accommodation of narrative, and to the "work" of law. When petitioners wrote complaints, especially complaints about violence, they were asking magistrates (external parties) to validate (written) claims about themselves. When the petition was subscribed, it was moved into the realm of adjudication, and here the offending party would have to reply in the same legal discourse. The offender would have to articulate a different vision of how the events transpired, and defend his or her actions in legal discourse.[94] He or she would have to claim that the acts of degradation were justified or excused and to put forward a competing normative vision of the world. And here it cannot be a question of splitting the difference, for there is in fact no difference to split. To recall Cover, once again: "different interpretive communities will almost certainly exist and will generate distinctive responses to any normative problem of substantial complexity." Here, perhaps ironically, different communities now have been reduced to different individuals, and to a degree, pluralism has become atomism. But once these "distinctive responses" become irreconcilable there is only adjudication, a decision between the two ideas of who was who and who was right. The results of the adjudication—as well as the petitions that led to it—were preserved in writing, capable of being manipulated in various ways in thinking through subsequent problems (as were the citations in the petition of Dionysia).

The fact that these narratives were accepted and validated, in practice and in theory, could not be made to square with "weak pluralism," the idea that there exist a package of nested citizenships or juridical statuses representing communities that would regulate their members internally but according to imperially palatable standards. Briefly put, the issue is this: the Roman-directed government in Egypt encouraged or at least tolerated, albeit in limited fashion and usually only at the margins, at least one element of strong legal pluralism: it allowed, and in fact encouraged, individuals, by means of petitions, to craft narratives containing normative claims that were capable of being compressed into justiciable questions; by being accepted by imperial authorities (at the local or the provincial level) these narratives were accepted into the body of materials that were potentially legally true.[95] These petitions were catalogued among the official documents, lived on in the archives, were recorded in the *commentarii* of officials, were passed through chains of bureaucrats like official documents, and in some cases could be reactivated in new contexts; as such, they sat at a vanishing point between what is narrative and rhetoric and what is law.[96]

But at the heart of these moments of strong pluralism, however limited and fleeting they were, there stands a tension: because these claims were made by individual members of groups, generally against other members of the same groups, they impinged on the ideology of local group self-regulation characteristic of the officially authorized weak versions of pluralism. Ultimately, then, these narratives posed a challenge to this official weak pluralism, in the sense that petitioners constantly undermined it by challenging its borders. It is in this dynamic—the push-and-pull between the challenge of pluralist borders by the provincial inhabitants and the coordinate attempt of the state (and several other powerful, sub-state actors) to police and reinscribe them—that we can best understand the longer-term, diachronic development of the provincial legal system in Egypt at least, and probably elsewhere as well. As for the question of violence, it sheds at least some light on what petitioners were doing when they went to court, and why violence seems to be a problem area in the law that strains not just the legal system's own understanding of what it is doing, but also why petitioners took it so seriously—namely, because through their complaints they had the power to challenge the validity of the very local structures that led to the violence in the first place. As I stated earlier, jurispathic judges can be a good thing indeed.

CHAPTER 6

Fusion and Fission

In previous chapters I sought to build models of violence from the individual level outward, asking how violent experiences were perceived, and how these experiences were translated into legally actionable issues. As such, it was salutary to treat individuals and their narratives as the core of the analysis. Such a method, however, overlooks what is almost certainly the key factor in an act (or complaint) of violence, and one that was hinted at in the previous chapter: violence and complaint are both about regulating the behavior of others and deciding the terms on which these relations will be carried forward. Violence is frequently a public act (or interpreted as such)—an attempt to "send a message" to the victim him or herself. But what was the content of this message? What were people "doing" when they used violence?

It is here that we find the scholarly categories for understanding the role of violence within disputes to be surprisingly limited. Violence between individuals in the ancient world—when discussed at all—is often described (through categories borrowed from the study of classical Athens) in terms of "feuding" behavior.[1] It is a term which can mean one of two things. It might refer to a culturally regulated system of tit-for-tat vengeance between kin groups, most often found in areas without a strong state presence (or with resistance to such a presence) and accompanied by a series of rules of recognition for identifying who must take vengeance and how. This, more or less, is the "blood feud" model, stated here primarily as an ideal type. The second sense of "feud" might simply be taken to mean an escalating process of conflict between two individuals or groups.[2] These are clearly two different things. In the first sense (the classical anthropological sense), violence is highly regulated and ritualized. It often rests on the back of a system of male "honor," which should be taken as meaning not just a vaguely inflated sense of self and personal inviolability, but also (crucially) a sense of male self built on the foundation of a rigid sexualized division of labor. In the second sense of feud, regulation has failed: parties escalate their disputes in a game of one-upsmanship; disputes begin as a series of real or perceived slights, move slowly and inchoately to a point where violence may eventually be introduced into the mix (though it need not), and continue to mutate through reciprocal violence or the movement of the dispute into a legal arena (and here we return to the theory that law is just one of a series of weapons that people use against one another). That such relatively different behaviors have both been called "feuds" by scholars should give pause.

It is relatively easy to deal with the first category of feud (the "blood feud" model) empirically: there is no evidence of it in the papyri. Never do we have evidence that in the case of personal injury a victim's family rallied back, creating back-and-forth, tit-for-tat feud featuring revenge, score-keeping, and the aligning of real or fictitious kin-groups against one another. There is similarly no good reason to think that violent behavior is the product of some kind of underlying sexualized "honor" system—and the presence of women in violent acts further militates against such a conclusion. The idea that there is some sort of unitary "Mediterranean honor system" to begin with, has, in my opinion, been thoroughly debunked by Michael Herzfeld; in light of Herzfeld's critiques, the burden of proof is now upon those who would assert that such a thing exists.[3] Likewise, I do not think that the lack of any talionic practices recorded in petitions is simply a failure of the documentation: as I discussed above (Chapter 5), the evidence for such sentiments in personal letters, for example, is slender and largely inconclusive.

The question remains, however, as to what to do with the second category (the "escalation" model). It feels sociologically floppy and under-theorized, but nevertheless seems to describe something commonsensical. The problem could be put like this: if we were to imagine that, instead of the rhetorical narratives of the papyri, our documentation of violence consisted in videotapes of the actual incident, we still would still have precious little knowledge about the incident in question. We might be able to say, for example, that when a petitioner claimed that he was assaulted "for no reason" that he had actually made a crude or threatening gesture. But this would still tell very little about *why* he had done such a thing to the offender. Common sense rightly tells us that violent conflicts are rarely random, even if presented as such. They are often the products of long-simmering debates, dislikes, and conflicts. Petitioners may (wisely) choose to conceal elements of these prehistories of violent encounters, but generally speaking, it is a rare instance when individuals who know each other, and sometimes know each other well (as we can tell from some narratives), one day meet in the street and start punching one another, without some precipitating factor or factors.

Unsurprisingly, Egyptian petitioners are seldom transparent about the nature and origins of the antipathies from which legal complaints arise. To take an example: in May A.D. 336, in a village near Oxyrhynchos, the pigs of Aurelia Allous got loose from their pen and ran around her land and onto the land of her neighbor, a man named Pabanos. The result of this interaction was that Pabanos attacked Allous with a chisel. Her complaint is written to the *syndikos*, an official who came to be in charge of providing affordable justice to individuals with limited means:

> ὑπατείας Οὐιρίου Νεπωτιανοῦ καὶ Τετ'τ[ί]ου Φακούνδου τῶν λαμπροτάτων {λαμπροτάτων}, [Πα]χὼν ς. Φλαουΐῳ Ἰουλιανῷ διοικοῦντι συνδικ̣ί̣[αν] Ὀ̣ξ̣υ̣ρυγχίτου παρὰ̣ Αὐρηλίας Ἀλλοῦτος Θωνίου ἀπὸ κώ̣μ̣ης Τ̣αα\μ/πεμοῦ ε πάγο̣υ̣. ἑσπεριναῖς ὥραις τῇ χ[θ]ὲ̣ς ἡ[μέρ]ᾳ̣ ἡμέτ̣ε̣ροι χοῖροι δύο τὴν [ὁ]ρ̣μὴν ποιού[μ]ενοι ἐ̣π̣ὶ̣ ἡ̣μ̣έτερον ἔ̣δ̣α̣φος γε̣νόμενοι <ἐν> ὑ̣δ̣ραγωγίῳ μ̣[η]χ̣α̣ν̣ῆς τῶν ἡ̣μ̣ε̣τ̣έ̣ρ̣ω̣ν̣ π̣[ε-]δ̣ῶ̣ν̣ κ̣α̣ὶ̣ Π̣α̣β̣ά̣ν̣[ου] τ̣ι̣ν̣ὸ̣ς̣ ἀ̣π̣ὸ̣ ̣ ῆ̣[ς] αὐτῆς κώ̣[μ]η̣ς, ὁ προειρημένος Παβᾶνος π̣[αρατυ]χὼν ἔχω̣ν̣ μετὰ χεῖρας ξοΐδιον ἀνελεῖν τοὺς χοίρους βουλόμ̣[ενος] καὶ τοῦτον ἐ̣π̣ι̣σ̣χοῦσα ὡς μηδαμῶς ἀδ[ικ-]η̣[θέντα] ὑ̣π̣ὸ̣ τῶν χοίρων καὶ ἀπο[σχό]μ̣ενο̣ς̣ [τῆς πρὸς] τ̣ο̣ὺ̣ς̣ [χοί-]ρ̣ους ἐπελεύσεως ἐ̣[μοὶ ἐπελήλυθε]ν̣ βου[λόμ]ενός μ̣ε̣ καταποντίσαι ἐ̣ν̣ ὑ̣δ̣ρ̣α̣[γωγίῳ ὡς εἰ] μ̣ὴ̣ ἔ̣κ̣ τ̣ινος προνοίας τ̣ὴν [...]ν τῶν ἐ̣π̣α̣ν̣τ̣λ̣ούντων βοῶν.....[........].[.].....[μη]ν̣ ὑπ' αὐτοῦ ἐν̣ [ὑδραγω-]γ̣ί̣[ῳ̣] . . .
>
> In the consulship of the most glorious Virius Nepotianus and Tettius Facundus, Pachon 6.
> To Flavius Iulianus, acting as the *defensor* of the Oxyrhynchite nome,
> From Aurelia Allous, daughter of Thonios, from the village of Taampemou in the 5th pagus. Yesterday evening our two pigs got out on to our property and ended up in the conduit for the waterwheel for our lands and those of a certain Pabanos from the same town. The aforementioned Pabanos happened upon us with a chisel in his hands and tried to kill the pigs, but I held him back. Although he had not been harmed by the pigs, but because he had been held

> back from his attack on them, he attacked me instead, trying to drown me in the conduit. (And he would have), unless by some providence . . . the oxen pumping . . . by him in the conduit . . . [4]

There is no reason for us to believe, either by imagining a counter-narrative or even on the basis of Allous' complaint itself, that Pabanos is by constitution a chisel-wielding psychopath, provoked into a frothing rage at the sight of some piglets ranging around on his land and the shared water-wheel. Even Allous' description of events militates against this, even if we might doubt that (a) her actions were in fact so benign and (b) his economic interests were not harmed by the pigs. We might guess that Pabanos' anti-porcine rage originates in a history of unpleasant relations; Allous does not allude to this in her complaint, nor should she have, lest she be seen as the real offender in this case by violating the boundary between her property and his, and possibly assaulting him when he tried to defend his economic interests.[5]

It is worth comparing the incident between Pabanos and Allous with an example from the modern United States. In one of the narratives presented by Sally Engle Merry in her work on the legal anthropology of small-claims courts in Massachusetts, we see a similar example of boundary-infringement and mutual abuse:

> The feud began with a simple quarrel over dogs. Mrs. Brown's elderly poodle urinated against the fence in front of Mrs. Smith's newly purchased house. Mrs. Smith pushed the dog away with a wooden clog shoe, and Mrs. Brown, incensed and eager to protect her dog, hit Mrs. Smith with a baseball bat. It was a small bat, a child's toy. Mrs. Brown was in her sixties, Mrs. Smith in her thirties. The two women had already been fighting over their dogs, Mrs. Smith's larger shepherd/Doberman mix and Mrs. Brown's poodle. Mrs. Smith called the police, who filed a major incident report charging Mrs. Brown with assault and battery with a deadly weapon (the baseball bat).[6]

The dispute Merry chronicles in this section of her book was an example of how individual perceptions of the "right" age and cultural composition of the Massachusetts neighborhood in question could turn into (sometimes violent) legal disputes. Her main point is directly relevant to questions of interpreting the evidence from Egypt: without a context-specific, extended case study cataloguing both the incidents in question and the social, cultural, and economic background to the conflict, there is no way for us to tell what the source of hostilities was. Merry had the advantage of being able to interview participants; papyrologists work from scraps.[7] Even when we can *nominally* reconstruct what one party says the cause of the debate was, we still generally only work at the level of dogs and piglets, not root causes.

In these terms, the "escalation" model runs up against a problem of historical knowledge and reconstruction. From the vast majority of the complaints about violence from the first six centuries of Roman rule it is clear that the parties in conflict knew one another, either through business relationships, geographical proximity, or other sorts of interpersonal ties. Sometimes petitioners claim that they were assaulted by people that they appear to know well; sometimes they describe the origins of the violent part of the conflict coming from an argument about money owed, which indicates an existing relationship of credit and trust.[8] These ties, even when admitted within the context of rhetorical performances, speak to a multiplicity of substantive relationships that hover below the radar of scholarly attention, which in the context of ancient history has focused primarily on two kinds of relationships: the atomistic level of the family or the pyramid of patronage and power.[9] That is, in ancient history the most intensive work on society has focused on mapping vertical relations of deference, rather than horizontal relations. Within the discourse of current scholarship, we lack even the basic conceptual vocabulary to define these relations, much less to theorize their dynamics.[10] This is not a fault of the escalation model itself, of course—it is to point out that the model leads us to a particular problem of reconstruction, and the need to rethink our basic categories of social relations. In that sense, it is highly useful.

Where it runs into trouble, however, is with its concept of the nature of fights and fighting. It is one thing to say that there is a prehistory to every conflict, a series of moves and counter-moves that can be mapped as a series of escalations leading to one party making a claim before the law in an attempt to win the battle of escalating injuries. But is there something special about violence in these situations of extended conflict? Does this mean that violent acts themselves carry no "message"—that they're fundamentally the same as earlier insults and later litigation? For reasons I outlined in the previous chapters, I doubt this; but what is necessary here is a method for figuring out *how* these acts are different. Likewise, does the escalation model necessarily push us to an instrumental vision of law? Is law *merely* one force among many—a form of violence that responds to another form of violence? If violence is something different from escalation, and law is a form of violence, is law something different from escalation? If it is different, precisely how is it different? And how are we to account for the fact that law and legal categories are often already implicated in these fights well before the moment of violence and the subsequent petition? In what follows I hope to improve upon the "escalation" model by trying to change the terms of the debate, moving away from the "feud" type of model toward a model grounded more in symbolic (rather than functional) anthropology. What follows starts by accepting the main insight of the "escalation" model—namely, that we have to try to rethink the universe of social relations that might be at stake in a violent encounter. Where I differ is in interpreting the act of violence itself.

My argument is this: the world that petitioners and their opponents inhabit prior to a violent act—the real world—is complex, multifaceted, and populated by individuals and groups with long-standing histories. This is not unique to Roman Egypt: all human relationships in complex societies can be described in such a way. But in the world of Roman Egypt, when these overlapping and complicated relationships come face to face with an individualistic ideology built on the premise of personal integrity and the relatively even dispersal of social power,[11] the interpersonal relationships that result can become *intolerably* complex and dynamic. In the case of violence, as Roger Bagnall has noted, people who are relatively equal—or, perhaps more correctly, people who *perceive* themselves as relatively equal—engage in disputes in which, by definition, there is not a clear set of rules or structures according to which one party can be expected to defer.[12] In these disputes there is necessarily a lack of clarity about the relationships between the individuals in question. In what follows, I argue that the use of violence is one way of bringing clarity and structure to these relationships, as are the legal relationships that result from pursuing violence through legal channels. Violence is not only a moment in a conflict where scholars can pinpoint the degeneration of conflict into something that may be unsolvable, but insofar as this degeneration is framed in legal categories ("violence") these categories provide a grammar through which individuals can reimagine and redescribe themselves. To continue with the linguistic metaphor: a grammar is not a language—it has no richness, no improvisations; it is by definition both constrained and prescriptive or normative. And that is its advantage. For it is in this sense that violence brings clarity to these tense and dynamic relations—by allowing people to channel them into less dynamic and therefore more manageable categories, and to redefine messy sets of personal antipathies through categories that individuals themselves draw from law.[13]

What follows proceeds in two parts. First, I attempt to render some meaning from attacks that seem to be deliberately overwhelming. I argue that these moments of overwhelming a petitioner can be "read" as public displays of group solidarity that attempt to clarify patterns of deference and compress complex disputes into claims that the terms on which the relationship will now go forward are essentially different. Here I adapt some concepts from Chris Wickham's important study of twelfth-century Tuscany. From there I move to violence within the family. Violence within the family is largely underrepresented in the papyri, for reasons that are generally obvious; but some of the most interesting and best-documented instances of violence—the petition of Chairemon quoted within the petition of Dionysia, and the petitions and contracts dealing with the estate of Kopres and the conflict between his daughter Aurelia Taesis and her uncle, Chairemon—come from conflicts within the family. Through an investigation of these somewhat exceptional cases, I argue, we can gain a better understanding of the ways in which violence is used to structure and, perhaps more important, restructure interpersonal relationships. In this second part I also work out the social force of a term I raised earlier (Chapter 3): obligation.

* * *

In contemporary America, fights are to be "taken outside," ideally to be finished as a duel between two people of roughly equal size and ability. Ganging up on someone is largely scorned. Hitting women is beyond the pale (if the attacker is male). Fighting, in other words, should be largely "fair"—there must be a possibility of a contest. If these "rules" get broken, especially if there is a future encounter, they may come to be reinforced, and an initial unfairness countered by a brutal and punishing unfairness: this, it appears, is the logic behind hockey fights.[14] The idea of "fair fighting" is powerful, and has even been generalized into a theoretical model claiming to explain a vast canvas of human behavior.[15] But the idea that conflicts ideally take place in a structured duel between two partners who are rough equals is largely culture-bound. Others may have different ideas, as illustrated by Italian journalist Luigi Barzini:

> The contemporary capitalistic world is still almost incomprehensible to most Italians, who admire, envy, and imitate, often very successfully, its outward aspect, its power, and its practical products, but miss its moral character. They even doubt if it exists at all.

> Many current rules of fair conduct strike the Italians as pure nonsense. Take the English saying, "never kick a man when he is down." They do not believe anybody really obeyed it. They know a man should not be kicked if he is old, if he is strong and can immediately kick back, if he can avenge himself later, if he has powerful friends or relatives, if he could be useful some day in any way, or if a policeman is watching. But why not "when he is down"? When else, if you please, should one kick a man more advantageously? When more safely and effectively? A famous handbook on how to play *scopa*, the most common Italian card game, written in Naples by a Monsignor Chitarella, begins: "Rule Number One: always try to see your opponent's cards." It is a good concrete practical rule.[16]

Regardless of the value of these sorts of vignettes as serious data, they may have some purchase for thinking through how violence can be given social meaning. In the American world, violence sits at the tail end of irresolvable conflicts—but once the contest has been had, there is settlement. In Barzini's description, an act of violence is always done with an eye to the future. It assumes that no repair is possible after giving a man a good kicking, but also that such a kicking is instrumental in other plans. Hence, in Barzini's example violence is likened to a move in card games—rational and calculated to maximize gains. By contrast, in colloquial American English violence is often said to occur when events "boil over" or when people are "blowing off steam"—the idea being that every man has his upper threshold of toleration, that irritation creates internal pressure, and that while he may once in a while "blow his top" he will also eventually "simmer down." The use of hydraulic metaphors to reflect moments of irrationality and irascibility here is interesting, if only as a window into cultural difference: I would imagine that in Roman Egypt, where the Nile bursting its banks and flooding the countryside was a source of survival if not prosperity, such language would be met with raised eyebrows.

In the Egyptian countryside outnumbering a victim was not uncommon and, it appears, also useful and important in the symbolic vocabulary of violence. The accounts of these group beatings are given in a number of ways. In some cases, petitioners are vague about the identity of their assailants. In some of these cases, it is because the petitioner does not know their identity, but can be sure of the person who appears to be the primary assailant. Thus, in his petition to the prefect discussed in Chapter 5, Satabous son of Herieus claims that Nestnephis came to his farm "with his family and some others" ([με]τὰ τῶν αὐτῶν καὶ ἑτέρων), but does not give the names of any of them.[17] Though he knows to distinguish members of the family from others, his narrative places the blame on Nestnephis alone. In his other petition, the one directed to the centurion Lucretius, he simply states that Nestnephis came against him "with many hands" (μετὰ πολυχειρίας).[18] In other cases, however, vagueness about the identity of co-conspirators comes from a lack of knowledge.[19] Nevertheless, as one would expect, most known accomplices are members of the nuclear family, though sometimes there are other participants who cannot be linked to the group of attackers in a specific way.[20] Attacks by fathers and sons, for example, show up in the documentary record. A father and a son are both implicated by a petitioner who claims that he was attacked by the son and a group of armed men (whose names he does not give); in the complaint, however, he details the offenses that both the father and the son had done to him in the past, and he asks that the father and son be arrested.[21] One petitioner claims that he was attacked by a man and his sons along with another man and his brother, claiming that they looked down on him because of his *apragmosyne* (inexperience or quietness) and his *schema* (looks or character). This group of men, he claims, attacked him on his land, since they wanted to farm it themselves.[22] In addition to male members of the family, female members also feature prominently in petitions concerning violence, both as victims and as attackers.[23] In some cases they appear alongside other members of their family, such as in the petition of Aurelia Eus discussed in the previous chapter. In this document the violence is done by a man named Isakis along with his sister and two other women.[24] Brothers and sisters also appear in a petition from Aurelia Thaesis, who claims that a group of five individuals assaulted her farmers in the course of a land dispute; of the five, there were two groups of siblings:

> ὑπατείας Οὐ[ι]β̣[ίου Νεπω]τιανοῦ καὶ Τετ'τίου Φακούνδου τῶν λαμπ[ρ(οτάτων), Φ]αῶφι κη. Φλαυίῳ Ἑρμείᾳ [σ]υνδίκῳ Ὀξυρυγ'χίτου παρὰ Αὐρηλίας Θαήσιος [Π]ρ̣όϊτος καταγεινομένης ἐν κώμῃ Φοβώου ε πάγου. γῆς μου πολλῷ χρόνῳ ὑποκλεπτομένης, ὑπὲ̣ρ ἧς ἐξ οἴκοθεν τὰ εὐσεβῆ τελέσματα ὑπομένω, ἀνήνεγ'κα περὶ ἀφορισμοῦ καὶ παραδόσεως ταύτης τῇ ἐπαρχικῇ ἐξουσίᾳ καὶ ἀκολούθως τοῖς προσταχθεῖσι παρεδόθη μοι ἀκολούθως προσφωνῇ Τιτόου γραμματέως τοῦ πάγου [κ]αὶ τῶν ̣[..]ει[- ca.14 -]..[- ca.12 -] ου γεωμέτρου κ̣αὶ ἐκμισθωσαμένη γεωργ[οῖ]ς ἐπὶ τοῦ πάγου τὰ τέλη αὐτοῦ. οἵδε ἐπεσχέθησ[αν] ὑπὸ Παρακλῆ καὶ Πτολλ̣ᾶ καὶ Θαήσιος γαμβρᾶς τοῦ Παρακλῆ καὶ παισὶ Ὀ[ν]νώφριος, πάντων ἀπὸ τῆς

αὐτῆς κώμης Φ[ο]βώου, καὶ ἐπελθόντες τοῖς γεωργοῖς πληγαῖ[ς] κατέκοψαν, ὅθεν αἰτιωμένη τούτοις τὰ βιβλία ἐπιδίδωμι, ἀξιοῦσα τὴν δέουσαν ἐπεξ[έλε]υσιν γενέσθαι καὶ ἐπαναγκασθῆναι τούτους ἀ[π]οσχέσθαι τῆς ἡμετέρας γῆς πρὸς τὸ δύνασ[θαι] καὶ ἐμὲ τὰ δημόσια τελέσματα ἀποδιδόν[α]ι.
(hand 2) Αὐρηλία Θαήσιος [ἐ]πιδέδωκα. Αὐρήλιος Θέων Θέωνος ἔγραψα ὑπὲρ αὐτῆς μὴ εἰδυίας γράμματα.

In the consulship of the most glorious Virius Nepotianus and Tettius Facundus, Phaophi 28.
To Flavius Hermeias, *defensor* of the Oxyrhynchite,
From Aurelia Thaesis, daughter of Prois, living in the town of Phoboos in the 5th pagus. For a long time now my land has been stolen, although I remain personally responsible for the blessed taxes on it. I applied to the provincial officials concerning the boundaries and the transfer of this land, and I was given in accordance with the rules and in accordance with the report of the scribe of the pagus and of . . . land surveyor and having let to the farmers in the pagus for its taxes. But these men were held back by Parakles and Ptollas and Thaesis, the sister-in-law of Parakles, and the children of Onnophris, all of them from the same town of Phoboos. They attacked the farmers and beat them up badly. Therefore I accuse them and submit this petition, requesting that they receive the necessary punishment, and that they be forced to stay off our land, so that I also can be able to pay the public taxes.
(hand 2) I, Aurelia Thaesis, have submitted this. I Aurelius Theon, son of Theon, wrote on her behalf, since she is illiterate.[25]

Thaesis' petition is useful in that it ties together a number of themes in these "group assault" petitions. First, and already remarked upon, is that the groups tend to have family connections. Second, property is key in a number of these petitions: Nestnephis and his family and friends assault Satabous in the course of an extended property dispute; in the case of Aurelia Eus, the assailants in a "tyrannical fashion knocked down the wall of the vacant lot, wishing to steal from me my building site and my mother's fallen house next to the yard, although I have the deeds of sale for it in my possession." Finally, not only do these group challenges deal with property, they deal, as is made especially clear in the case of Thaesis, with the public marking of property.[26]

To note these similarities is not to assert that these claims were always only "about" who owns what. It is probably not surprising that people fight over property, to be sure. But property can come to serve as more than simple resources. Anyone who has spent time watching the daytime courtroom shows that are popular in America has seen examples of this: plaintiffs in these shows often sue friends, families, and acquaintances over seeming tokens—the return of a favorite piece of jewelry, rights to a pet, or seemingly insignificant sums of money. The actual value of these tokens is not particularly at issue, however, except in their capacity as symbols of the interpersonal relationships themselves, and the fact that *as tokens* they have the power to force third parties to make decisions about right and wrong.[27] This is not, of course, to claim that the item in question—Eus' wall, or Satabous' millstone, for instance—were items of little or no value. Quite the opposite: apart from their value at market (which may be substantial), their value is only increased by the fact that they can come to be discussed through legal categories and thereby acquire the power to regulate relationships. Violence does this, too, as do the subsequent narratives that emerge from it.

To put these boundary and possession claims—and their associated acts of violent solidarity—into sharper focus, we might profitably look to a comparative example. In his discussion of Tuscany in the twelfth century, Chris Wickham makes the following point:

> Where disputes were so complex and hard to pin down, as in the agrarian cases we are looking at, public actions of all kinds helped to concentrate the mind. In disputes like the Ponte S. Petro case, public verbal statements were the points of reference that witnesses used to underpin their perceptions of which side was right. But forceful actions, as long as they were not secret, were the most rhetorically effective actions of all, for they also involved an opposing party who did not respond to the challenge, or who actively backed down. In the complexity of some of our disputes, then, when parties were short of clear-cut documentary proof, or of a secure body of informed witnesses, or in some cases where they sought to make a particularly clear point, they frequently resorted to public acts of a variety of kinds—speech, direct action, force, ritual—to create images, signs, of a situation which observers could absorb, understand, and remember.[28]

In these situations, Wickham describes the role of violence as "probative"—that is, it is used as a means of proof to gather people to your side. This was particularly important in a legal system in which *publica fama* (public talk, reputation) was recognized as having legal force within a subsequent investigation.[29] This was not the case in Egypt, however, and publicly doing violence to one's opponent would not be likely to help in the subsequent legal process. What is important about Wickham's work is that it provides an account of how violence can come to "mean" something within a state system with a relatively robust institutional infrastructure (that is, more robust than a clan or tribal structure, from which our "feud" models are derived).[30] It remains possible, within Wickham's system, to describe violence as a purely local means of regulating the conduct of individuals—as a sort of "rough justice," for example—but to see these interactions as existing in opposition to or independent of other institutions would be to miss the larger point. That is, that these acts of violence need to be understood as also being intimately connected to the kinds of legal processes that individuals relied upon to regulate their interpersonal relationships.

It is surely no accident that the groups that do violence against others are always structured in such a way that they outnumber their victim or victims. Violence in Egypt was often done in a symbolic, public, and communicative way. Being assaulted by a single individual in the course of a heated argument was one thing; being faced down by a number of individuals—a nuclear or extended family—made life more complicated. All individuals who could be named would then be implicated in the subsequent complaint, but some of them would certainly get away with doing violence. But here we still lack a sense of the meaning of such moments. To come closer we might look to a document from fifth-century Karanis:

> π(αρὰ).
> καὶ πρίν με γράψαι οὐκ ἀγνοεῖ σου ἡ θαυμασιότης ὡς ὅτι οὔκ εἰσι
> οἱ ἀπὸ Καρανίδος πρὸς τὸ οἰκῆσαι αὐτῶν τὴν κώμην οὔτε μὴν
> τελέσαι τῷ βασιλεῖ, καὶ γὰρ ἐν τῇ ἐχθὲς ῥιφθείς μοι ἦν (ὁ δεῖνα)
> παρὰ τῷ κεφαλαιωτῇ πρὸς μεθοδίαν φανεροῦ κέρματος. τοῦτον
> ζητήσας μεθοδεῦσαι περιερρόγχασέν μοι καὶ ἐβουλήθη μοι
> ἐπελθεῖν . . . καὶ διὰ τὸν εἰρήναρχον καὶ τὸν ἄλλον λειτουργὸν
> τοῦτον ἐδυνήθη μεθοδεῦσαι. οὐκ οἶδα δὲ τινὸς ἕνεκεν ὁ αὐτὸς
> ἐκεῖνος συνάξας αὐτοῦ τοὺς διαφέροντας κάθισμα ἐποίησεν τῷ
> εἰρηνάρχῳ, τοῦτον μέλλων ἀνελεῖν πρὸς τὸ τούτου γιγνομένου τοῦ
> λοιποῦ μήτε μερισμὸν μήτε ἄλλο τι ἀπόκρισιν αὐτοὺς ποιεῖν. καὶ
> γὰρ ἐν τῇ σήμερον οὔτ' εἰρήναρχος οὔτ' ἄλλος τις ἦλθε πρὸς μὲ δι'

> ὃ ἔπαθαν ἐν τῇ ἐχθές, ἀλλὰ ἁπλῶς οὕτω καθιζόμεθα, μηδὲν . . . ποιοῦντες.[31]
>
> From . . .
> Even before I write your Worship is not unaware that the people from Karanis are not concerned to inhabit the village or indeed to pay their taxes to the Emperor. And in fact yesterday I had (so-and-so) flung before the headman for exaction of a certain sum of money. When I attempted to collect from this man, he snorted his contempt for me and wanted to attack me . . . and thanks to the *eirenarch* and the other service official I was able to collect from this one. Yet, I know not why, that same man gathered his adherents and laid siege (*kathisma epoiesen*) to the *eirenarch*, intending to kill him, so that, when this was done, they should not in the future be answerable for their tax share or for anything else. And in fact today neither *eirenarch* nor anyone else has come to me because of the treatment which they suffered yesterday, but we simply sit as we are (*kathizometha*), not doing anything. (tr. Rea)[32]

This letter is amusing, if only because it provides an excellent example of the types of behavior Ammianus enjoyed mocking among the Egyptians. It is also an example of how group violence can be used profitably: as a result of the violence by the unnamed man and his supporters, the mechanisms of tax collection have broken down, and none of the local officials will support the writer. In his commentary on the text, Rea pointed out the difficulty in the term *kathisma*—literally a "chair" or a "seat"—and chose to translate it as "laid siege." Though this surely captures the sense, there is, I think, an additional layer of meaning in the author's use of the term. There are no straightforward parallels, but the sense of the term becomes clearer when compared with the result of the "seat" (*kathisma*)—that the writer and his partners just "sit here" (*kathizometha*) as a result of the attack of the man and his relatives. In English we would say that the individual in question "made a stand" (not a seat). This "stand" or "seat" is an act of group solidarity, in this case directed against officials, and in this case also exceedingly effective, since it kept the man and his family free of any further intervention by meddlesome government officials (who appear to be too afraid to go to work). Their "stand" puts the writer of the letter in a situation in which he is stuck. Petitioners were not themselves stuck, as they could bring the legal system to bear on their lives (where this official could not, since he *was* the legal system). Being faced with an instance of group solidarity, the petitioner is faced with a dilemma: complain or ignore. And it is a dilemma in the literal sense of the term—that is, it is a choice between two paths. It is especially important to note that in this system of doing violence there need be only *one* violent incident to set this process of transformation in motion.

* * *

With this in mind, we can adapt Wickham's insight for the Egyptian material. Violence might not have probative force in Egypt in the same way as it did in medieval Tuscany, but it seems certainly to have had decisive force—force that had the ability to transform the nature of the conflict itself. What is important in such a description of the "meaning" of violence is twofold. First, decisive force only works within a legal system in which violence is treated as a separate category. If a dispute can easily be ignored by magistrates or sent to mediation, we must assume that it would be. Roman magistrates were not prone to make too much new law, or open the system to an excessive number of complaints that could in theory be solved through mediation.[33] But, in a system in which there is no avenue for the mediation of violence, and one which makes ideological promises of the physical safety of its subjects and citizens,[34] violence channels the larger questions of mutual antagonism into a legally judicable issue. It also sidelines other issues. By forcing the dispute into a framework in which mediation is not possible, it also forces third parties to give a yes or no answer as to which party is "right."

Second, both violent showdowns and legal recourse serve to compress complex and multifaceted relations into single acts which represent claims that whatever previously had structured these relations has to change fundamentally, and proceed in the future on clearer, simpler terms. These violent acts, in other words, were moments of social fission—a moment where a show of unity against a perceived troublemaker (like Satabous, Eus, Thaesis, or the tax collector in Karanis) worked out, if only temporarily, a clear structure of deference. They were claims that "we are in charge here; you must suffer, or try your hand at complaining"—or, to echo the tax collector's letter, "we have made our stand; you must take your seat."

The argument that violence represented a moment of fission—a way of breaking through the strangulating multiplicity of histories, local contexts, and sublegal social ties—has two corollaries. The first is that the idea of "fission" is deeply intertwined with the concept of delict itself (the main reason why it is important that we retain local categories, and not collapse "violence" into "crime"). Delicts were classed, in the Roman tradition, as being within the broader category of obligations. Obligation is a powerful metaphor in the papyri, in part for reasons I outlined above in Chapter 3, but also because in Roman juristic thinking the other category that fits into the broad category of "obligations" is contract. The difference between a contract and a delict is that in one you choose the person with whom you wish to be obligated and the terms of those obligations themselves; in the other, obligations are forced upon you. And if delicts are moments of fission, then contracts are moments of fusion. The second part of my argument is that, in the papyrological record, one can on key occasions see traffic between the two categories in sorting out complex interpersonal relations. This is especially so in the case of family conflicts, where in a few particular cases we can see this process being worked out in detail.

* * *

Family and kin units were especially important in the proper deployment of violence in the Egyptian towns and villages, as the preceding discussion hoped to make clear. They were not, however, absolute units.[35] Though we do not have a lot of information on violence in the family in Roman Egypt, there is some evidence that is tantalizing: two documents from divorce proceedings, several petitions, and, most important, relatively full documentation of two separate family conflicts. One of these is the petition of Dionysia (P.Oxy. II 237), in which a dispute between Dionysia and her husband on one side and her father Chairemon on the other seems to have escalated into violence on one occasion. The petition of Dionysia is critical not only because of its length, but because Dionysia quotes Chairemon's petition and responds to his accusations. Thus, this is one of the precious few examples in the corpus of petitions where we more have than one side of an issue.[36] The other important set of documents is a series of contracts and petitions related to the division of the estate of Kopres, the father of the Aurelia Taesis whose petition was discussed above (Chapter 4). These documents provide a sort of "prehistory" of violent conflict in a way in which the very partial narratives of an individual petition cannot.

Violence within the family is a more complex problem than violence between families. In some respects, it follows similar pathways: existing disputes are channeled into an instance of violence that presents a dilemma for the victim. In families, however, it is safe to assume that participants might initially seek to have conflicts contained or reined in, and to prevent them from degenerating into a process of total fission between two groups or individuals.[37] If the moment of violence transforms the legal relationships between two groups by sending a message, then this message is much stronger when sent between members of a family, since family relations are necessarily personal and affective but also often fraught with tension. As one petitioner in the late third century recounts, "to be wronged by strangers is difficult; but to be wronged even by relatives is the worst" (τὸ ὑπὸ ξένων ἀδικεῖσθαι χα[λεπόν, ἀλλὰ τὸ ὑπὸ] καὶ συγγενῶν χαλεπώτατον).[38] Though ancient and modern thinkers alike tend to see the family as a system of social organization modeled around neatly organized structures of authority and obedience, one may reasonably suspect that families are often held together by rather more fluid understandings of mutual responsibility, unspoken expectations, and a mutual willingness to overlook specific definitions of obligation in favor of internal harmony, even if such a harmony is temporary.[39] When these fluid structures of deference and mutual obligation are undermined, family affairs become both complicated and interesting. Still, while there are patterns in the ways that conflict within the family plays out, in what follows it is worth bearing in mind Tolstoy's opening to *Anna Karenina*: "Happy families are all alike; every unhappy family is unhappy in its own way."

Two of the most interesting documents from Oxyrhynchos are not petitions, but documents that seem to be related to divorce proceedings. In both of these documents, women present lists of offenses done by their husbands, in the course of describing how marital relationships fell apart.[40] Both of these documents are from the fourth or fifth century. To what extent they are important for understanding the social position of women in late antiquity is a question that I will largely ignore here, in favor of looking at the structures of disputes within the family.[41] In the first document, a woman complains about the many *hybreis* done against her by her husband—that he locked up her slaves and foster children, beat them, and tried to get them to give him the petitioner's property. As the husband's abuses piled up, there was an intervention:

> ἀπήντησεν δὲ αὐτῷ Ζω[ίλ]ος ὅτι καὶ τὸν τρόφιμον αὐτοῦ ἐνέκλεισεν, καὶ εἶπεν αὐτῷ ὅτ[ι] διὰ τὸν τρόφιμόν σου ἦλθας ἢ διὰ τὴν τοίαν ἦλθας λαλῆσαι ἐπάνω αὐτῆς; καὶ ὤμοσεν ἐπὶ παρουσίᾳ τῶν ἐπισκόπων καὶ τῶν ἀδελφῶν αὐτοῦ ὅτι ἀπεντεῦθεν οὐ μὴ κρύψω αὐτῇ<ν> πάσας μου τὰς κλεῖς καὶ ἐπέχω \καὶ τοῖς δούλοις αὐτοῦ ἐπίστευσεν καὶ ἐμοὶ οὐκ ἐπίστευσεν/ οὔτε ὑβρίζω αὐτὴν ἀπεντεῦθεν. καὶ γαμικὸν γέγονεν, καὶ μετὰ τὰς συνθήκας ταύτας καὶ τοὺς ὅρκους ἔκρυψεν πάλιν ἐμὲ τὰς κλεῖς εἰς ἐμέ.

> Zoilos went to him, since he had locked up his foster-child as well, and he said to him, "Have you come on account of your foster-child, or have you come to talk about this woman?" He swore in the presence of bishops and his brothers that "From now on, I will not hide all of my keys from her"—he trusted his own slaves, but he didn't trust me—"and I will even stay away from her, nor will I do violence to her again." We made a marriage agreement, and after these agreements and the oaths, once again he hid the keys from me.[42]

The other document is similar, though written in the form of a petition (in this case, to the tribune Flavius Marcellus), rather than as an accompanying document. As such, it contains a fuller narrative of the structure of the marriage, which may have begun by abduction. Apparently the husband, a man named Paulos, abandoned the petitioner (named Attiaina) after having a child with her, and began to cohabit with another woman.[43] Whatever happened in that relationship is unclear, but it appears that at some point, accompanied by ecclesiastical mediators, he tried to reconcile with Attiaina:

> καὶ μετὰ χρόνον τινὰ πάλιν ἐξηπ̣ά[τησ]εν διὰ πρεσβυτέρων ἄχρις οὗ πάλιν συνεισενέγκω αὐτὸν εἰς τ̣ὸ̣ν̣ ἡμέτερον οἶκον γραψάμενός μοι συνπ̣α[ρ]αμ̣εῖναι τὴν συμβίωσιν̣ εἰ δὲ βουληθείη τὰ αὐτὰ ἀνελεύθερα πράγ'ματα διαπράξασθαι ἐκτίσειν αὐτὸν χρυσίου οὐγκίας δύο καὶ ὁ τούτου πατὴρ ἐνγράφως ἀνεδέξατο αὐτόν.

> After a while he tricked me once again with the help of presbyters, until once again I agreed to bring him back into our home. He made a contract with me in which he stated that the marriage would abide and if he wished to engage in such disgusting practices that he would pay a fine of two ounces of gold. His father provided a written guarantee of this.[44]

The relationship again fell apart, however, as Paulos, it seems, reverted to his preferred ways: beating Attiaina, robbing soldiers quartered in their home, and fleeing the town. Attiaina, accordingly, sent him a deed of divorce. Paulos, she claims, then reabducted and reimpregnated her, and now threatens to ruin her reputation. In her petition Attiaina asks to have Paulos stand before the tribunal, to be punished, and to be forced to divulge the monetary penalty (the two ounces of gold) he had promised in the contract. Again, here, we might remember the power of property as token.

That both of these intra-household disputes move from a process of disagreement to contract (the γαμικόν in the first document; the oath with surety in the second), and then to fission (divorce, or divorce and lawsuit), is, I think, important. Contracts provide a clarity that is often missing in relationships where social expectations—rather than rigid terms of performance—govern behavior. Furthermore, in a set of relationships where parties might have conflicting expectations of obedience and deference, the writing of contracts is done on the basis of a fictional equality: in theory, one is free to choose with whom one makes a contract. Since the law does not recognize a forced contract, both parties are theoretically able to choose not to make one. This equality of ability to enter into an agreement may come up against social sanctions—that is, Attiaina may have felt a social pressure to reconcile—but she is free also to state terms, her husband was free to agree to them, and his father stands as surety for him, the ultimate in community sanction and crucial for the process of restructuring and reconciliation these contracts are supposed to supply.

In the case study that follows, I will look closely at another dispute within the family where relationships are first restructured by contract, and then finally restructured—dissolved—by violence. Both violence and contract are essential concepts for understanding the dynamics of conflict within the family. Both channel larger issues into more manageable structures, in this case legal relationships. Invoking legal relationships—ideal structures of behavior framed as legal obligations—is a means of sidelining important and problematic requirements of behavior in otherwise deferential and hierarchical relationships; no less important, these legal relationships are enforceable by powerful third parties.

* * *

A previous chapter (4) discussed the violent imagery of *P.Cair.Isid.* 63, a petition of Aurelia Taesis, a young woman who was assaulted by the wife and children of her uncle Chairemon in the course of a dispute over her inheritance. In this section, I attempt to piece together the relationships that led to this incident, and trace the ways in which Taesis and Chairemon frame their conflict legally. The documentation for this dispute (and the case study that follows) is unique because we have, in a limited sense, parts of both perspectives. That is, while we have petitions only from Aurelia Taesis, we also have

Figure 6. The Family of Aurelia Taesis, based on A. E. R. Boak and H. C. Youtie, *The Archive of Aurelius Isidorus* (Ann Arbor: University of Michigan Press, 1960), 6.

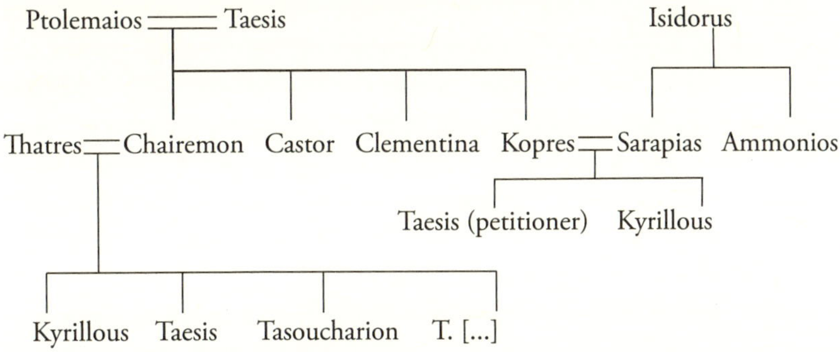

two contracts to which both parties agreed. The existence of these contracts is decisive for understanding the scope of the conflict itself, since they indicate instances in which both parties were able to agree to certain stipulations. Five documents pertain to this conflict, as well as one additional petition (*P.Cair. Isid.* 62) of Taesis against her stepmother, which is included because it seems to follow a trajectory that is structurally similar to the way that the conflict with Chairemon plays out. All of these documents come from the papers of Aurelius Isidorus (*P.Cair.Isid.*). I summarize them below.[45]

***P.Cair.Isid.* 62 (undated, but earlier than the other documents)**: Aurelia Taesis and her (possibly twin) sister Kyrillous, both under guardianship of their uncle, Ammonios, petition against their stepmother. They claim that when their father, Kopres, was on the brink of death, he asked his current wife (the unnamed stepmother) if he owed her anything, and she said no. But upon his death, they claim, the stepmother and her father took a group of twenty-seven sheep from his flocks. She appears to have gotten these. In addition, she claimed in front of mediators (διά τε μεσιτῶν φήσασα) that Kopres owed her a gold *mina*, but it appears that she did not offer sufficient proof of this. The stepmother later claims that Kopres had given her a half-share in a female slave, but again Taesis and Kyrillous feel that she has not provided sufficient proof. They petition a military officer (probably a *beneficiarius*) to force the stepmother to hand over the documents that prove her share in the slave.

***P.Cair.Isid.* 104 (20 November 297)**: Agreement between Aurelia Taesis, Kyrillous, and Chairemon, their uncle. Kyrillous and Taesis have not yet come of age, and are still under the guardianship of Ammonios, but are on the point of reaching their majority. In Kopres' estate there were two *arouras* of land, one of which Chairemon was given rights to, and the other which was given to Taesis and Kyrillous. Chairemon agrees that for the last thirteen years he has cultivated both *arouras* (one of which was rightfully part of the inheritance of Kyrillous and Taesis) without paying rent to Taesis and Kyrillous, but with payments of the *annona* and all public taxes. He cedes to Taesis and Kyrillous the right to cultivate both *arouras* for a period of thirteen years, the period for which he had cultivated it, provided they pay the *annona* and all public taxes due on it.

P.Cair.Isid. **105 (23 November 297)**: Another agreement (complete), this time among five parties, Taesis and Kyrillous (called by her nickname Allous in this document),[46] Chairemon, and Castor and Clementina. Taesis and Kyrillous have probably come of age, as there is no reference to their guardian, Ammonios.[47] Castor and Clementina are siblings of Chairemon. In this document, two mortars which are part of the inheritance are divided among the five, with Castor and Clementina getting one to share between them, and Taesis, Kyrillous, and Chairemon all having shares in the second one. Chairemon gets a half-share, and the sisters a half-share between them (a quarter-share each).[48] They agree on this division and affirm that if anyone brings suit against Chairemon for his half-share of the mortar, they will jointly defend him. Taesis and Kyrillous are given permission to do what they want with the half-share allotted to them.

P.Cair.Isid. **63 (21 December 297)**: Petition concerning violence. Taesis claims that as soon as she came of age, she brought suit against Chairemon for her share of the estate, which she claims that he appropriated and still has in his possession. She claims to have sent in two petitions against him. As a result of the second petition, she claims that the *beneficiarius* had ordered Chairemon to turn over to her what she was owed, though she claims that he did not do so. Instead, she claims, Chairemon's daughters Kyrillous, Tasoucharion, Taesis, and someone whose name is missing attacked her, along with their mother Thatres, beating her, dragging her by the hair, tearing her clothes, and knocking her to the ground in front of the village magistrates Hol and Kasios. The bottom of the document is missing.

P.Cair.Isid. **64 (after 63, but undated)**:[49] Taesis and Kyrillous both petition Aurelius Heron, the nome *strategos*, claiming that Chairemon still has not given over to them the movable property from their father's estate. They claim that Chairemon had handed over the *aroura* of land (the one discussed in *P.Cair.Isid.* 104), but they are unable to pay the rents on it. They say that they submitted a petition to a local official named Serenos, and that he had ordered Chairemon to hand over the property, but he refused. They ask again that the property be restored, and append a list, which includes sixty-one adult sheep, forty adult goats, one mill, three talents of silver, two *artabas* of wheat, two male slaves, and one female slave. They additionally claim that he has sold one of the slaves.

The trajectory of this dispute is complicated, since some of the petitions date from the revolt of Domitius Domitianus. Because of the revolt, there may have been a break in normal political and legal institutions. This is of particular import for the administrative context of *P.Cair.Isid.* 63, the petition concerning violence. In the opinion of J. D. Thomas, the rulings of the *beneficiarius* Gordianus, to whom Taesis sends her petition, would have not been enforceable after the end of the revolt of Domitianus.[50] Thus, when the government of the Tetrarchs was restored shortly after the attack, whatever was accomplished by the initial petition would have been moot and would have required reinitiating a process of legal appeals.

Even given this problem, the trajectory of the conflict is still visible in the documents. Within the conflict, we can isolate what appear to be two phases: first is the sequence of documents recording the division of the estate itself. The requests that Taesis and Kyrillous make are requests for restitution; the process is handled by contract and agreement. There is no reason that we should understand the contracts as being the result of anything besides a dispute—that is to say, the use of the mortars and the land appears to have been contested. The result of the contract concerning the use of the land is that the disputed behavior of Chairemon is handled by a process of restoration: the sisters get to have future rights to it in the *exact* amount that Chairemon has abused it. It is likewise important and telling, in my opinion, that the contract concerning the use rights of the mortars ends with a statement of familial solidarity, with all the contracting parties agreeing that they will come to Chairemon's defense if his rights to the mortars are challenged:

> {καὶ} ὁμολογοῦμεν κατὰ τήνδε τήν ἀσφάλειον ἐφ' ᾧ ἐάν τις ἐπέλθῃ ταύτης τῆς κοπτούρας τῆς παρὰ σοὶ τῷ Χαιρήμονι ἕνεκεν ἡμεῖς τὰ τέσσερα μέρη κοινῶς ἐξ ἴσου ἀποστήσομεν τὸν ἐπερχόμενον ἐκ τῶν ἰδίων ἀναλωμάτων.

> We agree according to this contract that, if someone should sue you, Chairemon, on account of the mortar you have, then we, the four parties, will defend you against the lawsuit from our own funds, as a group and with equal contributions.[51]

The assertion of a promise of common action and mutual support here is important. If I am right in placing these contracts in the broader context of dispute, and specifically, in the process of the resolution of an existing dispute, then the promise of aid in this contract—contained within the extended family—may perhaps be doing more work than simply providing a guarantee. In the context of the contract, assumptions of mutual aid are being spelled out specifically. One might assume that, as an organic unit, the family would be expected to maintain the claims of the other family members, especially in contexts where the claims were being made against properties that were shared among members (in this case, Chairemon, Taesis, and Kyrillous). But the provisions of this agreement are, to my knowledge, unique. The commitment to defense in case of a lawsuit is generally a feature of contracts of sale, not of division of inheritance, and it is generally only between the seller and the buyer (two parties, rather than many). Further, the papyri attesting to this system of mutual legal aid generally involve the promise of the seller to the buyer, rather than a distribution of responsibility.[52] In divisions of inheritance, parties may agree not to sue one another; but to my knowledge there are no other examples of families agreeing, in the context of an inheritance declaration, to protect each other from outside interference.[53] Additionally, the language seems to state specifically that only Chairemon himself is to be protected in this fashion. Still, the responsibility for the property shared among three members is to be actively protected by four members (Taesis, Kyrillous, Castor, and Clementina), and it is to be done *equally*, even though Castor and Clementina, who are obligated in this arrangement, have no specific interest in whether or not Chairemon holds on to his share of the mill. The equal contributions are also striking in light of the *un*-equal distribution of the resources—the two sisters pay as much as Castor and Clementina, even though they receive only a half-portion.

The two contracts, coming within days of one another, produce a series of overlapping relationships among all the parties, binding them to one another in countable, tangible ways. One might imagine that the negotiations that led to these documents were tense, and that protecting the interests of all the individuals while also defining their responsibilities to one another was a

Figure 7. The division of the mortars, and the distribution of legal responsibility for Chairemon's defense.

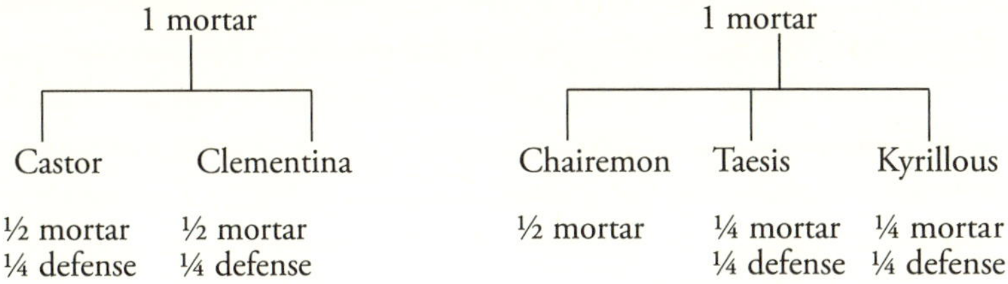

difficult process. This is probably especially true in the context of an inheritance, which can be both a tangible thing and a personal and symbolic matter (a token).[54]

As in the cases of divorce discussed above, these contracts arise from cases of tension and disagreement, and are especially important where the parties are unsure about the future conduct of the others involved because normal or expected social relationships have failed to ensure good behavior in the past. Contracts transform complex social relations (where "right" conduct is often based on trust and a sense of obligation) into legal relationships in which the terms of performance are spelled out explicitly. In this case, they recognize the tensions immanent in the question of the inheritance, and build a resulting relationship in which the tension is managed and admitted. If the tensions are not resolved, then at the least they are placed within a structure through which all parties can discuss terms. Legal agreements that structure relationships in terms of performance and cost (one share, one-half share, a quarter of legal expenses) can easily then serve as an expedient way of managing a system in which there are competing interests and expectations, especially when, as we might surmise, these expectations are already tainted with mutual acrimony. Whatever the tensions that caused the fallout over the succession to the estate of Kopres (and these we cannot know), the contract both literally and figuratively imposes a system of outright obligations and rights on all the parties involved, creating legally binding relationships in which resources are shared and family property is preserved, and in which the personal relationships between the agreeing parties are spelled out in terms of actual, tangible goods—that is, a fourth from each. On this reading, then, the use of contracts to settle (or at least manage) a dispute is one example of parties attempting to restructure social relationships by recasting them in the terminology of legal relationships.

Within a short period of time, the dynamics of the dispute shift perceptibly. Less than a month later, Taesis petitions the *beneficiarius* to restore her property; her petitions (and his decision) lead to violence; the attack is carried out by members of Chairemon's immediate family. It makes sense to revisit Taesis' complaint, and it is worth noting at the outset that Taesis' narrative is almost completely silent about the earlier phases of the dispute, the contracts into which she and her sister had entered, the pledges of mutual assistance, and the things that she had taken possession of in the meantime. This should be an important methodological warning concerning the kinds of conclusions about disputes that we might come to for documents that do not come from archives. *P.Cair.Isid.* 63 is missing its conclusion, but the preserved section reads:

> To Aurelius Gordianus, *beneficiarius* on duty,
> From Aurelia Taesis, daughter of Kopres, from the town of Karanis. I have suffered damage and illegal prosecution . . . by my paternal uncle, Chairemon, who is from the same town of Karanis. Not being able to bear these things, I have sought legal redress. When I was a young child I lost my parents, and I lived with my maternal uncle Ammonios, and was raised by him. But my paternal property was stolen and is being held by the aforementioned Chairemon. I remained passive about these matters while I was still a minor, but when thanks to the providence of god I came of age, I thought it necessary to sue the aforementioned Chairemon concerning the property which he was keeping from me. Not once but twice I petitioned the *beneficiarius* entrusted with the decadarchy, and he ordered Chairemon to return the things he was holding on to. But he did not return them. Yesterday, which was the 24th, his daughters Kyrillous, Tasoucharion, Taesis, T—, and Thatres, their mother . . . abused me with blows, pulled out (?) my hair, tore my clothes, and threw me on the floor. They did this in the presence of Hol and Kasios, officials from the same village, who pulled me away from the women . . . [55]

A number of scenarios might be plausible in this petition: the violence by the women against Taesis might have been done at the request of Chairemon, or the women might have disapproved of the arrangements between Chairemon and Taesis, and gone after Taesis to administer some "local justice."[56] There is no way to know if either of these two scenarios (or any other possible scenario) is the "true" version of events. Still, from the way that Taesis' complaint is structured, it seems reasonable to suspect that *she* frames the complaint as if the violence was done at the prompting of Chairemon. Petitions with elaborate narrations tend to provide background to specific aspects of the incident, and are designed to implicate the individuals understood to be responsible. The emphasis on Chairemon in the background to the specific complaint makes it likely that Taesis thinks that he is the party who bears ultimate responsibility for the attack.

Structurally, the dynamics of the petition and the contract could not be any more different. The contracts work between two groups (or more) of people who have a status that is essentially equal, at least in the most formal legal sense that contracts require and presume. Petitions bring third parties into the dispute, in the form of magistrates who, by definition, are more powerful than the parties involved in the dispute. Contracts are signed by willing parties; petitioning is an act that seeks to coerce other parties. The contract itself, no matter the extent to which one might have to hold his or her nose to sign it, is a document that can be worked out in private; a petition is a public proclamation of dispute. It may serve to escalate the dispute, but this need not be its only function. Taesis' initial petitions to the *beneficiarius* are not preserved, but her final one is (*P.Cair.Isid.* 64). This petition is directed to the *strategos* of the nome, suggesting that the dispute has escalated. If Thomas is right about the necessity of reinitiating legal proceedings after the restoration of imperial government, we may guess that *P.Cair.Isid.* 64 looks somewhat similar to the earlier petitions to which Taesis refers and which are no longer extant. This strategy of reading a later complaint to guess the substance of a nonextant earlier complaint is not without methodological problems, but may nonetheless be illustrative.

> Αὐρηλίῳ Ἥρωνι στρατηγῷ Ἀρσινοίτου παρὰ Αὐρηλίων Ταήσεως καὶ Κυριλλοῦτος ἀμφοτέρων Κοπρῆ ἀπὸ κώμης Καρανίδος. ὁ ἡμέτερος ἡμῶν πατὴρ, ἄριστε τῶν στρατηγῶν, τὸν βίον τελευτῶν κατέλειψεν κινητὰ εἴδη. ὁ δὲ τούτου ἀδελφὸς Χαιρήμων ἅπαντα τὰ κατέλειψεν ἐνκολπωσάμενος καὶ παρέσχετο ἡμῖν ταῖς γυναιξὶν σιτικὰς δημοσίας ἀρούρας ταῖς μὴ δυναμέναις ὑπαντᾶν τοῖς φόροις τῶν ἀρουρῶν. προσήλθαμεν δὲ καὶ τότε τῷ γενομένῳ πρωτοστάτῃ τῆς κώμης Σερήνῳ τῷ καὶ Ἁρπ[ο]κρᾷ καὶ ἐκέ[λ]ευσεν αὐτὸν ἅπαντα τὰ καταλειφθέντα ὑπὸ τ[ο]ῦ ἡμῶν πατρὸς ταῦτα ἡμῖν πα[ρ]ασχεῖν. ὃς δὲ οὐδεμίαν ἡμῶν φ[ρ]οντίδα πο[ι]εῖται, καὶ δι' αὐτὸ τοῦτο ἐντάξασαι τὰ καταλειφθέντα [δ]εόμεθα καὶ παρακαλοῦμεν

> τὴν σὴν φιλανθρωπίαν ὅπως κελεύσῃς αὐτῷ τῷ Χαιρήμονι ταῦτα ἡμῖν π[αρ]ασχεῖν ἵνα δυνηθῶμεν ὄνησιν ἔχ[ε]ιν τῶν ἰδίων.
> διευτύχει.
> ἔστι δὲ τὰ εἴδη· π[ρό]βατα τέλε[ια] ξα, αἶγες τέλειοι μ, μηχανὴ ἀλετικὴ α καὶ ἀργυρίου (τάλαντα) γ καὶ σίτου (ἀρτάβαι) β καὶ δουλικὰ σώματα δύο ἐξ ὧν κατεπώλησεν δούλην μίαν.

> To Aurelius Heron, *strategos* of the Arsinoite nome, from Aurelia Taesis and Aurelia Kyrillous, both daughters of Kopres from the town of Karanis. When our father died, O best of *strategoi*, he left some movable property. But his brother Chairemon took for himself all of what he left, and gave to us, the women, some arable *arouras* of public land. But we cannot pay the taxes on these *arouras*. We approached the administrator of the town, Serenos, also known as Harpokras. He ordered (Chairemon) to give us all of the things left by our father, but (Chairemon) paid no attention to us. We attach an account of the things left to us, and we ask your humanity to order this same Chairemon to give us these things, so that we can enjoy our property. Farewell.
> This is the list of property: 61 adult sheep, 40 adult goats, 1 mill, 3 talents of silver, 2 *artabas* of grain, and two slaves, of which he has sold one slave girl.

Two things are immediately noticeable. First, Chairemon's violence has been written out of this complaint. It may be that there was no longer any evidence of it, or that, since the petition comes from Taesis and Kyrillous jointly, the violence was not relevant to both of them, but this is simply speculation. The other thing that is noteworthy is that, in keeping with the request recorded in *P.Cair.Isid.* 63, the stakes have changed: no longer is the property in question simply two *aurouras* of land and a share in a mortar, but rather an extensive request for a great deal of movable property. The stakes are indeed higher, but perhaps telling is that the sisters' list also includes a grinding mill (μηχανὴ ἀλετική). It is likely that this is the same mill—or part of the mill—whose κοπτούρα they had previously agreed to share with Chairemon.[57]

Through her petitions, Taesis has changed the dynamics of the dispute, integrating third-party coercion and bringing the dispute into the public eye, as well as proceeding through various officials (the *prostates*, the *beneficiarius*, and finally, the *strategos*). By the same token, however, the simple act of petitioning is not in itself decisive, though one may guess that to the party who is being indicted it is at least embarrassing, frustrating, and potentially costly.[58] This person can also choose from several responses to a petition. Besides allowing the dispute to proceed through legal channels, the order can also be ignored (as it seems it often was), or it can be responded to with violence. These categories are not mutually exclusive, as the case of Chairemon proves.[59] Further, although the dynamics of the dispute are changed by means of bringing in third parties, the dispute could still potentially revert back to a process of settlement: Roman authorities encouraged settlement, and settlements could take place at various stages of the court proceedings that had been initiated by petition.[60]

Individuals, however, might not want to settle, and this is where violence becomes important.[61] Chairemon's violence against Taesis, then, would serve to finish the process that she started, transforming the dispute from something which could potentially be settled into a more permanent fission between the two parties. Taesis' complaint (*P.Cair.Isid.* 63) frames Chairemon's violence as such: in her narrative, Chairemon's violence is intimately linked to the course of the dispute as a whole and based on his refusal to obey the commands of the *beneficiarius* to return her inheritance. While we cannot reconstruct his motivations and intentions, we can tell from the complaint of Taesis herself that she sees this as a part of the process of disputing. With the instance of violence, Taesis ceases to be an insider—one with whom one negotiates—and is treated to the same sorts of group violence to which an outsider might be subjected. As a way of conceptualizing the transitions from contract to violence to complaint in Taesis' dispute, it is worth thinking about the ways that the Roman legal system would have classified these relationships. As I mentioned earlier, Roman legal theorists combined contract and delict under the broad heading of obligations.[62] As metaphors through which individuals understand their relationships, contract, delict, and obligation are powerful. In the case of Taesis and Chairemon, we see a process through which tense relationships are first restructured through contracts, and then, when these fail to satisfy, the relationships are again restructured as delicts. It is not stretching the symbolic vocabulary too far to read Taesis' description of Chairemon's violent behavior as reflecting the moment in which willingness to negotiate becomes transformed into an obligation in which she has no choice but to enter into a new sort of legal relationship—a relationship that begins, in the language of Justinian, from harm (*ex maleficio*). These legal categories almost certainly fail to describe the subtleties in the relationship between these two individuals. While this may seem paradoxical, that is also exactly why they are so important.

* * *

If we see in the course of the dispute between Taesis and her uncle a process by which clarity is introduced into the complexities of interpersonal relationships through contract, and then subsequently through the use of violence, then the petition of Dionysia provides a different perspective on the dynamics of dispute and the appropriation of legal relationships by both parties. The petition of Dionysia was discussed in part in Chapter 5, where I looked at the legal decisions of Roman magistrates included at the end of the lengthy document.[63] The judicial decisions that Dionysia appends to her petition, however, are but a single piece of the petition as a whole, which originally extended over eight columns on the *recto*; later in antiquity, the text was cut back to accommodate a copy of part of the *Iliad* on the *verso*. The first several columns consist only of small fragments, and the last is only a few lines. Considering how much is missing, a great deal is nevertheless preserved. The comprehensible text begins in column four, although parts of this column too are fragmentary and resist making connected sense. Column five is missing a fair amount of text on the left side, but columns six through the beginning of nine are generally well preserved, though missing some of their top lines. Generically, the petition is broken into two parts: the first, Dionysia's narrative of her conflicts with her father, Chairemon, which began with a debate over mortgaging a piece of property which was part of Dionysia's dowry; the second, a list of citations that support some of the key points in her case. As in the dispute of Taesis, then, the petition of Dionysia is one of the few instances in which we have the perspectives of both the victim and the violator; in an attenuated and mediated form, we also have the perspectives of the observers. Unlike the documents relating to the dispute of Taesis, however, in the petition of Dionysia the words of all of the participants are recorded in the text.[64]

The occasion for Dionysia's petition was a moment of escalation in the conflict by her father, namely, a petition in which he accused her of doing violence to him. I will return to this in a moment. As far as background goes, it seems fair to say that the relationship between Chairemon and Dionysia had probably been frosty for a period of probably several years before Chairemon's petition. Nevertheless, Dionysia presents the interactions leading up to Chairemon's lawsuit by dwelling on the language of agreement, citing a series of contracts regulating the rights to the piece of land in question that she made with her father.[65] Dionysia lists no fewer than three agreements, and dwells on the fact of repetition.[66] Though it is reasonable to gather that their finances were in a constant process of negotiation and renegotiation, and that these negotiations were probably strained, the emphasis on agreement is significant, for it introduces the problem of the language through which the subsequent relationships will be discussed.

In theory, at least, a contract is based on a moment of shared consent, embodied in a document that claims to register an agreement as to the types of actions that will govern the behavior of either party. But while the spelling out of particulars is key to the contract itself, it is worth asking why such agreements should be dwelt on at length by Dionysia. People make and break contracts all the time, and legal systems find ways of compensating the damaged party, either by prescribing a monetary award or (more rarely) by requiring specific performance which, if not achieved, then devolves again to a question of just compensation. At stake in Dionysia's complaint regarding these contracts is a question of her right—her unimpaired right (δίκαιον καθαρόν: vi.23–24)—to be free from her father's interference. The rights are the product of an agreement, or more precisely, a moment in which there was an assent to shared reason and language (the literal sense of ὁμολογία). The emphasis on remaining in the moment of shared language is key to her case: at stake is more than a moral claim of *pacta sunt servanda*; the logic, instead, is that through the magic of contract the complexities of interpersonal relations—those between father and daughter, with all their accompanying social baggage—melt away, treating the parties to the contract as being simply reducible to two individuals operating on equal terms.[67] The contracts represent agreement on legitimate communication—a shared truth within a strained relationship. The truths they express are further deposited in the town record office, adding the authority of a neutral third party—in this case, the state—to preserve and guarantee their truth. It seems, then, that the conflict between Dionysia and her father progresses in ways analogous to the break between Taesis and her uncle: both disputes use agreements to manage or dissipate tensions between the parties; in both cases the agreements themselves have fallen apart (though for what reasons we cannot know); and, most important, in both instances there is a violent incident that precipitates a legal intervention.

Though it is important that we have several perspectives on the dispute, we must also be careful to recognize that Chairemon's perspective only exists, for us, to the extent that Dionysia lets us hear it. There are a number of complaints by Chairemon that are referred to in Dionysia's petition; she has included just one of them, no doubt the one that she felt was potentially most injurious to his side and most beneficial to hers. While we may feel relatively secure that the documents included by Dionysia are real and unedited (changing or forging official records would be downright criminal as well as easily discovered), it is important to recognize that the complaint of Chairemon is framed by Dionysia to obtain maximum effectiveness.

Dionysia presents her understanding of Chairemon's complaint about violence before quoting the document itself (vi.4–12):

> ὁ δὲ πάλιν ἐπιθέμενός μοι οὐκ ἔληξε[ν], ἀλλ' ἐπιστάμενος ὅτι περὶ τῆς κατοχῆς οὐκέτι οἷόν τέ ἐστιν αὐτῷ ἐνκαλεῖν μετ̣ὰ̣ τὰς τοσαύτας ἐξετάσεις καὶ τοσαῦτα γράμματα, ἑτέρῳ ἐπέτρεψεν τὴν κατ' ἐμοῦ ἐπιβουλήν, καὶ σοῦ τοῦ κυρίου πάλιν καθ' ὁμοιότητα τῶν ἄλλων ἡγεμόνων ὑπογύως διαταξαμένου περὶ ἰδιωτικῶν ζητήσεων ἐπιστολάς σοι μὴ γράφειν, ὁ δὲ οὐ μόνον ἔγραψεν ἀλλὰ καὶ παρὼν ἠκρωτηρίασεν τὸ πρᾶγμα ὡς καὶ σὲ τὸν κύριον πλανῆσαι δυνάμενος. σιωπήσας γὰρ καὶ τὴν τοῦ Ῥούφου ἐπιστολὴν ἐφ' ὅτῳ ἐγράφη καὶ τὴν ἐντυχίαν τὴν ἐμὴν καὶ τὴν τοῦ Ῥούφου {την} ὑπογραφὴν καὶ τοῦ στρατηγοῦ τὴν ἐξέτασιν καὶ τῶν βιβλιοφυλάκων τὴν προσφώνησιν καὶ τὴν περὶ τούτων γραφεῖσάν σοι ὑπὸ τοῦ στρατηγοῦ ἐπιστολὴν καὶ τὴν πρὸς ταύτην ἐμοῦ ἐντυχούσης δοθεῖσαν ὑπὸ σοῦ τοῦ κυρίου ὑπογραφὴν καὶ τὰ ἐκ ταύτης τοῖς βιβλιοφύλαξι ἐπιστάλματα ψιλῶς σοι διὰ τῆς ἐπιστολῆς δεδήλωκεν τάδε·
>
> He did not cease, but went after me again, though he knew that it was impossible for him to accuse me about the mortgage (*katoche*) after so many investigations and so many written decisions. So he hatched another plan, and despite the fact that you, my lord, like the other prefects, had ordered that he not petition you concerning private suits. But he not only wrote you a petition, but appeared in person and mutilated the case, as if he were able to trick you, lord. He ignored the letter of Rufus and the circumstances under which he wrote it, and my complaint, and the subscription of Rufus, and the inquiry of the *strategos*, and the testimony of the record-keepers, and the letter written to you by the *strategos* concerning these things, and the subscription which was given by you, lord, at my request, as well as the letters to the record-keepers about this, and just wrote you the following . . .

The way Dionysia frames the complaint, and her conflict with Chairemon generally, is to assert that the actions of Chairemon are attempts to pursue a matter which has been settled decisively, and that any subsequent complaints by Chairemon are lies (as is implied in the charge that he "mutilated the case"). To reinforce this point, she quotes Chairemon's petition and the reply of the prefect,[68] and then makes reference to a long series of previous decisions by other magistrates. The importance of this strategy is clear when we look to the petition of Chairemon that she proceeds to quote. Chairemon's petition, dated to April or May A.D. 186 (vi.12–20) reads:

> Χαιρήμων Φανίου γυμνασιαρχήσας τῆς Ὀξυρυγχειτῶν πόλεως· τῆς θυγατρός μου Διονυσίας, ἡγεμὼν κύριε, πολλὰ εἰς ἐμὲ ἀσεβῶς καὶ παρανόμως πραξάσης κατὰ γνώμην Ὡρίωνος Ἀπίωνος ἀνδρὸς αὐτῆς, ἀνέδωκα ἐπιστολὴν Λογγαίῳ Ῥούφῳ τῷ λαμπροτάτῳ, ἀξιῶν τότε ἃ προσήνεγκα ạὐτῇ ἀνακομίσασθαι κατὰ τοὺς νόμους, οἰόμενος ἐκ τού<του> παύσεσθαι αὐτὴν τῶν εἰς ἐμὲ ὕβρεων· καὶ ἔγραψεν τῷ τοῦ νομοῦ στρατηγῷ (ἔτους) κε, Παχὼν κζ, ὑποτάξας τῶν ὑπ' ἐμοῦ γραφέντων τὰ ἀντίγραφα ὅπως ἐντυχὼν ọἷς p̣ạρ̣εθέμην φροντίσῃ τὰ ἀκόλουθα πρᾶξαι. ἐπεὶ οὖν, κύριε, ἐπιμένει τῇ αὐτῇ ἀπονοίᾳ ἐνυβρίζων μοι, ἀξιῶ τοῦ νόμου διδόντος μοι ἐξουσίαν οὗ τὸ μέρος ὑπέταξα ἵν' εἰδῇς ἀπάγοντι αὐτὴν ἄκουσαν ἐκ τῆς τοῦ ἀνδρὸς οἰκίας μηδεμίαν μοι βίαν γείνεσθαι ụφ' οὗτινος τῶν τοῦ Ὡρίωνος ἢ αὐτοῦ τοῦ Ὡρίωνος συνεχῶς ἐπαγγελλομένου. ἀπὸ δὲ πλειόνων τῶ[ν] p̣ẹρὶ το[ύ]των πραχθέντων ὀλίγα σοι ὑπέταξα ἵν' εἰδῇς. (ἔτους) κϛ, Παχών.
>
> From Chairemon son of Phanias, former gymnasiarch of the city of the Oxyrhynchites. Lord prefect, my daughter, Dionysia, has, at the instigation of her husband, Horion, often treated me impiously and illegally. I sent a letter to the most glorious Longaeus Rufus, asking that according to the laws I be able to take back what I had given her, thinking that by doing this she would stop her violence against me. He wrote to the *strategos* of the nome on Pachon 27 of year 25, appending copies of what I had written, so that he (the *strategos*) would examine what I attached and do what is fitting. Therefore, lord, since through her rebelliousness she continues doing violence to me, I ask, since the law gives me the power—and I attach below the section of it so you can see it—to take her, even if she is unwilling, from her husband's house, and I ask that no harm come to me at the hands of the agents of Horion or Horion himself, since he

> continually threatens it. I have attached below a few of the many (relevant) cases, for your information. Year 26, Pachon (?).

At first glance, Chairemon's request seems perverse: in order to stop Dionysia's violence against him, he claims to have requested that the property which was in dispute be transferred *to him*. Where we might have expected him to renounce his claim to this property in the interest of a mutually acceptable decision, his claim that the transfer of the disputed property to him to stop *her* violence against him (ἐκ τού<του> παύσεσθαι αὐτὴν τῶν εἰς ἐμὲ ὕβρεων) seems odd. In his second request, he asks for the ability to remove her from her husband's home, this time presented as a right to be exercised as a consequence of her violent behavior, rather than in the interest of stopping the violence that he claims is directed against him. Importantly, it is Dionysia who he claims is the perpetrator of the violence, not Horion himself, though in this case accusing Horion of violence would seem to make more sense. Likewise perplexing is his claim that Horion threatens him with *bia* (harm to property—perhaps by managing Dionysia's dowry?), and that he (Chairemon) should be protected against this *bia* when he comes to take her away from Horion's house. In Chairemon's view, the ultimate cause of the violence is Horion himself (he claims that Dionysia's violence is done "at his instigation"—κατὰ γνώμην), but this seems in no way to exonerate Dionysia's behavior.

Like the complaint of Aurelia Taesis, the petition of Chairemon presents a scenario in which there is an existing disagreement, in this case over a series of property relationships including land which is mixed up in a dowry, and the dispute over property has degenerated to a stage in which one party is using violence to make a point about the nature of the dispute itself. What makes the request of Chairemon so strange, however, is that unlike the petition of Taesis, he sees the *proper* response to the violence in reintegrating Dionysia into his home, along with the property that she claims from him. Why he requests this is unclear: perhaps he simply desires to degrade her, leaving her without her dowry, husband, or independent status. Dionysia herself claims as much in her response (discussed below), but since Chairemon does not explain his behavior we can only speculate. It would seem, if my argument holds, that the reintegration is predicated on the idea that, once she is in his house, the structures of power and deference will be made clear—especially since she will be without financial agency (her dowry) to complicate them further. What is important is that Chairemon understands that the dissolution of the marriage between Dionysia and Horion is now a critical factor in the dispute. In a fashion that bears a structural similarity to the case of Taesis, Chairemon seeks to change Dionysia's legal status and relationships as a way of responding to her violence; that he does this by trying to reintegrate her into his home rather than by promoting a full and complete break is odd, but ultimately comprehensible. The use of violence transforms the dispute from a simple matter over property (which seems to be the exclusive subject of discussion in the opening columns, mutilated though they are) into a dispute about status and relationships, where property is really only a proxy for the relationships themselves.

Dionysia's response to Chairemon's complaint is no less problematic (vi. 20–31):

> ὁ μὲν ταὺτην τὴν ἐπιστολὴν ἔγραψεν, ọὺ̣δ̣ẹμίαν μὲν οὔτε ὕβριν οὔτε ἄλλο ἀδίκημα εἰς αὐτὸν ἀπ' ἐμοῦ ἐφ' ῷ̣ μέμφεται δεῖξαι ἔ̣χων, ἐπὶ φθ̣ό̣νῳ δὲ μό̣ν̣ο̣ν̣ [λο]ịδορού̣μενος ὡς(?) δεινὰ πάσχων ἀπ' ἐμοῦ, λέγων ὅτι δὴ ὦτα παρέχω ἄνοα αὐτῷ̣, καὶ τῆς ὑπολειπομένης ἐμοὶ κατοχῆς τ̣ῆ̣ς οὐσίας ἵνα μ' αὐ̣τὴν ἀποστ<ερ>ῆται, κ̣ạὶ̣, τὸ κ̣ạι̣ν̣ό̣τερον, βίαν πάσχειν ὑ̣πὸ τοῦ ἀνδρός μου προφερόμενος τοῦ καὶ μετὰ {καὶ με̣[τὰ]} τ̣ὴ̣ν̣ πρὸς αὐ̣τόν μου συνγραφὴν ἐν ἧ̣ εἶχεν τὸ δίκαιον καθαρόν μου προσενηνεγμένον συνχωρήσαντός μοι κ̣αὶ̣ ἐπὶ τ̣ῆ̣ς μ[η]τρῴ̣ας οὐυίας συνευδοκῆσαι βουληθείσῃ αὐτῷ̣ ὑποτιθεμένῳ τὴν οὐσίαν ταύτην πρὸς ὅλα (τάλαντα) η, ἀφ' οὗ με ἀπαλλ[αττ...]...ειδη̣.ταυ̣ι̣ν̣ε̣υ̣κ̣ε̣ τοῦ ἀνδρός με στερῆσαι ἐπιχειρῶν, ἐπεὶ μὴ δύναται τῆς οὐσίας, ἵνα μηδ' ἀπ' αὐτοῦ χορηγε̣ῖ̣σ̣θ̣α̣ι̣ [......].. σενε̣[.]... δύ̣νωμ̣α̣ι̣ γυνή, ἀπὸ τοῦ πατρὸς μήτε ἣν ὑπέσχετο προῖκα μήτε τι ἄλλο ὑπάρχον λαβοῦσα ἀλλὰ μ̣η̣δὲ κ̣α̣τ̣ὰ̣ κ̣α̣[ι]ρὸν τὰς χορη[γηθ]ε̣ί̣σ̣ας τροφὰς ἀπολαμβάνουσα.

> So he wrote this letter, but he could show no instance of violence or of any other wrongdoing that I did to him for which he could hold me responsible. It was simply an insult, done out of malice, that he said he had suffered such terrible things at my hands, saying that I turned a deaf ear to him. As for the mortagaged property which was left, he wished to take it away from me, and, more worthless still, he claimed to suffer *bia* at my husband's hands—my husband who, after the writing of the marriage contract in which my pure right was conveyed, gave his consent to me concerning my maternal estate, and who also agreed when I wished to allow Chairemon to

> mortgage the property for a total of 8 talents. From this time . . . he tries to take me from my husband, since he can't take me away from my property, so that I (?), a married woman, can get nothing from him. And I've gotten nothing from my father, neither the dowry he promised nor anything else, not even the occasional allowances promised for my needs.

Dionysia's response returns quickly to the question of the property, which is discussed through the lens of Chairemon's broken promises. It is important to understanding her case, though, to note that she denies the violence of which Chairemon has accused her. Rather, she dismisses the accusation of violence as coming from malicious envy (*phthonos*). At the same time as she denies the violence, she accuses Chairemon of defamation (*loidoria*). Both *phthonos* and *loidoria* were serious accusations: as I argued in Chapter 4, complaints of *loidoria* fell under the general scope of violence itself. The question of *phthonos* is harder to pin down, but as I suggested earlier, *phthonos* is the language of the imbalance in proper social power, and, as I have argued elsewhere, these accusations tend to be mutual, for naming the actual source of social dysfunction is a complex and contested process.[69] In a sense, then, in this petition as well the accusations of violence go in both directions, with Dionysia claiming that Chairemon's accusations of violence are themselves an act of aggression.

It is, I think, no accident that Dionysia frames her relationship with her father in terms of contract. There are two sets of agreements that she discusses in her response: first, the marriage contract (συνγραφή) between herself and Horion, which, she claims, generates a "pure" or "unimpaired" right. By denying the fact of the violence, Dionysia is pursuing a consistent strategy. Chairemon has implied in his complaint that the dynamics of the conflict have shifted, and that he desires to have the matter dealt with; Dionysia denies that the shift has taken place, and switches the discussion from the violence back to the question of property, which is, in her interpretation, a settled matter. Dionysia goes on to quote the decision of the prefect Pomponius Faustus on Chairemon's petition, and from there she proceeds to give the lengthy list of legal decisions, some of which were discussed earlier (Chapter 5).

In the conflict between Chairemon and Dionysia, the style of legal conflict is about the nature of one's legal position. Both propose legal solutions to the problem; both of their legal solutions are grounded in personal appropriations of the legal category that they feel best structures their relationship. In the case of Chairemon, the legal relationship that is made necessary by the supposed violence—the challenge to his control—is to reassert his parental prerogatives and reintegrate Dionysia into his household.[70] Dionysia chooses to keep the dispute to the matters of contract and property; by denying that violence was used against Chairemon she argues that the legal system cannot again intervene in her affairs, since they are, according to her, settled matters, and the violence—since it does not exist—cannot force the courts to look back at the decisions that have been made. Even if it could, she continues to argue, the legal system would not support Chairemon's request. It is Chairemon's claim, I think, that is the most interesting for the question of violence: in a dispute about the nature of relationships, the moment of violence is the moment that affairs are restructured. That personal relationships are restructured through fictitious legal relationships is likewise critical.

* * *

In an important study, Richard Saller argued against making uncritical inferences about the nature of the family on the basis of legal texts. "In the historical era," he argued, "the Roman system of kinship terminology in its full form was a legal construct."[71] Saller pointed out that, whereas in the juristic treatments of kinship there was a complex multiplicity of possible legal relationships (he points out that the jurist Paulus counted 448 different ones), in day-to-day life these were ultimately less important than the immediate relationships of individuals within the *domus,* especially the nuclear family. Saller's most recent iteration of this thesis is supported by his earlier work (with Brent Shaw) on the tombstones of North Africa, which also supports his thesis that the nuclear family was the basic unit of social organization in the Roman world.[72]

On the basis of the evidence that I presented above, I believe that in some respects Saller's thesis can be pushed further. Saller is correct to assert that the "actual" relationships between individuals are never as neat and tidy as the jurists like to make them out to be. Roman jurists engaged in an abstract intellectual exercise that involved extending legal reasoning from a body of limited principles; there is little to indicate that the individuals who were being governed on a day-to-day basis really cared about the intricacies of this logic. However, as I emphasized in this chapter as well as in the previous one, there is every reason to believe that the inhabitants of Roman Egypt were conscious of law. Even if they may not have understood the finer details, there is ample evidence in the papyri that there was a consciousness of the privileges and protections that were offered to individuals through the legal system. Law provided a vocabulary for making requests and asking for tangible benefits, either negative (being protected from harm) or positive (asking for one's assailants to be punished). When people made these claims to benefits and protections from the legal system, they reinforced the Roman ruling ideology, according to which the strict but fair application of the laws of the province and Empire validated the rights of the Romans to rule in the first place. Thus, while Saller correctly claims that the vocabulary of law is not sufficient for understanding the dynamics of actual family relationships, we may add that when these relationships are strained to the point of breaking, individuals choose to use the language of law to validate their claims against one another.

What I have suggested in this chapter is that this vocabulary of law is of primary importance in understanding how individuals structured their personal universe in a time of crisis or conflict. In the cases of Dionysia and Taesis, legal relationships are made to substitute for the complexities of personal relationships. In the case of violence between groups, the moment of violence is the moment that achieves a certain kind of clarity between two hostile parties; it translates mutual animosities into a specific sort of legal relationship (an obligation, a clear and countable way of ordering relationships). What is most important about this new relationship is that it can subsequently be adjudicated by a third party. In both of these respects violence provides a moment where parties are forced to recast their relationships through the vocabulary of law. When I speak of law as providing a "vocabulary" or a "grammar," the point I wish to emphasize is that individuals invoke formal legal relationships as a means of reinventing their actual relationships. That is to say, for a petitioner the relationships evoked by the language of law are the relationships they *desire*, *not* the one in which they find themselves when writing a petition.

The legal system in Egypt was fluid; the trick was trying to pin it down. When Dionysia presented to the prefect the series of legal decisions that conclude the preserved portion of her petition, she made a claim to have the law on her side. That she did this through a series of precedents is important for understanding the nature of the Roman system in Egypt, as many scholars have noted. What most scholars ignore, however, is that Chairemon did the same thing: "I have attached below a few of the many (relevant) cases, for your information" (ἀπὸ δὲ πλείονων τῶ[ν] π̣ε̣ρὶ τού[των] πραχθέντων ὀλίγα σοι ὑπέταξα ἵν' εἰδῇς). Chairemon and Dionysia, in other words, each had distinct understandings of what they thought should be the legal relationship that governed their actual relationship. Yet both found a way to translate their claims upon one another into a vocabulary that presented a specific kind of understanding of their place in the world, and most important, into one that could subsequently be judged (and validated) by a magistrate.

Earlier on I made the claim that much of what makes violence interesting is that an individual must do more than declare that another person is "violent." The declaration is important and meaningful, of course, but one subsequently has to convince others that one'sinterpretation of events is the right one. In the Egyptian case, the convincing is done in the sphere of law, which necessarily implies that it is done in the context of a fluid system. Within this system the invocation of certain loaded terminology was a way of trying to start the discussion. It was also a way for an individual to declare that he or she wanted to be treated in a different way, that the relationship that had developed between the victim and the attacker had reached a point where external authorities needed to become involved in it. In the context of this process, it is a way of asserting a new type of relationship, one based not on the normal types of deference and tolerance but rather on conceptions of debts, obligations, and rights, and asking this relationship to be validated by external forces.

My argument that individuals used the vocabulary of law to redefine and restructure their interpersonal relationships has, I think, an important corollary. Many scholars of the Roman Empire have placed great emphasis on the importance of relationships of deference and reciprocity, and argued that these ties are a primary key for decoding the dynamics of social relationships. Yet while it is important to recognize and analyze these structures, the petitions from Egypt reveal a world in which we can access this system in a more dynamic way, albeit only at the micro-level. Certainly there was a sense of class structure and hierarchy in Egypt, but there is no reason to believe that these were absolute categories that governed every single interaction, or to believe that individuals would choose automatically to defer to someone who was just slightly above them on the pyramid. As I argued earlier (Chapters 3–4), the most important means that individuals used to differentiate themselves was to employ the distinction between free and slave—a binary distinction that also implies a fundamental equality between all the members of the "free" group. Likewise, what appears to be the abundant faith in the importance of contract—a relationship in which fictionally equal partners agree to terms and conditions of behavior—might be indicative of an *un*-hierarchical way of structuring one's world.[73] This is not to deny the realities of power and status, just to emphasize that these realities can be perceived and manipulated in many different ways. But this un-hierarchical way of perceiving the world comes with a price: when there is very little that separates individuals—as I sense that there was in Egypt—conflict plays an important role in clarifying one's place. So does violence.

Shows of community and family solidarity against outsiders or antagonists are one way of using violence to establish and reestablish what one thinks are the "proper" social relationships. Using contracts to clarify expectations and structures of responsibility within the family—or between families—is another way. These relationships can then be restructured again, through the use of violence; when violence is used, the stakes are raised, and third parties become integrated as judges and arbiters of right and wrong. Whatever governs the choices that lead people to use or not to use violence—and I think that these will continue to elude us—we cannot escape the conclusion that the use of violence was a core element in individual strategies for transforming their disputes, relationships, and positions vis-à-vis their opponents and the community at large.

CONCLUSION

Nomos and Its Narratives

Two types of conclusions can be drawn from the preceding essay. The first set of conclusions pertains primarily to the Roman world; the second to the relationship between violence, law, and society.

Papyri are a remarkable resource for writing the history of the Roman Empire. Though all ancient historians are likely to concede this point, there remains a paucity of studies using the papyri as sources for social history—sources, that is, which can illuminate the reasoning that people gave for their own actions. Scholars have made great progress throughout the "century of papyrology" and beyond in understanding the world that the papyri document, from the details of landholding regimes to the structures of administration. The next challenge is to consider how these structures were understood by the people who used them. The distribution of wealth, the patterns of inheritance, the system of taxation, the presence or absence of police forces, and many other aspects of daily life are well attested by the papyri. As "facts" these things are important. But the structures in which people live their lives do not in themselves have any intrinsic meaning. The meanings are construed on a daily basis and in divergent ways when the users of a system try to bend it to their own needs. It is an interactive process, and both sides of the question need to be given consideration. If I have emphasized agency, perception, and interpretation in this work at the expense of structure, then this is because perception is so seldom considered, while structure has already occupied the time and energy of so many conscientious scholars.

This emphasis on self-perception and interpretation—in other words, on the act of hermeneusis that can take place in the wake of a violent incident—also speaks to the importance of papyri in reconstructing the "colonial conversation" that structured governance, law, and society in the Roman Empire.

I borrow this concept from John and Jean Comaroff's magisterial historical anthropology of colonialism in South Africa,[1] but it is vitally important for the ways in which we describe and analyze the dynamics of ancient empires as well. The history of the Roman provinces has often been told as a story of acculturation—the slow and at times imperfect process by which people came to think of themselves as Roman. The history of Roman law in the provinces has been no exception to this rule. To a significant degree, such a question "makes sense"—in 30 B.C. there were very few Romans in Egypt; by the age of Justinian, everyone was Roman. There would seem to be a question there, something that demands explanation: what could such a change have signified? Was it merely a formal change of juridical status? Or was there something more meaningful at stake?

As interesting a question as this is, I have tried to sidestep it in this book, preferring instead to reconstruct something more akin to the Comaroffs' "conversation." Rather than mapping a move from one static cultural or legal pole to another, I have preferred to see in these petitions a dialectical process whereby people's understandings of themselves and their worlds come to be actuated, at least temporarily. Violent acts—and the petitions that arose from them—were moves in local dramas. But the petitions, at least, were different from other moves—by engaging law on its own terms but with sometimes differing immediate purposes, and by engaging the system through a form of writing that would come to live on in archives and contribute, in its own ways, to the shape of the laws themselves, these petitions structured interactions between subject and governor, ruler and ruled, in reciprocal ways. And these moves did not always go in the directions that the imperial government desired: the juridico-ethnic hierarchies that constituted an important means of domination for Roman governance were continually breaking down; the Roman commitment to legal pluralism was constantly shifting the boundaries of who should be in charge of whom and providing an engine for transformation; individual subjects processed some bits of Roman ideology, narrativized them, and turned them into normative claims on the government that the government did not always expect. The richness of this conversation ended up producing a set of temporary stabilities—moments of agreement—that made for a tolerable legal world.

My second point relates to the larger question of the relationships between violence, narrative, law, and the state. At the beginning of this study, I suggested that the importance of law, at least in the perhaps-idiosyncratic way that it worked in the Roman Empire, was that it had a hermeneutic function—that is, that it provided a vocabulary for describing one's suffering, and a genre of narration through which that relatively constrained and limited vocabulary could be activated. The end result was that two elements of a petition—the vocabulary of violence and the genre or grammar that made this vocabulary into a request—could serve as a means through which people came to locate themselves within a social world, and especially to redeem themselves in situations in which their everyday, taken-for-granted, pre-ontological understandings of themselves were suddenly and unpleasantly called into question. An excavation of the world of petitions led us back to the question of violence itself, and the role of violence in creating and maintaining communities.[2] Perhaps surprisingly, by the end of the inquiry violence and petitions came to look as though they were doing very similar things: defining the boundaries of communities; compressing complex relationships into clearly discernible categories; and forcing dilemmas—binary choices like complain/ignore, right/wrong, guilty/not guilty, obligated/unobligated, person/object—that had to be made either by victims or by judges about the terms on which relationships would proceed in the future.

Though violence and petition share some features, it would nonetheless be a grave error to equate an act of violence with a remedy for violence—or at least to do so without further comment—at the risk of trivializing both law and violence, both present and past. Put simply, a petition is not a punch in the face. A request that a magistrate punish a wrongdoer after a trial is not the same as beating that man, stripping his clothes, and making him crawl home while the rest of the village watched from the windows. This does not, of course, mean that the state could not partake of its own sorts of violence. As Robert Cover, whom I evoke in my title to this Conclusion, reminds us in his essay "Violence and the Word," "legal interpretation takes place in a field of pain and death.[3] One could rephrase: "even legal interpretation" does this—for aside from interpretation, the state has plenty of other violent tactics, too. Some would be brought to bear on the people about whom petitioners complained; sometimes, when things went wrong, they would be brought to bear on petitioners themselves. How, then, are we to distinguish a petition from a violent act—either by the person about whom a petitioner complains, or by the Empire which brings its interpretations and occasionally its whips and rods to bear on the original violator? In other words, is it just violence all the way down, and nothing more?

It is not. A petition—a narrative of self-understanding and self-redemption—is what Elaine Scarry calls a world-creating act.[4] To write a narrative about oneself in the form of a normative claim—to perform an act of interpretation—is to attempt to remake one's world after that world has been called into question. It is future-oriented, and therefore productive in the ways in which it motivates others to partake of that creation as well. Judith Butler has captured this productive element gracefully:[5]

> When we recognize another, or when we ask for recognition ourselves, we are not asking for an Other to see us as we are, as we have always been, as we were constituted prior to the encounter itself. Instead, in the asking, in the petition, we have already become something new, since we are constituted by virtue of the address, a need and desire for the Other that takes place in the language in the broadest sense, one without which we could not be. To ask for recognition, or to offer it, is precisely not to ask for recognition of what one already is. It is to solicit a becoming, to instigate a transformation, to petition the future always in relation to the Other. It is also to stake one's own being, and one's own persistence in one's own being, in the struggle for recognition.

Narrative and petition are productive acts; this production, for Scarry, constitutes an attempt to intervene in the world, to create within it; it is thereby also an act that is productive of civilization. These narratives create, in other words, a *nomos*—a tolerable, regular, predictable, rule-governed community. Violence—the infliction of pain—is essentially different (and here it pays to be metaphysical); it is, to follow Scarry, a world-destroying act. It seeks to evacuate the contents of consciousness, to make people "see stars" such that it renders linguistic expression impossible; it has the effect of forcing the one who suffers to take on the viewpoint of the one who makes him or her suffer. Insofar as it too can create a *nomos,* such a *nomos* is either illusory or created in bad faith.

How, then, was it possible for petitioners in Roman Egypt to make their worlds tolerable when they were caught between their local enemies and an imperial power that was both a prolific user of violence and a major innovator in its possible uses for governance?

Part of the answer, at least, seems to reside in an important historical irony, one located in the nature of law in Roman Egypt itself. The legal landscape of Roman Egypt was built from a series of conversations between the individuals who used and invoked it in times of need, especially at moments when they accessed it to pressure those in charge of such a system to solve their problems for them. The land of Egypt was not blanketed by Roman magistrates seeking to bring the populace into conformity with its laws. The use and development of law came from individual initiative, and was animated by the flood of individual narratives. Because of its ideology of responsiveness, and because it arrogated to itself the right to judge matters of violence, the Roman state tolerated these narratives. But it only *tolerated* them: as soon as it figured out technologies for eliminating them from its legal system—by suppressing them, for instance—it did. And here there is a parallel story in the development of Roman provincial law, a highly pessimistic story that runs parallel to—and of course in conversation with—the relatively optimistic view that characterizes the bulk of the preceding essay. In a world characterized by petitions—a world marked by the ability to petition vested in the rights-bearing subject who saw him or herself as fundamentally autonomous and inviolable—there is another world, the world of the governors and central authorities seeking ways to harness the power of his or her voice and narrative. Starting in the third century, the Roman state began developing new legal technologies, new ways of distinguishing what was "law" from what was not, and for determining whose voices would be allowed to participate in this process. The revolution in legal technology came by decoupling the narratives and petitions from the declarations of "what was law" that used to live on the bottoms of them—in subscriptions and in the courtroom. The central government began to compile these subscriptions—pulled from their narratives—and to bind them in authoritative handbooks: the *Codex Hermogenianus*, the *Codex Gregorianus*, and, most important, the *Codex Justinianus* that provides the chronological endpoint of this study. These were attempts to win the contest of whose voice would get to be authoritative—whose narrative, in other words, would be allowed to create a *nomos*. This is a story that needs to be told, too.

APPENDIX A: THE PAPYRUS ON THE PAGE

Many texts have been reproduced in this book, frequently in toto, offset in the text as block quotations. This insistence on quoting long stretches of text, and reproducing in the appendix that follows translations of my primary sources, is an important part of what I take to be good historical method—a way of showing one's cards, as it were. It is also something of an illusion. Papyri are, first and foremost, pieces of material culture. Through the careful work of conservators and textual scholars they have been made to yield texts that exist in two dimensions, rather than three. The purpose of this appendix is to introduce this process by which an artifact becomes a text, for interested readers who are not specialists in the arcana of papyrology. Readers who find this story exciting are encouraged to learn more by consulting Peter Parsons's wonderful survey, *City of the Sharp-Nosed Fish.*

Papyri emerge from their contexts, by either systematic or illicit excavation, in wadded rolls. They must be exposed to humidity to "release" the wads, then carefully cleaned of detritus, salt, and other intrusions (such as gesso, if the papyri were recycled in antiquity to make mummy cartonnage). The humidified text is carefully and painstakingly unrolled, its fibers straightened, and flattened before being mounted, usually under glass. Then the papyrus must be "read," producing a transcription of the "raw" text. "Reading" is different from publishing. To be properly published, an "edition" of the text must be made, featuring not only the transcription and a description of the unrolled artifact (with dimensions, description of color, provenance, and date), but usually also a line-by-line commentary on interesting or problematic features of the text and its contents. A photograph of the papyrus often accompanies publication. The goal is to produce an accurate representation of the text inscribed upon the original artifact. Accordingly, publications generally reproduce the text line-by-line, as it appears on the papyrus itself. For reasons of space, this arrangement largely has not been followed in this book, except in the rare instances in which the line-by-line presentation of the text is essential to the argument.

The previous paragraph compresses a number of features of this process that are consequential for historical interpretation. First is the matter of numbers. In the process of moving from conservation to publication there is attrition. Many papyri remain unconserved, unread, or unpublished. Some, once conserved, resist decipherment. Others, once deciphered, are for various reasons not published. Sometimes this is because they are only small fragments (a few letters, half a line); at other times this is because the editor, frequently overwhelmed with other publication responsibilities, deems a particular document uninteresting, or simply cannot "get to the bottom" of what is going on in the text to a level sufficient to produce a commentary. In general, it is likely that a text that is complete, relatively undamaged, and "interesting" will receive publication before one that is worm-eaten, abraded, and highly idiosyncratic, or a text that adds little to our knowledge of other examplars.

Second, reading and publication are not exact sciences. Transcribing the text is often a matter of reconstructing it, making educated and at times very sophisticated guesses at what it is "supposed" to say, on the basis of parallels from other texts. Writers in Greco-Roman Egypt use odd scripts and idiosyncratic cursives, make grammatical and orthographic errors, and generally use little, if any, punctuation. They often write Greek in the dialect they spoke. There are generally no breaks between words, and a string of letters can be divided into individual words in multiple ways that are at times consequential for understanding meaning. There are at times corrections in the original texts themselves. More important, this process of reconstruction is complicated by the fact that quite often pieces are literally missing from the text. Sometimes this can be a small bit here and there; other times this can be the entire top, bottom, left, or right side of a text. In some cases, guessing what parts of the text should be reconstructed is fairly safe. Some documents, such as contracts, follow fairly regular formulae. Others, such as personal letters, necessarily differ widely within their genre. Restoration is riskier in these cases. When preparing a printed version of the text on a papyrus, editors use a series of conventions to mark these guesses and restorations. Text printed within [square brackets] indicates that the editor has restored letters or words that no longer exist because the text is broken. Letters that are doubtful are marked by ṣụḅḷịṇẹạṛ ḍọṭṣ. Finally, writers of papyri used abbreviations. When an editor restores an abbreviation, it is printed within (parentheses). In my translations, I only use (parentheses) to make the text easier on the eyes; words (within parentheses) are my best guesses of what a lacuna in the text says.

Because this process is based on careful approximation and guesswork, the initial publication of a papyrus text (called by its Latin name, the *editio princeps*) is not necessarily the final version, or the version from which scholars choose to work. Subsequent editors will often see things in an accompanying photograph that the original editor did not see. Sometimes additional sense is made from a guess based on a letter form that can be read in a different way, or on the basis of a parallel text. On occasion, editors simply make mistakes. Periodically it becomes necessary to republish a text in its entirety, with a new and improved commentary. Other times only small corrections are necessary. These corrections are catalogued in a series of volumes known as the *Berichtigungsliste der greichischen Papyrusurkunden aus Ägypten* (abbreviated BL).

This process of reading and publishing has, in recent years, been revolutionized by the advent of digital technologies. Texts are still often published on paper (in articles or books), but they are also now digitally encoded as well. Thanks to a remarkable international collaboration, the text of all published documentary papyri is now freely available on the internet in a digitally searchable form. The website papyri.info contains the searchable Greek texts, many photographs, and substantial amounts of additional data (dates, provenances, bibliography on individual documents, and more). The digital revolution has allowed scholars to begin reediting and correcting texts online, logging changes in the text as they develop. Because of its nature as an open-access collaboration between scholars, the papyri.info text is generally the easiest reliable version to access. The texts printed above mostly derive from this site. It is important to note that, for purposes of accessibility, I use where possible a version of the text which has been normalized to use conventional Greek spelling, rather than printing the text precisely as it was written in antiquity.

The point here is to emphasize that the text printed on the page is a construct, a best guess based on the hard work of many people. The content of the text shifts constantly. Sometimes these shifts are minor—a sublinear dot is removed, a more convincing date is proposed—but at other times they are substantial and have significant consequences for historical interpretation.

APPENDIX B: TRANSLATIONS OF PETITIONS CONCERNING VIOLENCE

The translations that follow are of the extant petitions concerning violence, as well as a few other documents that have struck me as particularly illustrative because of their content or language (such as Chr.Mitt. 71, a *cessio bonorum*, in which the writer describes the violent consequences of being imprisoned on account of a debt; or BGU XI 2016, which may not be about violence). A few more petitions are likely to be about violence, but because of reasons of preservation we cannot be sure (P.Alex.Giss. 31; P.Flor I 58; SB XVIII 13127 = P.Bon. 22). These are only translations—they are not reeditions of texts. Whenever possible, I have built my translations on existing English translations. Additionally, all translations are interpretations of the best way to render a document into a modern language. I have tried to capture what I sense is the nature of these documents. This is, of course, tricky in the case of documents that combine colloquial language with formal legal terminology. It has seemed best to remain as consistent as possible with respect to the legal terminology, but to prefer more colloquial renderings for the remainder. At times this produces results that sound a bit strange. They probably sounded a bit strange in antiquity as well, as petitioners made their best effort to rethink themselves in restricted and imperfect legal categories.

A tricky issue in translations is official titles. I have sought to translate the meaning of the Greek, rather than reproduce the titles in Latin: thus, for example, κράτιστος ἐπιστρατηγός has been translated as "the most powerful *epistrategos*" rather than "the *epistrategos, vir egregius.*"

The translations are in chronological order. They can be looked up in the Index according to the checklist of editions.

1. BGU IV 1105 (Alexandria, 11–10 B.C.)

To Protarchos,
From Tryphaine, daughter of Dioskourides. Asklepiades, with whom I live, persuaded my parents—although I, Tryphaine, was unwilling—to give me to him as my guardian while they stayed in his home (?). According to the agreement made before your tribunal he married me, and as a dowry I brought forty drachmas worth of clothing and twenty silver drachmas. But the accused, Asklepiades, acted as if he were a foolish young man throughout the marriage, wasted the aforementioned (property) for nothing, does violence to me too with his maltreatment, and lays his hands on me, treating me worse than he would treat a slave. Therefore, having sent my father Dioskourides to present my complaint and completing the matters concerning my leaving, (I ask that you) send this to him (Asklepiades) through a member of your tribunal, who will complete the matters necessary for my leaving as is proper, and will give to Asklepiades a copy of this report, so that he will either contest this matter (?) without delay or pay me back 60 silver drachmas. Still more . . . to Dioskourides for the other expenditures, that is, 66 drachmas, and afterwards that you pursue Asklepiades with your hatred of malefactors for the expenses and for the harm, so that I may feel assisted.

2. SB XIV 11274 (= P.Mil.Cong. XIV, p. 37, Arsinoite, 4 B.C.)

(To NN), commander of the guards,
From Patermouthion, son of Akousilaos, Macedonian, son of Nepheros, one of those from Ibion Argaiou in the division of Polemon in the Arsinoite nome . . . with others . . . verbally abused me, and beat me with many blows all over the body. Therefore I ask, if it seems good to you, that you order a letter to be written to the commander of the town to send the accused before you, so that I can receive your justice and that he might receive fitting punishment as a warning to others, so that I can be helped. Farewell.
(hand 2) Forward to the commander, who will do what is necessary . . . Year 26 of Caesar, Epeiph 12.

3. SB XVIII 13087 (Arsinoite, 4 B.C.)

To Gaius Iulius —os, commander of the guards,

From Imouthos son of Ptolemaios. Papontas, son of Andron, one of those from Attinos Iseion of the division of Herakleides got from me (on loan) the price of fodder. He owes me as well three *artabas* of grain for the mortgage of a bath that I have on hire in the town of Ioulia and Libia. He gave me neither the fodder nor the grain, but instead with his sons and his wife he did violence to me. I filed the proper sort of complaint with Solon the commander of the guards. And after this my attendants got together and went to the town to get back the fodder and the grain. Papontas' wife Herakleia gave me a cloak as security through the village chief and the other elders. But this aforementioned wife of Papontas, Herakleia, and the son of both of them, Andron, came to my house and wounded me with great violence and blows, and they stole from me the cloak which they had left with me and another cloak which was ours, the value of which was 20 silver drachmas. Therefore I ask that you to order a letter to be written to the commander of the town to send Papontas and the others before you so that I can get back the fodder and the wheat and our cloak and that they can get what they deserve. Farewell.
(hand 2) To the guard. . . . do . . . Year 26 of Caesar, Epeiph.

4. SB XX 14086 (Arsinoite, 4 B.C.)

(To NN), commander of the guards,
From NN. On the 1st of the intercalary days of the present ? year of Caesar I was walking late at night. When I came near the . . . which I had in bundles . . . Heliodoros, along with some others whose names I do not know, beat me with many blows all over my body, also landing (a blow on) my right cheek, and as a result . . . a wound has appeared on it. Another one of them, Menyllos, broke my right thumb, and then (helped) this same Heliodoros (escape). I ask that you order them to appear before you so that I may receive . . .

5. P.Stras. VI 566 (Arsinoite, A.D. 7)

. . . from NN, son of Pathotes, a farmer, one of those from . . . On the 20th of Hathyr of the current 36th year of Caesar, on a holiday . . . the birthday of Tiberius . . . attacking with his rebellious party . . . one of those there beat me many times on the . . . and the other parts of my body, striking my left . . . from the blow my ? was spilled out . . . from the membrane (?) . . . Accordingly I am submitting petitions to you and to Lei—, the commander of the guards. Therefore I ask, if it seems good to you, that you order this petition to be kept on file with you and that there be given to this same . . . a copy through your attendant . . . so that he pay the fitting . . . (hand 2) . . . son of Arakon to . . . (hand 3) Year thirty-six of Caesar, eleventh of Phamenoth.

6. P.Louvre. I 1 (Soknopaiou Nesos, A.D. 13)

To Ko—, *strategos*,
From Pannephremmis, son of Teses, priest of the greatest god Soknopaios. On the 28th day of Mesore of the 42nd year of Caesar, Papais, son of Papais, one of the weavers from the town, approached my fig tree, and by force harvested whatever he wanted. When I had a discussion with him about this, he beat me many times and cracked me on the left hand with a rod, and took my tunic, my belt, my shovel, and my axe. Because of him I remain laid up: he did no small harm to me, mistreating me in the public fields which I farm. Therefore I ask that the accused be brought (before you) . . .

7. SB I 5235 (Soknopaiou Nesos, A.D. 14)

To Magius Maximus,
From Satabous son of Herieus, one of the priests from Soknopaiou Nesos in the division of Herakleides. On the 30th of Pachon of the 43rd year of Caesar Nestnephis son of Teses did irrational violence to me along with those associated with him. He did violence to me, laying many blows upon me with the intention of driving me off. Even though he was overpowered, he came with his family and some others at night in the manner of thieves . . . they removed the mortar from the mill that I have in the town. Concerning these things I have also filed a complaint with Dionysodoros. Since you have prohibited through edicts the mixing of such violence and beatings, I ask that you administer justice so that I may be assisted and the accused may get what he deserves as a deterrent to others. Farewell.

8. SB I 5238 (Soknopaiou Nesos, A.D. 14)

To Lucretius the centurion,
From Satabous, son of Herieus, the younger, one of those from the town of Soknopaiou Nesos in the division of Herakleides. In Soknopaiou Nesos I have a house which was a mill, in which I have a mortar, still . . . to those around me . . . (I don't know) for what particular reason Nestnephis, son of Teses, a priest, one of those from this same Soknopaiou Nesos, came upon it in the manner of thieves on the night before the 1st of Pauni of the 43rd year of Caesar. He went to the mortar in question and with the help of many others (lit., with many hands) took it away. For this reason I accused him in a petition before Diophantes who was acting on behalf of Dionysodoros as the *strategos* of the Arsinoite nome, and concerning this we prevailed in court and the accused was ordered to return the mortar. But he is unwilling to return it to me, and instead always directs inappropriate violence against me and my associates; not only this, but also he beats me up in the town. Since I cannot tolerate his abusive injustices and since I am in danger of having to leave my home . . . fitting . . . copy.

9. P.Oxy. II 281 (= Chr.Mitt. 66, Oxyrhynchos, A.D. 20–50)

To Herakleides, priest, *archidikastes*, and in charge of the *chrematistae* and the other courts,
From Syra, daughter of Theon. I married with Sarapion, giving him a dowry by agreement in the value of two hundred silver drachmas. I received him into my parents' home, since he was completely broke, and in all matters I conducted myself blamelessly. But Sarapion used up my dowry for whatever he wanted, and never ceased mistreating me, doing violence to me, laying hands on me, and leaving me in need of life's necessities. Later, he abandoned me in a state of poverty. Therefore I ask that you order him to be brought before you, so that he be compelled to return to me my dowry plus half. I persist in and will continue with all the other claims that are pending against him.

10. P.Sijp. 14 (Arsinoite, A.D. 22)

. . . my daughter whom I sent shopping for four drachmas worth of grain. In some way Taormotis and her daughter —ous, the two of them, surrounded my daughter, beat her multiple times, and stole her tunic and the four silver drachmas. Therefore I ask, if it seems fitting, to order the accused to be sent to you for the appropriate punishment. Farewell. Year 9 of Tiberius Claudius Caesar, 14 of the month of Sebastos.

11. P.Ryl. II 136 (Euhemeria, A.D. 34)

To Gaius Errius Priscus, commander of the guards
From Papos, son of Papos. In the month of Pachon in year 20 of Tiberius Caesar Augustus, while I was having a discussion with Ancherimphis the doorkeeper and his wife Thenapunchis, both from Euhemeria in the division of Themistos, about the tin cups, the small table, the other accessories, and the 60 silver drachmas which they took from my house like thieves, he attacked me with inappropriate violence. I ask that you write to the *archephodos* of the village to bring them before you for the appropriate punishment. Farewell.
(hand 2) To the *archephodos*: send them.
(hand 1) Year 20 of Tiberius Caesar Augustus, Pachon 9.

12. P.Ryl. II 141 (Euhemeria, A.D. 37)

To Gaius Trebius Iustus, centurion,
From Petermouthis, son of Herakleos, one of the public farmers from Euhemeria and collector of public taxes, as well as a tenant of Antonia wife of Drusus. On the 2nd of the present month of Pachon in the first year of Emperor Gaius Caesar, I was having a discussion with Papontos son of Orsenouphis and Apion who is called Kapareis, both of them shepherds, concerning what they owed me as damages for grazing their flocks. They beat me many times, being unashamed that they weren't returning the money, and in addition I lost the 40 silver *drachmas* which I had from the sale of poppy juice. I also lost a belt. Therefore I ask for protection so that nothing happens to any of the public taxes. Farewell.

13. SB X 10239 (= P.Oxy.desc. II 315, Oxyrhynchos, A.D. 37)

To Sotas, *strategos*,

From Tryphon, son of Dionysios, one of those from the city of Oxyrhynchos. Late at night on the *dies Augusta* of the present month of Epeiph, in the 1st year of Gaius Caesar Augustus, the woman Thenamounis from the Oasis (?) and her daughter, Demetrous, having no issue with me nor with my wife, Saraeus, attacked her for no reason and harmed her, despite her being pregnant and . . . blows . . . untimely birth (hand 2) therefore I approach you and ask that the accused be brought before you so that they get . . . and . . .

14. P.Ryl. II 144 (Euhemeria, A.D. 38)

To Athenodoros, commander of the guards,
From Ision, slave of Chairemon the *exegetes*. On the 2nd of the present month of Pauni, *dies augusta*, in the second year of Gaius Caesar Augustus Germanicus, I was present in Euhemeria of the division of Themistos due to some unfinished business, and I had an argument with Onnophris son of Silbon, one of those from the town, about a pledge that I have from him. But he, for his part, treated me with irrational violence, abused me in many unpleasant ways, and beat me. I lost my account book and 60 silver drachmas. Still he dared to cast envy at me, though for no good reason (?). Therefore I ask that you write for him to be brought before you for the necessary punishment. Farewell.

15. P.Ryl. II 145 (Euhemeria, A.D. 38)

To Athenodoros, commander of the guards,
From Diktas, who is in charge of the revenues of Theon, son of Theon. Chairemon, son of Moschas, who was the beer-brewer on our property, committed many acts of violence against my family, and, not satisfied with this, he seized Artemidoros, my current brewer, and beat him many times all over his body, and stole from him a female ass and a sack full of safflower along with 40 *drachmas* of silver and cloaks. I ask you to write to the *archephodos* of Taureinos, the town in which they dwell, to send the accused ones. Farewell.
(hand 2) To the *archephodos*: send them. Tubi 3, Year 3 of Gaius Caesar Augustus Germanicus.
(verso) To the *archephodos* of Taureinos.

16. P.Athen. 32 (Karanis?, A.D. 39)

To Probus, son of Tyrannos, Gaius Caesar Augustus Germanicus . . .
From Onnophris, son of Kastor, from the town of Karanis, farmer on the estate of Gaius Caesar Augustus Germanicus. On the 28th of Pachon in the present 3rd year of Gaius Caesar Augustus Germanicus, at a late hour, Diony—, son of Pyrrhos, and Amoeis who is called Allalie and his ? who is called K—, all from Karanis, approached my house in the manner of thieves. They carried off my clothing . . . all . . . equipment, and they beat me with many blows all over my body . . . at the 4th hour . . . attacking my house . . . young women . . . therefore I ask . . .
Onnophris, who is 45 years old, with a scar on his left brow. Year 3 of Gaius Caesar Augustus . . . Pachon (29).

17. P.Lond. III 1218 (Euhemeria, A.D. 39)

To Gaius Julius Pholus, commander of the guards,
From Dikaios son of Chairemon, one of those from Euhemeria and a royal farmer. On the 30th day of the present month of Mesore of the third year of Gaius Caesar Augustus Germanicus, Helenous, daughter of Tothis, with whom I've never had any sort of issue, did inappropriate violence to my wife . . . She called out . . . and yet . . . Therefore I ask you to write that the accused woman be brought before you for the necessary punishment. Farewell.

18. P.Ryl. II 150 (Euhemeria, A.D. 40)

To Gaius Iulius Pholus, commander of the guards,
From Sophos, son of Marcus Saturnilus. Dikaios, son of Chairemon, one of those from Euhemeria of the division of Themistos, overpowered me in the town and did immoderate violence to me, and he verbally abused me, (saying) many unpleasant things. In the fight I lost 40 *drachmas* of silver. I ask you to write to the *archephodos* of the village . . . no . . .
(hand 2) To the *archephodos*: send him. Year 5 of Gaius Caesar Imperator Augustus, in the month of Soter, day 22.
(verso) To the *archephodos* of Euhemeria.

19. P.Ryl. II 151 (Euhemeria, A.D. 40)

To Gaius Iulius Pholus, commander of the guards,
From Herakleos, son of Petermouthis, one of those from the town of Euhemeria in the division of Themistos. Herais wife of Heraklas son of P—, one of those from the town, came into the house I have in the town. She grabbed my daughter and beat her many times all over, ripped her purple tunic, and carried off 100 drachmas of the *gymnasiarch*'s silver which I administer. Therefore write to the *archephodos* . . .
(hand 2) To the *archephodos*: Send (her). Year 5 of Gaius Caesar Imperator Augustus, Savior. On the 20th, *dies augusta*.
(Verso) To the *archephodos* of Euhemeria.

20. P.Mich. VI 421 (Karanis, A.D. 41–68)

. . . on the night (before the ?) of Pharmouthi of year ? of the divine Claudius Caesar Augustus Germanicus Imperator, some men, acting in the manner of thieves, dug underneath the stable holding my donkeys, and once inside they took two adult white donkeys, valued at 290 *drachmas*. I presented a petition to Pankrates, the *archephodos* of Karanis, and together we loaded the other donkey with water and food and set off to track the offenders from where found their trail. We got to the division of Bacchias, and then finally to the hill. But Pasion, the *archephodos* of Bacchias, along with the guards at the customs house held us back when we were about to catch the offenders. They detained me and the *archephodos* of Karanis, broke our water jars, stole our rods, and detained us for three days so that we wouldn't catch the offenders. Then they took from us two packsaddles, our bread, a sheepskin, and two feed bags. They abused us with blows until the *komogrammateus* and the elders of the village ordered our release. I ask to be helped by you.

21. P.Oxy. II 283 (Memphis, A.D. 45)

(Fragment A) To Tiberius Claudius Ammonios (?), *strategos*,
From Sarapion . . . year ? of Tiberius Claudius Caesar Augustus Germanicus Imperator . . . the younger . . .

(Fragment B) . . . me . . . two . . . silver talents . . . I have suffered harm in addition to the attack against me . . . was present. Sailing to Alexandria, where Areios and Euporos and Apion's brother the procurator Kallidamas are, I arrived at Memphis on the 15th, the day of Julia Augusta, in the present month of Kaisareios. I captured the slave in question, Euporos, from whom it will be possible to learn the whole truth of the aforementioned matters. I have brought him before you, after being attacked and receiving a serious beating from him and those surrounding him. Therefore I have been brought to submit this petition, asking, if it seems good to you, that this slave be held securely, and that you send him to my lord, the prefect Julius Postumus, for the case I will bring about this whole matter, in whatever manner may be fitting. Year 5 of Tiberius Claudius Caesar Augustus Germanicus Imperator. Month of Kaisareios, 15th, day of Julia Augusta.

22. SB XX 15077 (Tebtynis, A.D. 45)

To Galates and Kronion and Didymos and Herakleides, commanders of Tebtynis and the surrounding towns,
From Orsenouphis, son of Phasos, a farmer, one of those from the aforementioned town of Tebtynis. On the 11th of the month of Epeiph of the present 5th year of Tiberius Claudius Caesar Augustus Germanicus Imperator, late at night as I was going to the country to inspect the grounds on the *arouras* that I farm, I ran into Eutychos, son of Eutychos, son of Takolleinis, along with the others he brought with him: Onnophris, son of Orsenouphis, son of Anchios, and Herakles, son of Akousilaos. These men, having absolutely no issue with me, grabbed me while I was at the canal in the desert at that time, and they beat me with many blows all over my body, using the axes and scythes that they had with them. As a result of the blows I am laid up and in danger of losing my life. I previously filed a complaint with the *exegetes* against the aforementioned Eutychos concerning the matter of the orphan, because of the lease with payments in the orphan's case. Eutychos was interrogated by the attendants of the *exegetes* in the month of Pauni in this same 5th year. Therefore I submit to you this petition so that they arrest the accused . . .

23. P.Mich. V 228 (Areos Kome, A.D. 47)

Roughly 26 years old, with a scar on the left side of his neck, and on his left forearm. Tanouris, daughter of Heronas, is his wife. Against Bentetis, son of Bentetis.

From Thouonis, son of Akousilaos, one of those from the town of Areios, on the 26th of the present month of Neos Sebastos, in the 8th year of Tiberius.

(hand 2) To Apollonios, *strategos* of the Arsinoite nome,

From Thouonis, son of Akousilaos, from the town of Areos in the division of Polemon. On the 26th of the present month of Neos Sebastos, in the 8th year of Tiberius, I was having a discussion with Bentetis, son of Bentetis, one of the herdsmen from the Oxyrhynchite in the same division, about the wages and payments that he owes me. But he did not wish to pay me, but instead tried to cheat me. He did violence to me and to my wife Tanouris, daughter of Heronas, in the aforementioned town of Areos. Still more, he beat my wife Tanouris with many unsparing blows on every part of her body that he could find, despite the fact that she is pregnant. As a result, the fetus came out dead, and now she is laid up and her life is in jeopardy. Therefore I ask you to write to the elders of Oxyrhynchos, and have them send the accused before you for the forthcoming punishment. Farewell. Eighth year of Tiberius Claudius Caesar Augustus Germanicus Imperator, on the 26th of the month of Neos Sebastos. Thouonis, roughly 26 years old with a scar on the left side of his neck and on his left forearm.

24. P.Mich. V 229 (Talei, A.D. 48)

To Apollonios, *strategos* of the Arsinoite nome,

From Petsiris son of Phoulemis, one of those from Talei. On the 5th of Tubi of the present 8th year of Tiberius Claudius Caesar Augustus Germanicus Imperator, while I was working in the vineyard that I rent from Ischyrion, son of Ptolemaios, in Talei, I myself saw Patynion son of Herakleides and his son . . . leading mules . . . in the vegetable patches. I had a discussion with them and they did inappropriate violence to me, and what's more, they beat me unsparingly with many blows all over my body. They laid into my side with their fists, so now I am laid up and in danger of losing my life. Therefore I ask you to write to the *archephodos* of Talei to send the accused to you for forthcoming punishment. Farewell. Eighth year of Tiberius Claudius Caesar

Augustus Germanicus Imperator. Tubi 9. Petsiris, roughly 45 years old, bald, with a scar on his left eyebrow, along the top.
(verso) Petition of Petsiris from Talei.

25. P.Mich. V 230 (Talei, A.D. 48)

To Apollonios, *strategos* of the Arsinoite nome,
From Papontos, son of Papontos, one of those from Talei in the division of Polemon and a farmer of the land called Psenamtis, in the same division of Polemon. Someone entered the house which I have in the aforementioned Talei in the manner of thieves, and took ten beams and a millstone. When the commander of Talei and I made an investigation, I myself saw five of the aforementioned beams in the house of Patynion son of Herakleos. When I had a discussion with him about this he used inappropriate violence, and in the melee a small child who was seated on my shoulder fell down to the ground, and because of this is in danger of losing his life. Therefore I ask you to write to the commanders of Talei and to have them send the accused man, Patynion, to you for forthcoming punishment. Farewell. Year 8 of Claudius, Mecheir 10. Papontos, roughly 45 years old, tall, brown, with a scar on the left side of his nose below the brow.

26. SB X 10244 (Oxyrhynchos, A.D. 50)

. . . they made an attack on us and beat us with many blows, with the result that my wife, Saraeus, although pregnant, is laid up and in danger of losing her life. Therefore I ask that this woman be brought before you bringing along the others, so that I can obtain a decision against them, if it seems good to you. Farewell.
I, Tryphon son of Dionysios, have submitted this petition. I, Zoilos, son of Zoilos, wrote on his behalf, since he is illiterate. Year 11 of Tiberius Claudius Caesar Augustus Germanicus Imperator, 11th of the month of Neos Sebastos.

27. P.IFAO I 16 (Provenance unknown, A.D. 50–100)

. . . for the office . . . he stole the libation and ruined the annual procession and assaulted me, tearing the garment that I wear for the office of *pteraphoros*. Therefore I ask, if it seems proper, give orders to write to the (*archephodos*) of the town . . . produce the accused . . . so that there occur . . . punishment. Farewell.

28. P.Bingen 63 (Oxyrhynchos, A.D. 66)

To Papiskos, *strategos* (?) . . . of the Oxyrhynchite, from Pto— . . . from the city of Oxyrhynchos . . . month . . . of Claudius . . . approaching . . . into Oxyrhynchos . . . the city . . . they wounded . . .

29. BGU I 36 (= Chr.Mitt. 125, duplicate is BGU II 436, Soknopaiou Nesos, A.D. 98–117)

To Messius Audax, centurion,
From Stotoetis, son of Apynchis, a priest from the town of Soknopaiou Nesos. Stotoetis, son of Stotoetis, also called Phanesis, and his brothers, Harpagathes and Horos, although they are in debt to me, make no effort to repay me, and instead ignore me and make excuses. What is more, they attacked me and did aggravated violence to me. They beat me and tore the tunic I was wearing, and they threaten to end my life. Therefore, since I am not able to be passive, I ask that they be sent to you for fitting punishment.

30. SB X 10218 (Theadelphia, A.D. 98–99)

. . . and (his) brothers . . . summer and winter . . . property . . . from the previous first . . . Trajan Augustus Germanicus . . . unless . . . sixty . . . another seven-hundred drachmas . . . Hilairidas and Erotas from Theadelphia . . . the pastures which they were about to buy . . . thirty, five hundred of the . . . they covered, and with many blows . . . I have fled to you . . . did work for me. But if . . . the share which I have . . . by stealing sheep, remorselessly turning back . . . threw five animals into the river and without . . . they compelled (us) to give them a guarantee on an *aroura* . . . it was impossible for you to approach . . . they kept me locked up . . . to the *archephodos* for six days until . . . so that I may be benefited . . . Imperator Caesar Nerva Trajan Augustus Germanicus . . .

31. P.Ryl. II 124 (Euhemeria, A.D. I)

From Hippalos, son of Archis, a public farmer, one of those from the town of Euhemeria in the division of Themistos. On the 6th of Tubi my wife Aplounous and her mother Thermis—Eudemonis, daughter of Protarchos, and Etthytais, daughter of Pees, and Deios, son of Ammonios, and Heraklous attacked them, and beat my wife Aplounous and her mother in the town bath. They hit her multiple times on all the parts of her body and as a result, she's laid up. And in the fight she lost a gold earring weighing a fourth . . . a plain bracelet the weight of sixteen drachmas, and a bronze cup worth 12 drachmas. Her mother Thermis lost a gold earring weighing two and a half quarters . . . they went out from . . . those in charge of the bath . . .

32. P.Stras. VI 521 (Provenance unknown, A.D. I)

. . . 27th of the (present) month of Sebastos...with his brother and Belleleines. There were so many of them who attacked me, and they abused me with many blows . . . my cloak, and had not the village scribe who was passing by helped me when I was . . . in the middle . . . so that (I am) in danger of my life. Therefore I submit this and ask (that they be brought) before you . . .

33. SB XII 11018 (Oxyrhynchos?, A.D. I–II)

. . . (not only) verbally abusing me with many shameful words, but also having men assault me. I ask that you order her to appear before you, so that she gets what she deserves. Farewell.

34. SB XVI 12470 (Provenance unknown, A.D. I–II)

. . . (business) in the . . . the fell upon (me?) . . . a public official . . . making an attempt . . . using such a degree of nastiness, he took the garment that had been given us as security for a loan. Not only this, but he grabbed me and my brother while we were alone, and did violence to me with blows, and tore my clothing . . .

35. P.Oxy. XXXVI 2758 (Oxyrhynchos, A.D. 110–12)

To Archias, *strategos*,
From Heraklas son of Pauseirion, from the city of Oxyrhynchos. Yesterday, on the 5th, late at night, Apollos, son of Herakleides, (hand 2) from the same city (hand 1) and who lives on the same block attacked my wife Taamois while she was standing in front of our house. He was drunk, and he verbally abused her and stripped her in the presence of many worthy men, whose names I will present at trial. Therefore I submit this petition, and I ask that I be avenged, so that for the future I can be unthreatened and be safe along with my family. (14th?) year of Imperator Caesar Nerva Trajan Augustus Germanicus Dacicus . . .

36. BGU I 22 (Bacchias, A.D. 114)

To Apion, *strategos* of the Arsinoite nome in the division of Herakleides,
From Tarmouthis, daughter of Phimon, vegetable-seller from the town of Bacchias, at present not having a guardian. On the 4th of the present month of Pharmouthi, Taorsenouphis, the wife of Ammonios also known as Phimon, the elder of the town of Bacchias, having absolutely no issue with me, came into my home and did irrational violence to me. She not only tore my tunic and my cloak, but in the course of this violent act she took from me 16 drachmas lying there from the money from the vegetables that I sold. And on the 5th of the same month, her husband Ammonios also known as Phimon came to my house as if to search for my husband. He took my lamp and entered my house, and then carried off the pair of bracelets lying there, the value of which by weight was 40 drachmas of uncoined silver, my husband being on a trip at the time. Therefore I ask that those accused be brought

before you for fitting punishment. Farewell. Tarmouthis roughly 30 years old, with a scar on her right foot. Year 17 of Imperator Caesar Nerva Trajan Augustus Germanicus Dacicus. Pharmouthi 6.

37. P.Hamb. IV 240 (Provenance unknown, A.D. 119–20)

. . . the same house . . . others . . . their husbands, Sis— and Phibis. She was having a (discussion) with Thaisarion and Thenapunchis about this, but they treated her nastily. They beat her and her sister many times on whatever parts of the body they could find. The attackers' husbands then ran to the house of Phibis. From the beating . . . Heros is laid up in bed, and since she is 7 months pregnant she is in danger of losing her life from the beating she received because of the lawlessness of the accused. But she saw her own sister is laid up and . . . weak. Therefore I flee to you, and ask that (the accused) be brought before you so that I may obtain my rights. Farewell.
Phibis, roughly 30 years old, with a scar . . . Year 4 Imperator Caesar Trajan Hadrian Augustus . . .

38. P.Stras. V 401bis (= P.Stras. IV 242, Provenance unknown, A.D. 123)

. . . (I was having a discussion) with NN, son of Hermogenes, a weaver from the town, concerning the taxes he owes. For no reason this man beat me with many blows, doing inappropriate violence to me, so that what I had in my purse—the money from the tax collection—was scattered. Not being able to be passive, I ask to receive your protection of my rights, so that I can be benefited. Farewell. Petesouchos, roughly 40, with a scar above his right eyebrow. Year 7 of lord Hadrian Caesar, 1st intercalary day.

39. P.Sarap. 1 (= BGU III 759, Thynis, A.D. 125)

To Aelius Hermesias, *strategos* of the Hermopolite nome,
From Pamounis, son of Pekysis, one of those from the town of Thynis, a shepherd. On the second of the present month of Kaisareios in the ninth year of lord Hadrian Caesar. Late at night certain people, acting in the manner of

thieves, attacked me while I was the plains of the town of Magdolon Mire, near the town in the northern parts of the farm where I was pasturing the animals of Anoubion, son of Sarapion. They beat me many times with their shepherds' crooks, beating me on my head and on the other parts of the body, and they took from me a tunic, a cloak, and an overcoat, as well as twelve silver drachmas. They also drove off three goats. Therefore I ask you to order the *nomophylax* and *archephodos* of Magdolon Mire to be brought before you so that they can present the guilty people, pay for the stolen things, and . . .

40. P.Tebt. II 331 (Tebtynis, A.D. 126–32)

To Andromachos, *strategos* of the Arsinoite nome in the division of Polemon, From Akous, son of Herakles, one of those from the town of Tebtynis. On the new moon of the present month of Thoth, Orsenouphis and Poueris, both sons of Mieus, and Theon and Sarapas, both sons of Chairas, and Poueris, son of Ptollion, and Maron, son of Orseus, and O—, son of Protas, all made a nasty attack on the house I have in the town. . . . in the gateway, when I was having a discussion with them, they beat me many times on all the parts of my body, and took some white tunics and clothing, a cloak, a white . . . scissors, beer, and a quantity of salt, and some other things which, at the moment, I'm not sure of. I have approached the *archephodos* of the town and Herakles, son of Herakleides. I ask that they be brought before you.

41. P.Oslo II 22 (= Pap.Choix. 5, Theadelphia, A.D. 127)

To Herodes, also called Tiberius, *strategos* of the division of Themistos in the Arsinoite nome,
From Sarapous, daughter of The—, from the town of Theadelphia. (Okymenes), son of NN, was made my guardian by you, though he is wretched in character and in his actions. Using his customary nastiness and daring, he continually assaults me. Now, in my own home, he does aggravated violence to me, not only by verbally abusing me, but also by abusing me with blows. Therefore, since I am not able to be passive and since for a long time, every day, I have daily been in danger of my life, I flee to you, weak and defenseless, and ask that he be brought before you for fitting punishment, so that I can obtain your help and relief, live peacefully in my property, and receive your

benefaction. Farewell. Year twelve of Imperator Caesar Trajan Hadrian Augustus. Hathyr 7.

42. BGU I 256 (Karanis, A.D. 137–42)

To Gaius Avidius Heliodorus, prefect of Egypt,
From —on, from the town of Karanis in the division of Herakleides in the Arsinoite nome. Being a public farmer on an imperial estate . . . father, lord, happened to die, and in his will he left all of his property to devolve to . . . of the Lucii Antistii Gemelli . . . he did this since I was in the public ? . . . they would preserve the property for me . . . up until the present I enjoy . . . profits, out of which I have paid the taxes . . . me by the officials of the nome . . . liturgy and the tax collectorship . . . I am ? of the town up to the present moment, lord . . . Therefore, lord . . . released from the army and . . . earlier dwelled . . . along with those accompanying Sabeinos and . . . for which I was holding out for years . . . abusing me with many blows . . . of my wife . . . a deed of one and a half talents . . . to Sabeinos who is currently in the army . . . I ask you, lord, if it seems good to your fortune . . . write to the *strategos* of the division of Herakleides (concerning my case against him) . . . (concerning) my property and concerning the violence . . . what I have to say against them . . . is capable, and I myself through your benefaction . . . return my property . . . Antistius Gemellus . . . (so that I may) receive your benefit. Farewell.
(hand 2) Petition the most powerful *epistrategos*, and he will do what is necessary.

43. P.Amh. II 77 (= Chr.Wilck. 277, Soknopaiou Nesos, A.D. 139)

To Julius Petronianus, most powerful *epistrategos*,
From Pabous son of Stotoetis son of Panomios, priest from the town of Soknopaiou Nesos of the division of Herakleides of the Arsinoite nome, Arab archer of the customs house of the same Soknopaiou Nesos . . . accuse . . . but seeing the state being defrauded by Polydeuces who has been supervising the aforementioned customs house for four years now (in spite of the prohibition on this) and by Harpagathos son of Ero—tax, I submitted to the overseers of the nomarchy a copy which I had of Harpagathos' accounts of the things that come in and out of the customs house. I requested an investigation of these

matters in order to ascertain whether the taxes on these items had been given over to the treasury. When Polydeukes found out he and some others whose names I do not know attacked me and abused me with many blows; not satisfied by this, he brought a certain Heraklas to me, one of the guards of the domains, and both of them by force lifted me up and carried me into the counting house of the overseer of the domains and did to me . . . I was whipped in order that I give Harpagathos' accounts to them. This became clear to the overseers of the nomarchy and the *beneficiarius* who was at that time in charge of these areas . . . therefore by necessity I hand over (this petition) and ask, if it seems right to you, to send for Polydeukes and Harpagathos, the ringleader in this wickedness and its mastermind, so that I might be able to proceed against them and receive your benefaction. Farewell. This is the copy of the accounts that Harpagathos made. (*the account follows*)

44. BGU II 589 (Berenikis Thesmophorou, A.D. 144)

To Isidoros, *strategos* of the divisions of Themistos and Polemon in the Arsinoite nome,
From Dios, son of Patynion, public farmer from the town of Berenikis Thesmophorou. The night before today, that is, the 8th of the month of Mesore, Kames and Lautanis and Kollouthos, from the town, all three of them threatened me and came to came into the (land) adjacent to Antener, in the public fields which I farm around the aforementioned town . . .

45. P.Ross.Georg. II 20 (Arsinoite?, A.D. 146)

To Lucius Valerius Proculus, prefect . . .
From NN, daughter of Sarapion, a citizen . . . to my brothers and to Hermias, the purchaser . . . its sale, I had many confrontations before —oreios, son of Kelearis, the official recorder and the *epi ton kekrimenon*, who rescinded the purchase since the price appeared unpaid in the course of the investigation. Sarapion was the *nomikos* who wrote up the transaction, who . . . following the forms that were there . . . before the most powerful official recorder . . . another (confrontation) with me . . . the purchaser Hermias from the announcement . . . a petition for bringing suit against us . . . Hermias being the highest bidder . . . from the confrontation we had

with him because he did not wish to pay the whole price at the appointed time . . . in order according to the judgment and therefore . . . I petitioned the official recorder many times . . . he ordered his attendants . . . but since Hermias scorned the judgments . . . he made. Unsatisfied with this . . . he does inappropriate violence to me with help from his brothers and some others. Therefore I ask, lord, that you pity me, a woman unjustly treated by men who are criminals . . . not abiding by the judgments and order . . . so that I may be benefited.
(hand 2) Given through Apion.
(hand 3) . . . the *epi ton kekrimenon* . . . will prosecute (on the basis of) the judgments . . .
(hand 4) citizen, (asks) that the judgments be enforced . . .

46. P.Mich. III 174 (Arsinoite, A.D. 146–47)

To Lucius Valerius Proculus, prefect of Egypt,
From Ptolemaios, son of Diodoros, also called Dioskoros, one of those from the Arsinoite nome. Your inborn benevolence, lord prefect, reaches all, and I ask to receive it as well. There are a certain number of people in my district who are called *nautokolymbetai.* These men are public officials and are in charge of the administration of water, and are attached to the shore-wardens and cultivators, and therefore they are also relieved of the entire poll-tax and exempt from every compulsory public service. They are even fed at public expense since they are completely prohibited from engaging in any other sort of work. One of these men is Isidoros son of Mareis, a truly reckless man with a surly character, who through his henchmen counterfeits official leases for the sake of extortion and profit—all of this I will prove to you at trial. Isidoros attacked me as well, by sending one of his henchmen, a man named Ammonios also known as Kaboi, a man who is worthy of blame and who has been proscribed on account of his immoderate lifestyle. He came after me despite the fact that I am the holder of an official lease and that I pay a great deal of money into the official treasury, and that I gave security for my lease. But this man does not allow me to enjoy my lease, but instead he shut me out of my house and beat me until he extorted money from me. Therefore I flee to you, the protector of all, and I ask you, since for the moment you have delayed your assizes in our nome, to order a letter to be written to the *strategos* of the division of Polemo and Themistos telling him to hear my case against him,

since I am able to bring proofs before him of the violence and extortion, so that I can continue to live unmolested in my private property, enjoying the most happy times of our great emperors and of your gracious governorship, and so that I may be helped. Farewell.
(hand 2) I, Ptolemaios son of Diodoros, have submitted the aforementioned petition.
(hand 3) The *strategos* of the nome will do what is fitting.
(hand 4) Return it.

47. PSI XIII 1323 (Arsinoite, A.D. 147–48)

To Marcus Petronius Honoratus, prefect of Egypt,
From Ptolemaios son of Diodoros, also called Dioskoros, from the Arsinoite nome. Begging your hatred of wickedness, just prefect, I have fled to you, the benefactor of all men. A certain Ptolemaios, son of Pappos the former *gymnasiarch* of the nome, lives the life of a moneylender: he is nasty and violent by nature because he thinks himself a ruler and that completed matters are his business. He has gone to such a point that he has collectors who work for him in the towns . . . roughly and with violence he besieges (me?) relentlessly on account of debts . . .

48. P.Wisc. I 33 (Arsinoite, A.D. 147)

To Marcus Petronius Honoratus, prefect of Egypt,
From Ptolemaios, son of Diodoros, also known as Dioskoros, one of those from the Arsinoite nome. I have attached a copy of the petition I submitted, along with the sacred subscription which you attached to it. The below-mentioned Sarapammon says that he will not yet attend your most sacred court, so that you can investigate the decision of the *strategos*. If it seems right to your most merciful fortune, order a letter to be written to the *strategos* of the division of Herakleides—if indeed Sarapammon is in that nome or in the Herakleopolite—and have him order Sarapammon to give security so that he will appear before your most sacred tribunal. I have appended the copy.
To Marcus Petronius Honoratus, prefect of Egypt,
From Ptolemaios, son of Diodoros, also called Dioskoros, one of those from the Arsinoite nome. Of all the horrid things in life, the worst is for free men

to suffer violence. Therefore I flee to you, lord: deal with this act of violence. A certain Sarapammon from the Herakleopolite nome, from the town of P—, scorns the *strategos* of the two divisions . . . and as a result, is in mortal danger. For this reason I inquired into what sort of person he was and how he had previously lived his life, and I found out that he had become village scribe and he left . . . I approached the most glorious Mamertinus asking . . . and yet such people have been freed for public purposes . . . to be *strategoi*, that is, to rule and to prevent and to crush and to beat and strike free men and to whip them like slaves. Therefore I approach you to obtain deterrence in your liberality . . . should it seem good to you, order a letter to be written to the *strategos* of the division of Herakleides to order (Sarapammon) to provide security until . . . your presence, so that I can receive the highest justice.
Copy of the subscription: When I judge the matters concerning the *strategos* . . . I have written. Year 11, Thoth 10. Farewell.
(hand 2) I, Ptolemaios son of Diodoros, have submitted this.

49. SB XX 14401 (Arsinoite, A.D. 147)

To the most powerful Publius Marcus Crispus, *epistrategos*,
From Ptolemaios son of Diodorus, also known as Dioskoros, one of those living in the Arsinoite nome. For free men the worst of all of life's insults is to be beaten and abused; this is especially the case when this is done by cheap slaves or parasites. This is worse than heinous violence. Although, lord, we often wished to get justice, we have been hampered by our distance from your justice. Of these men is Ptolemaios, son of a certain Pappos the former *gymnasiarch* of the same Arsinoite nome, but a man by nature nasty and violent, and who lives the life of a moneylender and does every sort of forbidden, foul thing, asking for a *stater* of interest on account of his power in the nome, disregarding the judgments of prefects and the commands of emperors. He has done this to others and to me, too, asking for a *stater* of interest, coming down into the town with a gang and doing great violence to anyone he manages to get his hands on. And often he has done precisely this to me, lord, having his underlings use senseless violence (against me), and when we wish to petition the *strategos* about his extortion, up until now he drags out these issues before the *strategos* and they in turn counsel the judge—thus it happens that we cannot get justice. I will show that one loan in a single town was given out at three and a half in turn takes interest of a *stater* so that annually it's a half as much again, and you will find among

others he has gotten an eight-fold return from someone, and from another he has done something which is certainly prohibited, namely, gotten in a few years more interest than the principal. Since people like this deserve to meet with a deterrent, I came to you, benefactor of all mankind, so that I can retain my property in the most bountiful times of our Lord Antoninus, and I ask that you order a letter to be written to the *strategos* of the division of Herakleides so that I might be protected, unthreatened and unviolated by Ptolemaios, and so that whatever I gave him in excess of a drachma per month be counted towards the principal, and, if it turns out that I owe him anything additional, I will gladly give it back to him. As for proof of these aforementioned things, order the *strategos* to order a certain Aphrodisios and a certain Zoilos, his clients, to be brought before him, along with those who are unharmed by his taking of interest, taking a surety for their appearance before your court, and from this that man's intrigue will become apparent, so that I can be helped by you. Farewell.
(hand 2) Year 11, Phaophi 21. Petition the *strategos*.
(hand 3) Return it

50. P.Lond. II 358 (= Chr.Mitt. 52, Soknopaiou Nesos, A.D. 150–54)

To Demetrius, also called Harpokration, *strategos* of the divisions of Themistos and Polemon in the Arsinoite nome,
From Stotoetis, son of Stotoetis, from the town of Soknopaiou Nesos in the division of Herakleides in the Arsinoite nome. I have something to say against Sotas, son of Theon, and his son, Ammonios, who are from the metropolis but who reside in the village called Areios, which is near the town of Herakleia in the division of Themistos. I suffered daring and harm in the act of extortion which they did to me. They brought with them the attendant, Herakleides, as though acting on the orders of Theon, who was *strategos* of the same division. Once they were in order they carried out a most wicked deed: using violence and blows they compelled me to hand over the documentation of a contract of sale and of a pledge and of a loan of four hundred drachmas in the name of my sister— who did not agree to this, because she was in fact not even there. The deed was put into the name of Satyriaina, the daughter of Sotas, who was alive at the time. (They did this) because they look down upon me because of the condition of my feet. They behave in a nasty way and they act as if unhindered, thinking that their lawless and unjust actions will bear fruit for them by not making the payments of *staters*. I could not be

passive about these things, so I petitioned the former prefect Honoratus, who in a subscription told me to petition Crispus, the former *epistrategos*. But thus far there has been no conclusion whatsoever to the matter, and since the issue needs the judgment of the prefect, the most glorious Munatius Felix, I ask that a copy of this petition be given to each of these men by one of your attendants, so that they know that they must be present at the most sacred tribunal of the prefect, where, when he convenes the *conventus* or assizes for the nome, I will be satisfied with his command, and my account will be preserved concerning all of the cases that I have lodged against them.

51. P.Sijp. 16 (Narmouthis, A.D. 155)

To the *beneficiarius* for the area,
From Neilos the goldsmith. Today, which is the 9th of the month of Hadrianus, a certain Thamounis, wife of a certain Kofos the donkey-driver, came to my workshop on the pretense of (looking at) some silver rings. Seizing the opportunity, she not only abused me indecently with many blows but she also took from my counter a golden earring weighing four-thirds. Therefore I submit (this), asking that she be brought before you (for) fitting punishment. Farewell.
Year 19 of Antoninus Caesar, lord, 9th of the month of Hadrianus.

52. SB XIV 12199 (Theadelphia, A.D. 155)

To Ptolemaios, royal scribe of the Arsinoite nome in the division of Polemon, who is also serving in charge of the *strategia* of the divisions of Themistos and Polemon,
From Horeion, son of Kastor, a public farmer from the town of Theadelphia. On the 20th of the present month of Phamenoth, late at night, a certain Herakleides, a mule-driver, and another man, a foreigner whose name I do not know, these 2 mule-drivers who have absolutely no issue with me, were drunk, and they attacked my house and did no little amount of violence to my family. But I have no issue with them. All the guards grabbed them . . .

53. P.Fouad I 26 (Ptolemais Euergetis, A.D. 158–59)

To Marcus Sempronius Liberalis, prefect of Egypt,
From Pharion Eutyches, son of Herakleides, one of those from the metropolis of the Arsinoite nome. I have attached a copy of the petition which I gave to you and the subscription which I was sent, on page 233 (of the roll) sent to Severus, the *epi ton kekrimenon*.
Since . . . My opponent, Heron son of Amatios, the former *exegetes* of the city of the Arsinoites is very powerful in the area because of his harmfulness and nastiness. I will not able to contend against him before such judges, since he is very powerful. To give you a sense of Heron's nastiness, a certain Paulinos, son of the *gymnasiarch*, petitioned Eudoros, *strategos* of the division of Themistos and Polemon, and made an accusation against Heron. The *strategos* sent for Heron, but the *strategos* too was violently abused (by him). A formal record of this has been made. Lord prefect, I have shown you my opponent's nastiness: I ask, lord, savior of Egypt, to hear me against him, so that I may remain in my home. Here is the copy of my petition.
To Marcus Sempronius, Prefect of Egypt, from Pharion Eutyches son of Herakleides. Since your inborn beneficence, lord prefect, has extended everywhere, and since I myself am violated and wronged in every way, I have hurried and fled to you to obtain justice. Here's what is going on: since I owe a debt, I have borrowed some small amount of money at various times from Heron, son of Amatios, former *exegetes* of the city of the Arsinoites. Since he is convinced that by the honor of his office he is very powerful in the area, he continually does violence and injustice to me although I pay him that which he forced me to pay, namely, a *stater*-worth of interest, which exceeds the principal by almost one-and-a-half times. Because of this, I am in danger of having to pick up and leave. Therefore I flee to you, savior of all, and ask, if it seems good to you, to hear me against him so that you can reckon what he has taken from me, and if it seems that something is justly owed to him once the books have been balanced, let him take it, so that I may receive your benefaction.

54. SB XXIV 16252 (Karanis, A.D. 163)

To the most powerful Vedius Faustus, *epistrategos*,
From Gaius Iulius Niger, veteran, of the Osirantinoan tribe and the Hermaian deme. I served honorably in the army, lord, and am a quiet person, but I have

been brought to a point where I need your justice. I have suffered violence at the hands of an Egyptian, Isidoros, son of Achillas, scribe of the supervisor of sequestered property in the town of Karanis in the division of Herakleides in the Arsinoite nome. Helping him in this was Didymos, his assistant. I present (the case of) inappropriate (violence).[1] I bought from the public . . . in the ? year of the deified Aelius Antoninus from the among the sequestered properties an *aroura* of olive-land near Psenarpsenesis in the same division, formerly belonging to Kastor, son of Pekysis. I completed the sale for (? drachmas) . . . then I was assigned to pay the taxes on it. Recently the aforementioned Isidoros, wishing to harm us . . . five days earlier . . . (*a gap of 9 or more lines in the text follows*) I flee to you . . . what he did . . . he threw out the pledges, and once again I made a report about this. Since his offenses against me are clear, I ask, as a Roman who has suffered such things at the hands of an Egyptian, that, if it seems good to you, order a letter to be written to the *strategos* of the division of Herakleides in the Arsinoite nome to send this man for your judgment, and hear my case against him, so that I may receive your justice and be benefited. Farewell.
(hand 2) I, Gaius Iulius Niger, have submitted this. Year 3, Mecheir 21.
(hand 3) If the *strategos* decides that there has been violence, he will alert me.
(hand 4) Return it.

55. P.Oxy. L 3561 (Arsinoite, A.D. 165)

To Vegetos, *strategos* of the Arsinoite nome in the division of Herakleides, through Zoilos the royal scribe serving as *strategos* of the same division,
From Dionysios, son of Eudaimon, grandson of—los, from the tribe of Sosikomeios and the deme of Althaia. Yesterday, which was the 12th of the present month, certain people, acting in the manner of thieves, attacked me near the village of Hiera Neikolaou, near the watchtower. They were armed with swords, and they abused me with many blows, with the result that I am in danger of losing my life. They not only did this, but they also carried off all my clothing and money, along with the gold ring that I had. Therefore by necessity I petition you, asking that my (complaint) be kept on file with you . . .

56. P.Harr. II 192 (Provenance unknown, A.D. 167)

Copy of the complaint of Pamounis.

To —ion, *strategos* . . .
From Pamounis, son of NN...living in . . . the current guardian of the peace . . . —outhis, son of Psois, (attacked me) . . . on the 16th of the present month of Mecheir . . . son of Hatres (?) and his . . . and Kolluthes son of Kor— . . . and many others . . . being convinced . . . my brother . . . his head . . . is half dead . . . *in extremis* . . . of peace . . . another time also these people . . . of the wife of Pausenyr— . . . by the son of . . . we submit this (petition asking that an attendant) come to observe him . . . *in extremis* . . . offenses . . . so that we may be helped. Farewell. Year 7 of Imperator Caesar Marcus Aurelius Antoninus Augustus Armeniacus Medicus Parthicus Maximus and Imperator Caesar Lucius Aurelius Verus Augustus Armeniacus Medicus Parthicus Maximus, Mecheir 17 . . . I, Pamounis, (son of NN), have submitted this. I, Hierokles, (son of NN), wrote on his behalf, since he is illiterate.

57. P.Tebt. II 304 (Tebtynis, A.D. 167–68)

To Longinus, decurion of the Arsinoite nome,
From Pakebkis, son of Onnophris, from the town of Tebtynis, a priest, exempted from taxes, of the well-known temple in that town. On the 30th of the month of Epeiph, when it was late at night, a certain Satorneilos, along with many others—I know not why—did irrational violence to me, to such a degree that they attacked me with rods. They grabbed my brother Onnophris and wounded him, and as a result he is in danger of losing his life. Therefore, lord, since I am being cautious about his deadly condition, I submit this petition asking that you order him to be brought before you so that what is fitting transpires and I can receive the necessary satisfaction.
Year 8 of Antoninus and Verus, lords, Augusti Armeniaci Medici Parthici Maximi.

58. P.Fay. 108 (Euhemeria, A.D. 169–71)

To Megalonymos, *strategos* of the divisions of Themistos and Polemon of the Arsinoite nome,
From Pasion, son of Herakleides, from the district of the Hellenion, and from Onesimos, son of Amerimnos, from the district of the gymnasium, both pig merchants of the metropolis. Yesterday, which was the 19th of the present

month of Thoth, we were coming up from the town of Theadelphia of the division of Themistos, and at dawn certain malefactors attacked us midway between Polydeukia and Theadelphia. They bound us, along with the tower-guard as well, abused us with many blows, and wounded Pasion. They took one of our pigs and stole Pasion's tunic . . . and . . . Onesimos . . . therefore we submit this petition and ask that it be kept on file and our account be preserved so that when the guilty ones appear we have a complaint against them about these things . . .

59. P.Oxy. XXXI 2563 (Oxyrhynchos, A.D. 170)

To the most powerful Aquilius Capitolinus, *epistrategos*,
From Sarapion, son of Hierax, from the city of Oxyrhynchos, overseer of the tribes of the Serapeum and the other temples of the city. I petitioned you, lord, and you agreed to send my petition, but up until now it has not been returned to me. It concerned the violence done by Ploution, son of Dionysodoros, and his brother-in-law. I also petitioned Herakleides, the royal scribe, who was serving as *strategos*, and he ordered one of his attendants, Thrasyllus, to investigate my condition in light of the violence I suffered. A doctor's report was produced concerning the wounds I had at that time. He abused with his blows not only me, but also my son and his nurse Heras on account of an inheritance . . . movable property which Heras' brother Sarapion left to Heras after his death. His will was registered with the *archidikastes*, making her heiress. But this one attacked us, acting nastily, in spite of his being a fellow-villager. I have fled to you, savior and benefactor of all: hear my case against him. There should be no harm (to anyone) in these most blessed (times) of our lords Aurelius Antoninus Caesar . . .

60. P.Gen.[2] I 3 (= Chr.Mitt. 122, Soknopaiou Nesos, A.D. 178–79)

To Frurius Proclus, centurion,
From Pabous and Harpalos, both sons of Melas, and priests of Soknopaiou Nesos. Our aforementioned father, lord, passed away, and made us his heirs, along with Stotoetis and Tanephron. The two of us were given the household goods which he left. For no reason, when I was away the aforementioned Stotoetis came, along with the aforementioned Tanephron, to the place where

the household goods were stored. Even though both of our seals were on the property, they took off the seals, entered the property, and took away everything that we had put in storage. When we arrived to divide the property, Stotoetis, convinced of his own power, attacked us and beat us inappropriately. Therefore we ask they be brought before you to give an account of the things that they did to us in such a way. Farewell. Year ?, Aurelii Antoninus and Commodus our lords, Augusti. Thoth 23.

61. SB XVI 12678 (Karanis, A.D. 179)

To the most powerful Tiberius Claudius Xenophon, *epistrategos*,
From Iulia Herais, an Antinoopolite citizen, through her son, Gaius Iulius Priscus. A copy of the petition that I gave to Titus Pactumeius Magnus, former prefect, and the sacred subscription that I received from him . . . is attached. I ask, if it seems good to you, to hear my case against Herakleides concerning taxes which he asks of me for no reason . . . but using his power he does violence to me, and . . . illegal exactions. This is it:
To Titus Pactumeius Magnus, prefect of Egypt,
From Iulia Herais, an Antinoopolite citizen, and however else I may be known. I approach you, lord prefect, with a matter that requires your judgment. Herakleides, son of Ammonios, collector of taxes on the register of the Arsinoite and other nomes, is a man who is by nature nasty. He threatened me when he tried to collect taxes from me on unproductive royal land. I do not owe these taxes, nor have they ever been collected. Therefore I have fled to you, my savior, and ask you to order the *epistrategos* of Heptanomia to hear my case against him, so that may not suffer any harm from Herakleides, and so that I may be benefited. Farewell. I, Iulia Herais, have submitted this through my son, Gaius Iulius Priscus. Copy of the subscription: Year 19, Mesore 3. Petition the most powerful *epistrategos*. I have subscribed this. Thoth 24.
(hand 2) I, Iulia Herais, have submitted this through my son, Iulius Priscus.

62. P.Col. X 266 (Arsinoite, A.D. 179–81)

To the most powerful Claudius Xenophon, *epistrategos*,
From Herakleia, also called Rufina, Antinoite, daughter of Didymos, son of Didymos, also called Lourios, from the tribe of Matidios and the deme of

Kallitekneios. Lord, since my opponent has often put off and avoided court dates, (after so many ?, wasting time, to call ?) . . . the deeds of evildoers . . . the proof is this . . . and in his wickedness . . . to overlook the ? from your tribunal . . . they did. And since I was involved in multiple injustices and was robbed by . . . and . . . my sister's, I submitted a long petition to Valens the *epistrategos* asking to be heard. Valens, seeing that my request was pertinent to the *epistrategia*, accepted it, and set it aside for a hearing through all his subscriptions. But my opponent could not be found, but fled the court . . . to put off the matter . . . since in the meantime . . . and him . . . on account of the harm inflicted by my opponent . . . according to the . . . asking . . . judgment . . . helpless . . .

63. SB XII 11113 (= P.Mich.Mchl. 11, Karanis, A.D. 180–210)

. . . the olive-grove I own in the plain of Psenarpsenesis in the town of Karanis, I saw Satabous, son of Satabous, also called son of Kinkiol, along with his son, cutting fruits from the date palms in that same plot. I tried to grab him, but with the pruning shears he had he tried to kill me and . . .

64. P.Lond. II 342 (Soknopaiou Nesos, A.D. 185)

To the *beneficiarius* stationed in the area,
From Pabous, son of Stotoetis, from the town of Soknopaiou Nesos. Today, which is the 27th, Sempronios, elder of the town, and his people attacked me and did irrational violence to me. They did this on the pretense of holding my relatives Hekysis and Apynchis for an offense. They got scared and disappeared, but then these people attacked my house and did violence to me, saying "you have to hand them over," and "we know who will get them from you." He is shameless in the town; he collects money all the time; he extorts the townsmen; he hunts down the recruits and let them go only once he was paid off. Therefore I submit this petition, asking that they be brought before you. Farewell. Year 25, Pauni 27.

65. P.Oxy. II 237.vi.12–20 (Oxyrhynchos, A.D. 186)

From Chairemon son of Phanias, former *gymnasiarch* of the city of the Oxyrhynchites. Lord prefect, my daughter, Dionysia, has, at the instigation of her husband, Horion, often treated me impiously and illegally. I sent a letter to the most glorious Longaeus Rufus, asking that according to the laws I be able to take back what I had given her, thinking that by doing this she would stop her violence against me. He wrote to the *strategos* of the nome on Pachon 27 of year 25, appending copies of what I had written, so that he (the *strategos*) would examine what I attached and do what is fitting. Therefore, lord, since through her rebelliousness she continues doing violence to me, I ask, since the law gives me the power—and I attach below the section of it so you can see it—to take her, even if she is unwilling, from her husband's house, and I ask that no harm come to me at the hands of the agents of Horion or Horion himself, since he continually threatens it. I have attached below a few of the many (relevant) cases, for your information. Year 26, Pachon (?).

66. BGU II 515 (= Chr.Wilck. 268 = Sel.Pap. II 286, Arsinoite, A.D. 193)

To Ammonios Paternus, centurion,
From Syros, son of Syrion, also called Petekas, from the metropolis. My brother and I have measured out the grain we owe in taxes for the month of Pauni, and similarly what we are obligated to pay in collective contributions for the town of Karanis, nine *artabas* of grain out of ten. While I was in the fields, the tax-collectors Pete—sios, son of Tkelo, and Sarapion, son of Maron, and their scribe, Ptolemaios and his attendant, Ammonios, came to my house on account of the remaining *artaba*. They took my mother's garment, and drove her off with kicks. Because of this she is laid up and cannot (work?) . . . I ask that they be brought before you, so that I may receive justice. Farewell. Description: roughly 47 years old, with a scar on his right leg, saying he is illiterate. Year 33 of lord Aurelius Commodus Caesar, 8th of the month of Pauni.

67. P.Mich. III 175 (Soknopaiou Nesos, A.D. 193)

To Ammonios Paternus, centurion,
From Melas, son of Horion, from the town of Soknopaiou Nesos, a priest of the god in that town. My cousins, Phanesis and Harpagathes, and I own a walled vacant lot in this same town in which we store our hay for the year. We own it jointly, in equal shares, as part of our inheritance from our grandfather

on my mother's side. Harpagathes died suddenly, and his share passed to both of us, in equal parts. Yesterday, which was the 22nd, I was stacking hay in the lot when Phanesis violently and nastily approached me, tried to take my hay, and prevented me from stacking it in our common part (of the lot). He tried to exclude me from the property, and to claim my share as his own. Not only this, but he did to me the most extreme form of violence. Therefore I ask you to order him to be sent up, so that I may obtain your clemency. Farewell. (hand 2) Year 1 of Publius Elbius Pertinax Augustus. Pharmouthi 23.

68. P.Ryl. II 116 (= Sel.Pap. II 287, Hermopolis, A.D. 194)

Copy of the petition of Saprion.
To Herakleides, *strategos* of the Hermopolite nome,
From Saprion, also known as Hermaios, son of Sarapion, former *kosmetes* and former *gymnasiarch* of greatest city of Hermopolis. When I was speaking with my mother, Eudaimonis, daughter of Eudaimon, elder of Sotas, concerning what was left to me by my father, Sarapion, according to the will that he made, my mother, distressed by her guilt over what she had taken from the household goods and items in storage and (hand 2) many other things—not a few of them—attacked me with the help of Serenos, also known as Tiberinos, the former *gymnasiarch*. This man is the husband of her sister. They not only did violence to me, but they also tore my clothes, since they wanted to take my property. Therefore I submit this petition and ask that it be kept on file as testimony until I proceed against them, without affecting my claims regarding all my (other) rights. Year 2, Imperator Caesar Lucius Septimius Severus Pertinax Augustus, Pachon 20. I, Saprion, also known as Hermaios, have submitted this.

69. P.Mich. VI 425 (Karanis, 198 A.D.)

To the most powerful Calpurnius Concessus, *epistrategos*,
From Gemellus, also known as Horion, son of Gaius Apolinarius, an Antinoite citizen. I have attached a copy of the petition which I sent to the illustrious prefect Aemilius Saturninus (hand 2) along with the (hand 3) sacred subscription which I received from him. I ask, if it seems good to your fortune, to write to the centurion in Arsinoite nome to send (the defendant) to your tribunal and to hear my case against him so that I can get obtain my rights. This is it:

To Quintus Aemilius Saturninus, prefect of Egypt, from Gemellus, also known as Horion, son of Gaius Apolinarius, an Antinoite citizen, and however else I might be known. I petition you, lord, against Kastor, assistant tax-collector of the village of Karanis in the division of Herakleides in the Arsinoite division. This man looks down on me as deformed, since I am one-eyed and do not see with the other eye although it looks like it works, and thus both my eyes are worthless. This man robbed me and earlier has done violence to me in public and to my mother, and after his many blows and his abusive treatment of her he broke down the four doors of my house with an axe, so that our entire house lies open and is easily accessible to whatever sort of criminal. Our house was demolished and we were beaten despite owing nothing to the treasury, since he dared neither to give a receipt lest he be judged through it to have done wrong or to have stolen from us. Therefore, since our savior has ordered those who have been done wrong to approach without fear and get what is ours, I ask to be heard by you, lord, and to be avenged, so that I may receive your benefaction, and my adversary be sent on your orders for a hearing. I, Gemellus, also known as Horion, have submitted this. I, Germanos, wrote on his behalf. Year 6, Mesore 18. Approach the most powerful *epistrategos*, who will not overlook his duties. Return it.
(hand 4) I, Gemellus, also known as Horion, have submitted this. I, NN, son of Panebtichis, wrote on his behalf, since he is illiterate.
(hand 5) (Year) 6, 3rd intercalary day of Mesore. Petition me when I am in your locality.
(hand 6) Return it.

70. BGU III 871 (Arsinoite, A.D. II)

To the most powerful Superbus (?), (*epistrategos*),
. . . From Kastor, son of Onnophris, from the town of . . . in the division of Herakleides . . . I sent you two petitions . . . concerning violence, harm, and theft . . . the accusations . . . my opponent . . . to Terentios . . . the things which were done . . . you subscribed my petition, saying, "send a petition (to the *strategos*)" . . . I petitioned the *strategos* . . . with a petition, but he . . . will remain in attendance at your tribunal . . . but again, not satisfied . . . the slave is a fool . . . I was not passive, but sent (a petition) . . . we will attest . . .

71. P.Stras. IV 241 (Arsinoite, A.D. II)

To NN, *strategos* of the division of Herakleides,
From Thaesis . . . a widow, presently not having a guardian. On the eighth of the present month of Kaisareios, Psenatoimis, surnamed Areothes, for (no) reason came up next to me, grabbed me, and beat me not a little, in the presence of witnesses, namely, Horion, son of Dioskoros, and Neoteros, son of Menches. Not only did he do this, but he also prevents . . . my (family) in Bacchias, recently up to the entrance and exit to my house in Bacchias. Therefore, since I am not able . . . to be passive . . .

72. SB VI 9458 (Tebtynis, A.D. II)

From Kronion, son of Pakebkis, son Harpokration, tax-exempt priest of the renowned temple of the town of Tebtynis and successor-prophet of the same temple. I have suffered inappropriate violence at the hands of a certain Kronios, a reckless man. This is what happened: He arrogated to himself the right to collect the taxes on the grain brought from the town to the harbor. But in return for the 19 *obols* per sack of grain given by him as taxes, because of his recklessness and nastiness he charges 30 *obols*. From what I measured out I gave him the total that he pays. But he wished to cheat me as well. Once I went away he came to my house and committed the most extreme violence, which reached such a point that he even brought my slave girls into the center of the public square and stripped their clothes. Not satisfied with this, he extorted them, too. Once I arrived I had a discussion with him about these things, but he paid me no heed, and went after me, too, with the same recklessness. Therefore of necessity I submit to you this petition and ask you to punish him for the things he has done so nastily, so that I may be helped. (hand 2) Farewell.

73. SB XX 14975 (Oxyrhynchos, A.D. II)

To Dionysios, *strategos* of the Oxyrhynchite nome,
From Heraklas, son of NN, from the city of Oxyrhynchos. A certain Amoitas, owing me sixteen silver drachmas, had his relative Hermes stand as surety on the loan, and this was witnessed by Herakleides the collector of the alum tax and Besa, and was attested by the *agoranomos*. When I went to find the

one who gave the surety, he dared to attack my house at night, and along with Hermes, they broke down my door with rocks, and abused me and my family with blows, almost to my doom. They broke my rib on my left side, which was even apparent to the watchmen who were on duty. Since you were in the nome at that time I showed the *agoranomos* my (broken) door, I submit this petition and ask that they be brought before you for punishment, should it seem good to you. Farewell.

74. SB VI 9238 (Arsinoite, A.D. 200–211)

To the *stationarius* in the area,
From Satorneilos, son of Amatios, and Ptolemaios, son of Tyrannos, both from the metropolis. We were leaving the temple, lord, when certain malefactors attacked us, being helped by . . . they prevailed over us . . . and they beat me on my knees and . . . we were almost dead, and they took from Ptolemaios a scarf (?), a light scarf, and a glass flask; and from me a *basidion* ring . . . Farewell. Year ? of our lords Imperatores Severus and Antoninus and Geta, Caesares Augusti . . . 29.

75. BGU I 45 (Soknopaiou Nesos, A.D. 203)

To Agathos Daimon, *strategos* of the Arsinoite nome in the division of Herakleides,
From Herieus, son of Pekysis, from the town of Soknopaiou Nesos. Yesterday, which was the 7th of the present month of Phaophi, my son Pekysis was working at the grain field which I own near the same town. A man named Stotoetis, who is also called Kalabelis, from the town of Herakleia—a violent man who through force does not perform his liturgies—along with his son and a man named Moros, attacked my son and abused him with many blows. Because of this he is laid up. Therefore I submit this petition and ask that a copy of it be kept on file so that I can bring a claim against them lest my son's injury prove mortal or if there be some threat to my family, and also concerning the things destroyed by them . . . Farewell.
Year 12 of Lucius Septimius Severus Pius Pertinax and Marcus Aurelius Antoninus Pius, Augusti, and Publius Septimius Geta Caesar Augustus, Phaophi 8.

76. BGU XI 2061 (Thenamounis, A.D. 210)

To Subatianus Aquila, prefect of Egypt,
From Temas, son of Phratres, from the town of Teinemounis in the division of Herakleides in the Arsinoite nome. Having confidence, lord, in your gracious prefecture, I flee to you to explain the harm that came to me at the hands of some . . . . The matter is as follows: I am a farmer, an upstanding man with respect to the sacred treasury. I am wronged by Orsenouphis, son of Tapa— . . . violent men. These men on each occasion attack me because of their power . . . . I gave it up and they carried it off. Not only did they do this, but . . . my land, threatening me even in the . . . of my property and its crops, which are nearby by which . . . (I flee to you, since I am unable) . . . to discuss their actions in the nome because of the fact that they close ranks (?) . . . in order to summon your hatred of malefactors to anger. For public officials . . . there is simply no one to disturb them. For last year . . . gathering up from the farm . . . such matters demand your judgment, so I ask you to hear my case against them . . . since I am not able to (get justice) in the nome . . . 1 Tubi. The most powerful *epistrategos* having investigated . . .
Year 16, Imperatores Caesares Lucius Septimius Severus Pius Pertinax Arabicus Adiabenicus Parthicus Maximus . . . Britannicus and Marcus Aurelius Antoninus Pius and Publius Septimius Geta Britannici Maximi Pii Augusti, 4 Tubi . . .
In Alexandria in Egypt, this was written and checked from the collection of petitions given to most glorious Subatianus Aquila, prefect of Egypt, and posted at the treasury in which there was also the attached petition along with the subscription. (*a copy of the same petition follows*)
(hand 2) . . . I, NN, have signed. I, Hierax, son of Dionysios, have signed. I, Serenos, have signed.

77. Stud.Pal. XXII 54 (Soknopaiou Nesos, A.D. 210)

To . . . Claudius Herennius, decurion,
From Posis, son of Mataitas, from the town of Soknopaiou Nesos in the division of Herakleides. The day before yesterday, lord, I wished to enter the place I have in the part of a house that belongs to me in the same town. The house is held in common with Kalabelis, son of Sotakas, from the same town. But Kalabelis did not allow me to enter, but instead abused me with many blows. Later, when I came into the house, I found that the window frames which I

had added to the place were stolen, and the place was left open. Therefore by necessity I submit to you this petition, and ask, if it seems good to you, to order him to be brought before you to account for this. Posis, roughly 60 years old, with a scar on his left knee. Year 19 of Lucius Septimius Severus Pertinax and Marcus Aurelius Antoninus and Publius Septimius Geta, Britannici Maximi Pii Augusti, Phaophi 13.

78. P.Oxy. XXXIII 2672 (Oxyrhynchos, A.D. 218)

To Aurelius Harpokration, *strategos* of the Oxyrhynchite nome,
From Aurelius Aphynchis, son of Sarapas, from the city of Oxyrhynchos. Today I found that Achilleus the pastry cook had assaulted Sarapias, the slave of my minor son, and that he had wounded her on the lip. Right away I confronted him and had a discussion with him about his remarkable nastiness, but he then attacked me too, and he did violence to me and cursed me out. Not only did he do this, but he also struck me in the head with a rock. Therefore I submit this petition and ask that he be brought before you to be prosecuted for the things he did, so that I can receive justice and so that my slave girl can receive medical treatment. Year 2 of Imperator Caesar Marcus Aurelius Antoninus Pius Felix Augustus, Phaophi ?. I, Aurelius Aphynchis, have submitted this . . .

79. P.Flor. I 59 (Provenance unknown, A.D. 225–79)

My mother's . . . he abused (me) with blows, along with them . . . and . . . on my sides . . . so that, having been beaten, I feel that I am . . . also in danger of being murdered at his hands . . . stripping (the garment) I had on . . . he took (it from me) . . . Therefore because of this . . . I necessarily submit to you this petition, asking, if it seems right to you, that you order one of your attendants and a public doctor to come examine my condition and make a joint report, so that I can (have a copy of) the report . . . attesting to this . . . so that my (condition) not remain unattested . . . to be punished . . . against him. Year 5 of Imperator Caesar Marcus . . . Pius Felix Augustus, Phaophi . . . Sarapion . . .

80. P.Oxy. XXXVIII 2853 recto (Herakleopolite?, A.D. 245/6)

To Iulius Ammonios, also called Euangelos, *strategos*,
From Aurelius Areios, son of Triadelphos, and Aurelius Ammonios, son of Dionysios, both in charge of the canal called Chiliarouras. Today, that is the 5th of Tubi, we came upon Soter and his brother, or however they call themselves, and we asked them to do the work on the canal which they are obligated to do. But for no reason they attacked us and abused us with blows. Therefore we submit this petition asking first of all they receive the necessary punishment, and then that they do their share of the canal-work so that we may be able to attend to the other parts. (Farewell. Year ?) . . . Imperatores . . .

81. P.Oxy. LVIII 3926 (This, A.D. 246)

To Iulius Ammonios, also called Euangelos, strategos of the Thinite nome,
From Aurelia Senpatous, daughter of Panouris, wife of Titoes, from This. Yesterday evening a group of malefactors came to our house in the town of This, and they hit my husband Titoes, son of Kortas, the shoemaker, with swords on the left shoulder and on the left hand, and they beat my son Psekes on the head. They carried off from my house whatever they could find, and broke down all our doors. Since I do not know the malefactors I submit this petition asking that you order your attendant to come investigate their condition, so that they can receive the necessary treatment.
Year 3 of Imperator Caesar Marcus Iulius Philippus Pius and Marcus Iulius Philippus most noble and most excellent Augusti, Mecheir 15.
(hand 2) I, Aurelia Senpatous, have submitted this. I, Aurelius Soter, son of Soter, wrote on her behalf since she is illiterate.
(hand 3) Sarapion the attendant has been sent. A copy of the petition of Senpatous is being sent to you, so that you can bring a public doctor and make a report on the condition of her son and husband once you have seen them. Year 4, Mecheir 15.

82. P.Oxy. XII 1556 (Oxyrhynchite, A.D. 247)

. . . (send) one of your attendants along with a public doctor to see me and report to you on my condition, and keep my petition on file to await the justice of the higher power. Year 4 of Imperatores Caesares Marci Iulii Philippi Pii Felices Augusti, Tubi 8.

83. SB IV 7464 (= P.Graux I 4 = Sel.Pap. II 291, Philadelphia, A.D. 248)

To Aurelius Marcianus, centurion,
From Aurelius Sarapion, son of Paseis, from the town of Philadelphia. There is nothing more horrid and miserable than violence. I have made it to this age—over eighty!—blamelessly serving as Arab archer. One of my daughter's piglets wandered off in the town. It was said to have ended up with Iulius, a soldier. I went to him and asked him to swear an oath (that he did not have it). But he grabbed me, though I am an old man, in the middle of the day and in public, as if the laws didn't exist, and abused me with blows in the presence of Nepotianus the procurator of the most eminent Valerius Titianus, and Mauros and Ammonios, the Arab archers. These men, scandalized that I was being beaten, tried to separate us, and I barely escaped the attempt on my life. Therefore of necessity I submit this petition, asking that he be brought up so that his offenses receive fitting punishment and that my account remain on file. Farewell. Sarapion, roughly 84 years old, with a scar on his right leg.
Year 6, Imperatores Caesares Marci Iulii Philippi Pii Felices Augusti, Hathyr 26.

84. P.Dubl. 18 (Hermopolite, A.D. 257–59)

To NN, *strategos* of the Hermopolite,
(From NN, son of) Hermes, also called Maximus, former *gymnasiarch* . . . Hermopolis the great . . . and however else he is known. Was sent . . . Mussius Aemilianus, who was in charge of the prefect's office . . . his greatness . . . by command of the prefect and . . . which is the 1st of Pauni, I know (not why) . . . I am brought here . . . unsatisfied . . . wickedly attacked me . . . abusing me with blows . . .

85. P.Sakaon 36 (= P.Ryl. II 114 = Sel.Pap. II 293, Thraso, A.D. 280)

To the most eminent Hadrianus Sallustius, prefect,

From Aurelia Artemis, daughter of Paesis, from the town of Thraso in the Arsinoite nome. Knowing your love of humble people, my master and prefect, and your care for all, especially women and widows, I make my approach to you asking to obtain your assistance. The matter is as follows: Syrion, having become the *dekaprotos* of the aforementioned town of Thraso, persuaded my husband, whose name was Kaet, to shepherd his flocks. But he unjustly stole back for himself sixty of the sheep and goats from my aforementioned husband. For as long as my aforementioned husband was alive, each man enjoyed what was his own, my husband what was his and the aforementioned his own. But when my aforementioned husband departed this world, lord, Syrion burst in, wishing, on account of his power in the area, to steal the property of my infant children from the very death bed of my husband as his body was still lying there. When I rushed to get back our things and to send off my husband, he sent me away with a threat, and up until today he still holds our animals. Therefore I ask you, master, to send me an assistant out of your command, so that I can get back my children's property and my own, since I am a widow, and so that I can mildly abide by what is commanded—for my aforementioned husband never was caught up any fraud pertaining to the treasury, but it is common for the aforementioned Syrion always to rob me, a widow with infant children, so that when he took corn from my deceased husband through NN, the assistant, he didn't give me a receipt for the coming dues—so that I am might be able to obtain my property through the philanthropic subscription of yours, lord and benefactor of all, and be able to remain in my property with my infant children, and to show my thanks to your good luck . . . Farewell.
(hand 2) Concerning the revenues what is fitting . . . The most powerful *epistrategos* will decide what is most just. Page 69, 1st volume.

86. PSI VII 807 recto (Oxyrhynchos, A.D. 280)

To Aurelius Philantinoos, *beneficiarius* of the prefect of Egypt stationed in the Oxyrhynchite nome,
From Aurelius Herakles, son of Nechtheneibis, whose mother is Tabolphis, from Ision Panga. The *dekaprotoi* of the upper toparchy of the previous third year illegally locked me up on account of land which I am not responsible for, since it is not part of my paternal inheritance nor do I farm or rent it. The laws command that no one should be arrested on account of others, neither a

father for a son, nor a son for a father, nor a brother for a brother. Therefore I submit this petition, asking to have my body free and inviolate, and not to be arrested on account of others, in accordance with what is decreed. Year 5 of Imperator Caesar Marcus Aurelius Probus Gothicus Maximus Persicus Maximus Germanicus Maximus Pius Felix Augustus. Mecheir 5.
I, Aurelius Herakles, son of Nechtheneibis, have submitted this. I, Aurelius NN, wrote on his behalf, since he is illiterate.

87. BGU XI 2069 (Arsinoite, A.D. 292)

. . . verbal abuse . . . did violence to me . . . (threw me) on the ground . . . unless I had fled . . . old . . . leaving . . . the slave, and I myself do not know if I might have suffered a mortal blow at his hands. Therefore I submit this petition certifying these things so that he be brought before you and his offences receive punishment according to the laws, and so that my account concerning him be preserved for the visit of my lord, the most eminent prefect Titius Honoratus, concerning the damage to my farm and the things which he dared to do to me. Farewell.
(hand 2) I, Aurelius Pennouphis, have submitted this. I, Aurelius Patron, wrote for him, since he is illiterate. I, Aurelius Pennouphis, have submitted this. I, Aurelius Patron, wrote for him, since he is illiterate.
(hand 3) Year 8 and 7 of our lords Diocletianus and Maximianus, Augusti, Tubi 2.

88. PSI IV 298 (Oxyrhynchos, A.D. 292–93)

To the most eminent Rupilius Felix, prefect of Egypt,
From Aurelius Phoibammon, son of Diogenes, son of Stephanos, former *archon* of the glorious and most glorious city of the Oxyrhynchites. On the fifteenth of the month of Phamenoth in the present year I gave a guarantee to sail on some of the many-oared public boats, and, according to the guarantee I wished to do the work, staying there for only one month . . . (but) the man in charge of these boats, Aurelius Klaudianos . . . first did not allow me the established time (to stay there), that is, to fill the six months, but instead he even threw out onto the ground all my provisions stored in that boat, and prevented me from sailing to there at all. And yet he has he not given me the

money for the month, although he himself has received all the . . . , still more, he does violence to me by beating me inappropriately, and by cursing me with the sorts of words that are forbidden to say among men . . . Helping him was Aurelius NN, the captain of the fleet . . . But I will provide as witnesses, if it should be necessary, those who were present with me at the station. And yet, though he does in no way understand the craft of seamanship, but simply for a long time . . . many-oared boats. Since I am not able to suffer the illegality of (his) violence, I am driven to flee to your feet, master, asking you to order, through your foresight and if it seems right to your greatness . . . to return to me . . . justly . . . punishment . . . farewell.
(hand 2) . . . I have submitted . . . Dionysios
(hand 3) . . . complaint . . . petition me . . . posted in the same place.

89. P.Cair.Isid. 63 (Karanis, A.D. 296)

To Aurelius Gordianus, *beneficiarius* on duty,
From Aurelia Taesis, daughter of Kopres, from the town of Karanis. I have suffered damage and illegal prosecution . . . by my paternal uncle, Chairemon, who is from the same town of Karanis. Not being able to bear these things, I have sought legal redress. When I was a young child I lost my parents, and I lived with my maternal uncle Ammonios, and was raised by him. But my paternal property was stolen and is being held by the aforementioned Chairemon. I remained passive about these matters while I was still a minor, but when thanks to the providence of god I came of age, I thought it necessary to sue the aforementioned Chairemon concerning the property which he was keeping from me. Not once but twice I petitioned the *beneficiarius* entrusted with the decadarchy, and he ordered Chairemon to return the things he was holding on to. But he did not return them. Yesterday, which was the 24th, his daughters Kyrillous, Tasoucharion, Taesis, T—, and Thatres, their mother . . . abused me with blows, pulled out (?) my hair, tore my clothes, and threw me on the floor. They did this in the presence of Hol and Kasios, officials from the same village, who pulled me away from the women . . .

90. P.Oxy. VIII 1120 (Oxyrhynchos, A.D. III)

Concerning what the husband of my daughter, Polydeukes, has suffered in this area, I have submitted a petition to the authorities against Eudaimon, who did the violence to him. But this man was powerful enough to have the petition quashed, so that he wouldn't appear liable to prosecution. Accordingly, I attest to his damages, since I am a weak and widowed woman: Thonis, being the curator of Seuthes, attacked my house, and dared to carry off my slave, Theodora, although he has no authority over her, since with all his strength he subjects me to harm.

91. PSI IV 292 (Oxyrhynchos, A.D. III)

. . . Pauni 23.
From Aurelius Hermias, son of Leonidas, whose mother is Ptolema, from Pela, in the western toparchy. The aforementioned divine imperial edict frees those who flee to you and who give up their property to those who put them forward (for liturgies). Your excellent ?, most powerful administrator . . . to the divine constitutions, and I myself ask such . . . divine benevolence . . . being a tax collector in the area . . . (I) presented (my case?) when the most powerful administrator was in the area . . . concerning what was owed to the administration . . . since I was made responsible for such a large amount of land . . . harassment followed, and bodily violence (to?) worthy men . . . of the *strategos*, those who ? the harvest and worth much . . . in the vineyard and in (my?) lots which had been previously seized because of taxes . . . (seized?), I renounced it to them . . . of the property, this (was) unregistered and from the *strategos* . . . unregistered, and from your greater power according to which . . . by necessity I flee to your footsteps, having ceded it to them . . . (asking) to have my body be unthreatened and unharmed, so that by your benevolence I can live unmolested in my homeland and . . . farewell. I, Aurelius Hermias, through me . . .

92. SB VI 9421 (Oxyrhynchos, A.D. III)

To Aurelius Alexander, one of those in charge of the peace,

From Aurelius A—, also known as Aphynchis, former *agonothetes* in the city of the Oxyrhynchites, Yesterday evening a certain Didyme, wife of Agathos Daimon, the cook, appeared at my house and, finding me standing there with my family, did violence to us, in ways both sayable and unsayable. She is a completely shameless woman, well-furnished with bravado. When I tried to restrain her and advised her to keep away from us, because of the darkness of night she reached such a peak of insanity that she attacked me, since she is naturally hot-tempered (?), reached out and struck me, and cursed out some of my granddaughters who were standing nearby. I have presented them as witnesses, and not only them, but also one of the officials of our city who was present as well. Having suffered such things and finding myself wounded, I submit to you this petition, asking you to order her to be brought before you, so that I may receive the benefaction you extend to all. Farewell.

93. PSI IV 313 (Oxyrhynchos, A.D. III–IV)

. . . on account of the sale of . . . I was present for the purchase . . . having the first wool (?). He received from me the agreed-upon price before witnesses. Today I approached him about the purchase. For reasons I don't understand, he did not wish to deliver (the products) to me, nor did he give me back the money. Instead he attacked me, beat me all over my body, tore my clothes, and left me wounded. Therefore I submit this petition, asking that he receive fitting punishment.
I, Aurelius Apphous, have submitted this.

94. PSI III 222 (Herakleopolis, A.D. III–IV)

To Aurelius Didymos, decurion in charge of the peace in the Herakleopolite nome,
From Aurelius Apion, son of K—, whose mother is E—, a collector of the tax on wild animals and birds. Horos son of NN, a hunter from the town of Thmoiamounis and Papnoutis, son of Tasonps, also a hunter from the town of Papas near Phebeichis, with great disobedience and illegality ignore the taxes ordered by the most eminent *iuridicus*. Every time I have approached them they fend me off with violence and verbal abuse, not (only) with clubs, but also by riling up others and disrupting collection of the tax on hunters. Because I am being harassed, by necessity I petitioned you, paying annually ten silver talents and ?

drachmas . . . I present to you this petition asking that they be brought before you to give an account of their disregard and disobedience.
Year ? and Year ?, Pauni ?.

95. P.Kell. I 20 (Kellis, A.D. 300–320)

To the most eminent Aurelius Herodes, *praeses* of the Thebaid,
From Aurelius Pamouris, son of Psais, from the town of Kellis of the city of the Mothites of the Great Oasis. There is nothing more terrible or more offensive, lord governor, than harm and extortion. In those times that were disordered by many (?), a certain Psais, from this same city of the Mothites, being a man who is very powerful in these parts, violently and tyrannically stole my donkey when I was still under age, and he beat me with mortal blows. Since I am a middling man . . . furnished with the means for life, I necessarily flee to you, master, asking and begging through this (petition) that you order . . .

96. P.Oxy. LXI 4122 (Oxyrhynchos, A.D. 305)

In the consulship of our masters Constantius and Maximianus, the most noble Caesars for the 5th time.
To Aurelius Scuthes, also known as Horion, *logistes* of the Oxyrhynchite nome,
From Aurelius Hierax, son of Asklepiades, from the same city. I have made a report which I publicly posted in which I attested to the things done illegally against my wife, Sarapias, by Psois and Tiron, his brother-in-law, and their wives and sons. Since my aforementioned wife has been abused by blows, and they beat her on the arm, by necessity I submit this petition, asking that a public doctor be sent by one of your attendants, along with the attendant himself, to investigate the condition of my wife and make a written declaration, and that this document remain in the register, so that it can serve as testimony and security for us and be preserved so that I can give my account before his greatness, the prefect, to receive satisfaction.
Year 21 and 13 of our lords Diocletianus and Maximianus, Augusti, and Constantius and Maximianus, most distinguished Caesars. Pauni 28.
(hand 2) I, Aurelius Hierax have submitted this.
(hand 3) I, Aurelius Horion, employee of the *logistes*, delivered it. Year 21 and 13, Pauni 28.

97. P.Grenf. II 78 (= Chr.Mitt. 63, Great Oasis, A.D. 307)

To the most eminent Satrius Arrianus, governor (of the Thebaid),
From Syros son of Petechon the younger, *exopylites* from the toparchy of Kysis in the city of the Hibites. I married a woman of my own sort, Tsek—, a free woman from free parents, and I have had children with her. But then Tabes, daughter of Ammonia the *exopylites*, and Leloi, her husband, along with their children Psenesis and Straton did a deed unworthy of the *paideia* that is enjoined upon everyone, but characteristic of their folly. Acting brashly, they confined my aforementioned wife and children in their home, attaching a slavish yoke to free individuals, though every one of them was born free, and have siblings who are still living who are also free. When I confronted them they seized me and abused me with undeserved blows. I considered it necessary to approach your highness, my governor and master, and to testify about these things, and to have my testimony sent to your excellence through —nis, who furnished me help as I was being abused and beaten by them, and I ask that my aforementioned children be freed from their unlawful detention and that my opponents be secured at your court . . . pressured . . . the judgment of your immaculate courtroom . . . with recourse to you I will convict my opponents of the insult to me and the illegal enslavement of my family.
Year 15 and Year 3 and Year 1 of our lords Maximianus and Severus, Augusti, and Maximinus and Constantinus, most noble Caesars, Phamenoth ?. I Syros, son of Petechon, the younger, the aforementioned exopylites, have submitted this. I, Aurelius NN, also known as NN, wrote on his behalf since he is illiterate.

98. P.Cair.Isid. 77 (= C.Pap.Jud. III 518c, Karanis, A.D. 320)

To Aurelius K—, *praepositus* of the 5th pagus,
From Aurelia Tales, daughter of Palemon, from the town of Karanis, through my husband Isidoros from the same town. That it is necessary for you, the *praepositi*, to . . . .to give all of your care to the poor farmers . . . he has made this clear to all. My father having died (intestate) fifteen years before, his property (?) was passed on to me and to my sister, whose name is Koulilla. We divided his estate, each of us managing the *arouras* distributed to each. Koulilla married her husband Aion, from the same town, but they both died, both my sister and her husband, leaving behind two young girls. The father of the girls (Aion) had

brothers named Sambathion and —nion and . . . land, six cows, two donkeys, two colts, and shares in . . . . But the aforementioned brothers of (the children's) father appropriated the property left by my sister and her husband, harvested the largest piece of the sown fields of Aion, and have left the remainder of this property unharvested, although the landholdings in these places were registered in the name of the father of the orphaned children . . . . They not only stole the inheritance, but they hold it back with the greatest illegality, since by law uncles are supposed to take care of the orphaned children. Yet while they are supposed to stand in place of the children's father, they nonetheless neglect the lands. When I went to have a discussion with them about this, they did inappropriate violence to me, even commanding me to . . . . Since I am not able to bear this, and since the time is pressing in for the oversight of the lands, by necessity I approach you. I ask that you summon them and compel them to provide an account of the entire inheritance, and to guarantee they assume all oversight of land, so that it can remain productive and not be sold out from under the orphans. They should also provide security that they will not actually do what they threatened to do to me, so that when the most eminent *praeses* Valerius Ziper makes his visit and I petition him they will be punished for everything according to the laws. Farewell.

I, Aurelia Tales, have submitted this, through me, Isidoros, her husband. I, Aurelius Paulos wrote on his behalf since he is illiterate.

In the consulship of our masters Constantinus Augustus for the 6th time, and Constantinus Caesar for the first time . . .

99. P.Kell. I 21 (Kellis, A.D. 321)

To Aurelius Faustianos, former *archon* of the city of the Mothites of the Great Oasis . . . *defensor* of the area.

From Aurelius Pamouris, son of Psais, from the town of Kellis of the city of the Mothites. If it were customary for matters of nastiness to prevail over each of us, and if the severity of the laws was not accustomed to follow, life would be unlivable for those of us who are middling men. So then: Sois, son of Akoutis, the *komarch* of this same town of Kellis, constantly plots against me, and every day attacks me, harassing my wife with a group of revelers including the soldiers stationed here and their attendants and the *expunctores*, and running me down. Yesterday, when I was away . . . splitting open the door with an axe, he entered along with the son of Psenamounis, a builder from

Pmoun Pano, who is not a liturgist nor is he a (fellow) townsman of mine. They attacked my wife with the club that they had and they beat her badly, such that the marks of the blows are apparent on her body. To this extent they do not follow the laws. Since such is the madness of the aforementioned *komarch* and the son of Psenamounis, I am not able to be passive, and so submit to your clemency this petition, asking that it be made known to the courage of my lord, the most eminent *praeses* Valerius Victorianus, so that their offense can receive the fitting punishment. Farewell.
After the consulship of our masters Constantinus Augustus for the 6th time, and Constantinus the most noble Caesar for the 1st time, 11 Tubi.
(hand 2) I, Aurelius Pamouris, son of Psais, the aforementioned, have submitted this. I, Aurelius Phibion, former archon of Hermopolis wrote for him, since he is illiterate.

100. P.Col. VII 171 (= P.Coll.Youtie II 77, Karanis, A.D. 324)

To Dioskoros Kaison, *praepositus* of the 5th pagus,
From Isidoros, son of Ptolemaios, from the town of Karanis, in your pagus. The animals of Pamounis and Harpalos ruined my planting, and their cow again pastured on my land, to the extent that my farming has been ruined. I captured the cow and was leading it back to the town when they came up to me in the fields with a large club. They knocked me to the ground and beat me, and took back the cow, as the marks from the blows that have appeared all over my body show. Had I not received help from Antoninus the deacon and Isaac the monk who were passing by, they would quickly have killed me. Therefore I submit this petition asking that they be brought before you, and that my account be preserved for the governor's court on account of both the sowing and the violence . . . In the year of the upcoming consuls for the 4th time, Pauni 12.

101. P.Oxy. LI 3620 (Oxyrhynchos, A.D. 326)

In the consulship of our masters Constantinus Augustus for the 7th time and Constantius the most August Caesar for the 1st time, Mecheir 8.
To Aurelius Aphthonios and Aurelius Timotheos, both *nyktostrategoi* of the glorious and most glorious city of the Oxyrhynchites,

From Aurelius Thonios, son of Onnophris, from the same (glorious) city. Yesterday evening when my wife was at home a woman named Tapesis, along with her slave, Victora, who live far away from our home, attacked my wife and did unspeakable violence to her. Not only did they tear her clothes, but her body (is also injured from the blows) they landed (on her) . . . my wife . . . gold. Therefore . . . I submit this petition asking . . . a midwife be sent by you to see her and attest to her condition in an official report, and once the report has been made and the offenses recorded they should provide a guarantee that if something should happen to my wife fitting punishment should occur in the immaculate courtroom of my lord, the governor of Egypt, the most eminent Tiberius Flavius Laetus.

102. P.Freib. II 11 (Oxyrhynchos, A.D. 336)

In the consulship of the most glorious Virius Nepotianus and Tettius Facundus, Phaophi 28.
To Flavius Hermeias, *defensor* of the Oxyrhynchite,
From Aurelia Thaesis, daughter of Piois, living in the town of Phoboos in the 5th pagus. For a long time now my land has been stolen, although I remain personally responsible for the blessed taxes on it. I applied to the provincial officials concerning the boundaries and the transfer of this land, and I was given in accordance with the rules and in accordance with the report of the scribe of the pagus and of . . . land surveyor and having let to the farmers in the pagus for its taxes. But these men were held back by Parakles and Ptollas and Thaesis, the sister-in-law of Parakles, and the children of Onnophris, all of them from the same town of Phoboos. They attacked the farmers and beat them up badly. Therefore I accuse them and submit this petition, requesting that they receive the necessary punishment, and that they be forced to stay off our land, so that I also can be able to pay the public taxes.
(hand 2) I, Aurelia Thaesis, have submitted this. I Aurelius Theon, son of Theon, wrote on her behalf, since she is illiterate.

103. P.Oxy. LIV 3771 (= P.Oxy. VI 901 = Chr.Mitt. 70, Oxyrhynchite, A.D. 336)

In the consulship of the most glorious Virius Nepotianus and Tettius Facundus, Pachon 6.
To Flavius Iulianus, acting as the *defensor* of the Oxyrhynchite nome,
From Aurelia Allous, daughter of Thonios, from the village of Taampemou in the 5th pagus. Yesterday evening our two pigs got out on to our property and ended up in the conduit for the waterwheel for our lands and those of a certain Pabanos from the same town. The aforementioned Pabanos happened upon us with a chisel in his hands and tried to kill the pigs, but I held him back. Although he had not been harmed by the pigs, but because he had been held back from his attack on them, he attacked me instead, trying to drown me in the conduit. (And he would have), unless by some providence . . . the oxen pumping . . . by him in the conduit . . .

104. P.Abinn. 57 (= P.Gen. I 49, Theoxenis, A.D. 342–51)

To Flavius Abinnaeus, *praefectus alae* of the soldiers stationed in the camps of Dionysias,
From Aurelius Ouranios, son of Dalmatios, former *praepositus*, and a landholder in the village of Theoxenis. On the fourteenth of the current month of Choiak, while I was walking through my fields, Dioskoros, son of Paul, the Libyan, told me that Peter, son of Agaon, and his other two brothers . . . were leading off my animals and appropriating my feed. (I confronted) them, and the three of them attacked me on the edges of Hermopolis, using their clubs. They nearly beat me to death. Therefore I ask you this, and beg your benevolence: arrest them and . . .

105. P.Abinn. 46 (Philadelphia, A.D. 343)

. . . and I have (the marks from) the blows still, although I owe them nothing (?). I can show this too through a mediator . . . took (?) me from them, half-dead. His name is —as. Therefore I submit to you this petition, *praepositus* . . . you judged that I owed them nothing. Farewell. Thoth 24. In the consulship of the most glorious Frurius Placitus and Flavius Fromollus. I, Aurelius Theodoros, have submitted this. I, NN, the attendant wrote on his behalf, since he is illiterate.

106. P.Sakaon 48 (Theadelphia, A.D. 343)

To Aurelius Ision, leading citizen, *praepositus* of the (8th) pagus of the Arsinoite nome,

From Aurelius Zoilos son of Melas, deacon of the universal church from the town of Theadelphia in the same nome. Those convicted of having a shameless and thievish character, O most pure of men, deserve to obtain the punishment of the laws. When my blessed son, Gerontios by name, was still alive, he came into the communion of marriage—were it never so!—with his wife Nonna, daughter of Annous, from the same town. Thinking goodwill and love itself prevailed for this marriage, the opposite happened. When my aforementioned son was laid up with an illness and was getting ready to die—I know not how—a certain man named Sakaon from the same town came to my house in a hostile fashion, and stole away the wife of my son, and he led this aforementioned Nonna to his own house, wrongfully and against all the laws. He had helpers in this remarkable illegality, namely, his brothers and the mother of (my son's) wife, the aforementioned Annous. At the time when my son died, right away I wished to avail myself of the help of the laws concerning the reckless deed that they dared to do—for I had indeed tried to live an unmeddlesome life. I know not why, but my other son, named Paseis, having seen his father being violated by utterly worthless men, and seeing his aforementioned clothing being chopped up (?), began to have a discussion with them about this. But they, for their part, taking up a most nasty attitude and filled with madness, attacked him too with axes and clubs, attempting to end his life—and they would have taken his life, had not an act of fortune intervened, namely, that he saved his life through flight. These men despise the good ordering of the present age and despise our lack of meddlesomeness. And indeed they stole and plundered the five sheep and eight cows and five asses which my sons had on loan—and I, a wretched man, am compelled by my masters to return them. Therefore I submit this petition, asking that they be brought before you and held securely, so that first they can be punished for their illegal and reckless deed, and second, that they be compelled to return the aforementioned animals. Or otherwise, I ask that they be sent on to the great tribunal of my lord the most eminent prefect of Augustopotamia [sic],

Flavius Olympius, so that the fitting punishment can be enjoined against them. Farewell.
In the Consulship of the most glorious Furius Placidius and Flavius Romulus. Pharmouthi 11.
(hand 2) I, Aurelius Zoilos, have submitted this . . . I, NN, wrote for him since he is illiterate.

107. P.Abinn. 51 (Hermopolis, A.D. 346)

To Flavius Abinnaeus, *praefectus alae* of the soldiers stationed in the camps of Dionysias,
From Aurelia Ataris, daughter of Melas the veteran, a landholder in the town of Hermopolis. On the third intercalary day at the tenth hour, I do not know why, and acting in the manner of thieves, when I was collecting a debt which he owes me, Poleion shut me up in his house, and along with Apion, the son of Horion the *eirenarch*, and Poleion's sister, Kyriake, and they practically beat me to death. I fled from their house and threw myself from it, escaping the violence and the damage that I suffered at their hands. Now I am at death's door. Therefore I ask you this, and beg your benevolence, lord: arrest these men and send them to my lord, the *dux*, for it is his job to punish people who dare to do such things. Once I achieve this I will owe you thanks, lord. Farewell.
I, Aurelia Ataris, have submitted this. In the consulship of our masters Constantius for the 4th time and Constans for the 3rd time, Augusti. Third intercalary day.

108. P.Abinn. 52 (Hermopolis, A.D. 346)

To Flavius Abinnaeus, *praefectus alae* of the soldiers stationed in the camps {camps} of Dionysias,
From Aurelia Ataris, daughter of Melas the veteran, landholder in the town of Hermopolis. On the third intercalary day at the tenth hour, I do not know why, and acting in the manner of thieves, when I was collecting a debt which he owes me, Pol, surnamed Obellos, and the son of Horion, Apion by name, and his sister Kyriake shut me up in his house. I escaped from his house . . . I am laid up, sitting at death's door . Therefore I ask you this, and beg your

benevolence: arrest these people, and that you send them to our lord, the *dux*, for it is his job to punish those who dare to do such things. Once I achieve this I will owe you thanks, lord. Farewell.
(hand 2) I, Aurelia Ataris, have submitted this. In the consulship of our masters Constantius for the 4th time and Constans for the 3rd time, Thoth 1.

109. P.Amh. II 141 (= Chr.Mitt. 126, Hermopolite, A.D. 350)

To Aurelius Diokles . . . *praepositus* of the 12th pagus of the Hermopolite nome,
From Aurelia Thaesis, daughter of Pathermouthis, from the town of Penne— in your pagus. My full brother, —ssos, lives with me, and there has never been any dispute between us. Unexpectedly, he attacked me, along with his wife Rhia. They pushed me to the ground with a considerable number of blows and with punches and kicks all over my body, so that now there are bruises on my face. They beat me half to death, and what's more, they even tore my clothing. Therefore, since I, a weak and widowed woman, am not able to be passive about this, I submit to your clemency this petition attesting to this and asking I be avenged by you. Farewell. In the consulship of the most glorious Sergius and Nigrinianus, Pharmouthi 12. I, Aurelia Thaesis, daughter of Pathermouthios, have submitted this. I, Flavius Ammonius, the veteran, wrote on her behalf as requested, since she is illiterate.

110. P.Kell. I 23 (Kellis, A.D. 353)

To the most eminent Flavius Faustinus, *praeses* (of the Thebaid),
From Aurelius Gena, son of Ouonsis, *komarch* of the town of Kellis in the Mothite nome. I was appointed as *komarch* of our town, lord, and along with the other liturgists in the presence of the vice-*exactor* and the other officials, as is customary, I made the liturgists declare their status to the office of the *strategos* in the customary fashion, and each of us in turn was selected by lot for his liturgy. But a certain man named Taa was selected with us, the client of Harpokration, the former *archon*. I had to go after him alone to get him to participate as well in public works along with the other liturgists. But this man is confident in the power of this Harpokration—which is quite great around here—and scorned my modestness. When he (Taa) was being held back by me and by my

colleague Gena, the other *komarch*, this aforementioned Harpokration, acting like a great tyrant, sent against me the *symmachoi* of the area, who are under his control, bearing clubs. These people attacked me as if in the midst of war, and thrashed me with deadly blows, dragged the public liturgist away from us, and hit me in the left eye and thrashed my sides. Since therefore I am at death's door I present to you this petition, lest I die before judgment and my murder go unpunished. And his slave Timotheos also participates in his tyranny each time . . . he has thought . . . our pigs, and squandering the dowry and willingly (stealing) the wine . . . taking my brother's pig, and as a result he too was interrogated by Psais, son of Pateminis, and Psekes, son of Psennouphis. And even all this was not enough for him, the . . . of the pig, but he ripped off my poor brother's clothing in public and caused him to flee to the Nile Valley since . . . he snuck into my house at night and took my wine, which I then produced from his house in public. As protection and corroboration of the violence he has done against me, I offer Pebos son of Tithoes Cheuos, who now has the clubs at his house, since he took them away from the *symmachoi* whose names are Troda, Psenpnouthes, Porphyrios, Theotimos, Leon, Sap—s, Korax . . . Pachoumis, —tos son of Labouates. Horion, son of Tithoes Cheuos is a witness of the attack, as are the daughter of Gena, son of Pakysis, and Sarapodoros, son of Eros. Therefore I submit these documents to Hermogenes, the vice-*exactor*, and swear before him by the divine and heavenly fortune of our eternally victorious masters, the Augustus and the Caesar, to bring to the court of my lord the prefect to whom I have taken flight, asking for punishment for the wrongdoings I have suffered, and I have given a copy to Ammonios, *stationarius* of the area. In the consulship of our masters Constantius Augustus, consul for the 6th time, and of Constantius, most noble Caesar, consul for the 2nd time.
(hand 2) I, Aurelius Gena, son of Ouonsis, the aforementioned, have posted this publicly.

III. BGU III 909 (= Chr.Wilck. 382, Philadelphia, A.D. 359)

From Aurelius Sarapion . . . from the town of Philadelphia, (a scribe) . . . in the month of Mesore on the ? intercalary day . . . (I was going) to a wedding at my sister's house. I do not know how, but Arios son of Agammon from the same town of Philadelphia waited for me to come out of the house to go to Kerkeosiris, and tried to attack me while bearing a sword. He had some others with him, whom he can identify. The *archephodoi* of the town and those living in the house can attest to this too. He attacked me, shouting many abusive words at my face. And last year this same Arion once again, along with his father, Agammon, who are among those in the village who have taken flight, attacked our house with reckless intentions, and bearing torches they burned it down to its foundations. Whereas, therefore, the offences that these men have dared to do to me are not few, and whereas the father of this man, the aforementioned Agammon, attacks and in every case is preventing the public service assignments which are taking place in the town, I submit my petition to you, and ask that the aforementioned Arion and his father be brought before you, that they be held securely in your presence, and that they provide a sufficient surety account of my salvation . . . others . . . I will petition the higher power. Farewell. In the consulship of most glorious Eusebius and Hypatius, Mesore on the ? intercalary day.

112. P.Oxy. XLIX 3480 (Oxyrhynchos, A.D. 360–90)

To Flavius Isidorianus, *beneficiarius* of the office of the governor of Augustamnica,
From Aurelius Gounthos, son of Penephis, from the city of the Oxyrhynchites. Didymos and Aion, children of my wife's sister, at the instigation of a certain Dorotheos, son of a certain Aphynchios, from the same city, approached me about doing some work . . . agreed to provide me a salary. But now my wife and I are being held to account . . . for the silver and gold tax levied on tradesmen . . . we approached the aforementioned Didymos and Aion about the aforementioned Dorotheos concerning the payment of the wages he owed to us for . . . that is, one *solidus*, for the . . . in the account. We do not know why, but in addition to being arrogant, along with some of his slaves he attacked us, both me and my wife. He beat us all over the body . . . my wife . . . our foster-child Heronas . . . therefore I submit this petition . . . owed . . . and the fitting (punishment) occur on account of the violence. I, Aurelius Gounthos, have submitted this. I, Aurelius Theon, have written for him, since he is illiterate.

113. P.Cair.Goodsp. 15 (Hermopolis, A.D. 362)

In the consulship of the most glorious Mamertius and Evittau.

To Aurelius Nilos son of Gennadios, and Aurelius Theodoros son of Komasios, *riparii* of the Hermopolite nome,
From Aurelia Eus daughter of Phibis from the village of Paploos in the same Hermopolite nome. The offenses committed against me in the time of such great peace commanded by our master, Emperor Flavius Julianus, eternal Augustus, must not be overlooked unavenged. I have had for 16 years according to a written guarantee a yard in the same town, and I have bought at the same time a vacant lot and the cistern in it on the north side of it from Tasous, mother of Taurinos. Along with the vacant lot and the yard I had a right of pasturage that I got at the same time as the purchase. I have put up a building on the vacant lot, have restored the collapsed embankments of the cistern, and I watered my cattle from the cistern up until this past year. And everyone from the town knows that I am the owner and have the right of pasturage. Now I have begun to build up the fallen wall. I know not how, but Isakis, son of Ammonion, and his sister Tapiomis along with Helene, daughter of Panitis, and Helene, wife of Petersos, and Ta— attacked me, wishing to finish me off—as they would announce to me constantly. And they would have, had I not found help in Taesis and her sister, Sophia. But Taesis was pregnant, and they made her expel the fetus because of their blows; and they stole Sophia's donkey, and they have it still. In a tyrannical fashion they knocked down the wall of the vacant lot, wishing to steal from me my building site and my mother's fallen house next to the yard, although I have the deeds of sale for it in my possession—I even showed them to the assistant of the *praepositus* at my official appearance. This same Isakis takes confidence in his money and his wealth, and he wishes to drive me from the town just as he drove off the father of my children, who is even now passing his time in other parts, and so now I have to pay taxes on 50 *arouras* of uninundated land. The accused scorns my distress just as many . . . from the village through the power of money. Therefore, since I am unable to be passive about this in any way, I am driven to give to your piety this petition asking . . . your concern . . . release from . . . in the . . . Farewell.

114. P.Oxy. XLVIII 3393 (Oxyrhynchos, A.D. 365)

In the consulship of our masters Valentinianus and Valens, eternal Augusti, Pauni 14.
To Aurelius Sarmates and Aurelius Diogenes, *riparii* of the Oxyrhynchite nome,

From Aurelius Dorotheos and Aurelius Papnouthios, both sons of Aphynchis, from the same city. A while ago we were urged by Eulogios the councilman to serve as assistants in the town of Terythis, and to make all payments in advance of our finding and collecting all the necessary taxes until we completed the collection for the aforementioned town. We agreed to these terms with him, and we carried out our work blamelessly. In the meantime, however, he provided no advance, but instead sent the tax-collectors against us, and with violence they extracted from us the taxes for the same village. Since we are totally impoverished and we own nothing whatsoever, we borrowed from moneylenders the required amount of silver and gold, which have also been paid for the same taxes. And since from the month of Tubi to the present we have also been prohibited by the same Eulogios from going to the aforementioned town, we now owe interest to the moneylenders who gave us the advance, even though we cannot collect on the sums owed to us. Indeed, he even sent his son Sarapion and his assistant Dorotheos to Terythis in our place, where they collected the money. Because of this we submit to your gracefulness this petition, and we ask that those officials who are responsible be sent for by you and that they be compelled to return everything that was advanced by us, so that we can pay back what we owe and remain in our homes and not be forced to become exiles from our homeland on account of this matter.

115. P.Mich XVIII 793 (Provenance unknown, A.D. 381)

. . . speaking at my face through his nose, he wished to end my life. And I would have long since been dead, if I had not obtained help from Pamoun my fellow villager. (Not) being able to bear this, I submit this petition to your gracefulness, attesting these things and asking that they be brought before you and that you do to them what the laws order, and that I can preserve my rights to possession and ownership of the vacant lot. Farewell. After the consulship of our masters Gratianus for the 5th time and Theodosius for the 1st, the eternal Augusti. I, Aurelia Eirene, have submitted this. I, Aurelius Herakleides, son of Apollonius, wrote on her behalf, since she is illiterate.

116. P.Lips. I 37 (Hermopolis, A.D. 389)

After the consulship of our master Theodosius the eternal Augustus for the 2nd time, and the most glorious Flavius Cynegius.
To Aurelius Zenodotos, son of Hermios, chief officer of the most glorious city of Hermopolis, and *riparius* of the Hermopolite nome,
From Flavius Isidoros, one of the *beneficiarii* of the office of the governor of the Thebaid. Many times now I have denounced to you Ionas, son of Eus, and Hatres, son of Herminos, shepherds from the village of Telbonthis and malefactors, since they have sent their herds of animals not once, not twice, not even three times, into our crops . . . But because no punishment has come down upon them, once again the day before yesterday, which was the (8th) of Pachon . . . customarily . . . they sent (their flocks) to our water trough to drink . . . of theirs on these very same lands of mine, (they) attempted to . . . our shepherd, whose name is —bios . . . but once they stripped him, straightaway with clubs they . . . they tore apart the clothes he was wearing and stole them, then they pounded him on the legs and on the other parts of his body, leaving him half-dead, such that the marks from the blows attested by those who came to see them remain apparent. Whether he will survive is unclear. Therefore I submit this petition to your eloquence, attesting to this and asking that they be held securely until the blessed visit of my lord, the governor. For I am absolutely ready to interrogate these confessed thieves and constant cattle rustlers in his immaculate courtroom, and to show that the aforementioned Ionas is a murderer.
After the aforementioned day, Pachon 10. I, Flavius Isidorus, the aforementioned have submitted this.
(verso) Petition of Isidoros, one of the *beneficiarii.*

117. P.Lips. I 39 (= Chr.Mitt. 127, Hermopolis, A.D. 390)

In the consulship of our master, Valentinianus, eternal Augustus, for the 4th time, and the most glorious Flavius Neoterius, Choiak 27.
To Aurelius Cyrus, son of Philammon, serving as *nyktostrategos* of the most glorious city of Hermopolis,
From Aurelia Demetria, daughter of Eugenios, from the same city. It is necessary that those who have once tempted the severity and fear of those in charge be restrained for the remainder of their time, and no longer harm anyone else. Kalandos, however, does the opposite of this. Among the things he dared to

do to me: after the entrance of my lord, the *comes*; after he had been given a deed of divorce by me; after the settlements had been made between us—after all of this, he came to my hearth—since among the barbarians there is no respect for the severity of the laws—and beat me mercilessly and broke my hands and as a result I also have black eyes from all of the (blows) . . . therefore I submit to your clemency my (petition) . . . asking . . .

118. P.Laur. IV 158 (Provenance unknown, A.D. 399–418)

After the consulship of our master, Honorius, eternal Augustus and . . .
. . . from (Flavius) Martyrios, son of Herakleos . . . those (in charge of) public order . . . since, therefore, a certain Saeis, a driver . . . —ammon, son of Pathos, from the village of Petr— . . . to the village, for the purpose of destroying . . . to withdraw, on account of his insanity . . . to the same landholdings . . . vineyard, and when I found it out, it was necessary . . . animals, beaten on the foot and . . . those attacking, one of our cows . . . from them . . . to your aptitude, asking your to order them to be brought . . . the cow that they took . . . the (punishment) according to the laws . . . I, (Flavius) Martyrios, have submitted this.

119. P.Amh. II 142 (= Chr.Mitt. 65, Herakleopolis?, A.D. IV)

. . . farewell.
To Marcus . . . most glorious . . . to the prefect of Augustamnica,
From Aurelius Germanos son of Horos from . . . I have near the village of Thmoiouthis (a property of) eighty *arouras* from the . . . up until now I have farmed some and rent some out to whoever wants for rents and taxes . . . conspiring with one another Palit, son of Horos, and his children, along with Perit son of Merkourios and his brother Kolluthes . . . in the manner of thieves came upon my land wishing to farm it. I approached them to have a discussion . . . all of them, both young and old, with clubs and swords, wanting to kill me, and (they used) foul language against me . . . to hear. By the grace of god I escaped from them, for if I hadn't, my life would have been in danger. Scorning . . . power . . . I petitioned your brother Philagrius about these things, and through memoranda he ordered . . . to return my land to me, in accordance with the *exactor* he sent to the *praepositus* of the pagus . . . a land surveyor. When they arrived to inspect the land and had measured the

plot they gave me . . . depositing with me a written declaration, which I will also present to you. Once again, after I farmed it for five years . . . and once again they don't allow me to farm it, since they look down on my lack of meddlesomeness and my appearance and my . . . by using their wealth and local tyranny they enjoy the fruits, although I pay the taxes . . . subscription, to order the *praepositus* of the camps of Hipponon of the nearest district (?) to compel the aforementioned . . . my land . . . and what's more, to return my rents from such a long while in order that, having received them, I can repay . . . the taxes that I pay for them. But if they argue that these have been sent, I ask to await your immaculate tribunal, since I am ready to . . . then I will give the greatest thanks forever at your feet. Farewell.
(hand 2) I, Aurelius Germanos the aforementioned, have submitted this; I, NN, son of Eudaimon, former archon of Herakleopolis, wrote for him since he is illiterate.

120. P.Flor. III 309 + P.Lond. III 983 (Hermopolite, A.D. IV)

. . . the slave of Melas, the silversmith. She attacked my house yesterday and did inappropriate violence to my wife and my young daughter, assaulting them with foul and shameful language. Since I cannot silently overlook the things said by her in contravention of the laws and of our way of life, I present to your clemency this petition, asking that she be detained to give an explanation and receive punishment for the things she said against us. Farewell. In the aforementioned consulship, Phaophi 11.
(hand 2) I, Aurelius Sarapion, son of Silbanos, have submitted this.

121. P.Herm. 20 (Provenance unknown, A.D. IV)

. . . from the . . . however much I find it . . . along with my relatives as well, at the hands of a certain Pemounios . . . and Anoubion, the athlete, and Hermeios and Euthymia. These people gathered together and attacked the same brother of mine along with their relatives. They beat him such that (the marks of) the blows are visible on this brother of mine, and he is in danger of losing his life. I have submitted to your clemency a petition against these people at an earlier time as well, and there was a report made about this. And . . . (since) this is no small offense, I submit to you this petition, asking that

the aforementioned Euthymia, along with all of her other aforementioned associates, be brought before you right away and held securely, while I make a petition against them to my lord the (*defensor*), for the purpose of greater punishment. Farewell.
I, Aurelius Beniamin, whose father is Ioses, wrote and have submitted this.

122. P.Lond. V 1830 (Provenance unknown, A.D. IV)

. . . into the road, malefactors . . . me, and (took) all of my things . . . left me naked . . . they enclosed me in the anointing room . . . I was locked up for days . . .

123. P.Oxy. VI 903 (= C.Pap.Jud. III 457d, Oxyrhynchos, A.D. IV)

Concerning all of the *hybreis* that he said against me:
He locked up in his basement his own slaves and my slaves, along with my foster-children and the overseer and his son—for nine whole days. He did violence to his slaves and to my slave, Zoe, (nearly) killing them with beatings. He set fire to my foster children, stripping them completely, which the laws forbid. He said to these same foster children, "Give me all her things." But they said, "She has nothing of ours." While the slaves were being whipped, he said, "What has she taken from my house?" They said, while being tortured, "She took nothing of yours. Your things are safe." Zoilos went to him, since he had locked up his foster child as well, and he said to him, "Have you come on account of your foster child, or have you come to talk about this woman?" He swore in the presence of bishops and his brothers that "From now on, I will not hide all of my keys from her"—he trusted his own slaves, but he didn't trust me—"and I will even stay away from her, nor will I do violence to her again." We made a marriage agreement, and after these agreements and the oaths, once again he hid the keys from me. When I went to church on the Sabbath he locked the outside doors, and yelled down at me, "Why have you gone to the church?" He said many foul things to my face, even speaking through his nose. As for the 100 *artabas* of grain due in taxes under my name, he has given not the first *artaba*. He locked up his account books and kept them from me, saying "Pay the bill of the 100 *artabas*," since as I said, he had not paid it. He said to his slaves, "bring the *symmachoi*, and

have them lock her up too." His assistance, Choous, was locked up in the public prison; Euthalamos paid bail for him, but it was not enough. I had a little money, and gave it to this man, Choous. I met him (my husband) while going to Antinoopolis. I had my bathing bag, in which I keep my jewelry, and he said to me, "If you have anything with you, I am going to take it on account of the bail you gave for Choous, my assistant, because of his tax problems." His mother will attest to all of these things. And concerning Anilla, his slave, he continually pressed my soul, both in Antinoopolis and here, (saying), "Get rid of this slave," since she knows he much he has. Perhaps he wanted to entangle me, and on this pretense to obtain what I have. But I refused to throw her out. Continually he said to me, "In a month I'm going to acquire a courtesan." God only knows.

124. P.Berl.Frisk 4 (= SB V 7518, Provenance unknown, A.D. IV–V)

. . . lest I say the other thing, encompassing everything alike in the price (?) . . . four each . . . but lacking the riffraff that was working together with him and the . . . hindering . . . approving the prior assize and sensing that a division had been stirred up by someone, he gathered up his relatives and approached. Of those he gathered, some were graced with human reason—but I know they had done something nasty—[[but one]] a certain Herakleon, son of Amazonios, who looks very much like that man, in fact practically the same, a man who takes pleasure in loose-living, suddenly hit me. I ask that he be sent up and pay the penalty, attesting to this so that I can live freely and safely and without hindrance enjoy what has been given to us by divine favor—which I have not been able to enjoy for the necessary time and not without danger (?), for although their envy was oppressive (?), it was not stronger than such a divine gift. For I was inexperienced . . . if even such a quantity of wealth has come into possession . . . of aid and censure, and once again to show the same thing to our fellow citizens. The witnesses of my clemency are the commoners of our city, and the decurions are witnesses of the attack. I will keep watch during my time to add other complaints against him to my case, for which one head would not suffice for punishment. And I will (not?) be silent, lest he free himself once again by destroying the investigation of such charges with money. So certifying these things, first and second I pray that to obtain a decision in the blessed and immaculate courtroom. I am not (afraid) . . . he has given the court . . . may this occur...concerning the insufferable offenses on account of the city and country . . . I swear on the divine and heavenly fortune . . . scribe . . . security.

125. P.Oxy. L 3581 (Oxyrhynchos, A.D. IV–V)

To Flavius Marcellus, tribune overseeing the peace,
From Aurelia Attiaina, from the city of the Oxyrhynchites. A certain Paulos, coming from the same city, is a reckless man who by force and compulsion abducted and married me . . . from him a daughter . . . bringing him into our home . . . his disgusting conduct, and all of my things . . . leaving me and my infant daughter . . . he lived with another woman and left me in solitude. After a while he tricked me once again with the help of presbyters, until once again I agreed to bring him back into our home. He made a contract with me in which he stated that the marriage would abide and if he wished to engage in such disgusting practices that he would pay a fine of two ounces of gold. His father provided a written guarantee of this. And so I brought him into our home, where he tried to do things worse than his previous actions. He scorned my orphan state, and not only did he pillage my home, he even robbed the soldiers quartered in the house and fled, whereupon I suffered violence and punishments until they allowed me only to live. Deciding that I wouldn't endanger myself further on his account I sent him a divorce decree through the *tabularius*, according to the imperial decree. Once again he acted recklessly, having his woman in the house, and bringing with him a crowd of disorderly men he snatched me away, locked me up in his house for (not) a few days, and when I became pregnant he left me once again to live with the woman he calls his wife. Now he threatens me, and stirs up envy against me. Therefore I call upon your firmness: order him to appear in court and return the two ounces of gold according to our written agreement, along with compensation for damages for what I suffered, and that he be punished for the things he did to me.
(hand 2) I, Aurelia Attiaina, have submitted this.

126. P.Rain.Cent. 91 (Provenance unknown, A.D. 419)

. . . I submit this petition to your virtue, asking that she be made to appear and that first I receive satisfaction on account of the violence, and then that a

judge be appointed concerning the other complaints about which I accuse her. If I receive this, I will owe thanks to your virtue, lord tribune.
I, Flavius Kyros, a veteran, have submitted this.
After the consulship of our masters Honorius for the 12th time and Theodosius for the 8th time, eternal Augusti.

127. SB XXIV 15970 (= P.Gron.Amst. 1, Oxyrhynchos, A.D. 455)

After the consulship of the most glorious Flavius Aetius and Flavius Studius, Phamenoth 18.
To Flavius Tatianus, reverential office-holder and *riparius* of the city of the Oxyrhynchites,
(hand 2) From Aurelius Touan, son of Sarapion, from the town of Tanaeus in the same nome.
(hand 1) Yesterday evening an association of malefactors attacked my field, riding on both horses and . . . because of the negligence of the guards who were responsible. (hand 2) I declare (hand 1) my cows were driven off, and my relative Mousaios was beaten up, leaving him half-dead and with all his limbs broken. Because of this I submit this petition to your aptitude, asking that a public doctor and an assistant come and examine the injured man, so that there can be a written report about his condition. I also ask that the guards in the area who are responsible, that is, the ones from the town of Sepho, be brought up and held securely until we get back the stolen animals and those who are responsible for such illegal offenses are produced to explain themselves. I am not afraid to go to court about this.
(hand 2) I, Aurelius Touan, son of Sarapion, have submitted this.

128. Chr.Mitt. 71 (= FIRA III 180, Hermopolis, A.D. 458–73)

To NN most glorious and most eloquent *scholasticus* and *defensor* of Hermopolis,
From Aurelius Sarapion son of Euthymios, whose mother is Chia, from the same city. With unwritten assurances I served as guarantor towards the repayment of certain debts for Sarapion, son of NN, from the same city. I don't know how, since the person whom I guaranteed was present and was not trying to flee, he accused me on account of that man, on the pretense that he (Sarapion) was careless about his obligations, and I was summoned and locked up in the public

prison on account of debts, and I was even tortured, which is prohibited by the laws . . . in my own home and then in the public prison, though your gloriousness did not know about this. Since everywhere the laws command that Romans are to have their bodies be free and inviolate, I have availed myself of this *cessio* . . . in exchange for the debts in full receive all of my property and money, and I ask that I reserve a sixth part, and that I be released from these bonds and tortures, and that I can have my body be free and inviolate according to the laws. I swear to the public scribe Apalos by the omnipotent lord and the piety and victory of our master Flavius Leon the eternal Augustus and Imperator so that what has been taken . . . this *cessio* of ours . . . and I give the greatest thanks to your gloriousness, glorious *defensor.*

(hand 2) I, Aurelios Sarapion, son of Euthymios, the aforementioned, have submitted this *cessio* as required . . . I, Aurelius Paulinos, son of Hermammon, the aforementioned, wrote for him at his request, since he is illiterate.

(hand 3) I, Aurelios Apalos, son of Papnouthios . . . of Hermopolis have received this *cessio* which was posted in public . . .

(hand 4) In the consulship of our master Flavius Leon the eternal Augustus for the 3rd time, and Flavius . . . twentieth of Epeiph, ? indiction.

129. P.Erl. 36 (Provenance unknown, A.D. V)

. . . blows . . . and . . . unless those who happened to be around . . . and tore my clothes . . . from (the blows) inflicted . . . (I flee) to your gracefulness, asking . . . for I am about to approach . . . against the laws . . . to his own brother.

130. SB IV 7449 (Oxyrhynchos, A.D. V)

To the holiest and most god-fearing Apa Theodoros, bishop of the glorious and most glorious city of the Oxyrhynchites,

From Aurelia Nonna, from the town of Spania in the Oxyrhynchite nome. Alypios, a monk who comes from our same town, who happens to be our nephew, wished to give my youngest daughter (in marriage) to Apaeion, also our relative. Those in charge of our property were eager to do this, and were unwilling to settle these things with me. Since, however, my daughter did not wish to be married to that man, the monk—acting contrary to his station—beat me and tore my clothes, making me appear helpless. Because of this I beseech your

holiness to pity me and to order him to be brought before you, so that I may receive a decision worthy of your holiness, most holy lord bishop.
(hand 2) I, Aurelia Nonna, have submitted this.

131. PSI VIII 876 (Oxyrhynchos, A.D. V–VI)

To the most reverential Flavius Sarapammon and Flavius Serenus, *proximoi* of this city of the Oxyrhynchites,
From Philoxenos, a builder, from the same city. —tis, a woman from this city who happens to be my neighbor, on account of (a debt?), when I was at the market, entered my stall with her family, and attacked my (wife) . . . (doing) unimaginable acts of violence . . . all of my neighbors are witnesses. Therefore I ask your aptitude to order her to be brought to court, and to hear our case and to produce a legal decision befitting your aptitude.

132. P.Wash.Univ. I 21 (Provenance unknown, A.D. V/VI)

. . . on order of the . . . (hand 2) when he was coming out of his village . . . they stopped him at the . . . in the documents . . . is found until you present . . . our brevity is under oath to your precision. I present this to you, attaching the single copy of the official report given to us . . . he is laid up and the . . . from the blows which he received . . . that which is presented to your greatness . . .

133. P.David. 17 (Hermopolis, A.D. 504)

In the consulship of the most glorious Flavius Cethegus, Hathyr 2, 13th indiction.
To the reverent Flavius Victor, *nyktostrategos* of southern division of Hermopolis,
From Aurelius Iosephios, son of Phoibammon, a farmer from the same city. If the strictness of the laws failed to overcome those who attack men, everyone would fall into madness and into other misfortunes. Since a certain Dionysios, a painter by trade, dared against all the laws to beat me so badly that (the marks from) the blows show up all over my body—and not only this, but he also sends his son to my hearth in the garden at night . . . all of the . . . the sowing of my land, (therefore) . . .

Verso: Petition of Iosephios son of Phoibammon

134. P.Oxy. XVI 1885 (Oxyrhynchos, A.D. 509)

To the most eloquent (Flavius Hermias), *scholasticus* and *defensor* of the city of the Oxyrhynchites,
From NN . . . of Theophilos . . .
. . . of this glorious city . . . to do the work befitting . . . beating him mercilessly on the head, and giving him a deadly blow, he threw him in the boat as he was, intending to destroy him. And as the wound upon him will attest, it was only by some sort of luck that he managed to live, though still he clings to life precariously. I ask your eloquence first of all to look at Sourous, then to order the public *tabularius* . . . and the *riparii* of this glorious city and have them view this man, Sourous, who was almost murdered, the state that he is in, and the wound upon his body, and to have your eloquence make all these things known to our lord, the most magnificent and most wise *praeses,* for the punishment for such acts, and to order that his seal be given to me in the customary manner through the public *tabularius*, my lord, most erudite *defensor*.
(hand 2) I, Theophilos . . . to the distinguished house, have submitted this.
(hand 1) In the consulship of most glorious Flavius Opportunus, Choiak 3.

135. SB VI 9239 (Oxyrhynchos, A.D. 548)

To Flavius Melas, reverential *tachygraphos* of the governor's office in the province of Arkadia,
From Christodora from the same city. To my misfortune, I gave my daughter in marriage to a certain Dorotheos, a silversmith, and I lived with him as well. I know not why, but acting in a tyrannical fashion with his customary recklessness he took my things and cast me out of the home we shared. He not only did this, but he also beat me with deadly blows. Therefore I call upon your gloriousness to order my aforementioned son-in-law to appear, and to hear the case between us and to give a just decision which befits our case, my master.
I, Christodora, have submitted this.
Reign of out most holy and pious master Flavius Justinianus, eternal Augustus and Imperator, year 22 and year 7 after the consulship of Flavius Basilius, most glorious, Phaophi 18.

PAPYRI IN CHECKLIST ORDER

P.Abinn. 52 (Hermopolis, A.D. 346) **108**
P.Abinn. 57 (= P.Gen. I 49, Theoxenis, A.D. 342–51) **104**
P.Amh. II 77 (= Chr.Wilck. 277, Soknopaiou Nesos, A.D. 139) **43**
P.Amh. II 141 (= Chr.Mitt. 126, Hermopolite, A.D. 350) **109**
P.Amh. II 142 (= Chr.Mitt. 65, Herakleopolis?, A.D. IV/post 341) **119**
P.Athen. 32 (Karanis?, A.D. 39) **16**
P.Berl.Frisk 4 (= SB V 7518, Provenance unknown, A.D. IV/V) **124**
P.Bingen 63 (Oxyrhynchos, A.D. 66) **28**
P.Cair.Goodsp. 15 (Hermopolis, A.D. 362) **113**
P.Cair.Isid. 63 (Karanis, A.D. 296) **89**
P.Cair.Isid. 77 (= C.Pap.Jud. III 518c, Karanis, A.D. 320) **98**
P.Col. VII 171 (= P.Coll.Youtie II 77, Karanis, A.D. 324) **100**
P.Col. X 266 (Arsinoite, A.D. 179–81) **62**
P.Coll.Youtie II 77 **100**
P.David. 17 (Hermopolis, A.D. 504) **133**
P.Dubl. 18 (Hermopolite, A.D. 257–59) **84**
P.Erl. 36 (Provenance unknown, A.D. V) **129**
P.Fay. 108 (Euhemeria, A.D. 169–71) **58**
P.Flor. I 59 (Provenance unknown, A.D. 225–79) **79**
P.Flor. III 309 + P.Lond. III 983 (Hermopolite, A.D. IV) **120**
P.Fouad I 26 (Ptolemais Euergetis, A.D. 158–59) **53**
P.Freib. II 11 (Oxyrhynchos, A.D. 336) **102**
P.Gen.2 I 3 (= Chr.Mitt. 122, Soknopaiou Nesos, A.D. 178–79) **60**
P.Graux I 4 **83**
P.Grenf. II 78 (= Chr.Mitt. 63, Great Oasis, A.D. 307) **97**
P.Gron.Amst. 1 **127**
P.Hamb. IV 240 (Provenance unknown, A.D. 119–20) **37**
P.Harr. II 192 (Provenance unknown, A.D. 167) **56**
P.Herm. 20 (Provenance unknown, A.D. IV) **121**
P.Ifao I 16 (Provenance unknown, A.D. 50–100) **27**
P.Kell. I 20 (Kellis, A.D. 300–320) **95**
P.Kell. I 21 (Kellis, A.D. 321) **99**
P.Kell. I 23 (Kellis, A.D. 353) **110**
P.Laur. IV 158 (Provenance unknown, A.D. 399–418) **118**
P.Lips. I 37 (Hermopolis, A.D. 389) **116**
P.Lips. I 39 (= Chr.Mitt. 127, Hermopolis, A.D. 390) **117**
P.Lond. II 342 (Soknopaiou Nesos, A.D. 185) **64**
P.Lond. II 358 (= Chr.Mitt. 52, Soknopaiou Nesos, A.D. 150–54) **50**

P.Ross.Georg. II 20 (Arsinoite?, A.D. 146) **45**
P.Ryl. II 114 **85**
P.Ryl. II 116 (= Sel.Pap. II 287, Hermopolis, A.D. 194) **68**
P.Ryl. II 124 (Euhemeria, A.D. I) **31**
P.Ryl. II 136 (Euhemeria, A.D. 34) **11**
P.Ryl. II 141 (Euhemeria, A.D. 37) **12**
P.Ryl. II 144 (Euhemeria, A.D. 38) **14**
P.Ryl. II 145 (Euhemeria, A.D. 38) **15**
P.Ryl. II 150 (Euhemeria, A.D. 40) **18**
P.Ryl. II 151 (Euhemeria, A.D. 40) **19**
P.Sakaon 36 (= P.Ryl. II 114 = Sel.Pap. II 293, Thraso, A.D. 280) **85**
P.Sakaon 48 (Theadelphia, A.D. 343) **106**
P.Sarap. 1 (= BGU III 759, Thynis, A.D. 125) **39**
PSI III 222 (Herakleopolis, A.D. III–IV) **94**
PSI IV 292 (Oxyrhynchos, A.D. III) **91**
PSI IV 298 (Oxyrhynchos, A.D. 292–93) **88**
PSI IV 313 (Oxyrhynchos, A.D. III–IV) **93**
PSI VII 807 recto (Oxyrhynchos, A.D. 280) **86**
PSI VIII 876 (Oxyrhynchos, A.D .V–VI) **131**
PSI XIII 1323 (Arsinoite, A.D. 147–48) **47**
P.Sijp. 14 (Arsinoite, A.D. 22) **10**
P.Sijp. 16 (Narmouthis, A.D. 155) **51**
P.Stras. IV 241 (Arsinoite, A.D. II) **71**
P.Stras. IV 242 **38**
P.Stras. V 401bis (= P.Stras. IV 242, Provenance unknown, A.D. 123) **38**
P.Stras. VI 521 (Provenance unknown, A.D. I) **32**
P.Stras. VI 566 (Arsinoite, A.D. 7) **5**
P.Tebt. II 304 (Tebtynis, A.D. 167–68) **57**
P.Tebt. II 331 (Tebtynis, A.D. 126–32) **40**
P.Wash.Univ. I 21 (Provenance unknown, A.D. V/VI) **132**
P.Wisc. I 33 (Arsinoite, A.D. 147) **48**
SB I 5235 (Soknopaiou Nesos, A.D. 14) **7**
SB I 5238 (Soknopaiou Nesos, A.D. 14) **8**
SB IV 7449 (Oxyrhynchos, A.D. V) **130**
SB IV 7464 (= P.Graux I 4 = Sel.Pap. II 291, Philadelphia, A.D. 248) **83**
SB V 7518 **114**
SB VI 9238 (Arsinoite, A.D. 200–11) **74**
SB VI 9239 (Oxyrhynchos, A.D. 548) **135**

SB VI 9421 (Oxyrhynchos, A.D. III) **92**
SB VI 9458 (Tebtynis, A.D. II) **72**
SB X 10218 (Theadelphia, A.D. 98–99) **30**
SB X 10239 (= P.Oxy. II 315, Oxyrhynchos, A.D. 37) **13**
SB X 10244 (Oxyrhynchos, A.D. 50) **26**
SB XII 11018 (Oxyrhynchos?, A.D. I–II) **33**
SB XII 11113 (= P.Mich.Mchl. 11, Karanis, A.D. 180–210) **63**
SB XIV 11274 (= P.Mil.Cong. XIV, p.37, Arsinoite, 4 B.C.) **2**
SB XIV 12199 (Theadelphia, A.D. 155) **52**
SB XVI 12470 (Provenance unknown, A.D. I–II) **34**
SB XVI 12678 (Karanis, A.D. 179) **61**
SB XVIII 13087 (Arsinoite, 4 B.C.) **3**
SB XX 14086 (Arsinoite, 4 B.C.) **4**
SB XX 14401 (Arsinoite, A.D. 147) **49**
SB XX 14975 (Oxyrhynchos, A.D. II) **73**
SB XX 15077 (Tebtynis, A.D. 45) **22**
SB XXIV 15970 (= P.Gron.Amst. 1, Oxyrhynchos, A.D. 455) **127**
SB XXIV 16252 (Karanis, A.D. 163) **54**
Sel.Pap. II 286 **66**
Sel.Pap. II 287 **68**
Sel.Pap. II 291 **83**
Sel.Pap. II 293 **85**
Stud.Pal. XXII 54 (Soknopaiou Nesos, A.D. 210) **77**

NOTES

INTRODUCTION: THE PRESENTATION OF THE SELF IN EVERYDAY LIFE

1. An issue posed, in a different register, in the important work of Samera Esmeir, *Juridical Humanity: A Colonial History* (Stanford, Calif.: Stanford University Press, 2012).

2. There are reasons for this doubling, of course: transformative projects in social theory were built at the same time as and in tandem with transformative projects in legal theory, which were, as it happens, also projects deeply invested in Roman law. The young Marx, after all, was undoubtedly influenced (both positively and negatively) by his teacher Savigny, the great advocate for the rehabilitation of the Roman legal project in a modern form; the young Weber, defending his dissertation, was interrogated and provoked toward his *Habilitationsschrift* by an aging Theodore Mommsen, Rome's most distinguished historian and responsible not only for the modern textual edition of Justinian's *Corpus Iuris Civilis* but for transformative (if failed) political projects as well. Interestingly enough, though none of these four men themselves were ever cold, abstract, mechanistic, or otherwise reductive, all four also stand at the root of social or historical projects that became so in distinctly different but largely analogous ways that have never been adequately explained. See further Yan Thomas, *Mommsen et "l'Isolierung" du droit (Rome, Allemagne, et l'état)* (Paris: de Boccard, 1984).

3. E.g., Jonathan Z. Smith, "In Comparison a Magic Dwells," in *Imagining Religion: From Babylon to Jonestown* (Chicago: University of Chicago Press, 1988), 19–35. Similarly provocative is William Ewald, "Comparative Jurisprudence (I): What Was It Like to Try a Rat?" *University of Pennsylvania Law Review* 143 (1995): 1889–2149.

4. Early discussions of "crime" in the papyri understood in light of the literary tradition: Barry Baldwin, "Crime and Criminals in Greco-Roman Egypt," *Aegyptus* 43 (1963): 256–63. Similar (though somewhat less prurient) is R. W. Davies, "The Investigation of Some Crimes in Roman Egypt," *Ancient Society* 4 (1973): 199–212. See also Naphtali Lewis, *Life in Egypt Under Roman Rule* (Oxford: Clarendon, 1983), 79–80. J. L. White, *The Form and Structure of the Official Petition: A Study in Greek Epistolography* (Missoula, Mont.: Society for Biblical Literature, 1972) is incomplete and primarily concerned with formal elements. Careful studies of violence are likewise hard to come by, even outside the Roman world. Classic is A. W. Lintott, *Violence in Republican Rome*, 2nd ed. (Oxford: Clarendon, 1999). See also Andrew M Riggsby, *Crime and Community in Ciceronian Rome* (Austin:

University of Texas Press, 1999). It was not until the bulk of this manuscript was finished that I could obtain a copy of Brent D. Shaw, *Sacred Violence: African Christians and Sectarian Hatred in the Age of Augustine* (Cambridge: Cambridge University Press, 2011); likewise, while I have benefited from certain details in the careful study of Benjamin Kelly, his *Petitions, Litigation, and Social Control in Roman Egypt* (Oxford: Oxford University Press, 2010) appeared too late to take detailed account of its broader arguments.

5. Slavoj Žižek, "Tolerance as an Ideological Category," *Critical Inquiry* 34 (2008): 675; John R. Searle, *The Construction of Social Reality* (New York: Free Press, 1995), 127–47; Max Gluckman, "The Peace in the Feud," *Past & Present* 8 (1955): 5. Important for this project as a whole is Robert M. Cover, "Nomos and Narrative," in *Narrative, Violence, and the Law: The Essays of Robert Cover*, ed. Martha Minow, Michael Ryan, and Austin Sarat (Ann Arbor: University of Michigan Press, 1992), 101: "A legal tradition is hence part and parcel of a complex normative world. This tradition includes not only a corpus iuris, but also a language and a mythos—narratives in which the corpus iuris is located by those whose wills act upon it. These myths establish paradigms for behavior. They build relationships between the normative and material universe, between the constraints of reality and the demands of an ethic. These myths establish a repertoire of moves—a lexicon of normative action—that may be combined into meaningful patterns culled from the meaningful patterns of the past."

6. Bruce W. Frier, "A New Papyrology?" *Bulletin of the American Society of Papyrologists* 26 (1989): 217–26; Roger S. Bagnall, *Reading Papyri, Writing Ancient History* (London: Routledge, 1995); Todd M. Hickey, "Writing Histories from the Papyri," in *The Oxford Handbook of Papyrology*, ed. Roger S. Bagnall (Oxford: Oxford University Press, 2009), 495–520.

7. Michel Foucault, ed., *I, Pierre Rivière, Having Slaughtered My Mother, My Sister, and My Brother. . .: A Case of Parricide in the 19th Century* (Harmondsworth: Penguin, 1978); Carlo Ginzburg, *The Cheese and the Worms: The Cosmos of a Sixteenth-Century Miller*, trans. John A. Tedeschi and Anne Tedeschi (Baltimore: Johns Hopkins University Press, 1980); Carlo Ginzburg, *The Night Battles: Witchcraft and Agrarian Cults in the Sixteenth and Seventeenth Centuries*, trans. John A. Tedeschi and Anne Tedeschi (Baltimore: Johns Hopkins University Press, 1992); Natalie Zemon Davis, *Fiction in the Archives: Pardon Tales and Their Tellers in Sixteenth-Century France* (Stanford, Calif.: Stanford University Press, 1987); Thomas N. Bisson, *Tormented Voices: Power, Crisis, and Humanity in Rural Catalonia, 1140–1200* (Cambridge, Mass.: Harvard University Press, 1998); Leslie P. Peirce, *Morality Tales: Law and Gender in the Ottoman Court of Aintab* (Berkeley: University of California Press, 2003); Chris Wickham, *Courts and Conflict in Twelfth-Century Tuscany* (Oxford: Oxford University Press, 2003); Daniel Lord Smail, *The Consumption of Justice: Emotions, Publicity, and Legal Culture in Marseille, 1264–1423* (Ithaca, N.Y: Cornell University Press, 2003).

8. I follow in the footsteps of an important recent trend in archaeology: Greg Woolf, *Becoming Roman: The Origins of Provincial Civilization in Gaul* (Cambridge: Cambridge University Press, 1998); Michael Dietler, "The Archaeology of Colonization and the

Colonization of Archaeology: Theoretical Challenges from an Ancient Mediterranean Encounter," in *The Archaeology of Colonial Encounters*, ed. Gil J. Stein (Santa Fe, N.M.: School of American Research, 2005), 33–68.

9. My arguments do, however, owe a debt to a particular social scientist, Pierre Bourdieu, most notably in his essay, "The Force of Law: Towards a Sociology of the Juridical Field," *Hastings Law Journal* 38 (1987): 814–53. It is noteworthy that, apart from a few bits of largely decontextualized terminology, his approach has largely failed to penetrate the "social science" approach characteristic of empirically oriented Anglophone scholarship.

CHAPTER 1. PTOLEMAIOS COMPLAINS

1. See J. E. G. Whitehorne, "P. Mich. Inv. 255: A Petition to the Epistrategus P. Marcius Crispus," *Chronique d'Égypte* 66 (1999): 251. On duplicates, see J. E. G. Whitehorne, "Strategus, Centurion, or Neither: BGU I 321 and 322 (= M.Chrest. 114 and 124) and Their Duplicates," *Bulletin of the American Society of Papyrologists* 40 (2003): 201–11. On Ptolemaios' archive, see the discussion on the Leuven homepage of papyrus archives: http://www.trismegistos.org/arch/archives/pdf/325.pdf (last accessed May 2011).

2. For a catalogue of duplicates, see Bruce E. Nielsen, "A Catalog of Duplicate Papyri," *Zeitschrift für Papyrologie und Epigraphik* 129 (2000): 187–214.

3. On the palaeography of subscriptions see J. David Thomas, "Subscriptions to Petitions to Officials in Roman Egypt," in *Egypt and the Hellenistic World*, ed. E. van't Dack, P. van Dessel, and W. van Gucht, Studia Hellenistica 27 (Leuven: Orientaliste, 1983), 378–81, who suggests a modification of the early treatment of Ulrich Wilcken, "Zu den Kaiserreskripten," *Hermes* 55 (1920): esp. 30–31.

4. SB XX 14401 (A.D. 147, 49), PSI XIII 1323 (A.D. 147–48, 47).

5. PSI XIII 1323.5, 47, with BL IX 321.

6. P.Wisc. I 33 48 (A.D. 147, 48).

7. Arkady B. Kovelman, "From Logos to Myth: Egyptian Petitions of the 5th–7th Centuries," *Bulletin of the American Society of Papyrologists* 28 (1991): 135–52; Jean-Luc Fournet, "Entre document et littérature: la pétition dans l'antiquité tardive," in *La pétition à Byzance*, ed. Denis Feissel and Jean Gascou, Centre de Recherche d'Histoire et Civilisation de Byzance, Monographies 14 (Paris: Association des Amis du Centre d'Histoire et Civilisation de Byzance, 2004), 61–74.

8. This is possibly also the correct restoration of σύ δὲ ἐκ Σαλωμῆ[ς τ]ῆς Ἰουδα[ίας υ]ἱ̣ὸς [. . .]βλητος in the Acts of Isidorus and Lampon (Musurillo, *Acts of the Pagan Martyrs*, 4a.3.12).

9. P.Wisc. I 33.11–12, 48; SB XX 14401.3–4, 49.

10. The papyrus in question is P.Wisc. I 33 (A.D. 147, 48). Sijpesteijn (ed. princ.) had read lines 2–3 as "Ptolemaios, son of Diodoros, one of the veterans in the Arsinoite nome" ([παρὰ Πτ]ο̣λεμαίου Διοδώρ̣ου το̣ῦ̣ κ̣α̣ὶ Διοσκόρ̣ο̣υ̣ τῶν ἀ̣π̣ὸ τοῦ Ἀρσ[ιν]οείτου̣ οὐετ̣[ρανῶν]). D. Hagedorn, "Bemerkungen zu einigen Wisconsin Papyri," *Zeitschrift für*

Papyrologie und Epigraphik 1 (1967): 158–59, reads instead of "veteran," οὗ ἐπ[ιδέδωκα ἀ-]ναφορίου. This is the preferable reading since it alleviates all chronological problems. I made this mistake in Ari Z. Bryen and Andrzej Wypustek, "Gemellus' Evil Eyes (P.Mich. VI 423–424)," *Greek, Roman, and Byzantine Studies* 49 (2009): 541. I thank Ben Kelly for pointing it out.

11. On subscriptions, see R. Haensch, "Die Bearbeitungsweisen von Petitionen in der Provinz Aegyptus," *Zeitschrift für Papyrologie und Epigraphik* 100 (1994): 487–546.

12. P.Yale I 61 (A.D. 209); Guiliana Foti-Talamanca, *Ricerche sul processo nell'Egitto Greco-Romano* (Milan: Giuffre, 1979), II.1, chap. 3, assembles the evidence for procedure; see also Naphtali Lewis, "The Prefect's Conventus: Proceedings and Procedures," *Bulletin of the American Society of Papyrologists* 18 (1981): 119–29; Lewis, *Life in Egypt*, 185–95; Lewis, "Judiciary Routines in Roman Egypt," *Bulletin of the American Society of Papyrologists* 37 (2000): 83–93; G. P. Burton, "Proconsuls, Assizes and the Administration of Justice Under the Empire," *Journal of Roman Studies* 65 (1975): 92–106.

13. A process sometimes imperfect: P.Oxy. XXXVI 2754 (A.D. 111).

14. Haensch, "Bearbeitungsweisen," 362, on the administrative background to this document. On problems with the *conventus*, see also P.Ryl. II 74 (= FIRA III 166, A.D. 136–37).

15. Deciphering the jurisdiction of these officials has consumed a great amount of scholarly energy. The various individuals will be discussed below as the cases arise, but ultimately, in my opinion, whether an individual was granted a specific form of jurisdiction was ultimately of less concern than whether he had the influence to get the petition looked at by the correct official. Among the vast bibliography, useful especially for the more minor officials is Sofía Torallas-Tovar, "The Police in Byzantine Egypt: The Hierarchy in the Papyri from the Fourth to the Seventh Centuries," in *Current Research in Egyptology, 2000*, ed. Angela MacDonald and Christina Riggs, BAR International Series 909 (Oxford: Archaeopress, 2000), 115–23, who collects references for the late antique magistrates. See also Dieter Hennig, "Nyktophylakes, Nyktostrategen, und die παραφυλακὴ τῆς πόλεως," *Chiron* 32 (2002): 281–95; J. E. G. Whitehorne, "Petitions to the Centurion: A Question of Locality?" *Bulletin of the American Society of Papyrologists* 41 (2004): 155–70; Michael Peachin, "Petition to a Centurion from the NYU Papyrus Collection and the Question of Informal Adjudication by Soldiers," in *Papyri in Memory of P J. Sijpesteijn*, ed. A. J. B. Sirks and K. A. Worp, American Studies in Papyrology 40 (Oakville, Conn.: American Society of Papyrologists, 2007), 79–97; Roger S. Bagnall, "Army and Police in Roman Upper Egypt," *Journal of the American Research Center in Egypt* 14 (1977): 67–86; Richard Alston, *Soldier and Society in Roman Egypt: A Social History* (London: Routledge, 1995), 86–94, who also provides a catalogue of petitions to centurions.

16. For the most current bibliography on the "orders to arrest" see James G. Keenan, "Roman Criminal Procedure," in *Law and Society in Egypt from Alexander to the Arab Conquest (330 B.C.–640 A.D.)*, ed. James G. Keenan, Joseph G. Manning, and Uri Yiftach-Firanko (Cambridge: Cambridge University Press, forthcoming 2013). In general, Sofía Torallas-Tovar, "Violence in the Process of Arrest and Imprisonment in Late

Antique Egypt," in *Violence in Late Antiquity: Perceptions and Practices*, ed. H. A. Drake (Burlington, Vt.: Ashgate, 2006), 103–12.

17. The basic study is R. A. Coles, *Reports of Proceedings in Papyri*, Papyrologica Bruxellensia 4 (Brussels: Fond. Égypt. R. Élisabeth, 1966), who is mostly concerned with formal elements; J. A. Crook, *Legal Advocacy in the Roman World* (Ithaca, N.Y.: Cornell University Press, 1995), supplements this and provides more analysis, treating the relevant papyri seriatim. These documents are treated more comprehensively in Benjamin Kelly, *Petitions*. Ann Ellis Hanson, "A Petition and Court Proceedings: P. Michigan Inv. 6060," *Zeitschrift für Papyrologie und Epigraphik* 111 (1996): 175–82, presents a case of a petition and a set of court proceedings found together on the same document, but the proceedings, while part of what appears to be an extended conflict, are not directly related to the petition itself.

18. See John Gavin Tait, "The Strategi and Royal Scribes in the Roman Period," *Journal of Egyptian Archaeology* 8 (1922): 166–73; J. E. G. Whitehorne, "The Role of the Strategia in Administrative Continuity in Roman Egypt," in *Proceedings of the XVI International Congress of Papyrology*, ed. Roger S. Bagnall (Chico, Calif.: Scholar's Press, 1981), 419–28; Whitehorne, "Recent Research on the Strategi of Roman Egypt," *ANRW* II.10.1 (1988): 598–617.

19. For the activities of the *strategos*, see Chr.Wilck. 41 (Sel.Pap. II 242, A.D. 232), the official log (*commentarii*) of the *strategos* of Elephantine, Aurelius Leontas.

20. SB V 7523 (A.D. 153), a sworn declaration of several witnesses that they saw a Roman veteran beaten with rods (ῥαβδοῖς) at the instigation of the *strategos*. This behavior was illegal, but it is nevertheless an interesting example of one extreme of behavior. See also P.Lips. I 40 (A.D IV), in which the *praeses* has an individual (in this case a slave) beaten during a trial.

21. P.Wisc. I 33 (A.D. 147, 48).

22. For example, P.Select 13 (A.D. 421). To my knowledge, however, this is the only document that records this sort of procedure; see further below, Chapter 5.

23. On criminal law in Egypt and the complicated question of the Berlin Legal Codex see James G. Keenan, "Roman Criminal Law in a Berlin Papyrus Codex (BGU IV 1024–1027)," *Archiv für Papyrusforschung* 35 (1989): 15–23.

24. I take this to be one of the central challenges of a comparative legal project. See Ewald, "Comparative Jurisprudence (I)," 1939–43, who frames the problem eloquently.

25. Charles Tilly, "Linkers, Diggers, and Glossers in Social History," in Tilly, *Explaining Social Processes* (Boulder, Colo.: Paradigm, 2008).

26. I use the term here in the sense of Cover, "Nomos and Narrative."

27. Veena Das, *Life and Words: Violence and the Descent into the Ordinary* (Berkeley: University of California Press, 2007).

28. Complete catalogues can be found in Kelly, *Petitions*; Bärbel Kramer, "P. Strasb. Inv. 1265 + P. Strasb. 296 Recto: Eingabe wegen Ἀνδραποδισμός (= Plagium) und Σύλησις (= Furtum)," *Zeitschrift für Papyrologie und Epigraphik* 69 (1987): 143–61; Jean-Luc Fournet and Jean Gascou, "Liste des pétitions sur papyrus des Ve–VIIe siècles," in *La pétition à Byzance*, ed. Denis Feissel and Jean Gascou, Centre de Recherche d'Histoire et

Civilisation de Byzance Monographies 14 (Paris: Association des Amis du Centre d'Histoire et Civilisation de Byzance, 2004), 141–96.

29. See Appendix B.

CHAPTER 2. VIOLENT EGYPT

1. James G. Keenan, "Egypt's 'Special Place'," in *Jesuit Education and the Classics*, ed. Edmund P. Cueva, Shannon N. Byrne, and Frederick Benda (Newcastle upon Tyne: Cambridge Scholars, 2009), 177–92; Giovanni Geraci, "L'Egitto romano nella storiografia moderna," in *Egitto e storia antica dall'ellenismo all'età Araba: Bilancio di un confronto*, ed. Geraci and Lucia Criscuolo (Bologna: CLUEB, 1989), 55–88.

2. Seneca's short work on Egypt is unfortunately not preserved.

3. The only similarity to this situation is the annexation of Cappadocia under Tiberius, which was governed by an equestrian procurator: see Stephen Mitchell, *Anatolia: Land, Men and Gods in Asia Minor* (Oxford: Clarendon, 1993), II: 63, on Strabo 12.1.4.

4. Tac. *Ann.* 2.59.

5. Alan K. Bowman and Dominic Rathbone, "Cities and Administration in Roman Egypt," *Journal of Roman Studies* 82 (1992): 120–25, have emphasized that this did *not* mean that communities (in this case, the metropoleis) had no local organs of administration.

6. J. Grafton Milne, "The Ruin of Egypt by Roman Mismanagement," *Journal of Roman Studies* 17 (1927): 1–13; John Garrett Winter, *Life and Letters in the Papyri* (Ann Arbor: University of Michigan Press, 1933), 1–6.

7. On the problems of lachrymose history, see, from a different context, David Nirenberg, *Communities of Violence: Persecution of Minorities in the Middle Ages* (Princeton, N.J.: Princeton University Press, 1998), 8–9.

8. This is the point of Naphtali Lewis's classic, *Life in Egypt Under Roman Rule*. Lewis's project was long in gestation: earlier versions of his theses can be found in the collection of his papers, *On Government and Law in Roman Egypt: Collected Papers of Naphtali Lewis*, ed. Ann Ellis Hanson, American Studies in Papyrology 33 (Atlanta: Scholars Press, 1995).

9. Benjamin H. Isaac, *The Invention of Racism in Classical Antiquity* (Princeton, N.J.: Princeton University Press, 2004), is an example of the limitations of such a method.

10. Erich S. Gruen, *Rethinking the Other in Antiquity* (Princeton, N.J.: Princeton University Press, 2011), 76–90. On Herodotus' ethnography more generally, see James Redfield, "Herodotus the Tourist," *Classical Philology* 80 (1985): 97–118; Ian S. Moyer, "Herodotus and an Egyptian Mirage: The Genealogies of the Theban Priests," *Journal of Hellenic Studies* 122 (2002): 70–90, to whose method I am most sympathetic.

11. Stephen Nimis, "Egypt in Greco-Roman History and Fiction," *Alif: Journal of Comparative Poetics* 24 (2004): 34–67.

12. I bracket here the discussions of Egypt and Egyptians in Philo of Alexandria, primarily because they seem to have made little contribution to the ways in which the Roman metropole understood Egypt and Egyptians.

13. A comprehensive narrative of Roman-Ptolemaic contacts through the second century can be found in Erich S. Gruen, *The Hellenistic World and the Coming of Rome* (Berkeley: University of California Press, 1984), 672–716.

14. Strabo 17.1.12. The passage is hopelessly corrupt: the Egyptians, according to the manuscript tradition, are said to be ὀξὺ καὶ πολιτικόν ("acute and inclined to civic life"); whether the text should instead read ὀξὺ καὶ ἀπολιτικόν ("ill-tempered and ungovernable") will depend on whether (a) one takes this to be an accurate paraphrase of Polybius and (b) whether Polybius "hates" (βδελύττεται) Alexandria because it is generally violent or because it represents an inversion of the proper state of affairs, where the Egyptians are the properly civic inhabitants and the mercenaries and Alexandrians are degraded. Frank W. Walbank, "Egypt in Polybius," in *Polybius, Rome, and the Hellenistic World: Essays and Reflections* (Cambridge: Cambridge University Press, 2002), 59–61, settles on οὐ πολιτικόν ("uncivilized"). See further Robert K. Ritner, "Implicit Models of Cross-Cultural Interaction: A Question of Noses, Soap, and Prejudice," in *Life in a Multi-Cultural Society: Egypt from Cambyses to Constantine and Beyond*, ed. Janet H. Johnson, Studies in Ancient Oriental Civilization 51 (Chicago: Oriental Institute, 1992), 287–88.

15. Tacitus, *Histories* 1.11.

16. Benjamin Kelly, "Tacitus, Germanicus and the Kings of Egypt (Tac. Ann. 2.59–61)," *Classical Quarterly* 60 (2010): 221–37.

17. Juvenal, *Satires*, 15.33–38.

18. 15.75–83.

19. Compare P.Oxy. LXII 3065.8 9 (A.D III), a personal letter describing a town in a state of "no longer war, but cannibalism" (νῦν ἀνθ̣ρ̣ωποφαγεία ἐστὶν καὶ οὐ πόλεμος). If the editors are correct that the letter is of Alexandrian provenance, it may well be that this author was playing on Juvenalian themes.

20. Here I differ with Richard Alston, "Conquest by Text: Juvenal and Plutarch on Egypt," in *Roman Imperialism: Post-Colonial Perspectives*, ed. Jane Webster and Nicholas J. Cooper, Leicester Archaeology Monographs 3 (Leicester: Leicester University Archaeological Research Centre, 1996), 104–8. *Sat.* 15.93–106 seems to block the possibility that Egyptians can integrate, since their behavior comes from preference (and natural defect), rather than necessity.

21. If Richard McKim, "Philosophers and Cannibals: Juvenal's Fifteenth Satire," *Phoenix* 40 (1986): 58–71, is right, *Sat.* 15 is a meta-joke in which the speaker spoofs Roman racism—this is perhaps possible, although Juvenal's poem has certainly convinced others of its claims: even Theodor Mommsen, *The Provinces of the Roman Empire from Caesar to Diocletian*, trans. William P. Dickson (London: Macmillan, 1909), II: 261, thought this story not only true, but "of very ordinary occurrence."

22. Lucian, *Toxaris* 27–33; Philostratus, *Vita Apollonii* 5.24. The papyrus containing Lollianus' *Phoinikika* attests to the fact that these bandit stories were popular in Egypt as well. Perhaps also useful is Philostratus, *VS* 603, contrasting local politics in Athens and Naukratis, where the politics of *Athens* are described as being tranquil (another learned joke?).

23. *HA* (Firmus) 7: *sunt enim Aegyptii, ut satis nosti, viri ventosi, furibundi, iactantes, iniuriosi, atque adeo vani, liberi, novarum rerum usque ad cantilenas publicas cupientes, versificatores, epigrammatarii, mathematici, haruspices, medici.*

24. 22.6.

25. See in general, Andrew Harker, *Loyalty and Dissidence in Roman Egypt: The Case of the Acta Alexandrinorum* (Cambridge: Cambridge University Press, 2008), who also provides an updated catalogue of the *Acta*. Claudius' speech is preserved on papyrus as P.Lond.VI 1912 = Sel.Pap. II 212.

26. An overview of changes in provincial society can be found in Greg Woolf, "Provincial Perspectives," in *The Cambridge Companion to the Age of Augustus*, ed. Karl Galinsky (Cambridge: Cambridge University Press, 2005), 106–29.

27. On the "new aristocracy" and the relations of the Flavians to the provinces, see Ronald Mellor, "The New Aristocracy of Power," and Jane M. Cody, "Conquerors and Conquered on Flavian Coins," both in *Flavian Rome: Culture, Image, Text*, ed. A. J. Boyle and W. J. Dominik (Leiden: Brill, 2003), 69–101 and 103–23, esp. 105–13, respectively. Certainly this was an extended process, with origins in the transition to the Principate (excepting a possible monument by Pompeius), and one not wholly localized in Rome: see R. R. R. Smith, "Simulacra Gentium: The Ethne from the Sebasteion at Aphrodisias," *Journal of Roman Studies* 78 (1988): esp. 70–77.

28. Mary Taliaferro Boatwright, *Hadrian and the Cities of the Roman Empire* (Princeton, N.J.: Princeton University Press, 2000).

29. See further Ari Z. Bryen, "Tradition, Precedent, and Power in Roman Egypt," in *Official Epistolography and the Language(s) of Power*, ed. Lucian Reinfandt and Sven Tost, Papyrologica Vindobonensia (Vienna, forthcoming 2013), on the problem of the introduction of new forms of "native" law in the late first century.

30. Philostratus *VS* 532 (on Polemon of Laodikea). I will return to the question of the sophists and the urban legal culture of the provinces in the high Empire in the future.

31. Greg Woolf, "Monumental Writing and the Expansion of Roman Society in the Early Empire," *Journal of Roman Studies* 86 (1996): 22–39.

32. Bryen, "Tradition."

33. *In Flaccum* 78–80.

34. P.Oxy. II 237.vii.39 (A.D. 186 but quoting a text from 87).

35. P.Giss. 40.17–30 (A.D. 212–15).

36. BGU V 1210 (A.D. 149); P.Oxy XLII 3014 is a partial copy from the first century.

37. As David Daube memorably put it (with reference to a distribution of material goods that I would not necessarily endorse), "In the urban areas at least, the vast majority of the residents were have-nots, with not much to litigate about and certainly lacking the means to litigate with. In theory, if a beggar's son hired out his services, the wages paid to him belonged to his father; so did the cigarette stubs he picked up from the gutter. The reality was totally different, he would never be bothered. Among the have-nots, whatever your status in the family, the little you acquired was yours from the age you had sufficient wits to acquire anything. In the slums, there was no distinction between a citizen and a

Greek or Jew. Poverty is a great equalizer." David Daube, *Roman Law: Linguistic, Social and Philosophical Aspects* (Edinburgh: Edinburgh University Press, 1969), 81. See also David Daube, "Fraud No. 3," in *The Legal Mind: Essays for Tony Honoré*, ed. Neil MacCormick and Peter Birks (Oxford: Clarendon, 1986), 1–17.

38. P.Oxy. II 237.viii.21–43 (A.D. 186, citing documents from A.D. 89).

39. Clearly, space could serve as an important factor, and on occasion a group could seek to police a particular space: Richard Alston, "Philo's 'In Flaccum': Ethnicity and Social Space in Roman Alexandria," *Greece & Rome* 44 (1997): 165–75, or with reference to the Hellenistic period, Kent J. Rigsby, "Founding a Serapeum," *Greek, Roman, and Byzantine Studies* 42 (2001): 123–24. My only point is that the opposite situation most typically prevailed.

40. Veterans: SB VI 9636 (A.D. 135–36); Antinoopolites: P.Mich. VI 423–24 (A.D. 197).

41. P.Giss. I 40.16–30 (A.D. 212–15), edict of Caracalla attempting to expel Egyptians from Alexandria.

42. In SB VI 9336.9–11, a personal letter, a man asks his friend to look after a newly discharged veteran, Terentianus, "and let him know what sorts of villagers we have here, so that he doesn't get hurt" (γνώτω ποταποὺς κωμήτας ἔχομεν, μὴ ἐπηρεάσθῃ).

43. Kent J. Rigsby, "An Ephebic Inscription from Egypt," *Greek, Roman, and Byzantine Studies* 19 (1978): 239–49. See the important study of Roger S. Bagnall, "Women's Petitions in Late Antique Egypt," in *Hellenistic and Roman Egypt: Sources and Approaches* (Aldershot: Ashgate, 2006), chap. xxiii.

44. P.Oxy. XLII 3061.12 (A.D. I); compare the famous Ptolemaic petition P.Enteux. 79 (218 B.C.), for which there is practically nothing similar from the Roman world save SB XXIV 16252 (A.D. 163, 54).

45. Clifford Ando, *Imperial Ideology and Provincial Loyalty in the Roman Empire*, Classics and Contemporary Thought 6 (Berkeley: University of California Press, 2000).

46. Brendan J. Haug, "The Egyptian Fayyum: Environment, Irrigation, Agriculture, and the End of Antiquity," Ph.D. dissertation, University of California at Berkeley, 2012, elucidates the intricacies of this balancing act for the Fayyum.

47. Michael Sharp, "Shearing Sheep: Rome and the Collection of Taxes in Egypt, 30 B.C.–A.D. 200," in *Lokale Autonomie und römische Ordnungsmacht in den kaiserzeitlichen Provinzen vom 1. bis 3. Jahrhundert*, ed. Werner Eck, Schriften des historischen Kollegs. Kolloquien 42 (Munich: R. Oldenbourg Verlag, 1999), 211–41; Andrea Jördens, *Statthalterliche Verwaltung in der römischen Kaiserzeit: Studien zum Praefectus Aegypti*, Historia Einzelschriften 175 (Stuttgart: Franz Steiner, 2009), deals in detail with the administrative responsibilities of the governor.

48. OGIS II 669.ii.1–9 = Chrest.Mitt. 102 = FIRA I 58 = SB V 8444, with parts preserved as BGU VII 1563. On governors and experience, see P. A. Brunt, "The Administrators of Roman Egypt," *Journal of Roman Studies* 65 (1975): 124–47.

49. Ari Z. Bryen, "Judging Empire: Courts and Culture in Rome's Eastern Provinces," *Law and History Review* 30 (2012): 771–811.

50. Alan K. Bowman, "Egypt," in *Cambridge Ancient History*, vol. X, *The Augustan Empire, 43 B.C.–A.D. 69*, ed. Alan K. Bowman, Edward Champlin, and Andrew Lintott (Cambridge: Cambridge University Press, 1996), 686.

51. On local initiative and "self-help" see also Rafael Taubenschlag, "Self Help in Greco Roman Egypt," in *Opera Minora*, ed. Vincenzo Arangio Ruiz (Warsaw: Państwowe Wydawn Naukowe, 1959), 135–42; Deborah W. Hobson, "The Impact of Law on Village Life in Roman Egypt," in *Law, Politics and Society in the Ancient Mediterranean World*, ed. Baruch Halpern and Deborah W. Hobson (Sheffield: Sheffield Academic Press, 1993), 193–219.

52. The classic discussion of precedents in Roman jurisprudence is H. F. Jolowicz, "Case Law in Roman Egypt," *Journal of the Society of Public Teachers of Law* 14 (1937): 1–16. See also Ranon Katzoff, "Precedents in the Courts of Roman Egypt," *Zeitschrift der Savigny-Stiftung fur Rechtsgeschichte (romanistische Abteilung)* 89 (1972): 256–92; Barbara Anagnostou-Canas, "La valeur des précédents judiciaires dans l'Égypte romaine: État de la question," *Droits et Cultures* 47 (2004): 47–65; Bryen, "Tradition"; on the question of precedent in the *ius civile*, see Ernest Metzger, "Roman Judges, Case Law, and Principles of Procedure," *Law and History Review* 22 (2004): 243–75, summarizing earlier literature.

53. J. E. Lendon, *Empire of Honour: The Art of Government in the Roman World* (Oxford: Clarendon, 1997), 18.

54. For a comparative example of how this process can become complicated, see John L. Comaroff, "Legality, Modernity, and Ethnicity in Colonial South Africa: An Excursion in the Historical Anthropology of Law," in *Law, Society, and Economy: Centenary Essays for the London School of Economics and Political Science, 1895–1995*, ed. Richard Rawlings (Oxford: Clarendon, 1997), 247–69.

55. Rafael Taubenschlag, *The Law of Greco-Roman Egypt in the Light of the Papyri, 332 B.C.–640 A.D*, 2nd ed. (Warsaw: Państwowe Wydawnictwo Naukowe, 1955), 29, proposing a "great basic law regulating the legal relations of both the Romans and peregrines"; Hans Julius Wolff, *Das Recht der griechischen Papyri Ägyptens in der Zeit der Ptolemäer und des Prinzipats*, Handbuch der Altertumswissenschaft 10.5 (Munich: Beck, 1978), 108–11, collects some subsequent references that may refer to a "provincial edict." Still the best treatments of the interaction of local tradition and Roman law are by Josef Mélèze Modrzejewski, "La règle de droit dans l'Égypte romaine (État des questions et perspectives de recherches)," in *Proceedings of the Twelfth International Congress of Papyrology*, ed. Deborah Samuel (Toronto: Hakkert, 1970), 317–77; Josef Mélèze Modrzejewski, "'La loi des égyptiens': Le droit grec dans l'Égypte romaine," in *Proceedings of the XVIII Congress of Papyrology*, ed. Basil Mandilaras (Athens: Greek Papyrological Society, 1988), 383–89.

56. On the dynamics of this process in Asia, see C. Kokkinia, "Ruling, Inducing, Arguing: How to Govern (and Survive) a Greek Province," in *Roman Rule and Civic Life: Local and Regional Perspectives*, ed. L. de Ligt, H. W Singor, and Emily Ann Hemelrijk, Impact of Empire 4 (Amsterdam: J.C. Gieben, 2004), 39–58.

57. Roger S. Bagnall, *Egypt in Late Antiquity* (Princeton, N.J.: Princeton University Press, 1993), 4–14.

58. Herwig Maehler, "Greek, Roman, and Egyptian Law," *Journal of Juristic Papyrology* 35 (2005): 125–26; Joseph G. Manning, *The Last Pharaohs: Egypt Under the Ptolemies, 305–30 B.C.* (Princeton, N.J.: Princeton University Press, 2010), chap.6.

59. Mélèze Modrzejewski, "La loi des égyptiens," 323; Bryen, "Judging Empire."

60. Ludwig Mitteis, *Reichsrecht und Volksrecht in den östlichen Provinzen des römischen Kaiserreichs* (Leipzig: Teubner, 1891). See also Bowman and Rathbone, "Cities and Administration in Roman Egypt," 113.

61. P.Oxy. XLVI 3285 (A.D. II). It is of course worth noting that we have *no* context for understanding how such a document was used, if in fact it was.

62. Hans Julius Wolff, "Das Vulgarrechtsproblem und die Papyri," *Zeitschrift der Savigny-Stiftung für Rechtsgeschichte (Romanistische Abteilung)* 91 (1974): 105, cited with approval by Maehler, "Greek, Roman, and Egyptian Law," 140.

63. See the summary treatment in Livia Capponi, *Augustan Egypt: The Creation of a Roman Province* (New York: Routledge, 2005), 51–63.

64. Mélèze Modrzejewski, "Règle," 329–30.

65. Mélèze Modrzejewski, "Règle"; Brunt, "The Administrators of Roman Egypt," 132–36; Bryen, "Judging Empire." There is a striking parallel in the New Testament: in John 18.31, Pilate discusses a question of jurisdiction with the Sanhedrin. Pilate instructs the Sanhedrin to try Jesus locally, "according to your own laws" (κατὰ τὸν νόμον ὑμῶν κρίνατε αὐτόν). Similar is Acts 18:12–17. See David Rensberger, "The Politics of John: The Trial of Jesus in the Fourth Gospel," *Journal of Biblical Literature* 103 (1984): 395–411.

66. Many of these show up on papyrus: the early Roman imperial edicts are collected by James Henry Oliver, *Greek Constitutions of Early Roman Emperors from Inscriptions and Papyri*, Memoirs of the American Philosophical Society 178 (Philadelphia: American Philosophical Society, 1989), which should be used with the supplement of V. I. Anastasiades and George A. Souris, *An Index to Roman Imperial Constitutions from Greek Inscriptions and Papyri: 27 B.C. to 284 A.D.* (Berlin: de Gruyter, 2000).

67. Julián González and Michael H. Crawford, "The Lex Irnitana: A New Copy of the Flavian Municipal Law," *Journal of Roman Studies* 76 (1986): 149, 203–4.

68. Bowman, "Egypt," 683.

69. See below, Chapter 5, and P. Fouad. 21 (A.D. 63) on the privileges of veterans; SB V 7523 (A.D. 153) on Roman citizens (where their legal protections are *not* granted).

70. The choice of location of the trial could be important, and the ability to have proceedings moved was a legal privilege. See P.Mich. VI 365 (A.D. 194).

71. *Digest* 1.18.8 (Julian, *Digest* book 1): "I have often heard our present emperor saying that a rescript, which states, 'you may approach the officer who presides over the province,' does not impose on the proconsul or legate or provincial governor the duty of personally undertaking the judicial examination. But he ought to weigh up whether to hear the case himself or to appoint a judge for that purpose" (*Saepe audivi Caesarem nostrum dicentem hac rescriptione: "eum qui provinciae praeest adire potes" non imponi necessitatem proconsuli vel legato eius vel praesidi provinciae suscipiendae cognitionis, sed eum*

aestimare debere, ipse cognoscere an iudicem dare debeat, trans. Alan Watson). See further William Turpin, "Imperial Subscriptions and the Administration of Justice," *Journal of Roman Studies* 81 (1991): 101–18; Lewis, "Judiciary Routines," 92; Hobson, "Impact of Law"; Serena Connolly, *Lives Behind the Laws: The World of the Codex Hermogenianus* (Bloomington: Indiana University Press, 2010).

72. Bagnall, "Army and Police," esp. 68. Compare P.Mich. VI 421 (A.D. 41–54, **20**), in which the local guards arrest and detain a man in hot pursuit of some donkey-thieves, whom he thinks the guards are protecting. In general, see Peter Brown, *Power and Persuasion in Late Antiquity* (Madison: University of Wisconsin Press, 1992), 35–70.

73. A possible exception might be SB XIV 12199 (A.D. 155, **52**).

74. Bagnall, *Egypt in Late Antiquity*, 161.

75. Jill Harries, *Law and Crime in the Roman World* (Cambridge: Cambridge University Press, 2007), 43–58. Labeling such anti-social acts "violence" produces the identical problem: Garrett G. Fagan, "Violence in Roman Social Relations," in *The Oxford Handbook of Social Relations in the Roman World*, ed. Michael Peachin (Oxford: Oxford University Press, 2011), 467–95.

76. So far as I know, no historian has come up with an adequate answer to this question. On "how violent," an interesting comparison is the case of nineteenth-century Wisconsin: James Willard Hurst, *Law and the Conditions of Freedom in the Nineteenth-Century United States* (Madison: University of Wisconsin Press, 1956); Michael Lesy, *Wisconsin Death Trip* (New York: Pantheon, 1973). A different approach is taken by Moushira Erfan et al., "Cranial Trauma in Ancient Egyptians from the Bahriyah Oasis, Greco-Roman Period," *Research Journal of Medicine & Medical Sciences* 4 (2009): 78–84, but I find it hard to generalize on the basis of their small and chronologically dispersed sample (in addition to the incomplete explanation of the nature of formation of the archaeological deposit in question).

CHAPTER 3. VIOLENCE, MODERN AND ANCIENT

1. Jonathan Simon, *Governing Through Crime: How the War on Crime Transformed American Democracy and Created a Culture of Fear* (Oxford: Oxford University Press, 2007).

2. An insight shared across disciplinary boundaries: compare, Judith Butler, *Precarious Life: The Powers of Mourning and Violence* (London: Verso, 2004), 19–28; Erving Goffman, *The Presentation of Self in Everyday Life* (New York: Anchor, 1959), 242.

3. Das, *Life and Words*, 38–58; Elaine Scarry, *The Body in Pain: The Making and Unmaking of a World* (New York: Oxford University Press, 1985), 27–59.

4. I refer here to the legal sense of the term, especially as it is used in *Digest* 47.10.1.

5. Paul Farmer, "An Anthropology of Structural Violence," *Current Anthropology* 45 (2004): esp. 317; Loïc Wacquant, *Urban Outcasts: A Comparative Sociology of Advanced Marginality* (Cambridge: Polity, 2008), 24–30, 67–69. I suspect that a concept of "structural violence" lurks at the center of Apuleius' *Metamorphoses*, although even though

Apuleius captures well what Farmer describes, he lacks the vocabulary to theorize it. I hope to return to this in another paper.

6. A list of standard definitions is given in Taubenschlag, *Law*, 435–42, and also in more detail in Rafael Taubenschlag, *Das Strafrecht im Recht der Papyri* (Leipzig: B.G. Turner, 1916), 81–84. See also Roger S. Bagnall, "Response to Hans Albert Rupprecht," in *Symposion 1990: Vorträge zur griechischen und hellenistischen Rechtsgeschichte*, ed. Michael Gagarin, Akten der Gesellschaft für griechische und hellenistische Rechtsgeschichte 8 (Köln: Böhlau, 1991), 149–52; Benjamin Kelly, "The Repression of Violence in the Roman Principate," Ph.D. dissertation, Oxford University, 2002.

7. See for instance Poll. *Onom.* 8.74–81, giving a list of possible ways to describe violence.

8. Paul, *Sent.* 5.4.1: *iniuriam patimur aut in corpus aut extra corpus.*

9. In no case that I know of is violence against a slave called *hybris*: thus for example P.Oxy. VIII 1120 (A.D. III, **90**), in which a woman complains of an attack against several people at her home: an attack against a woman's son-in-law is called *hybris* (the specifics are not preserved), while the attack against her slave girl is referred to as βία. On the problems of the restoring the term in the petition from Skaptopara, see Tor Hauken, *Petition and Response: An Epigraphic Study of Petitions to Roman Emperors, 181–249*, Monographs from the Norwegian Institute at Athens 2 (Bergen: Norwegian Institute at Athens, 1998), 115.

10. Taubenschlag, *Law*, 422–29. For a more detailed treatment, Wolfgang Dahlmann, "H BIA im Recht der Papyri," Ph.D. thesis, Cologne, 1968. For confusion between the two: Hobson, "Impact of Law," 221. Taubenschlag's discussion is slightly misleading. He claims that in the Roman period the definition does not change fundamentally from that of the Ptolemaic period. Yet the Ptolemaic evidence that he cites includes delicts against the person, including an example of physical assault (P.Lond. I 56 [223–221 B.C.]), which in the Roman period would probably not be considered *bia*, strictly speaking. Taubenschlag's distinction is maintained in the more recent work of Barbara Anagnostou-Canas, *Juge et sentence dans l'Égypte Romaine* (Paris: l'Harmattan, 1991). The distinction is questioned in Naphtali Lewis, "A Petition of A.D. 212," *Bulletin of the American Society of Papyrologists* 12 (1975): n.8, citing as an example BGU III 871 (A.D. II, 70), in which someone submits a complaint [περὶ ὕβρ]εως καὶ βίας καὶ ἁρπαγῆς. The petition, however, is too fragmentary to know precisely what the events in question constituted; it could have been all three.

11. For instance, in P.Lond. II 358 (= Chr.Mitt. 52, A.D. 150–54, **50**) the petitioner complains that he has been forced to sign away his rights to a sum of money. They forced him to do this with *hybreis* and beatings (μετὰ ὕβρεων καὶ πληγῶν). While there are thus two separate matters at hand, the *bia* and the *hybris*/assault, they are part of a single act. See also P.Rain.Cent. 91 (A.D. 419, **126**).

12. The echoes of this terminology in John Chrysostom are striking (so to speak), and suggest that they are not unique to Egypt: Joy A. Schroeder, "John Chrysostom's Critique of Spousal Violence," *Journal of Early Christian Studies* 12 (2004): 40.

13. This position is exemplified by Kathryn Burns, *Into the Archive: Writing and Power in Colonial Peru* (Durham, N.C.: Duke University Press, 2010).

14. Davis, *Fiction in the Archives*, 3–4.

15. Burns, *Into the Archive.*

16. See A. di Bitonto, "Le petitzione al re. Studio sul formulario," *Aegyptus* 47 (1967): 5–57; A. di Bitonto, "Le petizioni di funzionari nel periodo Tolemaico," *Aegyptus* 48 (1968): 53–107.

17. See Appendix A for a further discussion.

18. P.Mich. V 229, 230 (A.D. 48, **24, 25**).

19. In general Raffaella Cribiore, *Writing, Teachers, and Students in Graeco-Roman Egypt*, American Studies in Papyrology 36 (Atlanta: Scholars Press, 1996); Raffaella Cribiore, *Gymnastics of the Mind: Greek Education in Hellenistic and Roman Egypt* (Princeton, N.J.: Princeton University Press, 2001); Arthur Verhoogt, "Dictating Letters in Greek and Roman Egypt from a Comparative Perspective" (forthcoming). A working paper version of this study is available at http://sitemaker.umich.edu/verhoogt/files/dictating1.pdf.

20. Traianos Gagos, Jennifer E. Gates, and Andrew T. Wilburn, "Material Culture and Texts of Graeco-Roman Egypt: Creating Context, Debating Meaning," *Bulletin of the American Society of Papyrologists* 42 (2005): esp. 185, and below, Appendix A.

21. Pers.comm, 4/22/08.

22. See also Hauken, *Petition and Response*, 19, on the question of form in the petition of the *coloni* of the Saltus Burunitanus.

23. David M. Engel, "The Oven Bird's Song: Insiders, Outsiders, and Personal Injuries in an American Community," *Law & Society Review* 18 (1984): 551–82; John M. Conley and William M. O'Barr, *Rules Versus Relationships: The Ethnography of Legal Discourse* (Chicago: University of Chicago Press, 1990); Comaroff, "Legality, Modernity, Ethnicity"; Sally Falk Moore, "Certainties Undone: Fifty Turbulent Years of Legal Anthropology, 1949–1999," *Journal of the Royal Anthropological Institute* 7 (2001): 101–3; Lauren A. Benton, *A Search for Sovereignty: Law and Geography in European Empires, 1400–1900* (Cambridge: Cambridge University Press, 2010), 59–68, 112–20.

24. P.Oxy. VI 937.2–8 (A.D. III).

25. SB VI 9194.11 (A.D. III).

26. Apparently Chinese also offers a similar set of distinctions: see Barend J. ter Haar, "Rethinking 'Violence' in Chinese Culture," in *Meanings of Violence: A Cross Cultural Perspective*, ed. J. Abbink and Göran Aijmer (Oxford: Berg, 2000), esp. 136, on *wen* and *bao.*

27. Max Weber, "Politics as a Vocation," in *From Max Weber: Essays in Sociology*, ed. Hans Heinrich Gerth and C. Wright Mills (London: Routledge, 1991), 78; Max Weber, *Economy and Society: An Outline of Interpretive Sociology*, ed. Guenther Roth and Claus Wittich (Berkeley: University of California Press, 1978), 56. It is noteworthy that Ross and Wittich switch between force and violence in their translation.

28. Charles Tilly, *Big Structures, Large Processes, Huge Comparisons* (New York: Russell Sage Foundation, 1984), 56–59; Charles Tilly, *The Politics of Collective Violence* (Cambridge: Cambridge University Press, 2003).

29. North summarizes his work in Douglass C. North, "Institutions," *Journal of Economic Perspectives* 5 (1991): 97–112. On the question of violence and institutions more specifically, see Douglass C. North, John J. Wallis, and Barry R. Weingast, *Violence and Social Orders: A Conceptual Framework for Interpreting Recorded Human History* (Cambridge: Cambridge University Press, 2009).

30. Tilly, *The Politics of Collective Violence*, 55–80.

31. Standard is Martin Jay, *The Dialectical Imagination: A History of the Frankfurt School and the Institute of Social Research, 1923–1950*, Weimar and Now 10 (Berkeley: University of California Press, 1996). On Marcuse, see further Richard Wolin, *Heidegger's Children: Hannah Arendt, Karl Löwith, Hans Jonas, and Herbert Marcuse* (Princeton, N.J.: Princeton University Press, 2001), 134–72.

32. Hannah Arendt, *The Origins of Totalitarianism* (San Diego: Harcourt Brace, 1985), 441.

33. Max Horkheimer and Theodor W. Adorno, *Dialectic of Enlightenment: Philosophical Fragments*, ed. Gunzelin Schmid Noerr, trans. Edmund Jephcott (Stanford, Calif.: Stanford University Press, 2002), 33.

34. Ibid., 144.

35. Ibid., 138–39.

36. Ibid., 4, and, in a different vein, Reinhart Koselleck, *Critique and Crisis: Enlightenment and the Pathogenesis of Modern Society* (Cambridge, Mass.: MIT Press, 1988), 62–85.

37. The work of Frantz Fanon is crucial here.

38. Jay, *The Dialectical Imagination*, 255–61.

39. Nancy Scheper-Hughes and Philippe I. Bourgois, eds., *Violence in War and Peace: An Anthology*, Blackwell Readers in Anthropology 5 (Malden, Mass.: Blackwell, 2004). See further Nancy Scheper-Hughes, *Death Without Weeping: The Violence of Everyday Life in Brazil* (Berkeley: University of California Press, 1992); Abbink and Aijmer, *Meanings of Violence*; Das, *Life and Words*.

40. E.g., Arthur Kleinman, "The Violences of Everyday Life: The Multiple Forms and Dynamics of Social Violence," in *Violence and Subjectivity*, ed. Veena Das and Arthur Kleinman (Berkeley: University of California Press, 2000), 238. Michel Foucault famously reversed the first part of this formulation in *Discipline and Punish: The Birth of the Prison*, trans. Alan Sheridan (New York: Vintage, 1995), and the second part in *Security, Territory, Population: Lectures at the Collège de France, 1977–78*, ed. Michel Senellart, trans. Graham Burchell (New York: Picador/Palgrave Macmillan, 2009).

41. Michel Foucault, "Nietzsche, Genealogy, History," in *The Foucault Reader*, ed. Paul Rabinow (New York: Pantheon, 1984), 85–86.

42. Dominick LaCapra, *Writing History, Writing Trauma* (Baltimore: Johns Hopkins University Press, 2001), 23, 48, 80–81, 190, is persuasive on this point for the study of the Holocaust, but I suggest that his core claim can be easily generalized to the scholarly landscape writ large.

43. Susan Sontag, *Regarding the Pain of Others* (New York: Farrar, Straus and Giroux, 2003), 25. Certainly many are alert to this problem, though few have found ways

around it. See Philippe I. Bourgois, *Righteous Dopefiend*, California Series in Public Anthropology 21 (Berkeley: University of California Press, 2009), 9, in which Bourgois cautions against treating his photo-ethnography of heroin addiction as the "voyeuristic pornography of suffering" which it emphatically is.

44. John Paul Sartre, "Preface," in Frantz Fanon, *The Wretched of the Earth*, trans. Richard Philcox (New York: Grove Press, 2004), xliii–lxii, anthologized in Scheper-Hughes and Bourgois, *Violence in War and Peace*, 229–35.

45. Jean Baudrillard, *The Spirit of Terrorism and Other Essays*, trans. Chris Turner (London: Verso, 2003).

46. Hannah Arendt, "Letter to Gershom Scholem," in *The Portable Hannah Arendt*, ed. P. R. Baehr (New York: Penguin, 2000), 396.

47. For recent examples of such an expansive definition, see the articles collected in H. A. Drake, ed., *Violence in Late Antiquity: Perceptions and Practices* (Burlington, Vt.: Ashgate, 2006), and the monograph of Michael Gaddis, *There Is No Crime for Those Who Have Christ: Religious Violence in the Christian Roman Empire*, Transformation of the Classical Heritage 39 (Berkeley: University of California Press, 2005). Ramsay MacMullen's vision of the ancient towns and villages does not deal specifically with violence, but postulates an overwhelming vision of harsh coercion in which violence plays a major part: *Roman Social Relations, 50 B.C. to A.D. 284* (New Haven, Conn.: Yale University Press, 1974), 1–27.

48. Frier, "A New Papyrology?," 223.

49. What follows is analogous to the discussion of violence by David Riches, "The Phenomenon of Violence," in *The Anthropology of Violence*, ed. Riches (Oxford: Blackwell, 1986), 1–27. The political implications of the term "violence" are also strikingly analogous to the political implications of the label "social construction" discussed by Ian Hacking, *The Social Construction of What?* (Cambridge, Mass.: Harvard University Press, 1999), 58, 95.

50. Adam Bülow-Jacobsen, "Orders to Arrest: P.Haun. Inv. 33 and 54 and a Consolidated List," *Zeitschrift für Papyrologie und Epigraphik* 66 (1986): 93–98; Traianos Gagos and P. J. Sijpesteijn, "Towards an Explanation of the Typology of the So-Called 'Orders to Arrest'," *Bulletin of the American Society of Papyrologists* 33 (1996): 77–97; Fritz Mitthof and Roger S. Bagnall, "Order to Send a Person," in *Gedenkschrift Ulrike Horak (P. Horak)*, ed. Hermann Harrauer and Rosario Pintaudi, Papyrologica Florentina 34 (Florence: Gonnelli, 2004), 59–62; Keenan, "Roman Criminal Procedure."

51. The proper restoration of this phrase is a matter of dispute: the papyrus reads πθόνους, and I have here taken it as an accusative, the object of ἐπαγαγεῖν. The next phrase is jumbled: it may be a genitive absolute in which the gender has been bungled; alternatively, one might imagine that Ision is saying that "I am not the cause," but this would involve restoring some sort of *hapax* such as αἰτιάστης, which I am reluctant to do.

52. P.Ryl. II 144 (A.D. 38, 14).

53. On envy, see Bryen and Wypustek, "Gemellus' Evil Eyes."

54. Pierre Jouguet, *La vie municipale dans l'Égypte romaine* (Paris: Fontemoing, 1911), 315–18.

55. On interacting with slaves, compare P.Mich.Mchl.28 = SB XII 11130 (A.D. III/IV).

56. Compare P.Ryl. II 77.39–40 (A.D. 192), minutes of meeting concerning appointment to a liturgy, in which the appointed liturgist is said to have hit one of the others; the accusation is met with a curt denial, and seems to attract no one else's attention.

57. For this reason I find unlikely Peter Sijpesteijn's suggestion that the Euhemeria petitions represent the archive of the archephodos: "Petition to the Chief of Police," *Zeitschrift für Papyrologie und Epigraphik* 91 (1992): 101.

58. *Digest* 9.2.5.3–9.2.6.

59. Predictably, the entirety of the passage from *sed lege . . . non dubito* has been bracketed as an interpolation: e.g., R. Taubenschlag, "Lex Aquilia," *RE* XII.2, cols.2326–27. Reinhard Zimmermann, *The Law of Obligations: Roman Foundations of the Civilian Tradition* (Oxford: Oxford University Press, 1996), 105–6, summarizes the issue. The fact that it contradicts the classical principle, "*liberum corpus nullam recepit aestimationem*" ("the value of a free man's body does not admit of pricing": *Digest* 9.3.7) matters little. Certainly the passage is corrupt, but as Zimmerman makes clear, the use of the Lex Aquilia here is perfectly reasonable. Additionally, we have this passage preserved on papyrus, with marginal glosses: PSI XIV 1449 (A.D. IV, with restorations of Arangio-Ruiz): [. . . *esse actionem ex*] *locato pạ*[*tri eius Iul*(*ianus*)] *dicit, inịụ*[*riarum a*(*u*)*t*(*em*) *ne*]*gạt, quịa ṇọ*[*n iuniuriae fa*]*cięṇdae c*(*ausa*) *ịḍ* [*fecerit*], *sed praeci*[*piendi. Se*]*d et de Aquịl*[*ia quid sen-*] *tiamuṣ ạḷịọ* [(*com*)*m*(*en*)*tario tradi*]*dimus*. The gloss on the side reads: ['E]ν τῷ Aquilio τῶν de iud(iciis)· ἐδ̣έξατο δὲ ἐκ τού̣(του) ε̣ἶ̣ν̣αι *Aquil*(*ion*) ο[ὐτ(ίλιον)]. Even if not proof positive, this seems to indicate that the jurists at least entertained this idea.

60. Arangio-Ruiz, in his commentary on PSI XIV 1449, is doubtful, in part because of the "ripugnanza morale che una *fictio* del genere avrebbe suscitata in ogni *civis Romanus*," and in part because of the difficulty of the valuation (170). As a moral question, I am doubtful; as to the specifics of valuation, he concedes that this could possibly be done by some analogous process. Zimmerman, *Law of Obligations*, 1016, expresses similar doubts about the process that would structure valuation and compensation. On the interaction between fictions, law, and empire, see now Clifford Ando, *Law, Language, and Empire in the Roman Tradition* (Philadelphia: University of Pennsylvania Press, 2011), 1–18.

61. Roger S. Bagnall, "Official and Private Violence in Roman Egypt," *Bulletin of the American Society of Papyrologists* 29 (1989): 202, citing *Digest* 47.10.32.

62. Pierre Bourdieu, "The Sentiment of Honour in Kabyle Society," in *Honour and Shame: The Values of Mediterranean Society*, ed. John G. Peristiany (London: Weidenfeld and Nicolson, 1966), 205.

63. *Letters*, 3.14.6–7.

64. Scheper-Hughes, *Death Without Weeping*, 167–215; Pierre Bourdieu, *The Bachelors' Ball: The Crisis of Peasant Society in Béarn*, trans. Richard Nice (Chicago: University of Chicago Press, 2008), 86.

65. 3.14.2.

66. P.Oxy. LXIV 4441.i.1–16 (A.D. 315–16). For public doctors see Darrell W. Amundsen and Gary B. Ferngren, "The Forensic Role of Physicians in Ptolemaic and Roman

Egypt," *Bulletin of the History of Medicine* 52 (1978): 336–53; Sofía Torallas-Tovar, "La práctica forense en el Egipto Romano," *Cuadernos de Filología Clásica* 14 (2004): 183–200.

67. Susanna Elm, "Roman Pain and the Rise of Christianity," in *Quo Vadis Medical Healing: Past Concepts and New Approaches*, ed. Susanna Elm and Stefan N. Willich, International Library of Ethics, Law, and the New Medicine 44 (London: Springer, 2009), 41–54.

68. It bears mentioning that sometimes a silence can say more than language can: Das, *Life and Words*, 48–58; Ari Z. Bryen, "Dionysia's Complaint: Emotion, Truth, and Language in the Courtroom," in *Emotional Display, Persuasion, and Rhetoric in the Papyri*, ed. Chrysi Kotsifou (forthcoming 2013).

69. In thinking through these issues I have benefited greatly from discussions with Fahad Ahmad Bishara, who deals at greater length with the concept of obligation in "A Sea of Debt: Islamic Law, Empire and Commercial Society in the Western Indian Ocean, c. 1850–1940," Ph.D. dissertation, Duke University, 2012.

CHAPTER 4. NARRATING INJURY

1. *The End* (information available on http://www.imdb.com/title/tt1323914/), a 2010 documentary on cockney gangsters on London's East End, has been a valuable source here.

2. See, e.g., Michael Peachin, "Introduction," in *The Oxford Handbook of Social Relations in the Roman World* ed. Michael Peachin (Oxford: Oxford University Press, 2011), 22: "Each and every daily scenario had its protocol. But in all these situations, there occurred, in an utterly fundamental fashion, a continual ranking and re-ranking of people. Pretty well everything one said and did in any given Roman social interaction, served ultimately to position one in a hierarchy with respect to one's interlocutor. Thus, knowing how to negotiate this punctiliously graded universe with aplomb made you, at some very essential level, Roman, and simultaneously served to establish your proper place in the stratified maze that was ancient Roman society."

3. Bagnall, "Official and Private Violence"; Hobson, "Impact of Law"; Kelly, "Repression."

4. E.g., P.Fay. 108 (A.D. 169–70, **58**), from a group of pig merchants who were attacked on the road between Theadelphia and Polydeukia; P.Oxy. L 3561 (A.D. 165, **55**); P.Sarap. 1 (= BGU III 759, A.D. 125, **39**), a shepherd assaulted in his fields at night; SB VI 9238 (A.D. 200–211, **74**).

5. P.Abinn. 51, 52 (A.D. 346, **107**, **108**). The quoted text is P.Abinn. 51, Ataris' first petition.

6. Bagnall, *Egypt in Late Antiquity*, 134.

7. P.Abinn. 48 (A.D. 346), where Apion participates in illegal nocturnal sheep-shearing, along with one of Abinnaeus' men.

8. It is a very common occurrence, especially in petitions of first instance, that they date to within a day or two of the attack: Kelly, "Repression," 81.

9. P.Cair.Goodsp. 15.12–13 (A.D. 362, **113**): οὐκ οἶδ'(?) ὅπως Ἴσακις Ἀμμωνίωνος καὶ ἡ αὐτοῦ ἀδελφὴ Ταπίωμις καὶ . . .

10. P.Oxy. XXXVIII 2853.7–8 (A.D. 245/6, **80**), recto: οἱ δὲ μηδενὶ λόγῳ χρησάμενοι ἐπῆλθον ἡμῖν καὶ πληγαῖς ᾐκίσαντο . . .

11. SB I 5238.7 (A.D. 14, **8**): [ἀ]κολούθως τινί ποτ[ε] λόγῳ. Compare descriptions of the violent acts themselves as "irrational" (ἄλογον ἀηδίαν): BGU I 22 (A.D. 114, **36**), a complaint of a vegetable-seller attacked by a woman who had "absolutely no issue with me" (ἁπλῶς μηδὲν ἔχουσα πρᾶγμα πρὸς ἐμὲ), but whose husband reappeared the next night in order to fight the petitioner's husband; P.Ryl. II 144 (A.D. 38, **14**); P.Tebt. II 304 (A.D. 167–68, **57**).

12. e.g., P.Athen. 32 (A.D. 39, **16**); BGU XIII 2239 (A.D. 17), theft; P.Oxy. L 3561 (A.D. IV, **55**), theft with violence.

13. P.Amh. II 142 (= Chr.Mitt. 65, A.D. IV, **119**). This petition too is odd, since boundary-challenging claims are often described as being deliberately public: see further Bryen and Wypustek, "Gemellus' Evil Eyes," 553.

14. P.Sijp. 16 (A.D. 155, **51**).

15. SB XX 14401 (A.D. 147, **49**).

16. PSI XIII 1323.6–7 (A.D. 147, **47**).

17. Reckless (ῥιψοκίνδυνος): e.g., BGU III 909.15 (= Chr.Wilck. 382, A.D. 359, **111**); reckless and "utterly worthless" (πανκάκιστος): P.Sakaon 48.14 (A.D. 343, **106**).

18. SB VI 9421 (A.D. III, **92**).

19. Fergus Millar, "The World of the Golden Ass," in *Rome, the Greek World, and the East*, vol. 2, *Government, Society, and Culture in the Roman Empire*, ed. Hannah Cotton and Guy MacLean Rogers (Chapel Hill: University of North Carolina Press, 2002), 315–35, provides the classic survey of how practice may have measured up to theory.

20. This was a longstanding problem, dealt with in various ways: compare Augustus' letter concerning abuses in Cyrenaica (FIRA I 68) with Ulpian, *On the Duties of a Proconsul* (*Digest* 1.16.9.2–4).

21. P.Cair.Goodsp. 15.20–21 (A.D. 362, **113**): θαρρῶν . . . τοῖς χρήμασι αὐτοῦ καὶ τῷ πλούτῳ βούλεταί με ἐξελάσαι ἀπὸ τῆς κώμης . . . ; P.Berl.Frisk. 4.9 (A.D. IV–V, **124**), ἀταξίᾳ χαίρων.

22. SB XVI 12678.14–15 (A.D. 179, **61**): τῇ περὶ αὐτ[ὸν] [δυναστείᾳ] ἐξυβρίζοντα . . . ; P.Kell. I 20.9–10 (A.D. 300–320, **95**): [ἄν]θρωπος μεγάλα ἐπὶ τῶν τόπων δυνά[με]νος; P.Sakaon 36.16 (A.D. 280, **85**).

23. P.Fouad 26.15–17 (A.D. 158–59, **53**); SB XX 14401 (A.D. 147, **49**).

24. P.Amh. II 142.14 (= Chr.Mitt. 65, A.D. IV, **119**); P.Mich. VI 425 (A.D. 197, **69**), on which compare P.Mich. VI 422.29–31 (A.D. 197), concerning theft; P.Lond. II 358.11–12 (= Chr.Mitt. 52, A.D. 150, **50**).

25. P.Kell. I 23.18 (A.D. 353, **110**): οὐκ ἠρκέσθη α[ὐτῷ]; P.Amh. II 77.20–21 (= Chr. Wilck. 277, A.D. 139, **43**): an initial act of violence fails to satisfy; SB VI 9458.19 (A.D. II,

72), sexualized violence against slave women in public precedes theft; P.Ryl. II 145.10 (A.D. 38, **15**). The violence can also come second: P.Ross.Georg. II 20.21 (A.D. 146, **45**). Ambiguous or fragmentary cases: BGU III 871.14 (A.D. II, **70**); P.Ant. I 35.ii.10 (A.D. III); P.Dubl. 18.10 (A.D. 257–59, **84**); P.Stras. IX 825.5 (A.D. 98).

26. P.Kell. I 23.1–15 (A.D. 353, **110**).

27. Andrea Jördens, "Die ägyptischen Symmachoi," *Zeitschrift für Papyrologie und Epigraphik* 66 (1986): 105–11. Compare PSI VIII 872 (A.D. VI), where a man complains that his enemy has placed "barbarous slaves, (other?) slaves, and *symmachoi*" (βαρβάρους παῖδας καὶ οἰκέτας καὶ συμμάχους) in his house. The *oiketai* here may also be connected to the office of the *riparii*: P.Oxy. VI 904 (A. D. V), in which a man asks to be relieved from the duties of the *riparia* because he has been promised (but has not received) proper assistance: παρέχων μοι καὶ πρὸς βοήθειαν οἰκέτας τε καὶ συμμάχους καὶ [ἄ]λλους τοὺς ὀφείλοντας τὴν παραφυλακὴν τῆς πόλεως ποιεῖσθαι. Also P.Oxy. VI 904 (= C.Pap.Jud. III 457d, Oxyrhynchos, A.D. IV).

28. Naphtali Lewis, *The Compulsory Public Services of Roman Egypt*, 2nd ed., Papyrologica Florentina 28 (Florence: Edizioni Gonnelli, 1997), 156–60.

29. Bagnall, "Official and Private Violence," 211–12.

30. Gaius, *Institutes* 3.220.

31. SB X 10239 (= P.Oxy. II 315, desc., A.D. 37, **13**).

32. P.Oxy. II 282 (= Chr.Mitt. 117, A.D. 29–37), a petition from Tryphon accusing Demetrous and someone else (whose name is not preserved) of stealing his property when she left his home. Other pregnant victims: P.Mich. V 228 (A.D. 47, **23**); SB X 10244 (A.D. 50, **26**), also from Tryphon's papers; P.Hamb. IV 240 (A.D. 119–20, **37**); P.Cair.Goodsp. 15 (AD 362, **113**).

33. P.Cair.Isid. 63 (A.D. 296, **89**). On the documents associated with this conflict, see below, Chapter 6.

34. Thus, for instance, a soldier commits the murders of P.Mich. XIII 660 (A.D. VI). On the context of this document see Leslie S. B. MacCoull, "The Aphrodito Murder Mystery," *Journal of Juristic Papyrology* 20 (1990): 103–7, together with James G. Keenan, "The Aphrodito Murder Mystery: A Return to the Scene of the Crimes," *Bulletin of the American Society of Papyrologists* 32 (1995): 57–63.

35. P.Amh. II 77 (= Chr.Wilck. 277, A.D. 139, **43**).

36. P.Lips. I 37.19–25 (A.D. 389, **116**).

37. P.Col. VII 171.10 (A.D. 324, **100**).

38. P.Abinn. 57.19 (A.D. 342–51, **104**). On the range of tensions that might have existed between agriculturalists and pastoralists see James G. Keenan, "Village Shepherds and Social Tension in Byzantine Egypt," *Yale Classical Studies* 28 (1985): 245–59; James G. Keenan, "Pastoralism in Roman Egypt," *Bulletin of the American Society of Papyrologists* 26 (1989): 175–200.

39. SB XII 11113.12 (A.D. II–III, **63**), with uncertainty over the restoration of π̣[έλεκυ]ν̣ or δ̣[ρεπά]ν̣ῳ; compare SB XX 15077 (A.D. 45, **22**), featuring axes and scythes.

40. P.Sarap. 1.13–14 (A.D. 125, **39**).

41. P.Oxy. LVIII 3926.10 (A.D. 246, **81**).

42. P.Amh. II 142.8 (= Chr.Mitt. 65, A.D. IV, **119**).

43. P.Sakaon 48.15–17 (A.D. 343, **106**). See the genealogical discussions in Roger S. Bagnall, "The Population of Theadelphia in the Fourth Century," in *Later Roman Egypt: Society, Religion, Economy, and Administration* (Aldershot: Ashgate, 2003), chap. 6.

44. The text is printed as reading π̣ά̣ππον, "grandfather," but given the context, it must mean "father." The grandfather, Melas, is not attested after 315, and Bagnall, "Population," 44, estimates his birth c. A.D. 290. He may well have been dead by this point. For another example of the marriage politics of this village, see P.Sakaon 38 (= P.Flor. I 36 = Chr.Mitt. 64, A.D. 312), Melas and Sakaon at odds over a marriage.

45. Though his discussion of verbal assault is slender at best, and misleading at worst. He discusses it in the context of P.Hal. 1.117, the Ptolemaic *dikaiomata* papyrus, though this term appears nowhere within the text of the entire papyrus: Taubenschlag, *Strafrecht*, 14; Taubenschlag, *Law*, 435. Taubenschlag, *Law*, 440, claims PSI III 222 (A.D. IV, **94**) as an example of *convicium*, which is possible but hardly decisive. Likewise, he sees a possible sense of *convicium* in P.Lond. II 358 (= Chr.Mitt. 52, A.D. 150–52, **50**). Keenan, "Criminal Procedure," points to other instances in Taubenschlag's text where the footnotes do not support the argument.

46. Exceptions are P.Lond. II 342 (A.D. 185, **64**), where the petitioner quotes what seem to be veiled threats; P.Oxy. VI 903 (= C.Pap.Jud. III 457d, A.D. IV, **123**).

47. P.Enteux. 25, 74, 79, 86 (all from the third century B.C.); P.Tebt. III 765 (153 B.C.).

48. PSI III 222.12–15 (A.D. IV, **94**): με γενόμενον πρὸς αὐτοὺς μεθ' ὕβρεως καὶ [λοι]δοριῶν ἀπεπέμψαντο. *Loidoria* is paired with a physical assault in another example, this one from the early period of Roman rule: SB XIV 11274.9–10 (4 B.C., 2): με ἐ̣λ̣ο̣ι̣δ[όρη]σεν. Also belonging to this same papyrus roll are SB XX 14086 (4) and SB XVIII 13088. 14086 also involves violence, and 13088 is too fragmentary to discern the subject of complaint.

49. SB XII 11130.15–17 (= P.Mich.Michl. 28, A.D. III–IV): οὐδὲν μοι ἀπεφήνατο ἤ μὴ λοιδορεῖος καὶ ἐντελλόμενός μοι.

50. BGU XI 2069.1 (A.D. 292, **87**).

51. P.Oxy. XXXIII 2672.11–18 (A.D. 218, **78**).

52. PSI IV 298.14 (A.D. 292–93, **88**), where the complainant accuses someone of committing *hybris* by beating him and "cursing me with the sorts of words that are forbidden to say among men" ([β]λασφημῶν λόγοις οἵους οὐδὲ θεμιτὸν εἰπεῖν ἐν ἀνθρώ(ποις)), as well as P.Ryl. II 150.9–10 (A.D. 40, **18**): ἐκακολόγησεν πολλὰ καὶ ἀ-[σ]χήμονα. Nearly identical language is found in SB XII 11018.2 (A.D. I–II, **33**). See also P.Oslo II 22.9 (A.D. 127, **41**).

53. SB VI 9421.21–22 (A.D. III, 92).

54. P.Flor. III 309 + P.Lond. III 983 (A.D. IV, **120**). See also P.Amh. II 142.8 (= Chr. Mitt. 65, A.D. IV, **119**), in which the victim complains about an attack with clubs and swords, and includes that the attackers used "foul language" (ἀπρεπῆ ῥήματα); compare P.Tebt. III.1 802.15 (B.C. 135): φωνὰς ἀπρεπεῖς, a Ptolemaic example.

55. P.Mich. XVIII 793.2–5 (A.D. 381, **115**).

56. P.Col. VIII 242 (A.D. V): περιερρόγχασέν μοι καὶ ἐβουλήθη μοι ἐπελθεῖν. On this document see also John R. Rea, "P. Col. VIII 242: Caranis in the Fifth Century," in *Proceedings of the 20th International Congress of Papyrologists*, ed. Adam Bülow-Jacobsen (Copenhagen: Museum Tusculum Press, 1994), 266–72, and below, Chapter 6; P.Oxy. VI 903 (A.D. IV, **123**): πολλὰ ἀσελγήματα λέγων εἰς πρόσωπόν μου καὶ διὰ τῆς ῥινὸς αὐτοῦ. See also A. S. F. Gow, "Notes on Noses," *Journal of Hellenic Studies* 71 (1951): 81–84.

57. See below.

58. Erving Goffman, "On Face Work," in Goffman, *Interaction Ritual: Essays on Face-to-Face Behavior* (Garden City, N.Y.: Anchor, 1967), 5–45.

59. BGU III 909 (= Chr.Wilck. 382, A.D. 359, **111**).

60. BGU XIV 2371.6–7 (I B.C.).

61. For help with guild documents, I am grateful to Philip Venticinque, and look forward to the publication of his study of guilds (in progress): *Common Causes: Craftsmen, Merchants, and Communities in Roman and Late Roman Egypt.*

62. SB XII 10841. For the text, translation, and interpretation I work from the very helpful article of John R. Rea, "Two Christian Letters: PSI VII 831 and VIII 972," *Chronique d'Égypte* 45 (1970): 357–68. There is also commentary in Mario Naldini, *Il Cristianesimo in Egitto: Lettere private nei papiri dei secoli II–IV*, Studi e Testi di Papirologia 3 (Florence: Le Monnier, 1968), no.64.

63. Other instances of victims "discussing" with offenders: contrasted with verbal abuse, P.Amh. II 142.7 (= Chr.Mitt. 65, A.D. IV, **119**), P.Ryl. II 144.10–11 (A.D. 38, **14**); contrasted with physical violence, P.Mich. V 228.10–11 (A.D. 47, **23**), P.Mich. V 229.15–16 (A.D. 48, **24**), P.Mich. V 230.16 (A.D. 48, **25**), P.Ryl. II 136.4 (A.D. 34, **11**), P.Ryl. II 141.11–**12** (A.D. 37, 12), SB VI 9458.21–22 (A.D. II, **72**). In a similar vein, P.Sakaon 48.15 (A.D. 343, **106**): δικαιολογομένου; P.Cair. Isid. 77.20 (= C.Pap.Jud. III 518c, Karanis, A.D. 320, **98**).

64. Attempts to understand the role of gender in complaints include Maryline Parca, "Violence by and Against Women in Documentary Papyri from Ptolemaic and Roman Egypt," in *Le rôle et le statut de la femme en Égypte hellénistique, romaine et byzantine*, ed. Henri Melaerts and Leon Mooren, Studia Hellenistica 37 (Leuven: Peeters, 2002), 283–96; Bagnall, "Women's Petitions in Late Antique Egypt."

65. Chrysi Kotsifou will deal with this topic at greater length in a forthcoming paper.

66. For this suggestion I thank Clifford Ando. Domestic violence is largely underrepresented in the papyri, save for P.Amh. II 141 (= Chr.Mitt. 126, A.D. 350, **109**), P.Oxy. VI 903 (= C.Pap.Jud. III 457d, A.D. IV, **123**), P.Oxy. L 3581 (A.D. IV–V, **125**). See also Schroeder, "John Chrysostom's Critique."

67. J. E. G. Whitehorne, "Sex and Society in Greco-Roman Egypt," in *Actes du XVe congrès international de papyrologie*, ed. Jean Bingen and Georges Nachtergael, Papyrologica Bruxellensia 16–19 (Brussels: Fond. Égyptol. Reine Élisabeth, 1979), 240–46.

68. A fascinating comparandum on petitions and rape is Matthew Harvey Sommer, *Sex, Law, and Society in Late Imperial China* (Stanford, Calif.: Stanford University Press, 2000), 166–209.

69. E.g., P.Oxy. L 3581 (A.D. IV/V, **125**); possible also is P.Sakaon 48 (A.D. 343, **106**); a borderline case is SB IV 7449 (A.D. V, **130**), where a plans to arrange a marriage become violent, with the result that a monk beats the petitioner when her daughter rejects the marriage plan. See further Evans-Grubbs, "Abduction Marriage," 59–83; Cam Grey, "Two Young Lovers: An Abduction Marriage and Its Consequences in Fifth-Century Gaul," *Classical Quarterly* 58 (2008): 289.

70. P.Oxy. XXXVI 2758 (A.D. 110–12, **35**). In P.Kell. I 21.9 (A.D. 321, **99**) a petitioner also reports that the *komarch* of the village is ἐπικωμάζων ("propositioning?" "drunkenly flirting with?") his wife.

71. The text is problematic. It was originally published as P.Mich.Mchl. 12 (= SB XII 11114 [A.D. 163]). It was reedited as SB XXIV 16252 (**54**) (P. J. Sijpesteijn, "Complaint to the Epistrategus Vedius Faustus," *Zeitschrift für Papyrologie und Epigraphik* 110 (1996): 183–87) on the basis of a photograph that is probably of the first part of the document. However, the editor notes that the top and bottom parts cannot be joined, so there is a section of uncertain length missing from the *narratio*. I work here from the text of Sijpesteijn. For background on this family, see Richard Alston, *Soldier and Society in Roman Egypt: A Social History*. London: Routledge, 1995, 129–33. In a letter from Oxyrhynchos, a man complains to his son (a former *strategos* of the Panopolite nome) that some men had committed *hybris* against him, asks his son to send a "desert-guard" to deal with them, and comments, "you know how the Egyptians are" (οἶδας γὰρ τὸ τῶν Αἰγυπ(τίων)): *P.Oxy.* XLII 3061.13 (A.D. I). However, this is not an example of ethnic status playing a role in a legal complaint, *contra* Bagnall, "Official and Private Violence," 212.

72. On the roles of scribes in the appointment of liturgies, see Lewis, *Compulsory Public Services*, chap. 2.

73. Naphtali Lewis, "Notationes Legentis," *Bulletin of the American Society of Papyrologists* 34 (1997): 31–33, makes a great deal of this papyrus, asking it to support his theory that a few of the Ptolemaic *enteuxeis* featuring people with different names (Greco-Egyptian versus Greek) "illustrate[s] vividly the endemic hostility underlying the coexistence of the different population entities and erupting in conflicts most notably between indigenes and their privileged 'betters'" (31).

74. Lewis, "Judiciary Routines," 92. Likewise Hobson, "Impact of Law," 212: "though the imperial legal system was omnipresent to the little villager, as a source of authority and obligation, it is unlikely to have functioned very effectively as a source of protection and a guarantee of his personal rights," cited with approval recently by Michael Peachin, "Petition to a Centurion from the NYU Papyrus Collection and the Question of Informal Adjudication by Soldiers." In *Papyri in Memory of P. J. Sijpesteijn*, ed. A. J. B. Sirks and K. A. Worp, American Studies in Papyrology 40 (Oakville, Conn.: American Society of Papyrologists, 2007), 96; Connolly, *Lives Behind the Laws*, 120–21, operates with different assumptions concerning imperial responsiveness, but retains the emphasis on status.

75. MacMullen, *Roman Social Relations*, 204; Richard P. Saller, *Patriarchy, Property and Death in the Roman Family*, Cambridge Studies in Population, Economy, and Society in Past Time 25 (Cambridge: Cambridge University Press, 1994), 72. On terminology and the

distinction between class and status, see Brent D. Shaw, "Anatomy of the Vampire Bat," *Economy and Society* 13 (1983): 215–20. On *honestiores* and *humiliores* in Roman law, and the dual-penalty system specifically, see Peter Garnsey, "Why Penalties Become Harsher: The Roman Case, Late Republic to Fourth-Century Empire," *Natural Law Forum* 13 (1968): 141–62; Peter Garnsey, *Social Status and Legal Privilege in the Roman Empire* (Oxford: Clarendon, 1970); Rolf Rilinger, *Humiliores—Honestiores: Zu einer sozialen Dichotomie im Strafrecht der römischen Kaiserzeit* (Munich: R. Oldenbourg, 1988).

76. Bagnall, "Official and Private Violence," 201–2. See also Daube, *Roman Law*, 81–85.

77. Also *CJ* 9.35.1 (A.D. 222): *nec servis quidem alienis licet facere iniuriam.* The point, as I emphasized earlier, is that not *all* physical harm to slaves is either permitted or forbidden as *iniuria* (in the *Institutes* passage, raising a clamor or striking with a fist), but *certain* types of physical harm can and do constitute *iniuria* (setting a slave on fire, perhaps).

78. And only mild chastisement: *CJ* 9.35.6 (A.D. 290): *cum nec patronos iniuriam facere libertis iuris aequitas permittat, proponasque patronae heredes eum, qui libertatem a defuncta acceperat, iniuriis adficere, curabit praeses provinciae contumeliam heredum compescere.*

79. Tony Honoré, *Ulpian: Pioneer of Human Rights*, 2nd ed. (Oxford: Oxford University Press, 2002), 85, captures this distinction nicely.

80. On haves and have-nots, recent bibliography is collected in Walter Scheidel, "Stratification, Deprivation, and Quality of Life," in *Poverty in the Roman World*, ed. E. M. Atkins and Robin Osborne (Cambridge: Cambridge University Press, 2006), 40–59.

81. Bagnall, *Egypt in Late Antiquity*, 173.

82. P.Grenf. II 78 (= Chr.Mitt. 63, A.D. 307, **97**).

83. Herbert C. Youtie, "Notes on O. Mich. I," in *Scriptiunculae* (Amsterdam: Hakkert, 1973), 1: 90–97, 103.

84. For the suggestion that this petition concerns enslavement for debts I thank Cam Grey. Taubenschlag, *Law*, 75–76, argues that this petition deals with the enslavement of children from a slave mother, in which case we should understand the disagreement to be over possession of Syros's wife, understanding the side of the assailants to be that Tsek— was rightfully their slave, as were her children.

85. On *paideia* in late antiquity, see Brown, *Power and Persuasion in Late Antiquity*, 35–70; Raffaella Cribiore, *The School of Libanius in Late Antique Antioch* (Princeton, N.J.: Princeton University Press, 2007).

86. P.Amh. II 141 (= Chr.Mitt. 126, A.D. 350, **109**).

87. Petitioners generally refer to πληγαί, which can mean both blows and the marks from blows (i.e., bruises), or in some cases, πλήγματα.

88. P.Lips. I 39.12–13 (= Chr.Mitt. 127, A.D. 390, 117). For a similar construction see P.Kell. I 23 (A.D. 383, 110), where the left eye is specified. A late example comes from a letter in the papers of Dioskoros of Aphrodito, P.Cair.Masp. 67077.15–16 (A.D. VI): Ἰωάννης πλήγματα̣ [π]ολλὰ ἔχει περὶ τὴν ὄψιν; a Ptolemaic example can be found in P.Tebt. 797.19 (II B.C.).

89. P.Lips. I 40.7: τὰ πλήγματα φανερά.

90. Bryen and Wypustek, "Gemellus' Evil Eyes."

91. P.Sarap. 1.13–15 (= BGU III 759, A.D. 125, **39**); compare P.Oxy. 1885 (A.D. 509, **124**) and the fragmentary P.Harr. 192 (A.D. 167, **56**).

92. P.Berl.Frisk 4.19 (A.D. IV–V, **124**).

93. P.Lips. I 37 (A.D. 389, **116**); compare SB VI 9238 (A.D. 193–211, **74**).

94. For similar instances see P.Cair.Isid. 63 (A.D. 296–97, **89**); P.Ryl. II 151.13–15 (A.D. 40, **19**); SB XVI 12470.15–16 (A.D. I–II, **34**); and the small fragment preserved in P.Erl. 36.4 (A.D. V, **129**). On the stripping of clothes see Whitehorne, "Sex and Society in Greco-Roman Egypt," 240–46. For a similar example from the literary canon, see Dio Cassius 79.4.2–5, describing the public humiliation of Kilo, the tutor of Caracalla: "The soldiers tore the clothing off his body (τήν τε ἐσθῆτα αὐτοῦ περιέρρεξαν) and disfigured his face (τὸ πρόσωπον ἠ̣κίσαντο)."

95. In a few cases, the wounds themselves govern the activity of the verb: P.Col. VII 171.12–13 (= P.Coll.Youtie II 77, A.D. 324, **100**): αἱ περὶ ἐμὲ πληγαὶ δηλοῦσιν; P.Oxy. XVI 1885.10 (A.D. 509, **134**): ἡ̣ παρ' αὐτοῦ ἐ̣[πεν]εχθεῖσα μαρτυρή[σ]ει πληγή.

96. Simone Weil, "The Iliad, or the Poem of Force," trans. Mary McCarthy, *Chicago Review* 18 (1965): 5–30.

CHAPTER 5. THE WORK OF LAW

1. Jane Burbank and Frederick Cooper, *Empires in World History: Power and the Politics of Difference* (Princeton, N.J.: Princeton University Press, 2010), 1–22.

2. In my opinion the central shortcoming of two otherwise engaging discussions of courts: David Cohen, *Law, Violence, and Community in Classical Athens* (Cambridge: Cambridge University Press, 1995); Smail, *The Consumption of Justice*.

3. Bourdieu, "Force of Law," 832–33.

4. Hobson, "Impact of Law"; Bagnall, "Official and Private Violence"; Bagnall, *Egypt in Late Antiquity*, 168.

5. Useful background can be found in James Q. Whitman, *The Legacy of Roman Law in the German Romantic Era: Historical Vision and Legal Change* (Princeton, N.J.: Princeton University Press, 1990); Ewald, "Comparative Jurisprudence (I)," 1990–2044; Theodore Ziolkowski, *Clio the Romantic Muse: Historicizing the Faculties in Germany* (Ithaca, N.Y.: Cornell University Press, 2004), 105–32.

6. Important for placing this ideology of localism in historical context is Laura Nader, *Harmony Ideology: Justice and Control in a Zapotec Mountain Village* (Stanford, Calif.: Stanford University Press, 1990).

7. Jill Harries, *Law and Empire in Late Antiquity* (Cambridge: Cambridge University Press, 1999), 173. Welcome exceptions are Benjamin Kelly, *Petitions, Litigation, and Social Control in Roman Egypt* (Oxford: Oxford University Press, 2010); Cam Grey, *Constructing Communities in the Late Roman Countryside* (Cambridge: Cambridge University Press, 2011).

8. Hobson, "Impact of Law," 210; Bagnall, "Official and Private Violence," 209–11; Bagnall, "Response to Hans Albert Rupprecht"; Bagnall, *Egypt in Late Antiquity*, 168.

9. Kelly, "Repression," 70–81.

10. This would seem to undermine the claim that "the victim of violence faced a bewildering variety of remedies . . . . For the legal propagandists of emperors . . . choice was something to be welcomed by the victims. It would be more accurate, however, to argue that it was welcomed by lawyers for whom the number and variety of options offered opportunities to complicate matters and frustrate redress, especially for parties to suits who were weaker in terms of finance or the backing of patrons." Jill Harries, "Violence, Victims, and the Legal Tradition in Late Antiquity," in *Violence in Late Antiquity: Perceptions and Practices*, ed. H. A. Drake (Burlington, Vt.: Ashgate, 2006), 93.

11. BGU II 467 (A.D. 176–77).

12. BGU I 321.14–25 (= Chr.Mitt. 114, A.D. 216); for discussion, see Whitehorne, "Strategus, Centurion, or Neither."

13. BGU I 322.25–27.

14. SB XVIII 13087.27 (4 B.C., **3**); the fragmentary request in P.Sarap. 1 (A.D. 125, **39**) appears similar.

15. BGU XI 2069.15–16 (A.D. 292, **87**); a similar request about the *conventus*: P.Cair. Isid. 77 (= C.Pap.Jud. III 518c, A.D. 320, **98**).

16. P.Col. VII 171.18–20 (= P.Coll.Youtie II 77, A.D. 324, **100**).

17. E.g., P.Freib. II 11 (A.D. 336, **102**); P.Gen.2 I 3 (A.D. 178, **60**); P.Grenf. II 78 (= Chr.Mitt. 63, A.D. 307, **97**); P.Oxy. XXXIII 2672 (A.D. 218, **78**); P.Oxy. XXXVIII 2853 (A.D. 245/6, **59**); P.Sakaon 48 (A.D. 343, **106**); possible is P.Laur. IV 158 (A.D. 399–418, **118**); in P.Oxy. II 281 (= Chr.Mitt. 66, A.D. 20–50, **9**) the petitioner insists that she will persist in her other cases in addition to suing over a disputed dowry.

18. E.g., P.Ryl. II 136 (A.D. 30, **11**), P.Ryl. II 144 (A.D. 38, **14**), both from Euhemeria; BGU I 22 (A.D. 114, **36**); similar language, but not concerning violence: P.Oslo III 123 (A.D. 22).

19. *Ekdikia* often appears in cognate forms: e.g., P.Oxy. XVI 1885.16 (A.D. 509, **134**): νόμιμον ἐκδίκησιν; in the Abinnaeus archive, the job of the *dux* is "to punish people who dare to do such things" (τοὺς τὰ τοιαῦτα τολμῶντας ἐκδικεῖν): P.Abinn. 51, 52 (AD 346, **107, 108**).

20. ἐλεύθερον καὶ ἀνύβριστον: P.Ryl. II 117.26 (A.D. 269), concerning an inheritance; PSI VII 807.23–24 (A.D. 280), illegal imprisonment; Chr.Mitt. 71.10–11 (A.D. 462, **128**), a *cessio bonorum*; ἀνύβριστον καὶ ἀνεπηρέαστον: SB XX 14401.24 (A.D. 147), **49**; compare PSI IV 292.19 (A.D. III, **91**), dealing with a cession of land in exchange for exemption from a liturgy.

21. Kelly, "Repression," 77 n.246, citing SB XIV 12087 (A.D. 162) and PSI VII 807 (A.D. 280) which do not involve violence; P.Mich. III 174 (A.D. 145–47, **46**) and SB XVI 12678 (A.D. 179, **61**) in which petitioners also ask for proceedings; and P.Oxy. II 237 col. 6 (A.D. 186, **65**), Chairemon's complaint against Dionysia included in her petition. This final example is not, however, a petition of first instance, but rather a request for adjudication on

a matter of legal interpretation. On Chairemon's petition and the understanding of the magistrates, see Ranon Katzoff, "'Responsa Prudentium' in Roman Egypt," in *Studi in onore di Arnaldo Biscardi*, ed. Franco Pastori (Milan: Istituto Editoriale Cisalpino, 1982), 524.

22. Thus P.Freib. II 111.8–21 (A.D. 336, **102**): asking for restraint and punishment (ἀξιοῦσα τὴν δέουσαν ἐπεξ[έλε]υσιν γενέσθαι καὶ ἐπαναγκασθῆναι τούτους ἀ[π]οσχέσθαι τῆς ἡμετέρας γῆς); P.Mich. XVIII 793.7–10 (A.D. 381, **115**), asking for punishment and protection of land: αὐτοὺς ἀχθῆναι ἐπί σε καὶ τὰ ἀκόλουθα τοῖς νόμοις κατ' αὐ̣τῶν πρᾶξαι, φυλαχθῆναι δέ μοι τὴν τοῦ διαφέροντός μου ψιλοῦ τόπου νομὴ<ν> καὶ δεσπο̣τ̣ία<ν>; BGU III 909.25–26 (= Chr.Wilck. 382, A.D. 359, **111**), requesting ἵκανα ἀξιόχρεα for his σωτηρία; P.Flor. III 309 (A.D. IV, **110**) asking for offenders to be brought to court; P.Herm. 20.19 (A.D. IV, **121**): μείζονα ἐπέλευσιν; P.Oxy. XVI 1885.16 (A.D. 503, **134**): πρὸς τῶν γεγένημένων ἐκδίκησιν; in P.Oxy. XXXIX 3480.25–26 (A.D. 360–90, **112**): τὴν δέο[υσαν..] . . . . . . σιν γεν[έ]σθαι κ̣ατὰ τῆς ὕβρ[ε]ω̣ς (the lacuna should almost certainly read ἐπεξέλευσιν); PSI IV 313.13–14 (A.D. III–IV, **93**): ἐπεξε[λεύσεως] τυχεῖν τῆς προσηκούσης. An unclear example: PSI II 222.23–25 (A.D. IV, **94**): ἀξιῶν αὐτοὺς ἀχθῆναι [δώσοντας λόγο]ν τῆς ἀγνωμοσύ[νης καὶ] ἀ̣[πει]θίας.

23. "vague": Kelly, *Petitions*, 191 n.127.

24. For an extended meditation of the consequences of pricing injuries, see William Ian Miller, *Eye for an Eye* (Cambridge: Cambridge University Press, 2006).

25. The Romans were well aware of this problem: Gellius, *Attic Nights* 20.1.13 (recording a fragment of the jurist Labeo), on Lucius Veratius.

26. The issue of social differentiation and social mobility in the Roman Empire is vexed at best: see for late antique Egypt James G. Keenan, "On Law and Society in Late Roman Egypt," *Zeitschrift für Papyrologie und Epigraphik* 17 (1975): 237–50. For broad visions of the Roman empire as a whole, see MacMullen, *Roman Social Relations*, 88–120; Peter Garnsey and Richard P. Saller, *The Roman Empire: Economy, Society, and Culture* (Berkeley: University of California Press, 1987), 107–25. On the distribution of wealth in Egypt see especially Roger S. Bagnall, "Landholding in Late Roman Egypt: The Distribution of Wealth," *Journal of Roman Studies* 82 (1992): 128–49; Dominic Rathbone, "Poverty and Population in Roman Egypt," in *Poverty in the Roman World*, ed. E. M Atkins and Robin Osborne (Cambridge: Cambridge University Press, 2006), 100–114. Recently the question of status and mobility in Egypt in the third century has been revisited by Laurens Ernst Tacoma, *Fragile Hierarchies: The Urban Elites of Third Century Roman Egypt*, Mnemosyne Supplements 271 (Leiden: Brill, 2006).

27. See for example P.Mich. V 243 (A.D. 14–37). The Twelve Tables price injuries that are economically debilitating (such as a broken limb); this is not, however, a feature of the Roman law of delict in the classical and post-classical period.

28. Refusals to "be silent": e.g., P.Flor. III 309.5 (= P.Lond. III 983, A.D. IV, **120**), a petitioner not willing to overlook something "silently." Passivity, e.g.: BGU I 36.14 (= Chr.Mitt. 125, A.D. 98–117, **29**); BGU III 871.16 (A.D. II, **70**); P.Amh. II 141.15 (= Chr. Mitt. 126, A.D. 350, 109); P.Cair.Goodsp. 15.24 (A.D. 362, **113**); P.Kell. I 21.18 (A.D. 321,

99). Similar usages: CPR XIV 48.13 (A.D. 506), though the substance of this complaint is unclear; P.Berl.Frisk 4.19 (A.D. IV/V, **124**); P.Giss.Univ. III 27.16–17 (personal letter, a refusal to be silent at a tribunal, A.D. III); P.Mert. II 92.18 (A.D. 324).

29. P.Oxy. VIII 1120.7–10 (A.D. III, **90**).

30. Thus it seems that in BGU III 909.7 (Chr.Wilck. 382, A.D. 359, **111**), the offender lies in wait for the victim, planning to make an ἐπέλευσιν, which would seem capture the hostile sense of the term beyond its use in lawsuits.

31. Chr.Mitt. 78.5–6 (A.D. 376–78): ἐν στέρνοις ἔχω[ν] τὸν φόβον τοῦ δικαστηρίου ἀνέδραμον εἰς τὴν [ἔσω] Ὀᾶσ[ιν] . . .

32. P.Grenf. II 78 (= Chr.Mitt. 63, A.D. 307, **97**); P.Col. VII 171 (A.D. 324, **100**); P.Oxy. LI 3620 (A.D. 326, **101**); P.Rain.Cent. 91 (A.D. 451, **126**).

33. P.Lips. I 37 (A.D. 389, **116**).

34. SB XXIV 15970.16–17 (A.D. 455, **127**): οὐκ ὀκνήσω γὰρ κινῆσαι δικαστήρια περὶ τούτου. Likewise P.Berl.Frisk. 4.22 (A.D. IV–V, **124**).

35. Traianos Gagos and Peter van Minnen, *Settling a Dispute: Toward a Legal Anthropology of Late Antique Egypt*, New Texts from Ancient Cultures 1 (Ann Arbor: University of Michigan Press, 1994). Note, however, P.Haun. III 57 (A.D. 412–15) which may be an exception, as well as P.Abinn. 46 (A.D. 343, **105**), which refers to a violent attack. The petitioner seems to claim that the attack happened because his opponents thought he owed them money. He claims he does not, and that he will show this "through a mediator" (*dia mesitou*). The text, however, is fragmentary.

36. P.Oxy. VI 937.7–8 (A.D. III), where the writer says that he will "avenge himself" (ἐκδικήσω ἐμαυτόν). The sense of the Greek, however, is not nearly as clear as the sense of the English, and the writer may simply be referring to getting justice for himself—something which could very well take place in a courtroom.

37. P.Oxy. XLVIII 3480.24–25, 32 (A.D. IV, **112**).

38. P.Mich. VIII 492.21–22 (A.D. II). Another possible instance: P.Sarap. 92.12–13 (= P.Amh. II 133, A.D. 90–133).

39. P.Oxy. XLII 3061.8–12 (A.D. I), SB VI 9194.10–15 (A.D. III).

40. SB XIV 12084.4–9 (A.D. I).

41. P.Oxy. IV 706.12–13 (= Chr.Mitt. 81, A.D 73?): ἐάν σε μέμψηται [Ἡρακλείδης ?] ξυλοκοπηθῆναί σε κελεύσω. On the legal status of this document, see Mélèze Modrzejewski, "La loi des égyptiens'," 386–89.

42. P.Oxy. IX 1186 (A.D. IV), on which see Keenan, "Roman Criminal Procedure," on which this translation is based. Compare Hermogenianus in *Digest* 47.10.45, where free men are generally beaten with clubs (*fustibus*) as punishment for *iniuria*, and high-ranking individuals are exiled and subject to property confiscation. On judicial cruelty, see Garnsey, "Penalties"; Ramsay MacMullen, "Judicial Savagery in the Roman Empire," in *Changes in the Roman Empire: Essays in the Ordinary* (Princeton, N.J.: Princeton University Press, 1990), 204–14.

43. Above, note 42.

44. P.Wisc. I 33.19–20 (A.D. 147, **48**).

45. P.Lips. I 40.iii.20–21 (= Ch.L.A. XII 518, A.D. 381), trans. Keenan, "Roman Criminal Procedure." See also P.Flor. I 61 (= Chr.Mitt. 80, A.D. 85), where whipping is threatened during a hearing, but not carried out.

46. See Taubenschlag, Strafrecht, 106–9; Taubenschlag, Law, 557–58; Keenan, "Criminal Law." For penalties (but not in cases of violence) a decision concerning priests of Soknopaiou Nesos contains a clause against questioning or challenging official decisions, OGIS 664 (Soknopaiou Nesos, A.D. 54): "If someone challenges the things that have been once judged by me or invalidates what was ordered or plans to make a dispute, they will rightly be punished either monetarily or physically" (ἐὰν δέ τις ἐξελεγχθῆι τὰ ὑπ' ἐμοῦ ἅπαξ κεκριμένα ἢ προσταχθέντα κεινήσας ἢ βουληθεὶς ἀμφίβολα ποιῆσαι, κατ' ἀξιὰν ἢ ἀργυρικῶς ἢ σωματικῶς κολασθήσεται). P.Oxy. XII 1406 (A.D. 213–17) is an edict of Caracalla that appears to preserve a penalty of exile and infamia for a council member who hits a prytanis or another council member in the boule—that is, someone who uses violence in an official context. Likewise SB V 7523 (A.D. 153), a sworn declaration that a veteran was illegally beaten by a strategos. See also Garnsey, Social Status, 139.

47. P.Select 13 (A.D. 421).

48. Gagos and Minnen, *Settling a Dispute*, 30–31.

49. A useful survey is provided by Sally Engle Merry, "Legal Pluralism," *Law & Society Review* 22 (1988): 869–96.

50. On the reception of the concept of *patria potestas* in Egypt post A.D. 212, see Antti Arjava, "Paternal Power in Late Antiquity," *Journal of Roman Studies* 88 (1998): 147–65.

51. Clifford Ando, "Aliens, Ambassadors, and the Integrity of the Empire," *Law and History Review* 26 (2008): esp. 499–500.

52. Taubenschlag, *Law*, 6–7; Mélèze Modrzejewski, "Règle," 331–34. Uri Yiftach-Firanko, "Law in Greco-Roman Egypt: Hellenization, Fusion, Romanization," in *The Oxford Handbook of Papyrology*, ed. Roger S. Bagnall (Oxford: Oxford University Press, 2009), 555, is more strident than Taubenschlag, positing "the emergence of a new law, 'the law of the Egyptians,' which was applied by the *entire* population and consisted of Greek and Egyptian elements alike" (italics mine); for a different view, Bryen, "Judging Empire"; Bryen, "Tradition."

53. John Griffiths, "What Is Legal Pluralism?," *Journal of Legal Pluralism and Unofficial Law* 26 (1984): 1–55.

54. John 18:31; Acts 18:12–17. Rensberger, "The Politics of John," is key for remembering that this form of pluralism can sometimes be brutal.

55. Claudia Rapp, *Holy Bishops in Late Antiquity: The Nature of Christian Leadership in an Age of Transition* (Berkeley: University of California Press, 2005), 242–52, who is appropriately cautious with the papyrological material and the question of whether bishops exercised formal jurisdiction or simply power to mediate between parties. The petition directed to a bishop, Apa Theodorus, against a violent monk, would seem to indicate that, at least in limited circumstances, petitioners believed the bishop could have such authority: SB IV 7449 (A.D. V, 130).

56. The question of "custom" (*consuetudo*) in Roman law has generated a great deal of bibliography: useful still are the comments of J. A. Crook, *Law and Life of Rome* (London: Thames & Hudson, 1967), 27–28.

57. Philo, *In Flaccum* 53–54.

58. The classic discussion is Hendrik Hartog, "Pigs and Positivism," *Wisconsin Law Review* (1985): 899–935.

59. An interesting perspective on the intellectual traffic between official law and lawbreaking is Robert Weisberg, "Private Violence and Moral Action: The Law as Inspiration and Example," in *Law's Violence*, ed. Austin Sarat and Thomas R. Kearns (Ann Arbor: University of Michigan Press, 1992), 175–210. Philippe I. Bourgois, *In Search of Respect: Selling Crack in El Barrio* (Cambridge: Cambridge University Press, 1995) studies contemporary cultures of local norm enforcement. For a withering critique of the idea of embedded "codes" of morality in subordinated groups, see Loïc Wacquant, "Scrutinizing the Street: Poverty, Morality, and the Pitfalls of Urban Ethnography," *American Journal of Sociology* 107 (2002): 1486–93.

60. Benton, *A Search for Sovereignty*, 236–50, on hilly regions; Michael Herzfeld, *The Poetics of Manhood: Contest and Identity in a Cretan Mountain Village* (Princeton, N.J.: Princeton University Press, 1985), 26–33, on the problem of local law enforcement and its tensions with state ideology.

61. This would seem to be the point of the Christian martyr acts: compare the tense interaction between Polycarp and the governor in *Mart.Polycarp* 10, concerning whether the state will tolerate Polycarp's presentation of Christian doctrine as a judicial defense.

62. Cover, "Nomos and Narrative," 141, italics in original.

63. For a scathing critique, Brian Z. Tamanaha, "The Folly of the 'Social Scientific' Concept of Legal Pluralism," *Journal of Law and Society* 20 (1993): 192–217.

64. P.Oxy. II 237.vii.29–43 (A.D. 186).

65. On the availability and knowledge of laws in general I tend to agree with Michael H. Crawford, ed., *Roman Statutes*, Bulletin of the Institute of Classical Studies 64 (London: Institute of Classical Studies, 1996), 1: 27–34, who posits a wide diffusion of Roman law based primarily on epigraphic and literary sources; note also the judgment of Crook, *Law and Life of Rome*, 8: "it is likely that more Romans knew more about their legal institutions than Englishmen do about theirs."

66. See J. A. Crook, *Legal Advocacy in the Roman World* (Ithaca, N.Y: Cornell University Press, 1995), chap. 3, on advocates in the papyri, though his interest is more in the rhetorical capacities of advocates. To my knowledge, there has been very little research dedicated to the question of the availability of legal material in day-to-day life in Egypt outside the very cursory discussions of Taubenschlag, *Law*, 36–40; E. Seidl, *Rechtsgeschichte Ägyptens als römischer Provinz* (Sankt Augustin: H. Richarz, 1972), 49–55. See recently Serena Ammirati, "The Latin Book of Legal Content: A Significant Type in the History of the Book," in *Actes du 26e Congrès international de papyrologie,* ed. Paul Schubert, Publications de la Faculté des Lettres de l'Université de Genève 30 (Geneva: Librarie Droz) 19–25.

67. Ranon Katzoff, "Sources of Law in Roman Egypt: The Role of the Prefect," *ANRW* II.13 (1980): 833–43, who includes a catalogue of precedents cited in the papyri.

68. See Paul Weaver, "Consilium Praesidis: Advising Governors," in *Thinking like a Lawyer: Essays on Legal History and General History for John Crook on His Eightieth Birthday*, ed. Paul McKechnie, Mnemosyne Supplementum 231 (Leiden: Brill, 2002), 43–62; Brunt, "The Administrators of Roman Egypt." On the *nomikoi* see Wolfgang Kunkel, *Herkunft und soziale Stellung der römischen Juristen*, 2nd ed., Forschungen zum römischen Recht 4 (Köln: Böhlau, 1967), 263–70, 354–65.

69. Sally Engle Merry, *Getting Justice and Getting Even: Legal Consciousness Among Working-Class Americans* (Chicago: University of Chicago Press, 1990); Barbara Yngvesson, *Virtuous Citizens, Disruptive Subjects: Order and Complaint in a New England Court* (New York: Routledge, 1993), 15–31, on court clerks and their role in keeping certain complaints out of the legal arena.

70. *Contra* Richard Alston, "Violence and Social Control in Roman Egypt," in *Proceedings of the 20th International Congress of Papyrologists*, ed. Adam Bülow-Jacobsen (Copenhagen: Museum Tusculum Press, 1992), 517–21. See Anagnostou-Canas, *Juge et sentence*, 207–8. It is worth noting that emperors too on occasion used precedent in expanding legal definitions: see the Epistle of Severus to the city of Tyra (FIRA I 73).

71. P.Oxy. VIII 1120.9–10 (A.D. III, 90), and above, note 29.

72. P.Thomas 9 (A.D. I).

73. Though see William Turpin, "Apokrimata, Decreta, and the Roman Legal Procedure," *Bulletin of the American Society of Papyrologists* 18 (1991): 145–60, on the *Apokrimata* papyrus.

74. Katzoff, "Sources of Law," 834–41.

75. Notable exceptions are Miller, *Eye for an Eye*; Butler, *Precarious Life*.

76. For an overview, see Matthias Hagemann, *Iniuria: Von den XII-Tafeln bis zur Justinianischen Kodifikation*, Forschungen zum römischen Recht 43 (Köln: Böhlau, 1998).

77. Gaius, *Inst.* 3.225; Justinian, *Inst.* 4.4.9 (an expanded definition).

78. SB VI 9194.10–15 (A.D. III).

79. P.Hal. 1.192–213; see also P.Lille I 39 (= Chr.Mitt. 369 = Jur.Pap. 71, III B.C.); and the perceptive comments of Georges Nachtergael, "P.Brux.inv. E 7172," publishing a similar fragment from the Roman period.

80. SB XII 10929, cols.2–3 (A.D. 133–37?). The procedure outlined at the end of the third column has been the subject of some controversy: I tend to accept the view of Naphtali Lewis, advanced in a series of articles collected in Lewis, *On Government and Law in Roman Egypt*, 157–77.

81. For a comparative case from medieval Castile see Richard L. Kagan, *Lawsuits and Litigants in Castile, 1500–1700* (Chapel Hill: University of North Carolina Press, 1981); Richard L. Kagan, "A Golden Age of Litigation: Castile, 1500–1700," in *Disputes and Settlements: Law and Human Relations in the West*, ed. John Bossy (Cambridge: Cambridge University Press, 1983), 145–66. On negotiating the system in Egypt, Lewis, *Life in Egypt*, 189; Lewis, "Judiciary Routines"; Keenan, "On Law and Society in Late Roman

Egypt," 243–47; Bagnall, *Egypt in Late Antiquity*, 161; Jill Harries, "Resolving Disputes: The Frontiers of Law in Late Antiquity," in *Law, Society, and Authority in Late Antiquity*, ed. Ralph W. Mathisen (Oxford: Oxford University Press, 2001), 68–82.

82. Thus, for instance, P.Cair.Isid. 66 and 67 (A.D. 299, dealing with arson): these petitions are two drafts of the same complaint, with the signed version bearing a substantially different preface from the draft version. Likewise the relationship between the linguistic choices in P.Abinn. 51 and P.Abinn. 52 (A.D. 346, **107**, **108**) may be important, as the editor claims that "the writer has accidentally omitted some words." These omitted words happen to deal specifically with the type of violence committed and would make the difference between whether the complaint in P.Abinn. 52 maintains the charge of violence described in P.Abinn. 51. There is likewise an unpublished duplicate of P.Lips. I 39 (P.Lips.inv. 13).

83. Nielsen, "A Catalog of Duplicate Papyri."

84. SB I 5235 (A.D. 14, 7). See P.Sakaon 46 and 47 (= P.Abinn. 44, A.D. 342) for a similar case involving theft, along with the comments of Jean-Jacques Aubert, "Policing the Countryside: Soldiers and Civilians in Egyptian Villages in the Third and Fourth Centuries A.D.," in *La hiérarchie (Rangordnung) de l'armée romaine sous le Haut-Empire*, ed. Yann Le Bohec (Paris: Boccard, 1995), 257–65. A similar set of petitions might be found in P.Gen. I 16 (= Chr.Wilck. 354) and SB I 4282 (both A.D. 207).

85. SB I 5238 (A.D. 14, **8**).

86. For linguistic parallels, see P.Lond. II 342 (A.D. 185, **64**), P.Tebt. II 304 (A.D. 167–68, **57**), and P.Ryl. II 144 (A.D. 38, **14**), the petition of the slave Ision.

87. P.Mich. VIII 514.17 (A.D. III), referring to a quarrel between a woman and her husband; P.Mich. V 243.6 (A.D. 14–37), part of a guild ordinance.

88. Taubenschlag, *Law*, 441.

89. E.g., BGU IV 1187 (I B.C.); P.Oxy. XII 1465 (I B.C.); P.Sarap. 94 (A.D. II) appears to be the latest example.

90. For a chronology of the conflict see Paul R. Swarney, *The Ptolemaic and Roman* Idios Logos, American Studies in Papyrology 8 (Toronto: Hakkert, 1970), 41–46; Hans Albert Rupprecht, "Die Streitigkeit zwischen Satabous und Nestnephis," in *Symposion 1999: Vorträge zur griechischen und hellenistischen Rechtsgeschichte*, ed. Gerhard Thür and F. J. F. Nieto, Akten der Gesellschaft für griechische und hellenistische Rechtsgeschichte 14 (Köln: Böhlau, 2003), 481–92; Kelly, *Petitions*, 304–12.

91. See Whitehorne, "Petitions to the Centurion: A Question of Locality?"

92. SB X 10308 (A.D. 11).

93. Other examples of pregnant women harmed in conflicts: P.Mich. V 228 (A.D. 47, **23**); SB X 10239 (A.D. 37, **13**) and SB X 10244 (= P.Oxy. II 324 descr., A.D. 50, **26**). The last two are both from the papers of Tryphon the weaver.

94. Here my analysis is deeply indebted to Robert P. Burns, *A Theory of the Trial* (Princeton, N.J.: Princeton University Press, 1999).

95. Key for the dynamics of writing is Ando, *Imperial Ideology and Provincial Loyalty*, 73–130.

96. On the possibilities of this process for lawmaking, see Dennis P. Kehoe, *Law and the Rural Economy in the Roman Empire* (Ann Arbor: University of Michigan Press, 2007), 74–75; Bryen, "Tradition." Particularly illuminating is SB V 7601 (post A.D. 135), in which the fact that a petition is passed on provides an avenue for redress; the transcript from which we know this was itself recycled to make a legal claim.

CHAPTER 6. FUSION AND FISSION

1. An important exception here is Bruce W. Frier, *The Rise of the Roman Jurists: Studies in Cicero's* Pro Caecina (Princeton, N.J.: Princeton University Press, 1985).

2. E.g., Andrea Jördens, "Familenfehde in Hermupolis—Theophanes und Adelphios," *Bulletin of the American Society of Papyrologists* 45 (2008): esp. n.2; Bagnall, *Egypt in Late Antiquity*, 223; Kelly, *Petitions*, 304–9. An example of the difficulty of scholarly vocabulary can be found in Paul Hyams, "Feud and the State in Late Anglo-Saxon England," *Journal of British Studies* 40 (2001): 3–6, who notes the difficulties in translating the definitions from the medieval English literary and legal material into a current scholarly paradigm. In a medieval context see Thomas V. Cohen, "The Lay Liturgy of Affront in Sixteenth-Century Italy," *Journal of Social History* 25 (1992): 857–77, whose terminology is odd but whose attempt is admirable. Important in the early discussions of feud are Gluckman, "The Peace in the Feud"; Jacob Black-Michaud, *Cohesive Force: Feud in the Mediterranean and the Middle East* (Oxford: Blackwell, 1975); Christopher Boehm, *Blood Revenge: The Anthropology of Feuding in Montenegro and Other Tribal Societies* (Lawrence: University Press of Kansas, 1984); Miller, *Eye for an Eye*; Edward Muir, *Mad Blood Stirring: Vendetta and Factions in Friuli During the Renaissance* (Baltimore: Johns Hopkins University Press, 1993); Smail, *The Consumption of Justice*; Altina L. Waller, *Feud: Hatfields, McCoys, and Social Change in Appalachia, 1860–1900* (Chapel Hill: University of North Carolina Press, 1988). For a model of "tit-for-tat" conflict derived from game-theory see Robert M. Axelrod, *The Evolution of Cooperation* (New York: Basic Books, 1984), who presents this model as generating equilibria in a sense similar to Gluckman's early models. The question of feuds has also provoked an increasingly nasty debate in discussions of the evidence from fourth-century B.C. Athens: see D. Cohen, *Law, Violence, Community*, esp. 87; Gabriel Herman, *Morality and Behaviour in Democratic Athens: A Social History* (Cambridge: Cambridge University Press, 2006); E. M. Harris, "Feuding or the Rule of Law? The Nature of Litigation in Classical Athens, an Essay in Legal Sociology," in *Symposion 2001: Vorträge zur griechischen und hellenistischen Rechtsgeschichte*, ed. Robert W. Wallace and Michael Gagarin, Akten der Gesellschaft für griechische und hellenistische Rechtsgeschichte 16 (Vienna: Österreichischen Akademie der Wissenschaften, 2005), 125–41, and "Response to E. M. Harris" of Matthew Christ in the same volume.

3. Michael Herzfeld, "Honour and Shame: Problems in the Comparative Analysis of Moral Systems," *Man* 15 (1980): 339–51; Michael Herzfeld, "The Horns of the Mediterraneanist Dilemma," *American Ethnologist* 11 (1984): 439–54; Michael Herzfeld, "Of Horns and

History: The Mediterraneanist Dilemma Again," *American Ethnologist* 12 (1985): 778–80. Honor in Roman literature is discussed by Carlin A. Barton, *Roman Honor: The Fire in the Bones* (Berkeley: University of California Press, 2001); Lendon, *Empire of Honour*. Appropriately skeptical is William V. Harris, "The Mediterranean and Ancient History," in *Rethinking the Mediterranean*, ed. Harris (Oxford: Oxford University Press, 2005), 26–29.

4. The documents in question are P.Oxy. VI 901 (= Chr.Mitt. 70) and a duplicate, P.Oxy. LIV 3771 (**103**). The text printed is 3771, which is slightly fuller and incorporates restorations from 901. The status of the *syndikos* (also *ekdikos*, *defensor civitatis*) is complicated by a number of chronological factors: see B. R. Rees, "The Defensor Civitatis in Egypt," *Journal of Juristic Papyrology* 6 (1952): 73–102; Robert M. Frakes, *Contra Potentium Iniurias: The Defensor Civitatis and Late Roman Justice*, Münchener Beiträge zur Papyrusforschung und antiken Rechtsgeschichte 90 (Munich: Verlag Beck, 2001).

5. Other cases of wandering animals provoking violence between neighbors: P.Ryl. II 141 (A.D. 37, **12**), in which the cause of the violence is a debate between two parties over how much is owed in recompense because of earlier damages by animals; P.Col. VII 171.5–6 (= P.Coll.Youtie II 77, A.D. 324, **100**): τῆς β[οὸ]ς ạ[ὐτῶν] π̣ạ́λιν ἐν αὐτῷ τῷ τόπῳ καταβοσκηθείσῃς; P.Lips. I 37 (A.D. 390, **116**), claiming three petitions against shepherds allowing their flocks onto neighboring land; and SB IV 7464 (A.D. 248, **83**), another case of a stray piglet.

6. Merry, *Getting Justice*, 42.

7. Thus Gagos and Minnen, *Settling a Dispute*, 37, 44, on the impossibility of an "anthropology" of late antique Egypt.

8. To cite a few of the many examples: P.Mich. V 228 (A.D. 47, **23**), where violence between a man and a shepherd comes from the petitioner's attempt to reclaim what he was owed (ἐμοῦ λογοποιουμένου . . . περὶ ὧν ὀφείλει μοι); PSI IV 313 (A.D. III–IV, **93**), where the petitioner claims to have paid a debt, but was attacked anyway; also P.Abinn. 46 (A.D. 343, **105**), P.Stras. V 401 (A.D. 123, **38**), and above, Chapter 4.

9. On both topics, essential are Richard P. Saller, *Personal Patronage Under the Early Empire* (Cambridge: Cambridge University Press, 2002); Richard P. Saller, "Roman Kinship: Structure and Sentiment," in *The Roman Family in Italy: Status, Sentiment, Space*, ed. Beryl Rawson and P. R. C. Weaver (Canberra: Humanities Research Centre, 1997), 7–34. Anthropologists have sought to add greater sophistication to levels of interpersonal relationships, especially at the level of the family; the question of the density of social and familial institutions is critical in the early work on conflict. Though the bibliography is too vast to cite in its entirety, see Gluckman, "The Peace in the Feud"; John L. Comaroff and Simon Roberts, *Rules and Processes: The Cultural Logic of Dispute in an African Context* (Chicago: University of Chicago Press, 1981); Herzfeld, *The Poetics of Manhood*. It is admittedly an easier matter to track interpersonal relationships in societies with less social complexity. Recent and forthcoming work will hopefully add to our picture of the social organization of the Egyptian towns and countryside. For the sixth century, Giovanni Ruffini has attempted to reconstruct social networks by recourse to computer modeling: *Social Networks in Byzantine Egypt* (Cambridge: Cambridge University Press, 2008).

10. Noteworthy exceptions to this are David Konstan, *Friendship in the Classical World* (Cambridge: Cambridge University Press, 1997); Edward Champlin, *Final Judgments: Duty and Emotion in Roman Wills, 200 B.C.–A.D. 250* (Berkeley: University of California Press, 1991), 142–54; Grey, *Constructing Communities.*

11. On stratification and the distribution of wealth in the *chora,* see Bagnall, "Landholding in Late Roman Egypt"; Rathbone, "Poverty and Population in Roman Egypt."

12. Bagnall, "Official and Private Violence," and above, Chapter 4.

13. I borrow and adapt the idea of the "channeling function" of law and the role of formality from Lon L. Fuller, "Consideration and Form," *Columbia Law Review* 41 (1941): 799–824, a reference for which I thank Richard Epstein (who would surely not endorse my use of the term here). Also important are Conley and O'Barr, *Rules Versus Relationships*; Bourdieu, "Force of Law."

14. Ross Bernstein, *The Code: The Unwritten Rules of Fighting and Retaliation in the NHL* (Chicago: Triumph Books, 2006).

15. Axelrod, *The Evolution of Cooperation.*

16. Luigi Giorgio Barzini, *The Italians* (New York: Atheneum, 1965), 183.

17. SB I 5235.8 (A.D. 14, 7).

18. SB I 5238.12 (A.D. 14, **8**). For similar cases: P.Ross.Georg. II 20.22–23 (A.D. 146, **45**), in which the editors plausibly restore [οὐ τὰς τυχοῦσα]ς ὕβρεις μοι παρέχει σὺν τοῖς συνερ[γοῦσιν αὐτῷ ἀδελφοῖς καὶ] ἑτέροις; SB X 10244 (A.D. 50, **26**), from the papers of Tryphon the weaver.

19. See also Hobson, "Impact of Law," 204.

20. On the nuclear family see Richard P. Saller and Brent D. Shaw, "Tombstones and Roman Family Relations in the Principate: Civilians, Soldiers and Slaves," *Journal of Roman Studies* 74 (1984): 124–56.

21. BGU III 909 (= Chr.Wilck. 382, A.D. 359, **111**). Compare P.Sijp. 14 (A.D. 22, **10**), violence by a mother and her daughter.

22. P.Amh. II 142 (= Chr.Mitt. 65, A.D. IV, **119**).

23. Edgar Kutzner, *Untersuchungen zur Stellung der Frau im römischen Oxyrhynchos*, Europäische Hochschulschriften 392 (Frankfurt am Main: Peter Lang, 1989), 106–7; Parca, "Violence"; Bagnall, "Women's Petitions in Late Antique Egypt."

24. P.Cair.Goodsp. 15 (A.D. 362, **113**). Similar is P.Cair.Isid. 63 (A.D. 297, **89**).

25. P.Freib. II 11 (A.D. 336, **102**); similar is P.Amh. II 142 (= Chr.Mitt. 65, A.D. IV, **119**).

26. Compare P.Louvre I 1 (A.D. 13, **6**); BGU II 589 (A.D. 144, **44**); P.Mich. III 175 (A.D. 193, **67**).

27. In the American small-claims system these were often treated derisively by judges as "garbage cases"; there was an important movement in the 1970s to streamline the American legal system to push these cases to the side. The rise of Alternative Dispute Resolution, and the political consequences of this, have been crucial in the development of American legal anthropology: see Laura Nader, "Pushing the Limits—Eclecticism on Purpose," *PoLAR: Political and Legal Anthropology Review* 22 (2008): 106–9; Laura Nader,

"Moving On: Comprehending Anthropologies of Law," in *Practicing Ethnography in Law: New Dialogues, Enduring Methods*, ed. June Starr and Mark Goodale (New York: Palgrave Macmillan, 2002), 196–97.

28. Wickham, *Courts and Conflict in Twelfth-Century Tuscany*, 85.

29. See also Chris Wickham, "Gossip and Resistance Among the Medieval Peasantry," *Past & Present* 160 (1998): 3–24; Chris Wickham, "Fama and the Law in Twelfth Century Tuscany," in *Fama: The Politics of Talk and Reputation in Medieval Europe*, ed. Thelma S. Fenster and Daniel Lord Smail (Ithaca, N.Y.: Cornell University Press, 2003), 15–26.

30. An account of the strength of state and judicial institutions is in my opinion decisive for building a model of violence for Egypt, and has largely been left out of the discussions in previous scholarship. Alston, "Violence and Social Control in Roman Egypt," makes an attempt to integrate a discussion of institutions, but his account is based on a rigid understanding of the function of institutions and a reduced emphasis on the importance of individual initiative. Again, exceptions to this pattern are Frier, *The Rise of the Roman Jurists*; Gagos and van Minnen, *Settling a Dispute*. Both provide well-theorized accounts of their respective topics in the context of state institutions.

31. The original text was published with μηδὲν πόλεμον ποιοῦντες; Rea concluded that this was not supported by the photograph, and considered it an atypical usage as well.

32. P.Col. VIII 242 (A.D. V); see esp. Rea, "P. Col. VIII 242: Caranis in the Fifth Century," from whose article I print the normalized text and translation.

33. The Roman system was a non-interventionist system: Wilfried Nippel, *Public Order in Ancient Rome* (Cambridge: Cambridge University Press, 1995), 35–39. Though there were police officials, they bore no similarity to the system of modern policing that had its origins in early modern France. Still, claims have been made about the importance of police officials in the Roman world; it is a discussion that, to my mind, confuses terminology with substance. On Roman Egypt see Hennig, "Nyktophylakes," who is optimistic regarding the actual capabilities of these officials. For Ptolemaic Egypt see John F. Bauschatz, "Policing the Chora: Law Enforcement in Ptolemaic Egypt," (Ph.D. dissertation, Duke University, 2005), and for the Roman province of Asia (but also with reference to Egyptian material), Cédric Brélaz, *La securité publique en Asie Mineure sous le Principat (Ier–IIIème S. Ap. J.-C.): Institutions municipales et institutions impériales dans l'Orient romain*, Schweizerische Beiträge zur Altertumswissenschaft 32 (Basel: Schwabe Verlag, 2005). On *nyktostrategoi*, see the comments of Sijpesteijn *ad* P.David 17 (A.D. 509); on the situation in upper Egypt, see Bagnall, "Army and Police," who argues for corvée labor used in policing. On soldiers and centurions, Alston, *Soldier and Society*, 86–95; Whitehorne, "Petitions to the Centurion: A Question of Locality?"; Peachin, "Petition to a Centurion." For an instance where local officials were perhaps over-zealous in starting proceedings without following required procedure, see Hauken, *Petition and Response*, n.4, esp. 66–67 [Kemaliye].

34. A fact not lost on petitioners. See Chr.Mitt. 71.7–8 (A.D. 462, **128**), a *cessio bonorum* documenting what the writer claims is unjust imprisonment. The writer indicates the injustice by noting that "the laws command that everywhere Romans shall have their bodies free and unharmed"(ἐπειδὴ δὲ πανταχοῦ [οἱ] ν̣ό[μ]οι κελεύουσι Ῥ̣ω̣[μαίους <τὸ>] σῶμα [ἔχ]ειν ἐλεύθερο[ν κ]αὶ ἀνύβριστον).

35. Richard Alston, "Searching for the Romano-Egyptian Family," in *The Roman Family in the Empire: Rome, Italy, and Beyond*, ed. Michele George (Oxford: Oxford University Press, 2005), 129–58; Eleanor Dickey, "Literal and Extended Use of Kinship Terms in Documentary Papyri," *Mnemosyne* 57 (2004): 131–76.

36. Another instance is described by Deborah H. Samuel, "P. Berol. Inv. 8797 and P. Gen. 3: Two Versions of a Dispute over an Inheritance," *Zeitschrift für Papyrologie und Epigraphik* 37 (1980): 255–59.

37. Thus perhaps the importance of the use of *dialyseis* in family and inheritance conflict noted by Gagos and van Minnen, *Settling a Dispute*, 38.

38. P.Oxy. XXXIV 2713.3–4 (A.D. 297). In what follows I have benefited much from the discussion of Judith Evans-Grubbs, "'Wronged Even by Relatives': Petitions Against Family Members in Roman Egypt" (presented at the annual meeting of the Classical Association of the Midwest and South, 2007); important for the material from the Roman legal sources is Judith Evans-Grubbs, "Parent-Child Conflict in the Roman Family," in *The Family in the Roman Empire*, ed. Michele George (Oxford: Oxford University Press, 2005), 93–128.

39. A particularly persuasive description of the intricacies of family relationships can be found in Brent D. Shaw, "The Family in Late Antiquity: The Experience of Augustine," *Past & Present* 115 (1987): 3–51.

40. P.Oxy. VI 903 (A.D. IV, **123**); P.Oxy. L 3581 (A.D. IV, **125**); see Joëlle Beaucamp, *Le statut de la femme à Byzance, 4e–7e siècle*, Travaux et mémoires du centre de recherche d'histoire et civilisation de Byzance, Monographies 5–6 (Paris: Boccard, 1990), II: 91–94.

41. For discussion see Ilias Arnaotoglou, "Marital Disputes in Greco-Roman Egypt," *Journal of Juristic Papyrology* 25 (1995): 11–28; Judith Evans-Grubbs, *Women and the Law in the Roman Empire: A Sourcebook on Marriage, Divorce and Widowhood* (London: Routledge, 2002), 187–218, collects relevant source materials.

42. P.Oxy. VI 903.12–18 (= C.Pap.Jud. III 457d, A.D. IV, **123**).

43. On the dynamics of gendered violence, see Leslie Dossey, "Wife Beating and Manliness in Late Antiquity," *Past & Present* 199 (2008): 3–40; Schroeder, "John Chrysostom's Critique."

44. P.Oxy. L 3581.9–11 (A.D. IV–V, **125**). Compare P.Oxy. II 281 (= Chr.Mitt. 66, A.D. 20–50, **9**).

45. For the chronology of the conflict, I have relied on the work of J. David Thomas, "A Family Dispute from Karanis and the Revolt of Domitius Domitianus," *Zeitschrift für Papyrologie und Epigraphik* 24 (1977): 233–40. Similar to the petition of Taesis is the petition of Aurelia Didyme: P.Oxy. XXXIV 2713 (A.D. 297).

46. On the nickname see Naphtali Lewis, "Notationes Legentis," *Bulletin of the American Society of Papyrologists* 16 (1979): 206.

47. Thomas, "Family Dispute," 235–36.

48. In their note on the text, Boak and Youtie discuss the possibility that the mortars were actually left by Ptolemaios (grandfather of Taesis) rather than Kopres. The grammar of the text suggests the mortars were left by Kopres, though the nature of the division suggests they were left by Ptolemaios.

49. Thomas, "Family Dispute," 237, suspects it comes from early 298.

50. Thomas, "Family Dispute," 237.

51. P.Cair.Isid. 105.9–12.

52. The latest example I know of from the Roman period is BGU III 917 (A.D. 348), a sale of land. Other examples of the formula ἐάν τις ἐπέλθῃ . . . ἀποστήσω tend to be early: for example, BGU III 1002 (B.C. 55): sale of a house, from demotic, also recording that the property was the subject of a conflict (ὧν ἔχω ἐν ἀμφισβητ(ήσεως) [sic eds.], 4); SB I 5246 and its many duplicates (also originally in demotic), relating to the conflict between Satabous and Nestnephis (on which see above, Chapter 5); P.Ryl. II 95 (A.D. 71–72) also a contract mentioning a dispute. Other examples of the formula are Ptolemaic, coming from translations of demotic documents.

53. See P.Tebt. II 319 (A.D. 248). The closest analogue to this sort of promise may perhaps be found in guild charters: see P.Mich. V 243.6 (A.D. 14–37), which orders a fine for failure to come to the aid of another guild member.

54. On Roman wills and inheritances, see the excellent discussion of Champlin, *Final Judgments.*

55. The Greek text can be found in Chapter 4.

56. For this suggestion I thank T. Gagos.

57. See P.Mil.Vogl. II 53.11–12 (A.D. 152–153), a loan recording μυλαῖ[ο]ν, ἐν ᾧ [μη-] χαναὶ δύο ἀλε[τι]καὶ καὶ κοπτούραν.

58. See P.Mich. V 231 (A.D. 47–48), claiming that one individual committed suicide because of extensive legal harassment.

59. For another example see PSI III 222 (A.D. III–IV, **94**).

60. See Josef Mélèze Modrzejewski, "Private Arbitration and the Law of Greco-Roman Egypt," *Journal of Juristic Papyrology* 6 (1952): 239–56; Taubenschlag, *Law*, 510–13.

61. See P.Oxy. XXII 2342.11–18 (A.D. 102), in which there seems to be a social sanction against settlement. The petitioner claims that the offending party ἐπιτρίβεται ὑπὸ τῶν κακοτρόπων υἱων μὴ [ἀλ]ηθεύειν ὃ ἐχείρισεν μηδ' εἰς σύμβασιν [αὐ]τοῦ ἐλθεῖν οὔτε ἣν εἶχεν ἐνθήκης λόγ[ῳ] διευλυτοῦσα οὐδὲ τὰ γραπτὰ ἀναδ[ι]δοῦσα ἔχουσα τὸ πᾶν θέμα πλανῶσα [ἐμ]ὲ καθ' ἑκάστην ἡμέραν. ἤλθαμεν εἰς Δῖον τὸν στρατηγὸν εἰποῦσα . . . See likewise P.Oxy. XVI 1839 (A.D. VI).

62. Gaius, *Institutes* 3.88: *divisio in duas species diducitur: omnis enim obligatio vel ex contractu nascitur vel ex delicto*; restated with crucial expansions and changes in Justinian, *Institutes* 3.13.2: *sequens divisio in quattor species diducitur: aut enim ex contractu sunt aut quasi ex contractu, aut ex maleficio aut quasi ex maleficio.*

63. This petition is one of the lengthiest of the Roman period, though surprisingly, it has received relatively little attention beyond discussions of the judicial precedents included in it and the nature of the extent of *patria potestas* in Egypt. See Mélèze Modrzejewski, "La loi des Égyptiens'," 392–94; Katzoff, "'Responsa Prudentium' in Roman Egypt"; C. Kreuzaler and J. Urbanik, "Humanity and Inhumanity of the Law: The Case of Dionysia," *Journal of Juristic Papyrology* 38 (2008): 119–55; Uri Yiftach-Firanko, *Marriage and Marital Arrangements: A History of the Greek Marriage Document in Egypt, 4th Century B.C.E.–4th Century C.E.*, Münchener Beiträge zur Papyrusforschung und

antiken Rechtsgeschichte 93 (Munich: Beck, 2003). On the petition and *patria potestas* see Lewis, *On Government and Law in Roman Egypt*, 251–58; Arjava, "Paternal Power in Late Antiquity"; Evans-Grubbs, "Parent-Child Conflict in the Roman Family."

64. My analysis here is adapted from Bryen, "Dionysia's Complaint."

65. ὁμολόγημα: iv.6, iv.13, iv.26, iv.36, v.11; ὁμολογία: iv.33; ὁμολογοῦντα: iv.15.

66. πάλιν: iv.12, 13, 26, 31.

67. My analysis here is indebted to Richard A. Epstein, *Simple Rules for a Complex World* (Cambridge, Mass.: Harvard University Press, 1995), 74: "as long as you know there is an A and B, you have all the necessary information to figure out their *self*-definition of social roles by contract."

68. The form of the document, as Dionysia makes clear, seems to be a letter (*epistole*), rather than a petition. Certainly petitions evolved from an epistolary form, but the quoted petition/letter seems nevertheless odd: Chairemon's name at the top is in the nominative, rather than the genitive (which would be expected in both a petition and a letter).

69. Bryen and Wypustek, "Gemellus' Evil Eyes."

70. On control of children, provocative is David Daube, "Dividing a Child in Antiquity," *California Law Review* 54 (1966): 1630–37.

71. Saller, "Roman Kinship," 20.

72. Saller and Shaw, "Tombstones."

73. Thus it is probably no accident that the abusive behavior and *hybris* in the divorce decree discussed above is alternately called *aneleuthera pragmata*.

CONCLUSION: *NOMOS* AND ITS NARRATIVES

1. I borrow the concept of the colonial conversation from Jean Comaroff and John L. Comaroff, *Of Revelation and Revolution*, 2 vols. (Chicago: University of Chicago Press, 1991).

2. For a provocative discussion of the role of violence in policing the boundaries of communities, see Thomas Sizgorich, *Violence and Belief in Late Antiquity: Militant Devotion in Christianity and Islam* (Philadelphia: University of Pennsylvania Press, 2008), esp. 108–43.

3. Cover, "Violence and the Word," in *Narrative, Violence, and the Law*, 203.

4. Scarry, *Body in Pain*, esp. 50–51.

5. Butler, *Precarious Life*, 44.

APPENDIX B: TRANSLATIONS OF PETITIONS CONCERNING VIOLENCE

1. Sijpesteijn restores Διδύμου ὑπερέτου οὐ τὴν τυχοῦσαν. [τὸ δὲ π]ρ̣ᾶ̣[γμ]α̣ τίθημι. He restores the second sentence on the basis of P.Fouad. 26, but this cannot be correct: there needs to be a feminine noun to match the participle, for in no case in the extant papyri is the phrase οὐ τυχοῦσα used without a noun. Since on the basis of a photograph τίθημι seems secure, I have tried to render sense as best I can.

BIBLIOGRAPHY

Aijmer, Göran and Jon Abbink, eds. *Meanings of Violence: A Cross Cultural Perspective.* Oxford: Berg, 2000.

Alston, Richard. "Conquest by Text: Juvenal and Plutarch on Egypt." In *Roman Imperialism: Post-Colonial Perspectives,* ed. Jane Webster and Nicholas J. Cooper, 99–109. Leicester Archaeology Monographs 3. Leicester: Leicester University Archaeological Research Centre, 1996.

———. "Philo's 'In Flaccum': Ethnicity and Social Space in Roman Alexandria." *Greece & Rome* 44 (1997): 165–75.

———. "Searching for the Romano-Egyptian Family." In *The Roman Family in the Empire: Rome, Italy, and Beyond,* ed. Michele George, 129–58. Oxford: Oxford University Press, 2005.

———. *Soldier and Society in Roman Egypt: A Social History.* London: Routledge, 1995.

———. "Violence and Social Control in Roman Egypt." In *Proceedings of the 20th International Congress of Papyrologists,* ed. Adam Bülow-Jacobsen, 517–21. Copenhagen: Museum Tusculum Press, 1992.

Ammirati, Serena. "The Latin Book of Legal Content: A Significant Type in the History of the Book." In *Actes du 26e Congrès international de papyrologie,* ed. Paul Schubert, 19–25. Publications de la Faculté des Lettres de l'Université de Genève 30. Geneva: Droz.

Amundsen, Darrell W., and Gary B. Ferngren. "The Forensic Role of Physicians in Ptolemaic and Roman Egypt." *Bulletin of the History of Medicine* 52 (1978): 336–53.

Anagnostou-Canas, Barbara. *Juge et sentence dans l'Égypte romaine.* Paris: Harmattan, 1991.

———. "La valeur des précédents judiciaires dans l'Égypte romaine: État de la question." *Droits et Cultures* 47 (2004): 47–65.

Anastasiades, V. I., and George A. Souris. *An Index to Roman Imperial Constitutions from Greek Inscriptions and Papyri: 27 BC to 284 AD.* Berlin: de Gruyter, 2000.

Ando, Clifford. "Aliens, Ambassadors, and the Integrity of the Empire." *Law and History Review* 26 (2008): 491–519.

———. *Imperial Ideology and Provincial Loyalty in the Roman Empire.* Classics and Contemporary Thought 6. Berkeley: University of California Press, 2000.

———. *Law, Language, and Empire in the Roman Tradition.* Philadelphia: University of Pennsylvania Press, 2011.

Arendt, Hannah. *The Origins of Totalitarianism.* San Diego: Harcourt Brace, 1985.

———. *The Portable Hannah Arendt*. Ed. P. R. Baehr. New York: Penguin, 2000.

Arjava, Antti. "Paternal Power in Late Antiquity." *Journal of Roman Studies* 88 (1998): 147–65.

Arnaoutoglou, Ilias. "Marital Disputes in Greco-Roman Egypt." *Journal of Juristic Papyrology* 25 (1995): 11–28.

Aubert, Jean-Jacques. "Policing the Countryside: Soldiers and Civilians in Egyptian Villages in the Third and Fourth Centuries A.D." In *La hiérarchie (Rangordnung) de l'armée romaine sous le Haut-Empire*, ed. Yann Le Bohec, 257–65. Paris: Boccard, 1995.

Axelrod, Robert M. *The Evolution of Cooperation*. New York: Basic Books, 1984.

Bagnall, Roger S. "Army and Police in Roman Upper Egypt." *Journal of the American Research Center in Egypt* 14 (1977): 67–86.

———. *Egypt in Late Antiquity*. Princeton, N.J.: Princeton University Press, 1993.

———. "Landholding in Late Roman Egypt: The Distribution of Wealth." *Journal of Roman Studies* 82 (1992): 128–49.

———. "Official and Private Violence in Roman Egypt." *Bulletin of the American Society of Papyrologists* 29 (1989): 201–16.

———. *Reading Papyri, Writing Ancient History*. London: Routledge, 1995.

———. "Response to Hans Albert Rupprecht." In *Symposion 1990: Vorträge zur griechischen und hellenistischen Rechtsgeschichte*, ed. Michael Gagarin, 149–52. Akten der Gesellschaft für griechische und hellenistische Rechtsgeschichte 8. Köln: Böhlau Verlag, 1991.

———. "The Population of Theadelphia in the Fourth Century." In *Later Roman Egypt: Society, Religion, Economy, and Administration*. chap. vi. Aldershot: Ashgate, 2003.

———. "Women's Petitions in Late Antique Egypt." In *Hellenistic and Roman Egypt: Sources and Approaches*, chap. xxiii. Aldershot: Ashgate, 2006.

Baldwin, Barry. "Crime and Criminals in Greco-Roman Egypt." *Aegyptus* 43 (1963): 256–63.

Barton, Carlin A. *Roman Honor: The Fire in the Bones*. Berkeley: University of California Press, 2001.

Barzini, Luigi Giorgio. *The Italians*. New York: Atheneum, 1965.

Baudrillard, Jean. *The Spirit of Terrorism and Other Essays*. Trans. Chris Turner. London: Verso, 2003.

Bauschatz, John F. "Policing the Chora: Law Enforcement in Ptolemaic Egypt." Ph.D. dissertation, Duke University, 2005.

Beaucamp, Joëlle. *Le statut de la femme à Byzance, 4e–7e siècle*. Travaux et Mémoires du Centre de Recherche d'Histoire et Civilisation de Byzance Monographies 5–6. Paris: de Boccard, 1990.

Benton, Lauren A. *A Search for Sovereignty: Law and Geography in European Empires, 1400–1900*. Cambridge: Cambridge University Press, 2010.

Bernstein, Ross. *The Code: The Unwritten Rules of Fighting and Retaliation in the NHL*. Chicago: Triumph Books, 2006.

Bishara, Fahad Ahmad. "A Sea of Debt: Islamic Law, Empire and Commercial Society in the Western Indian Ocean, c. 1850–1940." Ph.D. dissertation, Duke University, 2012.

Bisson, Thomas N. *Tormented Voices: Power, Crisis, and Humanity in Rural Catalonia, 1140–1200*. Cambridge, Mass.: Harvard University Press, 1998.

di Bitonto, A. "Le petitzione al re: Studio sul formulario." *Aegyptus* 47 (1967): 5–57.

———. "Le petizioni di funzionari nel periodo Tolemaico." *Aegyptus* 48 (1968): 53–107.

Black-Michaud, Jacob. *Cohesive Force: Feud in the Mediterranean and the Middle East*. Oxford: Blackwell, 1975.

Blok, Anton. "The Meaning of 'Senseless' Violence." In Blok, *Honour and Violence*, 103–14. Cambridge: Polity, 2001.

Boatwright, Mary Taliaferro. *Hadrian and the Cities of the Roman Empire*. Princeton, N.J.: Princeton University Press, 2000.

Boehm, Christopher. *Blood Revenge: The Anthropology of Feuding in Montenegro and Other Tribal Societies*. Lawrence: University Press of Kansas, 1984.

Bourdieu, Pierre. *The Bachelors' Ball: The Crisis of Peasant Society in Béarn*. Trans. Richard Nice. Chicago: University of Chicago Press, 2008.

———. "The Force of Law: Towards a Sociology of the Juridical Field." *Hastings Law Journal* 38 (1987): 814–53.

———. "The Sentiment of Honour in Kabyle Society." In *Honour and Shame: The Values of Mediterranean Society*, ed. John G. Peristiany, 191–241. London: Weidenfeld and Nicolson, 1966.

Bourgois, Philippe I. *In Search of Respect: Selling Crack in El Barrio*. Cambridge: Cambridge University Press, 1995.

———. *Righteous Dopefiend*. California Series in Public Anthropology 21. Berkeley: University of California Press, 2009.

Bowman, Alan K. "Egypt." In *Cambridge Ancient History*, vol. 10, *The Augustan Empire, 43 BC–AD 69*, ed. Alan K. Bowman, Edward Champlin, and Andrew Lintott, 676–702. Cambridge: Cambridge University Press, 1996.

Bowman, Alan K., and Dominic Rathbone. "Cities and Administration in Roman Egypt." *Journal of Roman Studies* 82 (1992): 107–27.

Boyle, A. J., and W. J. Dominik, eds. *Flavian Rome: Culture, Image, Text*. Leiden: Brill, 2003.

Brélaz, Cédric. *La securité publique en Asie Mineure sous le Principat (Ier–IIIème S. Ap. J.-C.): Institutions municipales et institutions impériales dans l'Orient romain*. Schweizerische Beiträge zur Altertumswissenschaft 32. Basel: Schwabe Verlag, 2005.

Brown, Peter. *Power and Persuasion in Late Antiquity*. Madison: University of Wisconsin Press, 1992.

Brunt, P. A. "The Administrators of Roman Egypt." *Journal of Roman Studies* 65 (1975): 124–47.

Bryen, Ari Z. "Dionysia's Complaint: Emotion, Truth, and Language in the Courtroom." In *Emotional Display, Persuasion, and Rhetoric in the Papyri*, ed. Chrysi Kotsifou, forthcoming 2013.

———. "Judging Empire: Courts and Culture in Rome's Eastern Provinces." *Law and History Review* 30 (2012): 771–811.

———. "Tradition, Precedent, and Power in Roman Egypt." In *Official Epistolography and the Language(s) of Power*, ed. Lucian Reinfandt and Sven Tost. Vienna: Österreichischen Akademie der Wissenschaften, forthcoming 2013.

Bryen, Ari Z., and Andrzej Wypustek. "Gemellus' Evil Eyes (P.Mich. VI 423–424)." *Greek, Roman, and Byzantine Studies* 49 (2009): 525–55.

Bülow-Jacobsen, Adam. "Orders to Arrest: P.Haun. Inv. 33 and 54 and a Consolidated List." *Zeitschrift für Papyrologie und Epigraphik* 66 (1986): 93–98.

Burbank, Jane, and Frederick Cooper. *Empires in World History: Power and the Politics of Difference*. Princeton, N.J.: Princeton University Press, 2010.

Burns, Kathryn. *Into the Archive: Writing and Power in Colonial Peru*. Durham, N.C.: Duke University Press, 2010.

Burns, Robert P. *A Theory of the Trial*. Princeton, N.J.: Princeton University Press, 1999.

Burton, G. P. "Proconsuls, Assizes and the Administration of Justice Under the Empire." *Journal of Roman Studies* 65 (1975): 92–106.

Butler, Judith. *Precarious Life: The Powers of Mourning and Violence*. London: Verso, 2004.

Capponi, Livia. *Augustan Egypt: The Creation of a Roman Province*. New York: Routledge, 2005.

Champlin, Edward. *Final Judgments: Duty and Emotion in Roman Wills, 200 B.C.–A.D. 250*. Berkeley: University of California Press, 1991.

Christ, Matthew. "Response to E. M. Harris." In *Symposion 2001: Vorträge zur griechischen und hellenistischen Rechtsgeschichte*, ed. Robert W. Wallace and Michael Gagarin, 125–41. Akten der Gesellschaft für griechische und hellenistische Rechtsgeschichte 16. Vienna: Österreichischen Akademie der Wissenschaften, 2005.

Cody, Jane M. "Conquerors and Conquered on Flavian Coins." In *Flavian Rome: Culture, Image, Text*, ed. A. J. Boyle and W. J. Dominik, 103–23. Leiden: Brill, 2003.

Cohen, David. *Law, Violence, and Community in Classical Athens*. Cambridge: Cambridge University Press, 1995.

Cohen, Thomas V. "The Lay Liturgy of Affront in Sixteenth-Century Italy." *Journal of Social History* 25 (1992): 857–77.

Coles, R. A. *Reports of Proceedings in Papyri*. Papyrologica Bruxellensia 4. Brussels: Fond. Égypt. R. Élisabeth, 1966.

Comaroff, Jean, and John L. Comaroff. *Of Revelation and Revolution*. 2 vols. Chicago: University of Chicago Press, 1991.

Comaroff, John L. "Legality, Modernity, and Ethnicity in Colonial South Africa: An Excursion in the Historical Anthropology of Law." In *Law, Society, and Economy: Centenary Essays for the London School of Economics and Political Science, 1895–1995*, ed. Richard Rawlings, 247–69. Oxford: Clarendon, 1997.

Comaroff, John L., and Simon Roberts. *Rules and Processes: The Cultural Logic of Dispute in an African Context*. Chicago: University of Chicago Press, 1981.

Conley, John M., and William M. O'Barr. *Rules Versus Relationships: The Ethnography of Legal Discourse*. Chicago: University of Chicago Press, 1990.

Connolly, Serena. *Lives Behind the Laws: The World of the Codex Hermogenianus*. Bloomington: Indiana University Press, 2010.

Cover, Robert M. "Nomos and Narrative." In *Narrative, Violence, and the Law: The Essays of Robert Cover*, ed. Martha Minow, Michael Ryan, and Austin Sarat, 95–172. Ann Arbor: University of Michigan Press, 1992.

Crawford, Michael H., ed. *Roman Statutes*. 2 vols. Bulletin of the Institute of Classical Studies 64. London: Institute of Classical Studies, 1996.

Cribiore, Raffaella. *Gymnastics of the Mind: Greek Education in Hellenistic and Roman Egypt*. Princeton, N.J.: Princeton University Press, 2001.

———. *The School of Libanius in Late Antique Antioch*. Princeton, N.J.: Princeton University Press, 2007.

———. *Writing, Teachers, and Students in Graeco-Roman Egypt*. American Studies in Papyrology 36. Atlanta: Scholars Press, 1996.

Crook, J. A. *Law and Life of Rome*. London: Thames & Hudson, 1967.

———. *Legal Advocacy in the Roman World*. Ithaca, N.Y: Cornell University Press, 1995.

Dahlmann, Wolfgang. "*H BIA* im Recht der Papyri." Ph.D. Thesis, Cologne, 1968.

Das, Veena. *Life and Words: Violence and the Descent into the Ordinary*. Berkeley: University of California Press, 2007.

Daube, David. "Dividing a Child in Antiquity." *California Law Review* 54 (1966): 1630–37.

———. "Fraud No. 3." In *The Legal Mind: Essays for Tony Honoré*, ed. Neil MacCormick and Peter Birks, 1–17. Oxford: Clarendon, 1986.

———. *Roman Law: Linguistic, Social and Philosophical Aspects*. Edinburgh: Edinburgh University Press, 1969.

Davies, R. W. "The Investigation of Some Crimes in Roman Egypt." *Ancient Society* 4 (1973): 199–212.

Davis, Natalie Zemon. *Fiction in the Archives: Pardon Tales and Their Tellers in Sixteenth-Century France*. Stanford, Calif.: Stanford University Press, 1987.

Dickey, Eleanor. "Literal and Extended Use of Kinship Terms in Documentary Papyri." *Mnemosyne* 57 (2004): 131–76.

Dietler, Michael. "The Archaeology of Colonization and the Colonization of Archaeology: Theoretical Challenges from an Ancient Mediterranean Encounter." In *The Archaeology of Colonial Encounters*, ed. Gil J. Stein, 33–68. Santa Fe, N.M.: School of American Research, 2005.

Dossey, Leslie. "Wife Beating and Manliness in Late Antiquity." *Past & Present* 199 (2008): 3–40.

Drake, H. A., ed. *Violence in Late Antiquity: Perceptions and Practices*. Burlington, Vt.: Ashgate, 2006.

Elm, Susanna. "Roman Pain and the Rise of Christianity." In *Quo Vadis Medical Healing: Past Concepts and New Approaches*, ed. Susanna Elm and Stefan N. Willich, 41–54. International Library of Ethics, Law, and the New Medicine 44. London: Springer, 2009.

Engel, David M. "The Oven Bird's Song: Insiders, Outsiders, and Personal Injuries in an American Community." *Law & Society Review* 18 (1984): 551–82.

Epstein, Richard A. *Simple Rules for a Complex World.* Cambridge, Mass.: Harvard University Press, 1995.

Erfan, Moushira, Aly El-Sawaf, Muhammad Al-Tohamy Soliman, Azza Sarry El-Din, Wafaa A. Kandeel, Rokia Abd El-Shafy El-Banna, and Ayman Azab. "Cranial Trauma in Ancient Egyptians from the Bahriyah Oasis, Greco-Roman Period." *Research Journal of Medicine & Medical Sciences* 4 (2009): 78–84.

Esmeir, Samera. *Juridical Humanity: A Colonial History.* Stanford, Calif.: Stanford University Press, 2012.

Evans-Grubbs, Judith. "Abduction Marriage in Antiquity: A Law of Constantine (CTh IX. 24. I) and Its Social Context." *Journal of Roman Studies* 79 (1989): 59–83.

———. "Parent-Child Conflict in the Roman Family." In *The Family in the Roman Empire: Rome, Italy, and Beyond*, ed. Michele George, 93–128. Oxford: Oxford University Press, 2005.

———. *Women and the Law in the Roman Empire: A Sourcebook on Marriage, Divorce and Widowhood.* London: Routledge, 2002.

———. "'Wronged Even by Relatives': Petitions Against Family Members in Roman Egypt." Presented at annual meeting of the Classical Association of the Midwest and South, Cincinnati, 11–14 April 2007.

Ewald, William. "Comparative Jurisprudence (I): What Was It Like to Try a Rat?" *University of Pennsylvania Law Review* 143 (1995): 1889–2149.

Fagan, Garrett G. "Violence in Roman Social Relations," in *The Oxford Handbook of Social Relations in the Roman World*, ed. Michael Peachin, 467–95. Oxford: Oxford University Press, 2011.

Fanon, Frantz. *The Wretched of the Earth.* Trans. Richard Philcox. New York: Grove Press, 2004.

Farmer, Paul. "An Anthropology of Structural Violence." *Current Anthropology* 45 (2004): 305–25.

Foti-Talamanca, Guiliana. *Ricerche sul processo nell'Egitto greco-romano.* Milan: Giuffre, 1979.

Foucault, Michel. *Discipline and Punish: The Birth of the Prison.* Trans. Alan Sheridan. New York: Vintage, 1995.

———. "Nietzsche, Genealogy, History." In *The Foucault Reader*, ed. Paul Rabinow, 76–100. New York: Pantheon, 1984.

———. *Security, Territory, Population: Lectures at the Collège de France, 1977–78.* Ed. Michel Senellart, trans. Graham Burchell. New York: Picador/Palgrave Macmillan, 2009.

Foucault, Michel, ed. *I, Pierre Rivière, Having Slaughtered My Mother, My Sister, and My Brother ...: A Case of Parricide in the 19th Century.* Harmondsworth: Penguin, 1978.

Fournet, Jean-Luc. "Entre document et littérature: La pétition dans l'antiquité tardive." In *La pétition à Byzance*, ed. Denis Feissel and Jean Gascou, 61–74. Centre de Recherche d'Histoire et Civilisation de Byzance. Monographies 14. Paris: Association des Amis du Centre d'Histoire et Civilisation de Byzance, 2004.

Fournet, Jean-Luc, and Jean Gascou. "Liste des pétitions sur papyrus des Ve–VIIe siècles." In *La pétition à Byzance*, ed. Denis Feissel and Jean Gascou, 141–96. Centre de Recherche d'Histoire et Civilisation de Byzance. Monographies 14. Paris: Association des Amis du Centre d'Histoire et Civilisation de Byzance, 2004.

Frakes, Robert M. *Contra Potentium Iniurias: The Defensor Civitatis and Late Roman Justice*. Münchener Beiträge zur Papyrusforschung und antiken Rechtsgeschichte 90. Munich: Beck, 2001.

Frier, Bruce W. "A New Papyrology?" *Bulletin of the American Society of Papyrologists* 26 (1989): 217–26.

———. *The Rise of the Roman Jurists: Studies in Cicero's* Pro Caecina. Princeton, N.J.: Princeton University Press, 1985.

Fuller, Lon L. "Consideration and Form." *Columbia Law Review* 41 (1941): 799–824.

Gaddis, Michael. *There Is No Crime for Those Who Have Christ: Religious Violence in the Christian Roman Empire*. Transformation of the Classical Heritage 39. Berkeley: University of California Press, 2005.

Gagos, Traianos, Jennifer E. Gates, and Andrew T. Wilburn. "Material Culture and Texts of Graeco-Roman Egypt: Creating Context, Debating Meaning." *Bulletin of the American Society of Papyrologists* 42 (2005): 171–88.

Gagos, Traianos, and Peter van Minnen. *Settling a Dispute: Toward a Legal Anthropology of Late Antique Egypt*. New Texts from Ancient Cultures 1. Ann Arbor: University of Michigan Press, 1994.

Gagos, Traianos, and P. J. Sijpestcijn. "Towards an Explanation of the Typology of the So-Called 'Orders to Arrest'." *Bulletin of the American Society of Papyrologists* 33 (1996): 77–97.

Garnsey, Peter. *Social Status and Legal Privilege in the Roman Empire*. Oxford: Clarendon, 1970.

———. "Why Penalties Become Harsher: The Roman Case, Late Republic to Fourth Century Empire." *Natural Law Forum* 13 (1968): 141–62.

Garnsey, Peter, and Richard P. Saller. *The Roman Empire: Economy, Society, and Culture*. Berkeley: University of California Press, 1987.

Geraci, Giovanni. "L'Egitto Romano nella storiografia moderna." In *Egitto e storia antica dall'ellenismo all'età Araba: Bilancio di un confronto*, ed. Giovanni Geraci and Lucia Criscuolo, 55–88. Bologna: CLUEB, 1989.

Ginzburg, Carlo. *The Cheese and the Worms: The Cosmos of a Sixteenth-Century Miller*. Trans. John A. Tedeschi and Anne Tedeschi. Baltimore: Johns Hopkins University Press, 1980.

———. *The Night Battles: Witchcraft and Agrarian Cults in the Sixteenth and Seventeenth Centuries*. Trans. John A. Tedeschi and Anne Tedeschi. Baltimore: Johns Hopkins University Press, 1992.

Gluckman, Max. "The Peace in the Feud." *Past & Present* 8 (1955): 1–14.

Goffman, Erving. "On Face Work." In Goffman, *Interaction Ritual: Essays on Face-to-Face Behavior*, 5–45. Garden City, N.Y.: Anchor, 1967.

———. *The Presentation of Self in Everyday Life*. New York: Anchor, 1959.

González, Julián, and Michael H. Crawford. "The Lex Irnitana: A New Copy of the Flavian Municipal Law." *Journal of Roman Studies* 76 (1986): 147–243.

Gow, A. S. F. "Notes on Noses." *Journal of Hellenic Studies* 71 (1951): 81–84.

Grey, Cam. *Constructing Communities in the Late Roman Countryside*. Cambridge: Cambridge University Press, 2011.

———. "Two Young Lovers: An Abduction Marriage and Its Consequences in Fifth-Century Gaul." *Classical Quarterly* 58 (2008): 286–302.

Griffiths, John. "What Is Legal Pluralism?" *Journal of Legal Pluralism and Unofficial Law* 26 (1984): 1–55.

Gruen, Erich S. *Rethinking the Other in Antiquity*. Princeton, N.J.: Princeton University Press, 2011.

———. *The Hellenistic World and the Coming of Rome*. Berkeley: University of California Press, 1984.

ter Haar, Barend J. "Rethinking 'Violence' in Chinese Culture." In *Meanings of Violence: A Cross Cultural Perspective*, ed. Göran Aijmer and Jon Abbink, 123–40. Oxford: Berg, 2000.

Hacking, Ian. *The Social Construction of What?* Cambridge, Mass.: Harvard University Press, 1999.

Haensch, R. "Die Bearbeitungsweisen von Petitionen in der Provinz Aegyptus." *Zeitschrift für Papyrologie und Epigraphik* 100 (1994): 487–546.

Hagedorn, D. "Bemerkungen zu einigen Wisconsin Papyri." *Zeitschrift für Papyrologie und Epigraphik* 1 (1967): 143–60.

Hagemann, Matthias. *Iniuria: Von den XII-Tafeln bis zur justinianischen Kodifikation*. Forschungen zum römischen Recht 43. Köln: Böhlau, 1998.

Hanson, Ann Ellis. "A Petition and Court Proceedings: P. Michigan Inv. 6060." *Zeitschrift für Papyrologie und Epigraphik* 111 (1996): 175–82.

Harker, Andrew. *Loyalty and Dissidence in Roman Egypt: The Case of the Acta Alexandrinorum*. Cambridge: Cambridge University Press, 2008.

Harries, Jill. *Law and Crime in the Roman World*. Cambridge: Cambridge University Press, 2007.

———. *Law and Empire in Late Antiquity*. Cambridge: Cambridge University Press, 1999.

———. "Resolving Disputes: The Frontiers of Law in Late Antiquity." In *Law, Society, and Authority in Late Antiquity*, ed. Ralph W. Mathisen, 68–82. Oxford: Oxford University Press, 2001.

———. "Violence, Victims, and the Legal Tradition in Late Antiquity." In *Violence in Late Antiquity: Perceptions and Practices*, ed. H. A. Drake, 85–102. Burlington, Vt.: Ashgate, 2006.

Harris, E. M. "Feuding or the Rule of Law? The Nature of Litigation in Classical Athens, an Essay in Legal Sociology." In *Symposion 2001: Vorträge zur griechischen und hellenistischen Rechtsgeschichte*, ed. Robert W. Wallace and Michael Gagarin, 125–41.

Akten der Gesellschaft für griechische und hellenistische Rechtsgeschichte 16. Vienna: Verlag der Österreichischen Akademie der Wissenschaften, 2005.

Harris, William V. "The Mediterranean and Ancient History." In *Rethinking the Mediterranean*, ed. William V. Harris, 1–42. Oxford: Oxford University Press, 2005.

Hartog, Hendrik. "Pigs and Positivism." *Wisconsin Law Review* (1985): 899–935.

Haug, Brendan J. "The Egyptian Fayyum: Environment, Irrigation, Agriculture, and the End of Antiquity." Ph.D. dissertation, University of California at Berkeley, 2012.

Hauken, Tor. *Petition and Response: An Epigraphic Study of Petitions to Roman Emperors, 181–249*. Monographs from the Norwegian Institute at Athens 2. Bergen: Norwegian Institute at Athens, 1998.

Hennig, Dieter. "Nyktophylakes, Nyktostrategen, und die παραφυλακὴ τῆς πόλεως." *Chiron* 32 (2002): 281–95.

Herman, Gabriel. *Morality and Behaviour in Democratic Athens: A Social History*. Cambridge: Cambridge University Press, 2006.

Herzfeld, Michael. "Honour and Shame: Problems in the Comparative Analysis of Moral Systems." *Man* 15 (1980): 339–51.

———. "The Horns of the Mediterraneanist Dilemma." *American Ethnologist* 11 (1984): 439–54.

———. "Of Horns and History: The Mediterraneanist Dilemma Again." *American Ethnologist* 12 (1985): 778–80.

———. *The Poetics of Manhood: Contest and Identity in a Cretan Mountain Village*. Princeton, N.J.: Princeton University Press, 1985.

Hickey, Todd M. "Writing Histories from the Papyri." In *The Oxford Handbook of Papyrology*, ed. Roger S. Bagnall, 495–520. Oxford: Oxford University Press, 2009.

Hobson, Deborah W. "The Impact of Law on Village Life in Roman Egypt." In *Law, Politics and Society in the Ancient Mediterranean World*, ed. Baruch Halpern and Deborah W. Hobson, 193–219. Sheffield: Sheffield Academic Press, 1993.

Honoré, Tony. *Ulpian: Pioneer of Human Rights*. 2nd ed. Oxford: Oxford University Press, 2002.

Horkheimer, Max, and Theodor W. Adorno. *Dialectic of Enlightenment: Philosophical Fragments*. Ed. Gunzelin Schmid Noerr, trans. Edmund Jephcott. Stanford, Calif.: Stanford University Press, 2002.

Hurst, James Willard. *Law and the Conditions of Freedom in the Nineteenth-Century United States*. Madison: University of Wisconsin Press, 1956.

Hyams, Paul. "Feud and the State in Late Anglo-Saxon England." *Journal of British Studies* 40 (2001): 1–43.

Isaac, Benjamin H. *The Invention of Racism in Classical Antiquity*. Princeton, N.J.: Princeton University Press, 2004.

Jay, Martin. *The Dialectical Imagination: A History of the Frankfurt School and the Institute of Social Research, 1923–1950*. Weimar and Now 10. Berkeley: University of California Press, 1996.

Jolowicz, H. F. "Case Law in Roman Egypt." *Journal of the Society of Public Teachers of Law* 14 (1937): 1–16.

Jördens, Andrea. "Die ägyptischen Symmachoi." *Zeitschrift für Papyrologie und Epigraphik* 66 (1986): 105–18.

———. "Familenfehde in Hermupolis: Theophanes und Adelphios." *Bulletin of the American Society of Papyrologists* 45 (2008): 101–16.

———. *Statthalterliche Verwaltung in der römischen Kaiserzeit: Studien zum* Praefectus Aegypti. Historia Einzelschriften 175. Stuttgart: Franz Steiner, 2009.

Jouguet, Pierre. *La vie municipale dans l'Égypte romaine.* Paris: Fontemoing, 1911.

Kagan, Richard L. "A Golden Age of Litigation: Castile, 1500–1700." In *Disputes and Settlements: Law and Human Relations in the West*, ed. John Bossy, 145–66. Cambridge: Cambridge University Press, 1983.

———. *Lawsuits and Litigants in Castile, 1500–1700.* Chapel Hill: University of North Carolina Press, 1981.

Katzoff, Ranon. "Precedents in the Courts of Roman Egypt." *Zeitschrift der Savigny-Stiftung für Rechtsgeschichte (romanistische Abteilung)* 89 (1972): 256–92.

———. "'Responsa Prudentium' in Roman Egypt." In *Studi in onore di Arnaldo Biscardi*, ed. Franco Pastori, 523–35. Milan: Istituto Editoriale Cisalpino, 1982.

———. "Sources of Law in Roman Egypt: The Role of the Prefect." *ANRW* II.13 (1980): 807–44.

Keenan, James G. "The Aphrodito Murder Mystery: A Return to the Scene of the Crimes." *Bulletin of the American Society of Papyrologists* 32 (1995): 57–63.

———. "Egypt's 'Special Place'." In *Jesuit Education and the Classics*, ed. Edmund P. Cueva, Shannon N. Byrne, and Frederick Benda, 177–92. Newcastle upon Tyne: Cambridge Scholars, 2009.

———. "On Law and Society in Late Roman Egypt." *Zeitschrift für Papyrologie und Epigraphik* 17 (1975): 237–50.

———. "Pastoralism in Roman Egypt." *Bulletin of the American Society of Papyrologists* 26 (1989): 175–200.

———. "Roman Criminal Law in a Berlin Papyrus Codex (BGU IV 1024–1027)." *Archiv für Papyrusforschung* 35 (1989): 15–23.

———. "Roman Criminal Procedure." In *Law and Society in Egypt from Alexander to the Arab Conquest (330 BC–640 AD)*, ed. James G. Keenan, Joseph G. Manning, and Uri Yiftach-Firanko. Cambridge: Cambridge University Press, forthcoming 2013.

———. "Village Shepherds and Social Tension in Byzantine Egypt." *Yale Classical Studies* 28 (1985): 245–59.

Kehoe, Dennis P. *Law and the Rural Economy in the Roman Empire.* Ann Arbor: University of Michigan Press, 2007.

Kelly, Benjamin. *Petitions, Litigation, and Social Control in Roman Egypt.* Oxford: Oxford University Press, 2010.

———. "The Repression of Violence in the Roman Principate." Ph.D. Thesis, Oxford University, 2002.

———. "Tacitus, Germanicus and the Kings of Egypt (Tac. Ann. 2.59–61)." *Classical Quarterly* 60 (2010): 221–37.

Kleinman, Arthur. "The Violences of Everyday Life: The Multiple Forms and Dynamics of Social Violence." In *Violence and Subjectivity*, ed. Veena Das and Arthur Kleinman, 226–41. Berkeley: University of California Press, 2000.

Kokkinia, C. "Ruling, Inducing, Arguing: How to Govern (and Survive) a Greek Province." In *Roman Rule and Civic Life: Local and Regional Perspectives*, ed. L. de Ligt, H. W Singor, and Emily Ann Hemelrijk, 39–58. Impact of Empire 4. Amsterdam: Gieben, 2004.

Konstan, David. *Friendship in the Classical World.* Cambridge: Cambridge University Press, 1997.

Koselleck, Reinhart. *Critique and Crisis: Enlightenment and the Pathogenesis of Modern Society.* Cambridge, Mass.: MIT Press, 1988.

Kovelman, Arkady B. "From Logos to Myth: Egyptian Petitions of the 5th–7th Centuries." *Bulletin of the American Society of Papyrologists* 28 (1991): 135–52.

Kramer, Bärbel. "P. Strasb. Inv. 1265 + P. Strasb. 296 Recto: Eingabe wegen Ἀνδραποδισμός (= Plagium) und Σύλησις (= Furtum)." *Zeitschrift für Papyrologie und Epigraphik* 69 (1987): 143–61.

Kreuzaler, C., and J. Urbanik. "Humanity and Inhumanity of the Law: The Case of Dionysia." *Journal of Juristic Papyrology* 38 (2008): 119–55.

Kunkel, Wolfgang. *Herkunft und soziale Stellung der römischen Juristen.* 2nd ed. Forschungen zum Römischen Recht 4. Köln: Böhlau Verlag, 1967.

Kutzner, Edgar. *Untersuchungen zur Stellung der Frau im romischen Oxyrhynchos.* Europäische Hochschulschriften 392. Frankfurt am Main: Peter Lang, 1989.

LaCapra, Dominick. *Writing History, Writing Trauma.* Baltimore: Johns Hopkins University Press, 2001.

Lendon, J. E. *Empire of Honour: The Art of Government in the Roman World.* Oxford: Clarendon, 1997.

Lesy, Michael. *Wisconsin Death Trip.* New York: Pantheon, 1973.

Lewis, Naphtali. *The Compulsory Public Services of Roman Egypt.* 2nd ed. Papyrologica Florentina 28. Florence: Edizioni Gonnelli, 1997.

———. "Judiciary Routines in Roman Egypt." *Bulletin of the American Society of Papyrologists* 37 (2000): 83–93.

———. *Life in Egypt Under Roman Rule.* Oxford: Clarendon, 1983.

———. "Notationes Legentis." *Bulletin of the American Society of Papyrologists* 16 (1979): 205–12.

———. "Notationes Legentis." *Bulletin of the American Society of Papyrologists* 34 (1997): 21–33.

———. *On Government and Law in Roman Egypt: Collected Papers of Naphtali Lewis.* Ed. Ann Ellis Hanson. American Studies in Papyrology 33. Atlanta: Scholars Press, 1995.

———. "A Petition of AD 212." *Bulletin of the American Society of Papyrologists* 12 (1975): 159–64.

———. "The Prefect's Conventus: Proceedings and Procedures." *Bulletin of the American Society of Papyrologists* 18 (1981): 119–29.

Lintott, A. W. *Violence in Republican Rome*. 2nd ed. Oxford: Clarendon, 1999.

MacCoull, Leslie S. B. "The Aphrodito Murder Mystery." *Journal of Juristic Papyrology* 20 (1990): 103–7.

MacMullen, Ramsay. "Judicial Savagery in the Roman Empire." In *Changes in the Roman Empire: Essays in the Ordinary*, 204–14. Princeton, N.J.: Princeton University Press, 1990.

———. *Roman Social Relations, 50 B.C. to A.D. 284*. New Haven, Conn.: Yale University Press, 1974.

Maehler, Herwig. "Greek, Roman, and Egyptian Law." *Journal of Juristic Papyrology* 35 (2005): 121–40.

Manning, Joseph G. *The Last Pharaohs: Egypt Under the Ptolemies, 305–30 BC*. Princeton, N.J.: Princeton University Press, 2010.

McKim, Richard. "Philosophers and Cannibals: Juvenal's Fifteenth Satire." *Phoenix* 40 (1986): 58–71.

Mélèze Modrzejewski, Josef. "'La loi des égyptiens': Le droit grec dans l'Égypte romaine." In *Proceedings of the XVIII Congress of Papyrology*, ed. Basil Mandilaras, 383–99. Athens: Greek Papyrological Society, 1988.

———. "Private Arbitration and the Law of Greco-Roman Egypt." *Journal of Juristic Papyrology* 6 (1952): 239–56.

———. "La règle de droit dans l'Égypte Romaine (État des questions et perspectives de recherches)." In *Proceedings of the Twelfth International Congress of Papyrology*, ed. Deborah Samuel, 317–77. Toronto: Hakkert, 1970.

Mellor, Ronald. "The New Aristocracy of Power." In *Flavian Rome: Culture, Image, Text*, ed. A. J. Boyle and W. J. Dominik, 69–101. Leiden: Brill, 2003.

Merry, Sally Engle. *Getting Justice and Getting Even: Legal Consciousness Among Working-Class Americans*. Chicago: University of Chicago Press, 1990.

———. "Legal Pluralism." *Law & Society Review* 22 (1988): 869–96.

Metzger, Ernest. "Roman Judges, Case Law, and Principles of Procedure." *Law and History Review* 22 (2004): 243–75.

Millar, Fergus. "The World of the Golden Ass." In *Rome, the Greek World, and the East*, vol. 2: *Government, Society, and Culture in the Roman Empire*, ed. Hannah Cotton and Guy MacLean Rogers, 315–35. Chapel Hill: University of North Carolina Press, 2002.

Miller, William Ian. *Eye for an Eye*. Cambridge: Cambridge University Press, 2006.

Milne, J. Grafton. "The Ruin of Egypt by Roman Mismanagement." *Journal of Roman Studies* 17 (1927): 1–13.

Mitchell, Stephen. *Anatolia: Land, Men and Gods in Asia Minor*. 2 vols. Oxford: Clarendon, 1993.

Mitthof, Fritz, and Roger S. Bagnall. "Order to Send a Person." In *Gedenkschrift Ulrike Horak (P. Horak)*, ed. Hermann Harrauer and Rosario Pintaudi, 59–62. Papyrologica Florentina 34. Florence: Gonnelli, 2004.

Mitteis, Ludwig. *Reichsrecht und Volksrecht in den östlichen Provinzen des römischen Kaiserreichs.* Leipzig: Teubner, 1891.

Mommsen, Theodor. *The Provinces of the Roman Empire from Caesar to Diocletian.* Trans. William P. Dickson. London: Macmillan, 1909.

Moore, Sally Falk. "Certainties Undone: Fifty Turbulent Years of Legal Anthropology, 1949–1999." *Journal of the Royal Anthropological Institute* 7 (2001): 95–116.

Moyer, Ian S. "Herodotus and an Egyptian Mirage: The Genealogies of the Theban Priests." *Journal of Hellenic Studies* 122 (2002): 70–90.

Muir, Edward. *Mad Blood Stirring: Vendetta and Factions in Friuli During the Renaissance.* Baltimore: Johns Hopkins University Press, 1993.

Nader, Laura. *Harmony Ideology: Justice and Control in a Zapotec Mountain Village.* Stanford, Calif.: Stanford University Press, 1990.

———. "Moving On—Comprehending Anthropologies of Law." In *Practicing Ethnography in Law: New Dialogues, Enduring Methods*, ed. June Starr and Mark Goodale, 190–200. New York: Palgrave Macmillan, 2002.

———. "Pushing the Limits—Eclecticism on Purpose." *PoLAR: Political and Legal Anthropology Review* 22 (2008): 106–9.

Naldini, Mario. *Il Cristianesimo in Egitto: Lettere private nei papiri dei secoli II–IV.* Studi e Testi di Papirologia 3. Florence: Le Monnier, 1968.

Nielsen, Bruce E. "A Catalog of Duplicate Papyri." *Zeitschrift für Papyrologie und Epigraphik* 129 (2000): 187–214.

Nimis, Stephen. "Egypt in Greco-Roman History and Fiction." *Alif: Journal of Comparative Poetics* 24 (2004): 34–67.

Nippel, Wilfried. *Public Order in Ancient Rome.* Cambridge: Cambridge University Press, 1995.

Nirenberg, David. *Communities of Violence: Persecution of Minorities in the Middle Ages.* Princeton, N.J.: Princeton University Press, 1998.

North, Douglass C. "Institutions." *Journal of Economic Perspectives* 5 (1991): 97–112.

North, Douglass C., John J. Wallis, and Barry R. Weingast. *Violence and Social Orders: A Conceptual Framework for Interpreting Recorded Human History.* Cambridge: Cambridge University Press, 2009.

Oliver, James Henry. *Greek Constitutions of Early Roman Emperors from Inscriptions and Papyri.* Memoirs of the American Philosophical Society 178. Philadelphia: American Philosophical Society, 1989.

Parca, Maryline. "Violence by and Against Women in Documentary Papyri from Ptolemaic and Roman Egypt." In *Le rôle et le statut de la femme en Égypte hellénistique, romaine et byzantine*, ed. Henri Melaerts and Leon Mooren, 283–96. Studia Hellenistica 37. Leuven: Peeters, 2002.

Parsons, Peter. *City of the Sharp-Nosed Fish: Greek Lives in Roman Egypt.* London: Weidenfeld and Nicolson. 2007.

Peachin, Michael. "Petition to a Centurion from the NYU Papyrus Collection and the Question of Informal Adjudication by Soldiers." In *Papyri in Memory of P. J.*

Sijpesteijn, ed. A. J. B. Sirks and K. A. Worp, 79–97. American Studies in Papyrology 40. Oakville, Conn.: American Society of Papyrologists, 2007.

———. "Introduction." In *The Oxford Handbook of Social Relations in the Roman World*, ed. Michael Peachin, 3–36. Oxford: Oxford University Press, 2011.

Peirce, Leslie P. *Morality Tales: Law and Gender in the Ottoman Court of Aintab*. Berkeley: University of California Press, 2003.

Rapp, Claudia. *Holy Bishops in Late Antiquity: The Nature of Christian Leadership in an Age of Transition*. Berkeley: University of California Press, 2005.

Rathbone, Dominic. "Poverty and Population in Roman Egypt." In *Poverty in the Roman World*, ed. E. M. Atkins and Robin Osborne, 100–114. Cambridge: Cambridge University Press, 2006.

Rea, John R. "P. Col. VIII 242: Caranis in the Fifth Century." In *Proceedings of the 20th International Congress of Papyrologists*, ed. Adam Bülow-Jacobsen, 266–72. Copenhagen: Museum Tusculum Press, 1994.

———. "Two Christian Letters: PSI VII 831 and VIII 972." *Chronique d'Égypte* 45 (1970): 357–68.

Redfield, James. "Herodotus the Tourist." *Classical Philology* 80 (1985): 97–118.

Rees, B. R. "The Defensor Civitatis in Egypt." *Journal of Juristic Papyrology* 6 (1952): 73–102.

Rensberger, David. "The Politics of John: The Trial of Jesus in the Fourth Gospel." *Journal of Biblical Literature* 103 (1984): 395–411.

Riches, David. "The Phenomenon of Violence." In *The Anthropology of Violence*, ed. David Riches, 1–27. Oxford: Blackwell, 1986.

Riggsby, Andrew M. *Crime and Community in Ciceronian Rome*. Austin: University of Texas Press, 1999.

Rigsby, Kent J. "An Ephebic Inscription from Egypt." *Greek, Roman, and Byzantine Studies* 19 (1978): 239–49.

———. "Founding a Serapeum." *Greek, Roman, and Byzantine Studies* 42 (2001): 117–24.

Rilinger, Rolf. *Humiliores—Honestiores: Zu einer sozialen Dichotomie im Strafrecht der römischen Kaiserzeit*. Munich: R. Oldenbourg, 1988.

Ritner, Robert K. "Implicit Models of Cross-Cultural Interaction: A Question of Noses, Soap, and Prejudice." In *Life in a Multi-Cultural Society: Egypt from Cambyses to Constantine and Beyond*, ed. Janet H. Johnson, 283–90. Studies in Ancient Oriental Civilization 51. Chicago: Oriental Institute, 1992.

Ruffini, Giovanni. *Social Networks in Byzantine Egypt*. Cambridge: Cambridge University Press, 2008.

Rupprecht, Hans Albert. "Die Streitigkeit zwischen Satabous und Nestnephis." In *Symposion 1999: Vorträge zur griechischen und hellenistischen Rechtsgeschichte*, ed. Gerhard Thür and F. J. F. Nieto, 481–92. Akten der Gesellschaft für griechische und hellenistische Rechtsgeschichte 14. Köln: Böhlau, 2003.

Saller, Richard P. *Patriarchy, Property and Death in the Roman Family*. Cambridge Studies in Population, Economy, and Society in Past Time 25. Cambridge: Cambridge University Press, 1994.

———. *Personal Patronage Under the Early Empire.* Cambridge: Cambridge University Press, 2002.

———. "Roman Kinship: Structure and Sentiment." In *The Roman Family in Italy: Status, Sentiment, Space*, ed. Beryl Rawson and P. R. C. Weaver, 7–34. Canberra: Humanities Research Centre, 1997.

Saller, Richard P., and Brent D. Shaw. "Tombstones and Roman Family Relations in the Principate: Civilians, Soldiers and Slaves." *Journal of Roman Studies* 74 (1984): 124–56.

Samuel, Deborah H. "P. Berol. Inv. 8797 and P. Gen. 3: Two Versions of a Dispute over an Inheritance." *Zeitschrift für Papyrologie und Epigraphik* 37 (1980): 255–59.

Scarry, Elaine. *The Body in Pain: The Making and Unmaking of a World.* New York: Oxford University Press, 1985.

Scheidel, Walter. "Stratification, Deprivation, and Quality of Life." In *Poverty in the Roman World*, ed. E. M Atkins and Robin Osborne, 40–59. Cambridge: Cambridge University Press, 2006.

Scheper-Hughes, Nancy. *Death Without Weeping: The Violence of Everyday Life in Brazil.* Berkeley: University of California Press, 1992.

Scheper-Hughes, Nancy, and Philippe I. Bourgois, eds. *Violence in War and Peace: An Anthology.* Blackwell Readers in Anthropology 5. Malden, Mass.: Blackwell, 2004.

Schroeder, Joy A. "John Chrysostom's Critique of Spousal Violence." *Journal of Early Christian Studies* 12 (2004): 413–42.

Searle, John R. *The Construction of Social Reality.* New York: Free Press, 1995.

Seidl, E. *Rechtsgeschichte Ägyptens als römischer Provinz.* Sankt Augustin: H. Richarz, 1972.

Sharp, Michael. "Shearing Sheep: Rome and the Collection of Taxes in Egypt, 30 BC–AD 200." In *Lokale Autonomie und römische Ordnungsmacht in den kaiserzeitlichen Provinzen vom 1. bis 3. Jahrhundert*, ed. Werner Eck, 211–41. Schriften des historischen Kollegs. Kolloquien 42. Munich: R. Oldenbourg Verlag, 1999.

Shaw, Brent D. "Anatomy of the Vampire Bat." *Economy and Society* 13 (1983): 208–49.

———. "The Family in Late Antiquity: The Experience of Augustine." *Past & Present* 115 (1987): 3–51.

———. *Sacred Violence: African Christians and Sectarian Hatred in the Age of Augustine.* Cambridge: Cambridge University Press, 2011.

Sijpesteijn, P. J. "Complaint to the Epistrategus Vedius Faustus." *Zeitschrift für Papyrologie und Epigraphik* 110 (1996): 183–87.

———. "Petition to the Chief of Police." *Zeitschrift für Papyrologie und Epigraphik* 91 (1992): 101–2.

Simon, Jonathan. *Governing Through Crime: How the War on Crime Transformed American Democracy and Created a Culture of Fear.* Oxford: Oxford University Press, 2007.

Sizgorich, Thomas. *Violence and Belief in Late Antiquity: Militant Devotion in Christianity and Islam.* Philadelphia: University of Pennsylvania Press, 2008.

Smail, Daniel Lord. *The Consumption of Justice: Emotions, Publicity, and Legal Culture in Marseille, 1264–1423*. Ithaca, N.Y: Cornell University Press, 2003.

Smith, Jonathan Z. "In Comparison a Magic Dwells." In *Imagining Religion: From Babylon to Jonestown*, 19–35. Chicago: University of Chicago Press, 1988.

Smith, R. R. R. "Simulacra Gentium: The Ethne from the Sebasteion at Aphrodisias." *Journal of Roman Studies* 78 (1988): 50–77.

Sommer, Matthew Harvey. *Sex, Law, and Society in Late Imperial China*. Stanford, Calif.: Stanford University Press, 2000.

Sontag, Susan. *Regarding the Pain of Others*. New York: Farrar, Straus and Giroux, 2003.

Swarney, Paul R. *The Ptolemaic and Roman* Idios Logos. American Studies in Papyrology 8. Toronto: Hakkert, 1970.

Tacoma, Laurens Ernst. *Fragile Hierarchies: The Urban Elites of Third Century Roman Egypt*. Mnemosyne Supplements 271. Leiden: Brill, 2006.

Tait, John Gavin. "The Strategi and Royal Scribes in the Roman Period." *Journal of Egyptian Archaeology* 8 (1922): 166–73.

Tamanaha, Brian Z. "The Folly of the 'Social Scientific' Concept of Legal Pluralism." *Journal of Law and Society* 20 (1993): 192–217.

Taubenschlag, Rafael. *The Law of Greco-Roman Egypt in the Light of the Papyri, 332 B.C.–640 A.D.* 2nd ed. Warsaw: Państwowe Wydawnictwo Naukowe, 1955.

———. "Self Help in Greco-Roman Egypt." In *Opera Minora*, ed. Vincenzo Arangio Ruiz, 135–42. Warsaw: Państwowe Wydawn Naukowe, 1959.

———. *Das Strafrecht im Recht der Papyri*. Leipzig: B.G. Turner, 1916.

Thomas, J. David. "A Family Dispute from Karanis and the Revolt of Domitius Domitianus." *Zeitschrift für Papyrologie und Epigraphik* 24 (1977): 233–40.

———. "Subscriptions to Petitions to Officials in Roman Egypt." In *Egypt and the Hellenistic World*, ed. E. van't Dack, P. van Dessel, and W. van Gucht, 369–82. Studia Hellenistica 27. Leuven: Orientaliste, 1983.

Thomas, Yan. *Mommsen et "l'*Isolierung*" du droit (Rome, Allemagne, et l'état)*. Paris: Boccard, 1984.

Tilly, Charles. *Big Structures, Large Processes, Huge Comparisons*. New York: Russell Sage Foundation, 1984.

———. "Linkers, Diggers, and Glossers in Social History." In Tilly, *Explaining Social Processes*. Boulder, Colo.: Paradigm, 2008.

———. *The Politics of Collective Violence*. Cambridge: Cambridge University Press, 2003.

Torallas-Tovar, Sofía. "The Police in Byzantine Egypt: The Hierarchy in the Papyri from the Fourth to the Seventh Centuries." In *Current Research in Egyptology, 2000*, ed. Angela MacDonald and Christina Riggs, 115–23. BAR International Series 909. Oxford: Archaeopress, 2000.

———. "La práctica forense en el Egipto Romano." *Cuadernos de Filología Clásica* 14 (2004): 183–200.

———. "Violence in the Process of Arrest and Imprisonment in Late Antique Egypt." In *Violence in Late Antiquity: Perceptions and Practices*, ed. H. A. Drake, 103–12. Burlington, Vt.: Ashgate, 2006.

Turpin, William. "Apokrimata, Decreta, and the Roman Legal Procedure." *Bulletin of the American Society of Papyrologists* 18 (1991): 145–60.

———. "Imperial Subscriptions and the Administration of Justice." *Journal of Roman Studies* 81 (1991): 101–18.

Wacquant, Loïc. "Scrutinizing the Street: Poverty, Morality, and the Pitfalls of Urban Ethnography." *American Journal of Sociology* 107 (2002): 1468–1532.

———. *Urban Outcasts: A Comparative Sociology of Advanced Marginality.* Cambridge: Polity, 2008.

Walbank, Frank W. "Egypt in Polybius." In Walbank, *Polybius, Rome, and the Hellenistic World: Essays and Reflections*, 53–69. Cambridge: Cambridge University Press, 2002.

Waller, Altina L. *Feud: Hatfields, McCoys, and Social Change in Appalachia, 1860–1900.* Chapel Hill: University of North Carolina Press, 1988.

Weaver, Paul. "Consilium Praesidis: Advising Governors." In *Thinking Like a Lawyer: Essays on Legal History and General History for John Crook on His Eightieth Birthday*, ed. Paul McKechnie, 43–62. Mnemosyne Supplementum 231. Leiden: Brill, 2002.

Weber, Max. *Economy and Society: An Outline of Interpretive Sociology.* Ed. Guenther Roth and Claus Wittich. Berkeley: University of California Press, 1978.

———. "Politics as a Vocation." In *From Max Weber: Essays in Sociology*, ed. Hans Heinrich Gerth and C. Wright Mills, 77–128. London: Routledge, 1991.

Weil, Simone. "The Iliad, or the Poem of Force." Trans. Mary McCarthy. *Chicago Review* 18 (1965): 5–30.

Weisberg, Robert. "Private Violence and Moral Action: The Law as Inspiration and Example." In *Law's Violence*, ed. Austin Sarat and Thomas R. Kearns, 175–210. Ann Arbor: University of Michigan Press, 1992.

White, J. L. *The Form and Structure of the Official Petition: A Study in Greek Epistolography.* Missoula, Mont.: Society for Biblical Literature, 1972.

Whitehorne, J. E. G. "P. Mich. Inv. 255: A Petition to the Epistrategus P. Marcius Crispus." *Chronique d'Égypte* 66 (1999): 250–56.

———. "Petitions to the Centurion: A Question of Locality?" *Bulletin of the American Society of Papyrologists* 41 (2004): 155–70.

———. "Recent Research on the Strategi of Roman Egypt." *ANRW* II.10.1 (1988): 598–617.

———. "The Role of the Strategia in Administrative Continuity in Roman Egypt." In *Proceedings of the XVI International Congress of Papyrology*, ed. Roger S. Bagnall, 419–28. Chico, Calif.: Scholar's Press, 1981.

———. "Sex and Society in Greco-Roman Egypt." In *Actes du XVe congrès international de papyrologie*, ed. Jean Bingen and Georges Nachtergael, 240–46. Papyrologica Bruxellensia 16–19. Brussels: Fond. Égyptol. Reine Élisabeth, 1979.

———. "Strategus, Centurion, or Neither: BGU I 321 and 322 (= M.Chrest. 114 and 124) and Their Duplicates." *Bulletin of the American Society of Papyrologists* 40 (2003): 201–11.

Whitman, James Q. *The Legacy of Roman Law in the German Romantic Era: Historical Vision and Legal Change.* Princeton, N.J.: Princeton University Press, 1990.

Wickham, Chris. *Courts and Conflict in Twelfth-Century Tuscany.* Oxford: Oxford University Press, 2003.

———. "Fama and the Law in Twelfth-Century Tuscany." In *Fama: The Politics of Talk and Reputation in Medieval Europe*, ed. Thelma S. Fenster and Daniel Lord Smail, 15–26. Ithaca, N.Y.: Cornell University Press, 2003.

———. "Gossip and Resistance Among the Medieval Peasantry." *Past & Present* 160 (1998): 3–24.

Wilcken, Ulrich. "Zu den Kaiserreskripten." *Hermes* 55 (1920): 1–42.

Winter, John Garrett. *Life and Letters in the Papyri.* Ann Arbor: University of Michigan Press, 1933.

Wolff, Hans Julius. *Das Recht der griechischen Papyri Ägyptens in der Zeit der Ptolemäer und des Prinzipats.* Handbuch der Altertumswissenschaft 10.5. Munich: Beck, 1978.

———. "Das Vulgarrechtsproblem und die Papyri." *Zeitschrift der Savigny-Stiftung für Rechtsgeschichte (romanistische Abteilung)* 91 (1974): 54–105.

Wolin, Richard. *Heidegger's Children: Hannah Arendt, Karl Löwith, Hans Jonas, and Herbert Marcuse.* Princeton, N.J.: Princeton University Press, 2001.

Woolf, Greg. *Becoming Roman: The Origins of Provincial Civilization in Gaul.* Cambridge: Cambridge University Press, 1998.

———. "Monumental Writing and the Expansion of Roman Society in the Early Empire." *Journal of Roman Studies* 86 (1996): 22–39.

———. "Provincial Perspectives." In *The Cambridge Companion to the Age of Augustus*, ed. Karl Galinsky, 106–29. Cambridge: Cambridge University Press, 2005.

Yiftach-Firanko, Uri. "Law in Greco-Roman Egypt: Hellenization, Fusion, Romanization." In *The Oxford Handbook of Papyrology*, ed. Roger S. Bagnall, 541–60. Oxford: Oxford University Press, 2009.

———. *Marriage and Marital Arrangements: A History of the Greek Marriage Document in Egypt, 4th Century BCE–4th Century CE.* Münchener Beiträge zur Papyrusforschung und antiken Rechtsgeschichte 93. Munich: Beck, 2003.

Yngvesson, Barbara. *Virtuous Citizens, Disruptive Subjects: Order and Complaint in a New England Court.* New York: Routledge, 1993.

Youtie, Herbert C. "Notes on O. Mich. I." In Youtie, *Scriptiunculae*, vol. 1, 63–104. Amsterdam: Hakkert, 1973.

Zimmermann, Reinhard. *The Law of Obligations: Roman Foundations of the Civilian Tradition.* Oxford: Oxford University Press, 1996.

Ziolkowski, Theodore. *Clio the Romantic Muse: Historicizing the Faculties in Germany.* Ithaca, N.Y.: Cornell University Press, 2004.

Žižek, Slavoj. "Tolerance as an Ideological Category." *Critical Inquiry* 34 (2008): 660–82.

INDEX

Page references in italics refer to illustrations; those in bold refer to papyri.

ACKNOWLEDGMENTS

This book has its origins in an all-too-rare act of generosity and good faith at the annual meeting of the American Philological Association. Perhaps too late at night I approached a relatively senior scholar in my field who had co-authored an important book on the anthropology of disputes and settlements in Roman Egypt. I liked and respected the book, and in fact it has served as the main point of departure for my own work. But for some reason I decided to say something to the effect of, "that was a really interesting book, but I think it totally missed the point." It was lucky that the senior scholar was Traianos Gagos; most others would have (justifiably) walked away (or worse). Instead we spoke that night for over an hour about the challenges and possibilities of writing an anthropologically oriented social history of disputes and conflicts in Roman Egypt, a conversation that continued during a visit to Jordan when Traianos was editing the Petra papyri, and thereafter. Traianos' death in 2010 was a terrible moment; his candor and his openness to new approaches to papyrology and ancient history were instrumental in giving a significant number of young scholars an interest in the world of the papyri and the confidence to try new things and to enjoy intellectual play. He is sorely missed.

This project then developed while I was at the University of Chicago. It is hard to imagine an atmosphere more intellectually engaging than Chicago, or a group of scholars more generous than my mentors there: Walter Kaegi, Clifford Ando, James Keenan, and David Martinez. I thank Walter for his patience and his uncanny ability to be on the lookout out for my best interests well before I knew what they were; Cliff, for his enthusiasm for this project, his encouragement of the practice of reading widely, his tireless advocacy, and the opportunity to publish the results in his series with Penn Press; Jim, for his kindness to young scholars, his sense of humor, and his deep respect for the humanity of the people we study, a respect that has encouraged me to build on the foundations he's laid; and David for his respect for craft and attention to detail. An additional thank-you is due to Jonathan Hall. A conversation with Jonathan about the practice of writing history is an exciting, rigorous, and thought-provoking experience; I have been lucky to have had many such conversations, and to have enjoyed his friendship and support. This project would have gone nowhere were it not for the opportunity to present early findings in the Ancient Societies Workshop. I was also fortunate to have spent my time at Chicago with a large cohort of smart, thoughtful, funny, and generous people. Conversations with Vanessa Davies, Chris DiTeresi, Fanny Dolansky, Kathy Fox, Cam Grey, John and Sharon Hyland, Paul and Kathleen Keen, Chad Levinson, John Paulas, and Phil Venticinque have helped me through impasses at all stages of this project.

If there is an advantage to being peripatetic, it is that you get to meet wonderful people. In my time at the Institute for the Study of the Ancient World at New York University, Georgetown University, and the University of California, Berkeley, it has been my privilege to discuss material from this book with Anna Boozer, Marianne Constable, Susanna Elm, Samera Esmeir, Loren Goldman, Emily Mackil, Jessica Nitschke, and Carlos Noreña. Additionally, Roger Bagnall, Todd Hickey, Chuck Jones, Leslie Kurke, Charles McNelis, Michèle Lowrie, Josiah Osgood, Michael Peachin, and Alex Sens all went out of their way to make me feel welcome when I was new to their institutions; such small touches that make moving much easier. Grants from the Franke Institute for the Humanities, ISAW, the Mellon Foundation, and the American Council of Learned Societies' New Faculty Fellows program have made all of these conversations possible, in addition to granting me precious time off to complete this manuscript. In the early phases of writing I was also lucky enough to attend the Hurst Summer Institute for Legal History; conversations with Barbara Young Welke, Fahad Bishara, Nate Holdren, Keramet Reiter, Kim Welch, and others have made this project much better.

Over the course of writing, I have been greatly helped by a number of readers. Loren Goldman and Samera Esmeir saved me from a number of errors; Clifford Ando, Cam Grey, Noel Lenski, Sofía Torallas-Tovar, Phil Venticinque, and Kim Welch read and commented on the entire manuscript. My research assistant at Berkeley, Derin McCleod, had the formidable task of checking my translations, and saved me from more errors than I would care to admit to. Finally, conversations with P. T. D. Bryen have shed light on important points of detail. I naturally regret whatever mistakes remain.

Permission to use photos of papyri has kindly been granted by the Papyrology Collection of Hatcher Library of the University of Michigan, the Center for the Study of Ancient Documents at Oxford University, the Association Internationale de Papyrologues, and the Photographic Archive of Papyri in the Cairo Museum. Adam Bülow-Jacobsen generously agreed to share his photographs, and Charles Crowther and Alan Bowman (Oxford) and Adam Hyatt (Michigan) have been helpful in obtaining digital images.

A preliminary version of what has become Chapters 4 and 5 was published in *Greek, Roman, and Byzantine Studies.*

Cam, Cliff, Phil, and Kim have made a long, tiring process weigh lightly, and have my heartfelt thanks. My parents and sisters have been a constant source of support and encouragement, in too many different ways to detail here. This book is rightly dedicated to them.